Handbook of Big Data Privacy

Kim-Kwang Raymond Choo • Ali Dehghantanha
Editors

Handbook of Big Data Privacy

 Springer

Editors
Kim-Kwang Raymond Choo ⓘD
University of Texas at San Antonio
San Antonio, TX, USA

Ali Dehghantanha ⓘD
Cyber Science Lab
School of Computer Science
University of Guelph
Guelph, ON, Canada

ISBN 978-3-030-38559-0   ISBN 978-3-030-38557-6 (eBook)
https://doi.org/10.1007/978-3-030-38557-6

This Springer imprint is published by the registered company Springer Nature Switzerland AG.
The registered company address is: Gewerbestrasse 11, 6330 Cham, Switzerland

Contents

1   **Big Data and Privacy: Challenges and Opportunities**...............   1
Amin Azmoodeh and Ali Dehghantanha

2   **AI and Security of Critical Infrastructure**...........................   7
Jacob Sakhnini, Hadis Karimipour, Ali Dehghantanha,
and Reza M. Parizi

3   **Industrial Big Data Analytics: Challenges and Opportunities**   37
Abdulrahman Al-Abassi, Hadis Karimipour, Hamed HaddadPajouh,
Ali Dehghantanha, and Reza M. Parizi

4   **A Privacy Protection Key Agreement Protocol Based on ECC
for Smart Grid**   63
Mostafa Farhdi Moghadam, Amirhossein Mohajerzdeh,
Hadis Karimipour, Hamid Chitsaz, Roya Karimi, and Behzad Molavi

5   **Applications of Big Data Analytics and Machine Learning
in the Internet of Things**   77
Shamim Yousefi, Farnaz Derakhshan, and Hadis Karimipour

6   **A Comparison of State-of-the-Art Machine Learning Models
for OpCode-Based IoT Malware Detection**   109
William Peters, Ali Dehghantanha, Reza M. Parizi,
and Gautam Srivastava

7   **Artificial Intelligence and Security of Industrial Control Systems**....   121
Suby Singh, Hadis Karimipour, Hamed HaddadPajouh,
and Ali Dehghantanha

8   **Enhancing Network Security Via Machine Learning:
Opportunities and Challenges**...   165
Mahdi Amrollahi, Shahrzad Hadayeghparast, Hadis Karimipour,
Farnaz Derakhshan, and Gautam Srivastava

9 Network Security and Privacy Evaluation Scheme for Cyber
   Physical Systems (CPS) 191
   Mridula Sharma, Haytham Elmiligi, and Fayez Gebali

10 Anomaly Detection in Cyber-Physical Systems Using Machine
   Learning 219
   Hossein Mohammadi Rouzbahani, Hadis Karimipour,
   Abolfazl Rahimnejad, Ali Dehghantanha, and Gautam Srivastava

11 Big Data Application for Security of Renewable Energy
   Resources 237
   Hossein Mohammadi Rouzbahani, Hadis Karimipour,
   and Gautam Srivastava

12 Big-Data and Cyber-Physical Systems in Healthcare:
   Challenges and Opportunities... 255
   Jesus Castillo Cabello, Hadis Karimipour, Amir Namavar Jahromi,
   Ali Dehghantanha, and Reza M. Parizi

13 Privacy Preserving Abnormality Detection: A Deep Learning
   Approach 285
   Wenyu Han, Amin Azmoodeh, Hadis Karimipour, and Simon Yang

14 Privacy and Security in Smart and Precision Farming:
   A Bibliometric Analysis... 305
   Sanaz Nakhodchi, Ali Dehghantanha, and Hadis Karimipour

15 A Survey on Application of Big Data in Fin Tech Banking
   Security and Privacy 319
   Mahdi Amrollahi, Ali Dehghantanha, and Reza M. Parizi

16 A Hybrid Deep Generative Local Metric Learning Method
   for Intrusion Detection.. 343
   Mahdis Saharkhizan, Amin Azmoodeh, Hamed HaddadPajouh,
   Ali Dehghantanha, Reza M. Parizi, and Gautam Srivastava

17 Malware Elimination Impact on Dynamic Analysis:
   An Experimental Machine Learning Approach........................ 359
   Mohammad Nassiri, Hamed HaddadPajouh, Ali Dehghantanha,
   Hadis Karimipour, Reza M. Parizi, and Gautam Srivastava

18 RAT Hunter: Building Robust Models for Detecting Remote
   Access Trojans Based on Optimum Hybrid Features 371
   Mohammad Mehdi BehradFar, Hamed HaddadPajouh,
   Ali Dehghantanha, Amin Azmoodeh, Hadis Karimipour,
   Reza M. Parizi, and Gautam Srivastava

19 Active Spectral Botnet Detection Based on Eigenvalue Weighting.... 385
   Amin Azmoodeh, Ali Dehghantanha, Reza M. Parizi,
   Sattar Hashemi, Bahram Gharabaghi, and Gautam Srivastava

Contributors

Abdulrahman Al-Abassi School of Engineering, University of Guelph, Guelph, ON, Canada

Mahdi Amrollahi School of Engineering, University of Guelph, Guelph, ON, Canada

Amin Azmoodeh Cyber Science Lab, School of Computer Science, University of Guelph, Guelph, ON, Canada

Mohammad Mehdi BehradFar Computer Engineering Department, Pishtazan Institute of Higher Education, Shiraz, Iran

Jesus Castillo Cabello School of Engineering, University of Guelph, Guelph, ON, Canada

Hamid Chitsaz Department of Computer, Vahdat Institute of Higher Education, Torbat-e-Jam, Iran

Ali Dehghantanha Cyber Science Lab, School of Computer Science, University of Guelph, Guelph, ON, Canada

Farnaz Derakhshan Department of Electrical and Computer Engineering, University of Tabriz, Tabriz, Iran

Haytham Elmiligi Department of Computing Sciences, Thompson Rivers University, Kamloops, BC, Canada

Mostafa Farhdi Moghadam Department of Computer, Vahdat Institute of Higher Education, Torbat-e-Jam, Iran

Fayez Gebali Electrical and Computer Engineering, University of Victoria, Victoria, BC, Canada

Bahram Gharabaghi School of Engineering, University of Guelph, Guelph, ON, Canada

Shahrzad Hadayeghparast School of Engineering, University of Guelph, Guelph, ON, Canada

Hamed HaddadPajouh Cyber Science Lab, School of Computer Science, University of Guelph, Guelph, ON, Canada

Wenyu Han School of Engineering, University of Guelph, Guelph, ON, Canada

Sattar Hashemi Department of Computer Science and Engineering, Shiraz University, Shiraz, Iran

Amir Namavar Jahromi School of Engineering, University of Guelph, Guelph, ON, Canada

Hadis Karimipour School of Engineering, University of Guelph, Guelph, ON, Canada

Roya Karimi Department of Computer Engineering, Ferdowsi University of Mashhad, Mashhad, Iran

Amirhossein Mohajerzdeh Department of Computer Engineering, Ferdowsi University of Mashhad, Mashhad, Iran

Behzad Molavi Department of Computer Engineering, Ferdowsi University of Mashhad, Mashhad, Iran

Sanaz Nakhodchi Cyber Science Lab, School of Computer Science, University of Guelph, Guelph, ON, Canada

Mohammad Nassiri Computer Engineering Department, Urmia University, Urmia, Iran

Reza M. Parizi College of Computer and Software Engineering, Kennesaw State University, Marietta, GA, USA

William Peters Cyber Science Lab, University of Guelph, Guelph, ON, Canada

Abolfazl Rahimnejad School of Engineering, University of Guelph, Guelph, ON, Canada

Hossein Mohammadi Rouzbahani School of Engineering, University of Guelph, Guelph, ON, Canada

Mahdis Saharkhizan School of Electrical and Computer Engineering, Shiraz University, Shiraz, Iran

Jacob Sakhnini School of Engineering, University of Guelph, Guelph, ON, Canada

Mridula Sharma Electrical and Computer Engineering, University of Victoria, Victoria, BC, Canada

Suby Singh University of Mumbai, Mumbai, India

Gautam Srivastava Department of Mathematics and Computer Science, Brandon University, Brandon, MB, Canada

Simon Yang School of Engineering, University of Guelph, Guelph, ON, Canada

Shamim Yousefi Department of Electrical and Computer Engineering, University of Tabriz, Tabriz, Iran

Chapter 1
Big Data and Privacy:
Challenges and Opportunities

Amin Azmoodeh and Ali Dehghantanha (iD)

1 Introduction

The contemporary decade is distinguished for the explosion of information that is generating, transferring, and storing over vast and complex networks [1]. Technological advancements in information technology are creating a sea change in today's life. A majority of public and private sectors [2] beyond different industries are utilizing digital devices and procedures to provide their clients with high quality and reliable services. This widespread usage ranging from healthcare [3] and transport systems [4] to smart grids [5] and military services [6] has resulted in an inconceivable volume of data being generated and processed. The importance and sensitivity of such big data have turned it into an invaluable target for cybercriminals.

The privacy of big data has acquired new urgency due to the different issues linked to it [7, 8]. Regulating the pace of data growth with confidentiality, integrity, and availability of data processing technique is a challenging issue [9] which should be addressed. Moreover, investigation of big data on cloud-based platforms to identify and recover traces of criminal activities for forensic investigations is a time-consuming process [10] that demands novel approaches to overcome this challenge. Besides, big data storage, processing, sharing and management are crucial procedures [11] that should be carefully tuned because it may increase attack surface for malicious activities and data leakage.

On the other hand, and in terms of big data advantages, big data provides exemplary opportunities to leverage the high volume of data. It is projected that increasing data will lead to in-depth knowledge about the domain of data. Consequently, extracting in-depth knowledge from big data paves the way for proposing robust and

A. Azmoodeh (✉) · A. Dehghantanha
Cyber Science Lab, University of Guelph, Guelph, ON, Canada
e-mail: amin@cybersciencelab.org; ali@cybersciencelab.org

© Springer Nature Switzerland AG 2020
K.-K. R. Choo, A. Dehghantanha (eds.), *Handbook of Big Data Privacy*,
https://doi.org/10.1007/978-3-030-38557-6_1

outstanding mechanisms for protecting data and securing information technology networks [12]. Besides, storing big data and recovery mechanisms designed for it provides forensic investigators with more pieces of evidence that lead them to quick and accurate decision making [13].

2   Book Outline

This handbook presents existing state-of-the-art advances from both academia and industry, in big data and privacy. The remainder of the book is structured as follows. The second chapter [14] reviews security challenges and concerns related to critical infrastructure and methods that utilize artificial intelligence to protect these infrastructures. In the third chapter [15], authors survey new concepts, methodologies, and applications to achieve full autonomy in industry 4.0. In the fourth chapter [16], Moghadam et al. propose a privacy protection key agreement protocol for smart grid based on energy consumption controllers (ECC).

The fifth chapter [17] reviews the application of machine learning for the Internet of Things and discuss about their challenges and issues. In the subsequent chapter [18] (sixth chapter), Peters et al. apply different machine learning methods on the Internet of Things malware dataset and compare their performance and discuss the results. Singh et al. [19](seventh chapter) survey about the latest artificial intelligence based researches and methodologies undertaken for measuring and managing industrial cyber threats risks and security metrics that have been identified as a barrier to implementing these methodologies.

Eighth chapter [20] gives information about traditional machine learning based threat detection techniques for network security that are incapable of facing with huge amount of data so as to obtain more efficient knowledge to design and choose such techniques. In the next chapter, Sharma et al. [21] propose a multi-level network security and privacy evaluation scheme to evaluate and assess the security of cyber physical systems. Chapter 10 [22] is dedicated to machine learning approaches for cyber physical system anomaly detection. Then, through a case study, authors demonstrate the effectiveness of machine learning techniques for classifying False Data Injection attacks. The next chapter (Chapter 11) [23] briefly introduces renewable energy resources as well as different aspects and relations of security and big data for power systems using such resources. In the subsequent chapter, Cabello et al. [24] describe the importance of using cyber-physical systems and big data in healthcare sector. Chapter 13 [25] proposes a deep learning approach for abnormality detection while preserve privacy for a medical images dataset.

In order to provide a clear insight about researches related to security of smart farming, Nakhodchi et al. [26] in the fourteenth chapter propose a bibliometric analysis to comprehensively assess security and privacy of smart agriculture systems and related literature. In the next chapter, Amrollahi et al. [27] highlight the impact of big data and privacy in financial systems and survey the work related to FinTech banking cyber security concerns and detection methods. Chapter 16 [28] proposes a hybrid deep generative metric learning approach for intrusion detection and protect critical infrastructures. Nassiri et al. [29] present a method that combines the static and dynamic machine learning based malware detection methods. They experimentally demonstrate the performance of their proposed method. In the subsequent chapter [30], BehradFar et al. introduce a machine learning algorithm that applies a two-layer feature selection to obtain the optimum set of features for Remote access Trojan (RAT) detection and achieve high performance for RAT detection. In the last chapter [31], Azmoodeh et al. propose an active spectral clustering method to tackle problem of massive data in botnet detection research sphere that consumes the minimum number of similarity between network nodes to identify botnets.

References

1. A. Azmoodeh, A. Dehghantanha, K.-K.R. Choo, *Big Data and Internet of Things Security and Forensics: Challenges and Opportunities* (Springer International Publishing, Cham, 2019), pp. 1–4
2. V. Ho, A. Dehghantanha, K. Shanmugam, A guideline to enforce data protection and privacy digital laws in Malaysia, in *2010 Second International Conference on Computer Research and Development* (IEEE, Piscataway, 2010), pp. 3–6
3. S. Walker-Roberts, M. Hammoudeh, A. Dehghantanha, A systematic review of the availability and efficacy of countermeasures to internal threats in healthcare critical infrastructure. IEEE Access **6**, 25167–25177 (2018)
4. G. Epiphaniou, P. Karadimas, D. Kbaier Ben Ismail, H. Al-Khateeb, A. Dehghantanha, K.R. Choo, Nonreciprocity compensation combined with turbo codes for secret key generation in vehicular Ad Hoc social IoT networks. IEEE Internet Things J. **5**(4), 2496–2505 (2018)
5. H. Karimipour, A. Dehghantanha, R.M. Parizi, K.R. Choo, H. Leung, A deep and scalable unsupervised machine learning system for cyber-attack detection in large-scale smart grids. IEEE Access **7**, 80778–80788 (2019)
6. A. Azmoodeh, A. Dehghantanha, K.R. Choo, Robust malware detection for internet of (battlefield) things devices using deep eigenspace learning. IEEE Trans. Sustain. Comput. **4**(1), 88–95 (2019)
7. R. Bao, Z. Chen, M.S. Obaidat, Challenges and techniques in big data security and privacy: a review. Secur. Priv. **1**(4), e13 (2018)
8. S. Yu, Big privacy: challenges and opportunities of privacy study in the age of big data. IEEE Access **4**, 2751–2763 (2016)
9. S. Nepal, R. Ranjan, K.R. Choo, Trustworthy processing of healthcare big data in hybrid clouds. IEEE Cloud Comput. **2**(2), 78–84 (2015)
10. Y. Teing, A. Dehghantanha, K.R. Choo, Z. Muda, M.T. Abdullah, Greening cloud-enabled big data storage forensics: syncany as a case study. IEEE Trans. Sustain. Comput. **4**(2), 204–216 (2019)
11. C. Yang, Q. Huang, Z. Li, K. Liu, F. Hu, Big data and cloud computing: innovation opportunities and challenges. Int. J. Digital Earth **10**(1), 13–53 (2017)
12. P.J. Taylor, T. Dargahi, A. Dehghantanha, *Analysis of APT Actors Targeting IoT and Big Data Systems: Shell_Crew, NetTraveler, ProjectSauron, CopyKittens, Volatile Cedar and Transparent Tribe as a Case Study* (Springer International Publishing, Cham, 2019), pp. 257–272
13. Y.-Y. Teing, A. Dehghantanha, K.-K.R. Choo, CloudMe forensics: a case of big data forensic investigation. Concurr. Comput. Pract. Exp. **30**(5), e4277 (2017)

14. J. Sakhnini, H. Karimipour, A. Dehghantanha, R.M. Parizi, AI and security of critical infrastructure, in *Big Data and Privacy*, ed. by K.-K.R. Choo, A. Dehghantanha (Springer, Cham, 2020). https://doi.org/10.1007/978-3-030-38557-6_2
15. A. Al-Abassi, H. Karimipour, H.H. Pajouh, A. Dehghantanha, R.M. Parizi, Industrial big data analytics: challenges and opportunities, in *Big Data and Privacy*, ed. by K.-K.R. Choo, A. Dehghantanha (Springer, Cham, 2020). https://doi.org/10.1007/978-3-030-38557-6_3
16. M.F. Moghadam, A. Mohajerzdeh, H. Karimipour, H. Chitsaz, R. Karimi, B. Molavi, A privacy protection key agreement protocol based on ECC for smart grid, in *Big Data and Privacy*, ed. by K.-K.R. Choo, A. Dehghantanha (Springer, Cham, 2020). https://doi.org/10.1007/978-3-030-38557-6_4
17. S. Yousefi, F. Derakhshan, H. Karimipour, Applications of big data analytics and machine learning in the internet of things, in *Big Data and Privacy*, ed. by K.-K.R. Choo, A. Dehghantanha (Springer, Cham, 2020). https://doi.org/10.1007/978-3-030-38557-6_5
18. W. Peters, A. Dehghantanha, R.M. Parizi, G. Srivastava, A comparison of various machine learning models for opcode based internet of things malware detection, in *Big Data and Privacy*, ed. by K.-K.R. Choo, A. Dehghantanha (Springer, Cham, 2020). https://doi.org/10.1007/978-3-030-38557-6_6
19. S. Singh, H. Karimipour, H. HaddadPajouh, A. Dehghantanha, Artificial intelligence and security of industrial control systems, in *Big Data and Privacy*, K.-K. R. Choo, A. Dehghantanha (Springer, Cham, 2020). https://doi.org/10.1007/978-3-030-38557-6_7
20. M. Amrollahi, S. Hadayeghparast, H. Karimipour, F. Derakhshan, G. Srivastava, Enhancing network security via machine learning: opportunities and challenges, in *Big Data and Privacy*, ed. by K.-K.R. Choo, A. Dehghantanha (Springer, Cham, 2020). https://doi.org/10.1007/978-3-030-38557-6_8
21. M. Sharma, H. Elmiligi, F. Gebali, Network security and privacy evaluation scheme for cyber physical systems (CPS), in *Big Data and Privacy*, ed. by K.-K.R. Choo, A. Dehghantanha (Springer, Cham, 2020). https://doi.org/10.1007/978-3-030-38557-6_9
22. H.M. Rouzbahani, H. Karimipour, A. Rahimnejad, A. Dehghantanha, G. Srivastava, Anomaly attack detection in cyber-physical systems using machine learning, in *Big Data and Privacy*, ed. by K.-K.R. Choo, A. Dehghantanha (Springer, Cham, 2020). https://doi.org/10.1007/978-3-030-38557-6_10
23. H.M. Rouzbahani, H. Karimipour, G. Srivastava, Big data application for renewable energy resource security, in *Big Data and Privacy*, ed. by K.-K.R. Choo, A. Dehghantanha (Springer, Cham, 2020). https://doi.org/10.1007/978-3-030-38557-6_11
24. J.C. Cabello, A.N. Jahromi, H. Karimipour, A. Dehghantanha, R.M. Parizi, Big-data and cyber-physical systems in healthcare: challenges and opportunities, in *Big Data and Privacy*, ed. by K.-K. R. Choo, A. Dehghantanha (Springer, Cham, 2020). https://doi.org/10.1007/978-3-030-38557-6_12
25. W. Han, A. Azmoodeh, H. Karimipour, S. Yang, Privacy preserving abnormality detection: a deep learning approach, in *Big Data and Privacy*, ed. by K.-K.R. Choo, A. Dehghantanha (Springer, Cham, 2020). https://doi.org/10.1007/978-3-030-38557-6_13
26. S. Nakhodchi, A. Dehghantanha, H. Karimipour, Privacy and security in smart and precision farming: a bibliometric analysis," in *Big Data and Privacy*, ed. by K.-K.R. Choo, A. Dehghantanha (Springer, Cham, 2020). https://doi.org/10.1007/978-3-030-38557-6_14
27. M. Amrollahi, A. Dehghantanha, R.M. Parizi, A survey on application of big data in fin tech banking security and privacy, in *Big Data and Privacy*, ed. by K.-K.R. Choo, A. Dehghantanha, (Springer, Cham, 2020). https://doi.org/10.1007/978-3-030-38557-6_15
28. M. Saharkhizan, A. Azmoodeh, H. HaddadPajouh, A. Dehghantanha, R.M. Parizi, G. Srivastava, A hybrid deep generative local metric learning method for intrusion detection, in *Big Data and Privacy*, ed. by K.-K.R. Choo, A. Dehghantanha (Springer, Cham, 2020). https://doi.org/10.1007/978-3-030-38557-6_16

29. M. Nassiri, H. HaddadPajouh, A. Dehghantanha, H. Karimipour, R.M. Parizi, G. Srivastava, Malware elimination impact on dynamic analysis: an experimental analysis on machine learning approach, in *Big Data and Privacy*, ed. by K.-K.R. Choo, A. Dehghantanha (Springer, Cham, 2020). https://doi.org/10.1007/978-3-030-38557-6_17
30. M.M. BehradFar, H. HaddadPajouh, A. Dehghantanha, A. Azmoodeh, H. Karimipour, R.M. Parizi, G. Srivastava, Rat hunter: building robust models for detecting rats based on optimum hybrid features, in *Big Data and Privacy*, K.-K.R. Choo, A. Dehghantanha (Springer, Cham, 2020). https://doi.org/10.1007/978-3-030-38557-6_18
31. A. Azmoodeh, A. Dehghantanha, R.M. Parizi, S. Hashemi, B. Gharabaghi, G. Srivastava, Active spectral botnet detection based on eigenvalue weighting, in *Big Data and Privacy*, ed. by K.-K.R. Choo, A. Dehghantanha (Springer, Cham, 2020). https://doi.org/10.1007/978-3-030-38557-6_19

Chapter 2
AI and Security of Critical Infrastructure

Jacob Sakhnini, Hadis Karimipour, Ali Dehghantanha ⓘ, and Reza M. Parizi

1 Introduction: Towards Smart Urbanization

Smart technologies are a part of many aspects of our daily lives. The advancement of society is directed in the path of interconnected devices aimed at improving every-day life. From smartphones and tablets, to smart appliances and internet-controlled lights, smart technologies are involved in many elements of daily life; Fig. 2.2 shows some of these elements which include security and surveillance, remote control and automation, as well as smart entertainment. Aside from our daily lives, information and communication technologies (ICTs) have played a major role in shaping economic activities and urban infrastructure. Such exponential technological growth incited substantial buzz in the topics of integrating ICTs in urban development projects such as the smart grid and smart cities.

Cities and communities today have embraced ICT in their development strategies utilizing digital infrastructure for regulatory and entrepreneurial purposes [1]. For the last two decades, this phenomenon has been referred to by various names, such as "wired cities" [2], "cyber cities" [3], "digital cities" [4], and the most popular of these terms, "smart cities" [5]. Each of these terms is used to conceptualize the relationship between modern urbanism and ICT in a particular way. However, modern interpretation of the use of ICT in urban development has been largely

J. Sakhnini · H. Karimipour (✉)
University of Guelph, Guelph, ON, Canada
e-mail: jsakhnin@uoguelph.ca; hkarimi@uoguelph.ca; Canada-hkarimi@uoguelph.ca

A. Dehghantanha
Cyber Science Lab, School of Computer Science, University of Guelph, Guelph, ON, Canada
e-mail: ali@cybersciencelab.org

R. M. Parizi
College of Computer and Software Engineering, Kennesaw State University, Marietta, GA, USA
e-mail: rparizi1@kennesaw.edu

© Springer Nature Switzerland AG 2020
K.-K. R. Choo, A. Dehghantanha (eds.), *Handbook of Big Data Privacy*,
https://doi.org/10.1007/978-3-030-38557-6_2

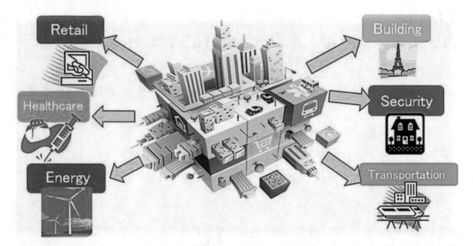

Fig. 2.1 Virtualization of a smart city [1]

referred to with the label "smart cities", a term which has gained substantial attention in business, government, and academia.

The meaning of "smart city" has been controversial in literature, but can be broadly defined by the increasing extent to which urban areas are composed of pervasive computing and digital devices built into the fabric of urban environments that are used to monitor and regulate city processes [6]. Applications of such devices in the urban platform include fixed and wireless telecom networks, digitally controlled transport infrastructure, and sensor and camera networks designed to strengthen and optimize urban flows and processes, as highlighted in Fig. 2.1. Furthermore, mobile computing and the use of smartphones and other devices provides substantial data that can be used to model and predict urban processes and simulate likely future outcomes in urban development [7]. The use of such public data is argued to make a city knowable and controllable, as well as provide a more consolidated, efficient, and sustainable network [8].

Another definition of the notion of "smart city" is the broad development of a knowledge economy within a city [9]. In other words, a smart city is a city in which the economy and governance is being driven by technological innovation and entrepreneurship. The importance of ICT still stands in this definition of a smart city; it is seen as the platform for realizing ideas and innovations. In fact, ICT plays an integral role in both aforementioned definitions of smart city. In the first conceptual definition, a smart city uses ICT in managing and regulating the city from a technological perspective. However, in the second definition, policies related to education, economic development, and human capital are enhanced by ICT constituting networked infrastructures as the enabler of innovation and creativity which facilitates environmental, economic, social and cultural development [8]. In both cases, ICT plays a major role in urban development (Fig. 2.2).

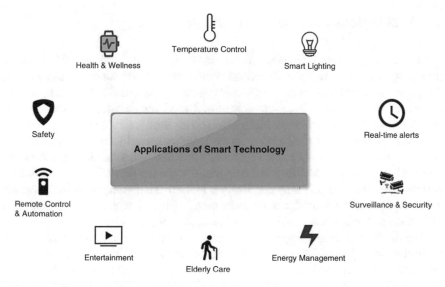

Fig. 2.2 The applications of smart technologies in everyday life

The integration of smart technology goes beyond the applications obvious to the general public. Networked infrastructure, smart devices, and sensors are used in various other applications ranging from healthcare to energy generation. Internet of Things (IoT) is the phenomenon referring to the integration of internet in various devices; such devices are used to increase the efficiency in a number of areas, including transport, healthcare, and manufacturing [9]. The integration of networks and ICT in all aspects of the community evokes larger security risks. Furthermore, the use of networks to connect various devices creates vulnerabilities in which attacks can cascade from a small device into a network where it can create significant damage to a community. As such, security is a critical topic and crucial to the exponential development of technologies in all aspects of the community. Furthermore, the increased complexity of technological and networked systems being used today induces the need for intelligent defense mechanisms.

In this chapter, the focus will be on the integration of networks and smart technologies in critical infrastructure and the use of artificial intelligence (AI) and big data for security of these infrastructures. The following sections will discuss the applications smart technologies, the vulnerabilities and security challenges associated with these applications, as well as some defense mechanisms discussed in literature. Furthermore, this chapter will dive into the applications of AI and importance of big data in cybersecurity.

2   Applications of Smart Technologies

Smart technology, referring to the incorporation of sensors and networked infrastructures, is used in many applications today. The use of smart technology has
the potential to enhance every service or product. Furthermore, the incorporation
of smart technology has been introduced and used for decades. For example, in
the 1980s, students at Carnegie Melon University used internet-connected sensors
to a vending machine to keep count of soft drinks served [10]. This allowed the
product providers to keep track of product count in each vending machine for
more efficient product delivery and service. Such examples of smart technology
adoption are abundant in many applications and are continually growing in variety
and complexity. These applications can be seen in Fig. 2.3, which shows the number
of IoT smart devices connected world wide in each application.

Among the prominent applications of smart technology and IoT, healthcare is
a significant and promising area. IoTs, in combination with Cloud Computing,
are receiving increased attention and value in the development of healthcare
services [12]. According to market analyst Grand View Research, the healthcare
IoT market is expected to grow to $330 billion by 2020 [13]. The integration
of internet connections in medical devices can increase the capability of health
monitoring and diagnosis [14]. The medical industry is expanding towards the
use of IoT and network infrastructures. These IoT based healthcare techniques are
proposed to analyze problems like heart rate, ECG, and oxygen saturation in the

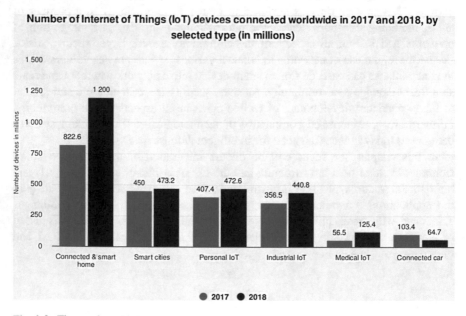

Fig. 2.3 The number of IoT devices connected worldwide in 2017 and 2018 [11]

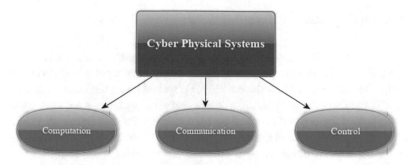

Fig. 2.4 The three major components of CPS; which are communication, control, and computation

blood [15]. Furthermore, cloud-based health monitoring systems have also been proposed for increased monitoring by medical personnel to improve healthcare and reduce costs [16].

Another pivotal set of applications of smart technology is in critical infrastructure. Sensors are used along city infrastructure and buildings for data collection to be used in more efficient modelling and prediction of likely outcomes. The concepts of smart meters, smart buildings, and smart grids are often discussed as the pinnacle of smart urbanization [17]. With data flowing across a city's infrastructure, relevant information can be used in various analysis, most notably efficient energy generation. Knowledge of energy consumption along a city's infrastructure enhances the predictive analysis of control centers, which in turn allow for more efficient energy distribution. Furthermore, the increased demand for green energy calls for a smart networked infrastructure capable of efficient use of energy sources. As such, the concept of the smart grid plays a major role in shaping the technological advancement of urban areas (Fig. 2.4).

The idea of the smart grid comprises of integrating smart meters and sensors and advanced computing technologies into the power systems [18, 19]. This smart grid technology greatly enhances the power generation efficiency and prompts the incorporation of various sources of energy generation into one system [20, 21]. Network communications and control centers accommodate the combination of green energy sources; and the association of smart meters and sensors along the power grid network allows the generation centers access to real-time power demand information, which can be used to implement an efficient generation and distribution plan [22]. As such, integration of these technologies into the power system infrastructure has greatly increased the energy efficiency as well as reduced the price of electricity[23]. The combination of communication networks and physical systems, referred to as cyber physical systems, are discussed in the next section.

3 Cyber Physical Systems

The integration of cyber components into physical systems is a phenomenon known as Cyber Physical Systems (CPS). CPS are systems that operate on various levels through different layers. These layers are the physical layer, which comprises of the physical components of the system, a sensor and actuator layer, a network layer, and a control layer. Sensors and actuator are used to communicate information between the physical components and the network, and the control layer is to send commands to the various aspects of the system. These layers are illustrated in Fig. 2.5.

As shown in Fig. 2.4, CPS can be defined by its three major components: communication, control, and computation [24]. CPS are characterized by the following actions that they perform:

- Detection and capturing events or data such as pressure, temperature, presence of an object, electrical demand, user data, etc.
- Actuators or physical components that affect a physical process within the system.
- Interactions with other CPS.
- Evaluation of saved data.
- Use of global data.
- Human machine interfaces [25]

As such, many industries adopted the use of CPS. Some examples of these applications include:

- Healthcare
- Transportation
- Manufacturing
- Energy generation and distribution
- Critical Infrastructure
- Agriculture [26].

The most prominent applications of CPS are discussed in the subsections that follow.

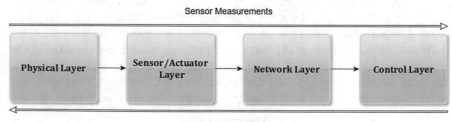

Fig. 2.5 The four layers of CPS; which are communication, control, and computation

3.1   CPS in Healthcare

Recent developments in medical devices have shifted towards integrating complex computing networks classifying them as CPS [27]. This shift in technology allows continuous monitoring and control of patients' physiological processes and functions. The integration of CPS in medical devices also provides the ability to remotely observe patients' condition [28]. Furthermore, the embedded sensing, computing, communications, and integration with physical elements and processes allow these CPS to achieve a level of functionality that is beyond simpler passive systems. CPS also have the potential to reach the body using minimally invasive techniques. They also lower costs, enhance mobility, independence, and quality of life. The sensitive nature of dealing with medical issues makes the design of CPS in healthcare challenging. Continuous exponential development of medical devices calls for comprehensive and efficient testing. Furthermore, the standards of healthcare are among the highest in all fields of technology. Security and privacy are also among the largest concerns with CPS in the healthcare. The flow of sensitive data and the access of CPS to the body means attacks can have devastating, and sometimes life-threatening, impacts.

3.2   CPS in Transportation

To meet the increasing demands of society, transportation systems are growing and evolving towards increasing complex systems. The European Rail Traffic Management System (ERTMS) as an excellent example of CPS integration in transportation. ERTMS use GSM communication, or global system for mobile communication, to connect the trains and infrastructure system for better management. Many other companies and organizations are integrating CPS in transportation. Cloud Computing and online databases are used in keeping track and optimization of bus or train schedules. Additionally, smart phones play a growing role in transportation; a smart phone can act as a train ticket, a GPS tracker, and, in some cases, connect to and operate some parts of a vehicle. Modern solutions for mobility emphasize automated forms of transportation, with interconnected vehicles, to address the societal goals of increased security, safety, convenience, and efficiency.

3.3   CPS in Manufacturing

Manufacturing has been a forerunner in automation. Automation tools, such as industrial robots and autonomous machines, are initiated in manufacturing before moving to other domains. Manufacturing encompasses CPS in various forms, ranging from 3D printers to cloud manufacturing. As such, integration of CPS in manufacturing creates opportunities for customized manufacturing schemes that can be beneficial and affordable to small businesses. Additionally, Life-cycle integration is introduced by industrial companies, which involves tracing data back to development and manufacturing for future improvement. CPS also provide solutions for increased sustainability through accurate and continuous monitoring of physical systems.

3.4 CPS in Power Systems: The Smart Grid

Among the most prominent and studied applications of CPS is the smart grid, the power systems of the next generation. The development of today's power systems is aimed towards integrating smart meters and sensors and advanced computing technologies to enhance the power generation efficiency[29]. The association of smart meters and sensors along the power grid network allows the generation centers access to real-time power demand information, which can be used to implement an efficient generation and distribution plan [30–32]. As such, integration of these technologies into the power system infrastructure has greatly increased the energy efficiency as well as reduced the price of electricity. The smart grid system consists various resources and technologies. Smart meters are incorporated to collect consumption data for more efficient power distribution. Additionally, interconnection of supervisory control and data acquisition (SCADA) allows for more expanded centralized distribution along large geographical areas [32–34]. The smart grid also allows for interaction among transmission and distribution grid, building controllers, as well as various sources of energy generation.

With the increased use and integration of CPS, security risks and challenges are raised and considered. The next section outlines and describes these challenges.

4   Security Challenges in Cyber Physical Systems

Most of today's critical infrastructures are based on cyber-physical systems [35]; meaning that they contain both physical and virtual aspects that operate on technology. This cyber-physical structure exposes critical infrastructure to cyber risks that can have devastating physical consequences. These cyber risks lead to security penetration that can go beyond breaking into the system and progress to controlling it [36]. And since CPS are used in many aspects of life, compromising these systems can have devastating and potentially lethal impact. In healthcare, for example, many machines and devices are connected to a network; compromising these devices can have destructive impact. Compromising an X-ray machine, for example, can alter the level of radiation given to a patient and causing serious harm or death [37]. Another example of compromised CPS that can have devastating impacts is the smart grid. Compromising some of the smart meters can result in faulty measurements passed to the control centers, which can result in wrongful energy generation and distribution inducing a blackout or physical damage to some infrastructure [38]. As such, safety and security of CPS is crucial. A secured and functioning CPS is defined by satisfying the following categories:

Confidentiality   The ability to prevent unauthorized individuals from disclosing information.
Integrity   Inability to modify or alter data without authorization.
Availability   The ability of the CPS to provide the intended services.
Authenticity   Ensuring safe data communication and transmission [39].

Ensuring the security of CPS begins by identifying the types of threats that endanger these systems. There are various types and subtypes of attacks that exploit different vulnerabilities of a CPS. These attacks can be subdivided into two categories: passive and active attacks [40]. Passive attacks have the purpose of being undetected over a long period of time. These attacks are aimed at intercepting sensitive data without causing any destruction. Active attacks, however, are aimed at causing direct damage or taking control of a system [41]. In general, CPS can endure any of the following attacks:

1. Eavesdropping
2. Spoofing
3. Denial of Service (DoS)
4. Code Injection
5. Malware
6. Control Hijacking

Each of the above attacks have unique purposes and exploit specific vulnerabilities. Furthermore, each of these attacks have various subtypes. These attacks and subtypes are defined and described in the following sections and demonstrated in Fig. 2.6.

4.1   Eavesdropping

Eavesdropping attacks are aimed at stealing data and information from a system. Subtypes of these attacks include Man-in-the-Middle, traffic sniffing, and replay attacks [42]. The first is an active type of attack in which an intruder intervenes between the communicating entities to intercept the packets. Traffic sniffing is a passive attack with the purpose of traffic analysis. Replay attacks aim to intercept authentication information.

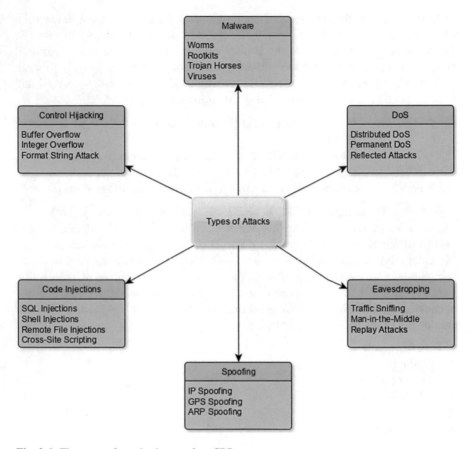

Fig. 2.6 The types of attacks that can face CPS

4.2 Spoofing

The main types of spoofing are GPS spoofing, ARP spoofing, and IP spoofing [43]. IP spoofing uses a modified IP to pass through security systems. This type of attack is typically the first stage of a complex intrusion. GPS spoofing, however, is based on broadcasting incorrect signals of higher strength than received from the satellites to deceive the victim. ARP spoofing is where falsified ARP (Address Resolution Protocol) messages are used to link the attacker's MAC address with the IP address of the victim; thus all data in the compromised system will pass through the intruder.

4.3 Denial of Service (DoS)

DoS attacks are subdivided into permanent DoS, distributed DoS, and reflected attacks [44]. Permanent DoS is a type of attack where the intruder tries to exploit unpatched vulnerabilities to install modified firmware to the system. However, a distributed DoS attack is an attack where several systems are sending requests to a victim system to occupy resources like bandwidth and processor time [45]. With this attack, the victim system is unable to provide services or continue its usual tasks. Reflected attacks are attacks that send forged requests to a large number of systems with the IP address set to that of the target victim. This results in the target victim being flooded with the responses. Smurf attacks and Fraggle attack are some of the variations of reflected attacks and they use ICMP packets and UDP packets respectively.

4.4 Code Injection

The four main types of code injection attacks are as follows:

SQL Injection Attack Involves insertion of malicious SQL statements leading to failure of input data.

Cross Site Scripting Exploits open script vulnerabilities and adds malicious code into web application for execution.

Remote File Injection Files with malicious code are downloaded on the server side of web applications and are executed on the server.

Shell Injection Malicious shell code is inserted into the code string for further interpretation by the shell [46].

4.5 Malware

Malware is any program or file that is harmful to a computer user and includes viruses, Trojan horses, rootkits, and worms [42, 47]. Each of these types are defined as follows:

Virus A type of malware that infects files and programs in the system.

Trojan Horse A type of malware that intrudes the system under the disguise of a legitimate software.

Rootkit A set of software, such as scripts, executable files, and configuration files, with the ability to hide itself and other malicious software.

Worm A type of malware software with the ability to replicate itself resulting in a waste of network bandwidth.

4.6 Control Hijacking

This type of attack is aimed at taking control of a target machine or system. This is done through the three main subtypes of control hijacking attacks each designed to exploit a specific vulnerability. These attacks are listed and defined as follows:

Buffer Overflow Attack An attack designed to force the target system to write data outside its given buffer.

Integer Overflow Attack An attack aimed at creating an integer overflow error, which occurs due to the system's inability to represent numerical values within its given storage space.

Format String Intrusion An intrusion in which the input string is executed as a command.

Considering the variety of attack types, particular types of CPS are more prone to specific attacks. For example, medical devices are prone to eavesdropping attacks such as replay and traffic sniffing. Critical infrastructure, while also prone to eavesdropping attacks, have additional vulnerabilities with high potential impact. Therefore, security of critical infrastructures, such as the smart grid, is a much more elaborate task. Furthermore, certain types of CPS, such as the smart grid, are prone to specific types of attacks designed just for these systems. For example, False Data Injection (FDI) attacks are a type of attack in which malicious data is injected into the smart meters to deceive the control centers with inaccurate power demand data [48]. This type of attack, when successful, can potentially cause blackouts or serious infrastructural damage to power stations.

The variety of vulnerabilities and attack methods in CPS calls for comprehensive defense strategies at various levels of the systems. The next section describes the defense mechanism used and proposed to date.

5 Defense Mechanisms

Considering the important applications and complexity of CPS, ensuring their security is crucial. Furthermore, the distributed nature of modern CPS is a key concern; complex CPS consist of various components at different levels, all of which with their own vulnerabilities. Therefore, ensuring a secured CPS involves securing each of the components and considering all possible consequences of a compromised component on the whole system [49]. As such, numerous challenges can arise from securing a CPS, with distinct challenges for each type of CPS.

Security approaches in literature vary upon the application and the type of CPS. However, a general methodology to secure networks and infrastructure is proposed by CISCO [50], and contains the following elements:

- *Security Policy (SP):* Procedures of conducting necessary measures to maintain security. This involves all relevant security measures such as firewalls, authentication, and authorization. A well-established security policy is defined by the following aspects [51]:

  - A set of security measures for particular threats
  - Role distribution.
  - Clear definition of normal or accepted behavior.
  - Resource classification based on sensitivity.
  - Communication process organization.
  - Reporting and logging of essential information.

- *Monitoring and Response:* Includes routine knowledge extraction about the environment of the system and potential threats, as well as conventional responses to potential threats.
- *Testing:* Constant checking of the system abilities to react to threats as well as the response time. The purpose is to maintain constant control of state or configuration of the security system and detecting weaknesses.
- *Management and Improvement:* Organizing efficient use of security assets and acting on identified security gaps. This includes maintaining proper functioning of the system and keeping security systems up to date.

An important component of cyber security systems is intrusion detection. Intrusion detection systems (IDS) aim to inform the system or the operator of an intrusion or attack through collecting relevant historic data and analyzing subsequent gathered data [52]. According to the National Institute of Standards and Technology (NIST), there are four main types of IDS listed as follows [53]:

- *Network Based:* Focuses on network traffic and considers network protocols, traffic, and devices.
- *Wireless:* Similar to network based, however protocols are in the scope of the IDS used.
- *Network behavior analysis:* Considers network traffic flows and identifies suspicious patterns and policy violations.
- *Host-based IDS:* Monitors activities related to a certain host such as traffic, application activities, operations, and configurations. This type of IDS is usually applied in critical infrastructure.

When it comes to detecting the threats, however, most modern IDS can be divided into three subgroups, which are based on their algorithmic operations [54]. These subgroups are listed and defined as follows:

- *Anomaly-based:* Detects behavioral patterns in system's data which are different of normal system's functioning.

- **Signature-based:** Identifies threats using a set of threat models. This requires an up-to-date storage of various types of threats and their models.
- **Specification-based:** Suspicious activity is detected using the specifications of the system as well as its components

Many techniques are proposed in literature that claim a high threat detection accuracy. One approach uses trusted devices, or sensors with guaranteed security, and compares data from these devices to other devices with potential threats in order to detect attacks on the system [55]. Such model-based techniques are not practical due to their vulnerability to passive attacks as well as DoS attacks. While each CPS is associated with its own security challenges, resource and time constraints are issues that prevail in the security of almost all systems. Considering the importance and sensitivity of the applications of CPS, time and resources are scarce and must be used wisely. Furthermore, detection of intrusions and attacks must occur in a precise and timely manner, in which security mechanisms and protocols are given the appropriate time and resources to act and mitigate the threat. To solve for the issue of resource constraint, scheduling techniques are proposed in which responsibilities are shared among the various components of a CPS [56]. However, it is difficult to propose a model-based technique that is both time-efficient and highly accurate. As such, intelligent systems are proposed, which employ Artificial Intelligence (AI) and Big Data for more accurate and time-efficient attack detection. The next section discusses the applications of AI in the security of CPS and its importance in designing comprehensive security systems.

6 Applications of AI in Cyber Security

Artificial Intelligence (AI) is a fast-growing field in the technology industry. Many researchers and developers are implementing methods and techniques that simulate human-like intelligence in algorithmic operations. AI and the emergence of deep learning has increased the potential of many applications. AI, unlike ordinary programming tools, does not require a clearly modelled process; in many cases, AI can use input-output data to learn and generate system parameters that can classify and predict unlearned data. Such a tool can have a wide range of applications, such as speech recognition, facial recognition, and robotics. Cyber security is also one of the largely studied applications of AI [57, 58]; in fact, most organizations working with AI focus on detecting and deterring security intrusions, as per Fig. 2.7. Intelligent systems are also used for malware monitoring and intrusion detection. Furthermore, machine learning (ML) algorithms are commonly used to classify and detect cyber threats in CPS. The abundant use of AI in cyber security is due to its high potential efficiency and scalability. As opposed to model-based solutions, intelligent systems have the capability of learning and thus adapting to larger systems.

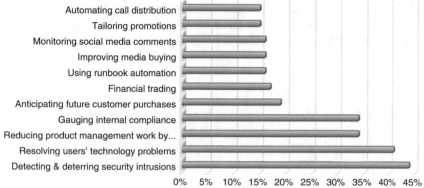

Fig. 2.7 The types of applications of AI sorted by number of organizations working in each field [59]

The issue with the use of ML in cyber security mainly comes from the dependence of these algorithms on a set of variables or features. When designing an ML algorithm for detecting a malware, for example, key features of a malware must be identified. And if certain variables are not used as features, the ML algorithm will ignore them. As such, feature selection or feature extraction is a key concept in developing ML algorithms. As such, to maintain a high classification accuracy, ML algorithms must employ a comprehensive and efficient feature extraction technique [60–63]. To overcome this flaw, researchers began to migrate from traditional ML algorithms to deep neural networks or deep learning (DL).

DL is a sub-domain of ML with the ability to directly train on original data without extracting its features. In the past decade, DL has greatly improved the performance in the fields of computer vision, speech recognition, and text recognition achieving a historic leap in the AI field [64]. The main advantages of DL are its ability to detect nonlinear relationships and support new file types; and therefore, it can detect unknown attacks in systems, which is an attractive trait for cyber security. DL, as well as general ML algorithms, can be categorized into the following three categories:

Supervised Learning Requires the use of labeled input data to train a classification or regression algorithm. Classification is used to analyze data and allocate it to a specific class while regression is used to output a prediction value of continuous nature.

Unsupervised Learning Uses unlabeled input data. This class of algorithms is often used to cluster data or reduce its dimensions.

Reinforcement Learning Based on a reward system that rewards satisfactory actions. These types of algorithms can be considered as a fusion of supervised and unsupervised learning, and are mainly suitable for tasks that have long-term feedback [65].

There are many ML and DL algorithms that fall within the above categories, many of which are used in various areas of cyber security. The following sections discuss traditional ML algorithms and DL algorithms and their applicability to cyber security.

6.1   Traditional ML Algorithms for Cyber Security

Traditional ML solutions consist of the following four main steps [66]:

1. Feature Extraction
2. Choosing an appropriate ML algorithm
3. Training models with varying parameters and selecting the model with optimal performance.
4. Classify or predict unknown data using the trained model.

Examples of ML algorithms include support vector machines (SVM), K-nearest neighbor (KNN), decision trees, and artificial neural networks. There are other ML algorithms, however, the aforementioned four algorithms are among the most used ML algorithms in cyber security. The following subsections discuss each of those algorithms and their application to cyber security.

6.1.1   Support Vector Machines (SVM)

SVM is a supervised learning algorithm that can be used for classification and regression, which are known as support vector classification and support vector regression respectively. SVM works by separating the input data through the construction of an appropriate split plane. The most common way of creating such a split plane is through the use of a Gaussian Kernel, which is defined by the following equation:

$$K\left(x_i, x_{i'}\right) = \exp\left\{-\gamma \sum_{j=1}^{p} \left(x_{ij} - x_{i'j}\right)^2\right\} \qquad (2.1)$$

where γ is the kernel coefficient and x represents the data. This split plane is used to divide and distinguish between classes of data. An example visualization of this split plane can be seen in Fig. 2.8.

SVM has been used in various applications of cybersecurity including the detection of distributed DoS attacks in software-defined network and real time detection of malware uniform resource locator (URL) [67, 68]. SVMs are also used

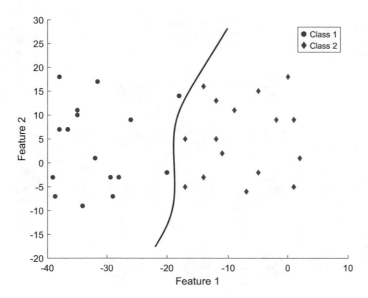

Fig. 2.8 An example of SVM classifications

in detection of false data injection (FDI) attacks in the smart grid [69, 70]. In each of these implementations of SVM, it was proved, when compared to other ML algorithms, that SVM has the potential of achieving high classification accuracy and a low false positive rate. The main disadvantage, however, is the long training time.

6.1.2   K Nearest Neighbor (KNN)

K-nearest neighbors (KNN) algorithm is another supervised learning method that classifies data based on its closest k neighbors. The closeness between the data is determined using the Euclidean distance,

$$d_{ij} = \left\| \mathbf{s_i} - \mathbf{s}_j \right\|, \mathbf{s}_j \in S \tag{2.2}$$

where S and s correspond to labelled and unlabeled data respectively, and $k > 1$ corresponds to the number of neighbors. The KNN algorithm has been proposed for various applications in cybersecurity. The main use of this classifier is for intrusion detection. One method represents program behavior by frequencies of system calls which are classified as normal or intrusive via the KNN algorithm [71]. KNN was also used with particle swarm optimization (PSO) for intrusion detection. PSO was claimed to increase the classification accuracy by 2% [72].

Hidden Layers

Input Layer   Output Layer

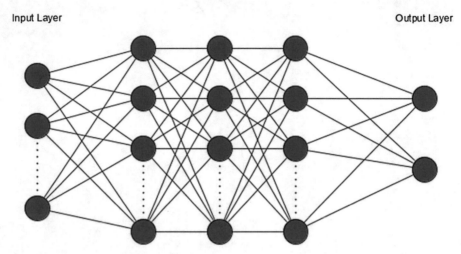

Fig. 2.9 An example ANN architecture [73]

6.1.3 Artificial Neural Network (ANN)

ANN is an algorithm composed of interconnected elements, called neurons or nodes, which process information based on specific weights. ANN can be constructed in various methods and architectures and typically consist of an input layer, hidden layers, and an output layer each consisting of several nodes. Each of the input nodes contains a feature of the data; these nodes are activated through various types of activation functions which process the information into the next layer of nodes. This activation process occurs in every layer until the data is classified in the output layer of the ANN (Fig. 2.9).

ANNs are used in many areas of cyber security. One study developed an intrusion detection system for supervisory control and data acquisition (SCADA) systems [74]. The ANN monitors the physical behavior of the SCADA system to successfully detect man-in-the middle response injection and DoS attacks. Another study proposed a computationally efficient ANN for intrusion detection [75]. The experimental results showed promising results in reducing runtime and memory requirements; which are key concerns associated with neural networks.

6.2 Deep Learning Algorithms

Through automatic feature selection, deep learning (DL) attempts to obtain deeper and more accurate relationships in the input data. Most commonly used DL algorithms include recurrent neural networks (RNN), convolutional neural networks

(CNN), deep belief networks (DBN), and automatic encoders. The functionality and applications of each of the DL algorithms are discussed in the following subsections.

6.2.1   Deep Belief Networks (DBN)

DBN is a learning algorithm based on probabilistic generative models, and is composed of stochastic hidden units acting as feature detectors. A typical architecture of DBN consists of two top layers with symmetric connections between them forming an associative memory, and two bottom layers receiving top-down directed connected from the above layers. This creates an efficient layer-by-layer procedure in which generative weights determine how variables in one layer depend on the variables in the layer above. After learning, the DBN classifies and predicts data through a bottom-up pass that starts with the data vector at the bottom layer, and uses the generated weights in the reverse direction. The unique feature of DBNs is their efficient greedy learning, in which the network learns one layer at a time by treating the values of the previous layers and training data for the next layer.

In cyber security, DBN has been implemented in malware detection in android applications [76]. The results of this study prove the superiority of DBN over traditional ML algorithms such as SVM and ANN. Another study proposed a novel intrusion detection scheme that combines DBN with a probabilistic neural network (PNN) and particle swarm optimization (PSO) [77]. In this technique, DBN is used to extract characteristics from the raw data, PNN is used to classify the low-dimensional data, and PSO is used to optimize the number of nodes in each hidden layer.

6.2.2   Recurrent Neural Networks (RNN)

RNNs are a class of ANN in which connections between nodes form a directed graph along a temporal sequence. This allows RNNs to use previous predictions as part of the input data. In other words, RNNs have memory and use present and recent past inputs in their decision making. This is done through a feedback loop connecting past decisions to current inputs in the RNN architecture. The most prominent type of RNNs are long short-term memory (LSTM) networks. LSTM networks have been notably used in language modelling, machine translation, and speech recognition [78].

In cyber security, LSTM-RNNs are used to classify permission-based Android malware due to their ability to learn from temporal behaviors in sparse representations, in which they achieved accuracy as high as 89.7% [79]. A cloud-based intrusion detection scheme for Internet of Vehicles (IoV) has also been proposed [80]. This pointed out very promising results, as the LSTM learned temporal context of various attacks such as DoS, command injection, and malware. The high computational demands of RNN, as well as other DL methods, were also addressed through the use of cloud-based computational offloading.

6.2.3   Convolutional Neural Networks (CNN)

CNNs are another class of deep neural networks that use convolutional layers. The use of convolutional layers is an approach towards regularization, in which hierarchical patterns in data are used to break down complex patterns into smaller and simpler patterns. The main use of CNNs is for image classification and facial recognition [81, 82]. In cyber security, however, CNN was proposed in the use of malware classification based on malware gene sequences [83]. CNN, due to its convolutional property, proved successful in identifying malwares based on patterns in the gene sequences representing the malwares attributes. Another approach of using DL for cyber security presented the use of CNN for intrusion detection, coupled with two traditional ML classifiers, SVM and KNN, which performed few-shot intrusion on the outputs of each layer of the CNN [84].

6.2.4   Automatic Encoders

Unlike the aforementioned DL algorithms, automatic encoder, also known as autoencoder, is an unsupervised learning algorithm. Autoencoders are very different from traditional learning algorithms; instead of classifying or predicting data, autoencoders attempt to reduce the dimensions of the data by learning representations or encoding for a dataset. In other words, autoencoders attempt to reduce and reconstruct the data to be as close as possible to the original input. This method is extremely useful for dimensionality reduction or automatic feature selection.

Autoencoders are extensively used in the field of cyber security. Stacked autoencoders are used for unsupervised DL that can classify cyberspace attacks in fog-to-things computing [85]. Autoencoders are also used for anomaly detection. One study used autoencoders and de-noising autoencoders and concluded optimal performance in detecting attacks from unlabeled data [86]. Additionally, detection of DoS attacks in applications was also tackled by the use of autoencoders. This scheme analyzes communications between a web server and its clients and distributes them using a stacked autoencoder and DL algorithms to detect DoS-related attacks [87]. The benefit of this scheme is that it does not require decryption of the encrypted traffic, thus obeying the ethical norms concerning privacy.

7   Deep Learning: Adapting to the Real World

Most intelligent algorithms are developed and tested in a simulated environment or on miniaturized systems. As such, generalization of these techniques is of great importance for the purpose of scalability and application to larger real-time systems. Since the main goal of an intelligent system is to adapt to unseen data, generalization demonstrates the dependency of a trained model on unseen training set. This is expressed by the generalization gap, which represents the difference between empirical risk and expected risk, which are statistical terms expressing the adaptability of the learning algorithm to new data through testing and numerical estimation.

$$Generalization\ Gap := R\left[f_{A(S)}\right] - R_S\left[f_{A(S)}\right] \qquad (2.3)$$

Where $R\left[f_{A(S)}\right]$ is the expected risk and $R\left[f_{A(S)}\right]$ is the empirical risk. The goal is empirical risk minimization, which is minimizing the computable empirical risk in order to minimize the non-computable expected risk. The primary challenge of analyzing the generalization gap stems from the dependence of the learning function on the dataset. Several approaches in statistical learning theory have been developed to handle this dependence [88, 89], which include:

- **Hypothesis-space complexity:** This approach handles the dependency by decoupling the model function from its training data and considering the worst-case gap for functions in the hypothesis space.
- **Stability:** The stability approach deals with the dependence of the model on the dataset by considering the stability of the learning algorithm with respect to different datasets. This considered stability is a measure of the effect of changing a data point in the original dataset.
- **Robustness:** The robustness approach avoids certain details of the dependence of the model function on the dataset by considering the robustness of the learning algorithm for all possible datasets. As opposed to stability, robustness measures the loss value variation with respect to the input space. This approach, however, requires a known and fixed partition of the input space.

The main goal of adapting AI systems to real-world application is achieved through minimizing the generalization error. The various strategies of generalization fall under the definition of regularization, which is any modification to the algorithm that reduces the generalization error without reducing the training error [90]. There are two categories of regularization: implicit and explicit [91]; both are defined as follows.

Implicit Regularization regularization using the characteristics of the learning algorithm, the network architecture, or the data. Examples of this include the use of convolution layers or batch normalization.

Explicit Regularization regularization that is not through a structural part of the network architecture, algorithm, or the data. These methods of regularization can be added or removed easily and include dropout layers, data augmentation, and weight decay.

Regularization plays a critical role in developing a successful and efficient AI system. This is because regularization improves the scalability and adaptability of the intelligent system on larger applications. Therefore, the shift from a theoretical model to an applicable model must involve some regularization methods. The commonly used regularization methods in deep learning are:

- **Weight Decay:** Also known as L2 Regularization, weight decay is an explicit regularization method that constrains and decreases the complexity of a neural network. Limiting the weights or parameters prevents the learning algorithm from producing too large values, which can in turn increase the computational cost [92].
- **Dropout:** The dropout technique revolves around using dropout layers within the neural network. The dropout layers avoid over-fitting by randomly dropping units from the network forcing the network to learn using varying combinations of features [93].
- **Sparsity Regularization:** Sparsity refers to layers with most coefficients being zero. The idea behind this is that the model can learn by reduced number of variables, which leads to reduction of computational and memory requirements. Sparsity can be enforced by either implicit or explicit regularization [94]. Implicitly, sparsity regularization can be achieved through convolution layers. In explicit regularization, however, sparsity can be achieved by including a loss function that penalizes non-zero weights.
- **Weight Sharing:** This method consists of sharing a single weight among many nodes in the neural network. In other words, groups of neuron nodes share weight values such that each group processes a local region of the input [95]. This technique results in a shift-invariant system aiding in the generalization capability of the model. It also reduces the complexity and computational cost due to the reduced number of parameters.
- **Data Augmentation:** An explicit regularization technique where additional generated data is used in the training of the model [90]. This additional data is usually fake and generated to train the model on additional adversaries.
- **Pooling:** An operation used in almost all CNNs which makes output representations invariant to small translation of the input image. Pooling layers function by progressively reducing the spatial size of the data representation to reduce the amount of parameters and computation in the network [90]. This strategy helps avoid overfitting.
- **DropConnect:** A recently introduced regularization method for neural networks. In this method, randomly selected subsets of weights are replaced by zero [96]. This introduces dynamic sparsity within the network which can help it adapt to more adverse and variant data. In certain cases, this can be considered as an improvement to dropout, but not always [97].
- **Adversarial Training:** The process of explicitly training the model on adversarial examples to increase robustness and reduce test error on clean input samples [90]. This is useful because malicious inputs can be designed to fool a machine learning model, and adversarial training can aid in avoiding that [98].

As previously highlighted, AI tools have the potential of solving many cyber-related challenges. Although advanced intelligent solutions are essential for the unsolved challenges of cyber security, such solutions raise technical questions and uncertainties for the consequences of employing AI tools, particularly in critical infrastructure. There is a number of serious ideological, ethical, and legal concerns that could arise from the use of such advanced and intelligent technology in sensitive areas like critical infrastructure. There are also challenges associated with the immaturity of the subject itself. These challenges are discussed in the next section.

8   Challenges of AI in Cyber Security

The integration and development of AI in security of CPS is concluding towards the use of deep learning methods. DL provides a rich collection of models that can approximate any function and adapt to any data. Furthermore, DL provides a scalability factor, which is essential for large critical infrastructure. These attributes are desirable because CPS typically have high dimensional data coming from a large number of sensors. Furthermore, CPS are constantly updated with new data with consistent growth; as such DL is extensively used in cyber security of CPS. However, there are many challenges associated with DL.

One of the major problems with DL approaches is the lack of theoretical background in the topic. Most studies in the topic demonstrate the impressive performance of DL methods without detailed explanation of how they generalize well [89]. This lack of transparency has reduced peoples' trust in DL approaches [99]. Furthermore, it has made it difficult to implement proper regularization techniques for real world applications.

Regularization is an integral part of applying AI methods to any application; it involves modifications of parameters to ensure scalability to the real world systems. For example, in classic ML theories, regularization typically involves changing parameters so that the number of training samples outweighs the number of parameters in the ML algorithms [100]. In DL methods, however, good generalization has been achieved even with over-parameterized settings [89]. Some DL methods require different techniques for good generalization such as weight sharing, weight decay, drop out layers, and data augmentation. While these techniques are often used, their importance is seldom highlighted and expressed.

Another critical challenge in implementing AI, and specifically DL methods, is the selection of the correct parameter and setting balance of the algorithm. Increased development of GPU has increased the potential of DL algorithms. This increased processing power has encouraged researchers to train broader and deeper networks [101]. These deeper networks have the potential of learning more complex patterns. However, it has been shown that networks with larger capacities reduce the practicality of regularization methods, such as dropout or weight decay, as well as requiring longer training time [90, 102]. As such, researchers and AI developers must find the balance between implementing deeper architectures and usage of regularization methods. This is a key to increasing the robustness of DL methods, which can be sensitive to adversarial samples [103].

The exponential development and integration of AI in cyber security, and all aspects of technology, has raised ideological and ethical concerns as well. Reports outline that reliance on AI could create new vulnerabilities that could be exploited by adversaries [104]. As such, some attention should be focused on technological or policy-oriented solutions that can mitigate malicious applications of these AI tools. The integration of AI also introduces new difficulties in interactions between machines and humans. Interpreting information from complex autonomous systems can become increasingly difficult. Speculations also exist regarding the creation of autonomic mechanisms for judgements and decisions that can be deemed too affected by information overload or human emotions [105].

Some technical recommendations were suggested for the design and development of intelligent systems include [106]:

- A guarantee of appropriate control under all circumstances
- Strict constraints are set for the algorithm's behavior
- Careful testing and validation is performed to satisfy safety concerns
- Restricted environment in which the intelligent system is permitted to operate on known platforms.

Another concern to be further examined is the protocol of communication. A main concern is whether communication should be one-way, only allowing gathering of information, or two-way, allowing swift actions to be taken. Two-way communication can have advantages such as faster reaction time but is also prone to additional security concerns such as loss of control over the intelligent system. Comprehensive communication protocols also have a larger potential in dealing with multi-agent threats, or threats that deal with possible cooperative behavior or various agents. Such multi-agent formations have high potential in application of cyber operations. Inter-agent communications can be used for more comprehensive cooperation to achieve more general goals [106]. However, unwanted coalitions between agents can occur if agents are given too much autonomy in decision-making. This can have severe consequences that can be difficult to reverse [107]. The technical solutions suggested for such problems include the use of safeguards such as back-doors and forced destruction.

Clarity questions and uncertainties also surround the legal implications of the development of intelligent mechanisms. Some suggest that autonomous agents are similar to any other tool and should therefore exist under international law [107]. However, it is unclear to whether a developer could be held responsible if an intelligent agent exceeds its assigned tasks and makes unauthorized decisions. As such, the use of mandatory signatures or watermarks as well as automatic safeguards can have beneficial effects on the integration of AI into society.

9 Conclusion

The increased integration of smart technology into critical infrastructure is accompanied with many advantages. However, the reliance of these technologies on communication networks raises many concerns regarding security. Moreover, the use of these cyber physical systems in critical infrastructure, such as healthcare, transportation, and power generation, induces severe consequences that accompany these security concerns. With the advancement of technology in the direction of networked devices, security of such cyber physical systems has become a topic of great interest. As such, many security measures and defense mechanisms were introduced to tackle the security issues of these systems.

There are many challenges associated with the security of cyber physical systems. The variety of threats and vulnerabilities deems model-based techniques ineffective. The diversity of the system types, as well as the types of cyber attacks that may inflict them, calls for more comprehensive techniques capable of detecting threats of varying nature. These comprehensive detection methods must rely on artificial intelligence in order to accurately classify these threats. This is because non-intelligent model-based systems require substantial complexity to attain sufficient results. As such, the use of AI is an ideal solution to security of cyber physical systems and critical infrastructure.

In this chapter, the importance of smart technology and the adoption of cyber physical systems in everyday life, specifically pertaining to critical infrastructure. Additionally, the security challenges of these systems are highlighted and discussed. The use of AI for cyber security is also examined in this chapter; various machine learning and deep learning techniques are identified and their applications are explained. Furthermore, generalization methods are discussed, which aim at increasing the robustness and scalability of these algorithms to large complex systems. While the significance and advantages of using AI in security of critical infrastructure is strongly recommended, associated challenges and risks, also discussed in this chapter, must be considered. Therefore, it can be concluded that while AI offers many advantages and shortcuts, thorough testing and monitoring must take place to minimize the associated risk while taking advantage of the solutions these AI algorithms can provide.

References

1. Z. K. A. Mohammed and E. S. A. Ahmed, Internet of things applications, challenges and related future technologies. World Sci. News, **67**(2), 126–148 (2017)
2. W. Dutton, J. Blumler, K. Kraemer, *Wired Cities: Shaping the Future of Communications*. Communications library (Washington Program, Annenberg School of Communications, Washington, 1987)
3. S. Graham, S. Marvin, Planning cybercities? Integrating telecommunications into urban planning. Town Plan. Rev. **70**(1), 89–114 (1999)
4. T. Ishida, K. Isbister (eds.), *Digital Cities: Technologies, Experiences, and Future Perspectives*. Lecture Notes in Computer Science (Springer, Berlin, 2000)
5. R.G. Hollands, Will the real smart city please stand up? Intelligent, progressive or entrepreneurial? City Anal. Urban Trends Cult. Theory Policy Action **12**(3), 303–320 (2008)
6. A. Greenfield, *Everyware: The Dawning Age of UbiquitousComputing*, 1st edn. (New Riders, Berkeley, 2006)
7. G. Hancke, B. Silva, G. Hancke, Jr., The role of advanced sensing in smart cities. Sensors **13**, 393–425 (2012)

8. S. Allwinkle, P. Cruickshank, Creating smart-er cities: an overview. J. Urban Technol. **18**, 1–16 (2011)
9. D. Miorandi, S. Sicari, F. De Pellegrini, I. Chlamtac, Internet of things: vision, applications and research challenges. Ad Hoc Netw. **10**, 1497–1516 (2012)
10. R. Vetter, Internet kiosk-computer-controlled devices reach the internet. Computer **28**, 66 (1995)
11. IHS, Global connected IoT devices by type 2017 and 2018. Available online at: https://www.statista.com/statistics/748737/worldwide-connected-iot-devices-by-sector/
12. F. Firouzi, A.M. Rahmani, K. Mankodiya, M. Badaroglu, G. Merrett, P. Wong, B. Farahani, Internet-of-Things and big data for smarter healthcare: from device to architecture, applications and analytics. Futur. Gener. Comput. Syst. **78**, 583–586 (2018)
13. C. Perera, C.H. Liu, S. Jayawardena, M. Chen, A survey on internet of things from industrial market perspective. IEEE Access **2**, 1660–1679 (2014)
14. K. Gautam, V. Puri, J.G. Tromp, C.V. Le, N.G. Nguyen, Internet ofthings and healthcare technologies: a valuable synergy from design to implementation. Int. J. Mach. Learn. Netw. Collab. Eng. **2**, 128–142 (2018)
15. J.J.P.C. Rodrigues, D.B. De Rezende Segundo, H.A. Junqueira, M.H. Sabino, R.M. Prince, J. Al-Muhtadi, V.H.C. De Albuquerque, Enabling technologies for the internet of health things. IEEE Access **6**, 13129–13141 (2018)
16. M. Hassanalieragh, A. Page, T. Soyata, G. Sharma, M. Aktas, G. Mateos, B. Kantarci, S. Andreescu, Health monitoring and management using Internet-of-Things (IoT) sensing with cloud-based processing: opportunities and challenges, in *2015 IEEE International Conference on Services Computing*, New York City (IEEE, Piscataway, 2015), pp. 285–292
17. A. Luque-Ayala, S. Marvin, Developing a critical understanding of smart urbanism? Urban Stud. **52**, 2105–2116 (2015)
18. I. Colak, G. Fulli, S. Sagiroglu, M. Yesilbudak, C.-F. Covrig, Smart grid projects in Europe: current status, maturity and future scenarios. Appl. Energy **152**, 58–70 (2015)
19. J. Sakhnini, H. Karimipour, A. Dehghantanha, Smart grid cyber attacks detection using supervised learning and heuristic feature selection, in *2017 IEEE International Conference on Smart Energy Grid Engineering (SEGE)* (2019)
20. M.C. Such, C. Hill, Battery energy storage and wind energy integrated into the smart grid, in *2012 IEEE PES Innovative Smart Grid Technologies (ISGT)* (2012), pp. 1–4
21. H.M. Rouzbahani, A. Rahimnezhad, H. Karimipour, Smart households demand response management with micro grid. *IEEE Innovative Smart Grid Technologies (ISGT 2019)* (2019)
22. H. Yang, J. Zhang, J. Qiu, S. Zhang, M. Lai, Z.Y. Dong, A practical pricing approach to smart grid demand response based on load classification. IEEE Trans. Smart Grid **9**, 179–190 (2018)
23. H. Karimipour, V. Dinavahi, On false data injection attack against dynamic state estimation on smart power grids, in *2017 IEEE International Conference on Smart Energy Grid Engineering (SEGE)* (2017), pp. 388–393
24. N. Wu, X. Li, RFID applications in cyber-physical system, in *Deploying RFID – Challenges, Solutions, and Open Issues* (IntechOpen, London, 2011)
25. D.B. Rawat, J.J.P.C. Rodrigues, I. Stojmenovic, *Cyber-Physical Systems: From Theory to Practice* (CRC Press, Boca Raton, 2015). Google-Books-ID: _CzSCgAAQBAJ
26. National Academies of Sciences, Engineering, and Medicine, *A 21st Century Cyber-Physical Systems Education* (The National Academies Press, Washington, 2016)
27. I. Lee, O. Sokolsky, Medical cyber physical systems, in *Design Automation Conference* (2010), pp. 743–748
28. A. Milenković, C. Otto, E. Jovanov, Wireless sensor networks for personal health monitoring: issues and an implementation. Comput. Commun. **29**, 2521–2533 (2006)
29. H. Karimipour, V. Dinavahi, Accelerated parallel WLS state estimation for large-scale power systems on GPU, in *2013 North American Power Symposium (NAPS)* (2013), pp. 1–6
30. X. Fang, S. Misra, G. Xue, D. Yang, Smart grid – the new and improved power grid: a survey. IEEE Commun. Surv. Tutorials **14**, 944–980 (2012)

31. H. Karimipour, V. Dinavahi, Parallel domain decomposition based distributed state estimation for large-scale power systems, in *2015 IEEE/IAS 51st Industrial Commercial Power Systems Technical Conference (I CPS)* (2015), pp. 1–5
32. H. Karimipour, V. Dinavahi, Extended Kalman Filter-based parallel dynamic state estimation. IEEE Trans. Smart Grid **6**, 1539–1549 (2015)
33. The Smart Grid Interoperability Panel–Smart Grid Cybersecurity Committee, Guidelines for smart grid cybersecurity, Technical Report NIST IR 7628r1, National Institute of Standards and Technology (2014)
34. H. Karimipour, V. Dinavahi, Robust massively parallel dynamic state estimation of power systems against cyber-attack. IEEE Access **6**, 2984–2995 (2018)
35. R. Rajkumar, I. Lee, L.R. Sha, J. Stankovic, Cyber-physical systems: the next computing revolution, in *Proceedings of the 47th Design Automation Conference, DAC '10* (2010), pp. 731–736
36. R. Langner, *Robust Control System Networks* (Momentum Press, New York, 2011)
37. L. Ayala, *Cybersecurity for Hospitals and Healthcare Facilities – A Guide to Detection and Prevention | Luis Ayala | Apress* (Apress, New York, 2016)
38. Z.E. Mrabet, N. Kaabouch, H.E. Ghazi, H.E. Ghazi, Cyber-security in smart grid: survey and challenges. Comput. Electr. Eng. **67**, 469–482 (2018)
39. E.K. Wang, Y. Ye, X. Xu, S.M. Yiu, L.C.K. Hui, K.P. Chow, Security issues and challenges for cyber physical system, in *Proceedings of the 2010 IEEE/ACM Int'L Conference on Green Computing and Communications & Int'L Conference on Cyber, Physical and Social Computing*, GREENCOM-CPSCOM '10, Washington, pp. 733–738 (IEEE Computer Society, Washington, 2010)
40. Y. Shoukry, P. Martin, P. Tabuada, M. Srivastava, Non-invasive spoofing attacks for anti-lock braking systems, in *Proceedings of the 15th International Conference on Cryptographic Hardware and Embedded Systems*, CHES'13, Berlin (Springer, Berlin, 2013), pp. 55–72. Event-place: Santa Barbara, CA
41. Y. Chen, S. Kar, J.M.F. Moura, Cyber-physical attacks with control objectives. IEEE Trans. Autom. Control **63**, 1418–1425 (2016)
42. D. Papp, Z. Ma, L. Buttyan, Embedded systems security: threats, vulnerabilities, and attack taxonomy, in *2015 13th Annual Conference on Privacy, Security and Trust, PST 2015* (Institute of Electrical and Electronics Engineers Inc., Piscataway, 2015), pp. 145–152
43. P. Jokar, N. Arianpoo, V.C.M. Leung, Spoofing detection in IEEE 802.15.4 networks based on received signal strength. Ad Hoc Netw. **11**, 2648–2660 (2013)
44. P.G. Neumann, *Computer Related Risks* (ACM Press/Addison-Wesley Publishing Co., New York, 1995)
45. O. Osanaiye, H. Cai, K.-K.R. Choo, A. Dehghantanha, Z. Xu, M. Dlodlo, Ensemble-based multi-filter feature selection method for DDoS detection in cloud computing. J. Wirel. Commun. Netw. **2016**, 130 (2016)
46. Z. Su, G. Wassermann, The essence of command injection attacks in web applications, in *Conference Record of the 33rd ACM SIGPLAN-SIGACT Symposium on Principles of Programming Languages*, POPL '06, New York (ACM, New York, 2006), pp. 372–382. Event-place: Charleston, South Carolina, USA
47. A. Souri, R. Hosseini, A state-of-the-art survey of malware detection approaches using data mining techniques. HCIS **8**, 3 (2018)
48. J. Tian, B. Wang, X. Li, Data-driven and low-sparsity false data injection attacks in smart grid. Secur. Commun. Netw. **2018**, 1–11 (2018)
49. C. Perkins, G. Muller, Using discrete event simulation to model attacker interactions with cyber and physical security systems. Proc. Comput. Sci. **61**, 221–226 (2015)
50. M. Sweeney, C.T. Baumrucker, J.D. Burton, I. Dubrawsky, *Cisco Security Professional's Guide to Secure Intrusion Detection Systems*, 1st edn. (Syngress Publishing, Mountain View, 2003)

51. R.U. Rehman, *Intrusion Detection Systems with Snort: Advanced IDS Techniques Using Snort, Apache, MySQL, PHP, and ACID*. Bruce Perens' Open Source Series (Prentice Hall PTR, Upper Saddle River, 2003). OCLC: ocm52996780
52. R. Mitchell, I.-R. Chen, A survey of intrusion detection in wireless network applications. Comp. Commun. **42**, 1–23 (2014)
53. K.A. Scarfone, P.M. Mell, Guide to Intrusion Detection and Prevention Systems (IDPS). Technical Report NIST SP 800-94, National Institute of Standards and Technology, Gaithersburg (2007)
54. C. Alcaraz, L. Cazorla, G. Fernandez, G. Fernandez, *Context-Awareness Using Anomaly-Based Detectors for Smart Grid Domains*. Risks and Security of Internet and Systems (Springer, Cham, 2015)
55. M. Naghnaeian, N. Hirzallah, P.G. Voulgaris, Dual Rate Control for Security in Cyber-physical Systems. arXiv:1504.07586 [cs] (2015)
56. W. Abbas, A. Laszka, Y. Vorobeychik, X. Koutsoukos, Scheduling intrusion detection systems in resource-bounded cyber-physical systems, in *Proceedings of the First ACM Workshop on Cyber-Physical Systems-Security and/or PrivaCy*, CPS-SPC '15, New York (ACM, New York, 2015), pp. 55–66. Event-place: Denver, Colorado, USA
57. D. Kiwia, A. Dehghantanha, K.-K.R. Choo, J. Slaughter, A cyber kill chain based taxonomy of banking Trojans for evolutionary computational intelligence. J. Comput. Sci. **27**, 394–409 (2018)
58. M. Conti, T. Dargahi, A. Dehghantanha, Cyber threat intelligence: challenges and opportunities, in *Cyber Threat Intelligence*, ed. by A. Dehghantanha, M. Conti, T. Dargahi, Advances in Information Security (Springer International Publishing, Cham, 2018), pp. 1–6
59. C. T. Association, AI's application areas in organizations 2018. Statista (2018). Available online at: https://www.statista.com/statistics/805348/world-ai-application-areas-in-enterprise/
60. V.A. Golovko, Deep learning: an overview and main paradigms. Opt. Mem. Neural Netw. **26**, 1–17 (2017)
61. H. Karimipour, A. Dehghantanha, R.M. Parizi, K.R. Choo, H. Leung, A deep and scalable unsupervised machine learning system for cyber-attack detection in large-scale smart grids. IEEE Access **7**, 80778–80788 (2019)
62. S. Mohammadi, H. Mirvaziri, M. Ghazizadeh-Ahsaee, H. Karimipour, Cyber intrusion detection by combined feature selection algorithm. J. Inf. Secur. Appl. **44**, 80–88 (2019)
63. H. Haddadpajouh, R. Javidan, R. Khayami, A. Dehghantanha, K.-K. Raymond Choo, A two-layer dimension reduction and two-tier classification model for anomaly-based intrusion detection in IoT backbone networks. IEEE Trans. Emerg. Top. Comput. **PP**, 1–1, 11 (2016)
64. L. Deng, Deep learning: methods and applications. FNT Signal Process. **7**(3–4), 197–387 (2014)
65. K. Arulkumaran, M.P. Deisenroth, M. Brundage, A.A. Bharath, Deep reinforcement learning: a brief survey. IEEE Signal Process. Mag. **34**, 26–38 (2017)
66. Y. Xin, L. Kong, Z. Liu, Y. Chen, Y. Li, H. Zhu, M. Gao, H. Hou, C. Wang, Machine learning and deep learning methods for cybersecurity. IEEE Access **6**, 35365–35381 (2018)
67. R.T. Kokila, S. Thamarai Selvi, K. Govindarajan, DDoS detection and analysis in SDN-based environment using support vector machine classifier, in *2014 Sixth International Conference on Advanced Computing (ICoAC)*, Chennai (IEEE, Piscataway, 2014), pp. 205–210
68. M. Olalere, M.T. Abdullah, R. Mahmod, A. Abdullah, Identification and evaluation of discriminative lexical features of malware URL for real-time classification, in *2016 International Conference on Computer and Communication Engineering (ICCCE)*, Kuala Lumpur (IEEE, Piscataway, 2016), pp. 90–95
69. P.-Y. Chen, S. Yang, J. A. McCann, J. Lin, X. Yang, Detection of false data injection attacks in smart-grid systems. IEEE Commun. Mag. **53**, 206–213 (2015)
70. M. Esmalifalak, L. Liu, N. Nguyen, R. Zheng, Z. Han, Detecting stealthy false data injection using machine learning in smart grid. IEEE Syst. J. **11**, 1644–1652 (2017)

71. Y. Liao, V. Vemuri, Use of K-nearest neighbor classifier for intrusion detection. Comput. Secur. **21**, 439–448 (2002)

72. A.R. Syarif, W. Gata, Intrusion detection system using hybrid binary PSO and K-nearest neighborhood algorithm, in *2017 11th International Conference on Information & Communication Technology and System (ICTS)*, Surabaya (IEEE, Piscataway, 2017), pp. 181–186

73. F. Bre, J.M. Gimenez, V.D. Fachinotti, Prediction of wind pressure coefficients on building surfaces using artificial neural networks. Energ. Build. **158**, 1429–1441 (2018)

74. W. Gao, T. Morris, B. Reaves, D. Richey, On SCADA control system command and response injection and intrusion detection," in *2010 eCrime Researchers Summit*, Dallas (IEEE, Piscataway, 2010), pp. 1–9

75. T. Vollmer, M. Manic, Computationally efficient Neural Network Intrusion Security Awareness, in *2009 2nd International Symposium on Resilient Control Systems*, Idaho Falls (IEEE, Piscataway, 2009), pp. 25–30

76. D. Zhu, H. Jin, Y. Yang, D. Wu, W. Chen, DeepFlow: deep learning-based malware detection by mining android application for abnormal usage of sensitive data, in *2017 IEEE Symposium on Computers and Communications (ISCC)*, Heraklion (IEEE, Piscataway, 2017), pp. 438–443

77. G. Zhao, C. Zhang, L. Zheng, Intrusion detection using deep belief network and probabilistic neural network, in *22017 IEEE International Conference on Computational Science and Engineering (CSE) and IEEE International Conference on Embedded and Ubiquitous Computing (EUC)*, Guangzhou (IEEE, Piscataway, 2017), pp. 639–642

78. A. Sherstinsky, Fundamentals of Recurrent Neural Network (RNN) and Long Short-Term Memory (LSTM) Network, arXiv:1808.03314 [cs, stat] (2018)

79. R. Vinayakumar, K. Soman, P. Poornachandran, S. Sachin Kumar, Detecting Android malware using Long Short-term Memory (LSTM). J. Intell. Fuzzy Syst. **34**, 1277–1288 (2018)

80. G. Loukas, T. Vuong, R. Heartfield, G. Sakellari, Y. Yoon, D. Gan, Cloud-based cyber-physical intrusion detection for vehicles using deep learning. IEEE Access **6**, 3491–3508 (2018)

81. A. Krizhevsky, I. Sutskever, G.E. Hinton, ImageNet classification with deep convolutional neural networks, in *Advances in Neural Information Processing Systems 25*, ed. by F. Pereira, C.J.C. Burges, L. Bottou, K.Q. Weinberger (Curran Associates, Inc., Red Hook, 2012), pp. 1097–1105

82. S. Lawrence, C.L. Giles, A.C. Tsoi, A.D. Back, Face recognition: a convolutional neural-network approach. IEEE Trans. Neural Netw. **8**, 98–113 (1997)

83. X. Meng, Z. Shan, F. Liu, B. Zhao, J. Han, H. Wang, J. Wang, MCSMGS: malware classification model based on deep learning, in *2017 International Conference on Cyber-Enabled Distributed Computing and Knowledge Discovery (CyberC)*, Nanjing (IEEE, Piscataway, 2017), pp. 272–275

84. M.M.U. Chowdhury, F. Hammond, G. Konowicz, C. Xin, H. Wu, J. Li, A few-shot deep learning approach for improved intrusion detection, in *2017 IEEE 8th Annual Ubiquitous Computing, Electronics and Mobile Communication Conference (UEMCON)*, New York City (IEEE, Piscataway, 2017), pp. 456–462

85. A. Abeshu, N. Chilamkurti, Deep learning: the frontier for distributed attack detection in Fog-to-Things computing. IEEE Commun. Mag. **56**, 169–175 (2018)

86. R.C. Aygun, A.G. Yavuz, A stochastic data discrimination based autoencoder approach for network anomaly detection, in *2017 25th Signal Processing and Communications Applications Conference (SIU)*, Antalya (IEEE, Piscataway, 2017), pp. 1–4

87. M. Zolotukhin, T. Hamalainen, T. Kokkonen, J. Siltanen, Increasing web service availability by detecting application-layer DDoS attacks in encrypted traffic, in *2016 23rd International Conference on Telecommunications (ICT)*, Thessaloniki (IEEE, Piscataway, 2016), pp. 1–6

88. K. Kawaguchi, L.P. Kaelbling, Y. Bengio, Generalization in Deep Learning, arXiv:1710.05468 [cs, stat] (2017)

89. B. Neyshabur, S. Bhojanapalli, D. McAllester, N. Srebro, Exploring generalization in deep learning, in *Proceedings of the 31st International Conference on Neural Information Processing Systems*, NIPS'17 (Curran Associates Inc., Red Hook, 2017), pp. 5949–5958. Event-place: Long Beach, California, USA
90. I. Goodfellow, Y. Bengio, A. Courville, *Deep Learning* (MIT Press, Cambridge, 2016). http://www.deeplearningbook.org.
91. A. Hernández-García and P. König, Data augmentation instead of explicit regularization, arXiv:1806.03852 [cs] (2018)
92. A. Krogh and J.A. Hertz, A simple weight decay can improve generalization, in *Advances in Neural Information Processing Systems 4*, ed. by J.E. Moody, S.J. Hanson, R.P. Lippmann (Morgan-Kaufmann, Burlington, 1992), pp. 950–957
93. N. Srivastava, G. Hinton, A. Krizhevsky, I. Sutskever, R. Salakhutdinov, Dropout: a simple way to prevent neural networks from overfitting. J. Mach. Learn. Res. **15**, 1929–1958 (2014)
94. C. Szegedy, W. Liu, Y. Jia, P. Sermanet, S. Reed, D. Anguelov, D. Erhan, V. Vanhoucke, A. Rabinovich, Going Deeper with Convolutions, arXiv:1409.4842 [cs] (2014)
95. S.J. Nowlan and G.E. Hinton, Simplifying neural networks by soft weight-sharing. Neural Comput. **4**, 473–493 (1992)
96. L. Wan, M. Zeiler, S. Zhang, Y. LeCun, R. Fergus, Regularization of neural networks using dropconnect, in *Proceedings of Machine Learning Research* (2013), p. 12
97. E.A. Smirnov, D.M. Timoshenko, S.N. Andrianov, Comparison of regularization methods for ImageNet classification with deep convolutional neural networks. AASRI Proc. **6**, 89–94 (2014)
98. C. Szegedy, W. Zaremba, I. Sutskever, J. Bruna, D. Erhan, I. Goodfellow, R. Fergus, Intriguing properties of neural networks, arXiv:1312.6199 [cs] (2013)
99. C.S. Wickramasinghe, D.L. Marino, K. Amarasinghe, M. Manic, Generalization of deep learning for cyber-physical system security: a survey, in *IECON 2018 – 44th Annual Conference of the IEEE Industrial Electronics Society* (2018), pp. 745–751
100. C. Zhang, S. Bengio, M. Hardt, B. Recht, O. Vinyals, Understanding deep learning requires rethinking generalization, arXiv:1611.03530 (2016)
101. K. Simonyan, A. Zisserman, Very deep convolutional networks for large-scale image recognition, arXiv:1409.1556 (2014)
102. A. Hernandez-garcia and P. Konig, Data augmentation instead of explicit regularization, arXiv:1806.03852 (2018)
103. A. Kurakin, I.J. Goodfellow, S. Bengio, Adversarial examples in the physical world, arXiv:1607.02533 (2016)
104. Ministry of Defence, *Global Strategic Trends*. Swindon, England. Available online at: https://espas.secure.europarl.europa.eu/orbis/sites/default/files/generated/document/en/MinofDef_Global%20Strategic%20Trends
105. D. Bilar, B. Saltaformaggio, Using a novel behavioral stimuli-response framework to defend against adversarial cyberspace participants, in *2011 3rd International Conference on Cyber Conflict* (2011), pp. 1–16
106. E. Tyugu, Command and control of cyber weapons, in *2012 4th International Conference on Cyber Conflict (CYCON 2012)* (2012) pp. 1–11
107. A. Guarino, Autonomous intelligent agents in cyber offence, in *2013 5th International Conference on Cyber Conflict (CYCON 2013)* (2013), pp. 1–12

Chapter 3
Industrial Big Data Analytics: Challenges and Opportunities

Abdulrahman Al-Abassi, Hadis Karimipour, Hamed HaddadPajouh, Ali Dehghantanha ⓘ, and Reza M. Parizi

1 Introduction

Manufacturing industries have faced several industrial revolutions to withstand competition in global production capacity, quality and cost [1]. Industrial revolutions in the past have been influenced by several technical innovations, as illustrated in Fig. 3.1. The first industry revolution was introduced at the end of the eighteenth century [2]. It is generally considered to be the steam-powered mechanical machines which made the steam power exploitable opening the industry age [1, 2]. The second industry revolution, which targets mass production and assembly lines [3] was first introduced at the beginning of the twentieth century [1]. In this division, we see an introduction of programmable logic controllers (PLCs) to automation industries in applications of electricity to create mass production [2]. The third industry revolution focuses on digitalization and automation [4]. It is usually linked to the extensive use of electronics and information technology to automate production [2].

Even though the three industrial revolutions are based on break-through scientific discoveries [2], experts believe that internet will play a major role in running industrial facilities through Cyber Physical Systems (CPS) [1]. Therefore, Industry 4.0 refers to the fourth industrial revolution introduced in 2011 [5] (Lu, Industry 4.0: A Survey on Technologies, Applications and Open Research Issues [6]) and

A. Al-Abassi · H. Karimipour
School of Engineering, University of Guelph, Guelph, ON, Canada
e-mail: aalaba03@uoguelph.ca; hkarimi@uoguelph.ca; Canada-hkarimi@uoguelph.ca

H. HaddadPajouh · A. Dehghantanha
Cyber Science Lab, School of Computer Science, University of Guelph, Guelph, ON, Canada
e-mail: hamed@cybersciencelab.org; ali@cybersciencelab.org

R. M. Parizi (✉)
College of Computer and Software Engineering, Kennesaw State University, Marietta, GA, USA
e-mail: rparizi1@kennesaw.edu

© Springer Nature Switzerland AG 2020
K.-K. R. Choo, A. Dehghantanha (eds.), *Handbook of Big Data Privacy*,
https://doi.org/10.1007/978-3-030-38557-6_3

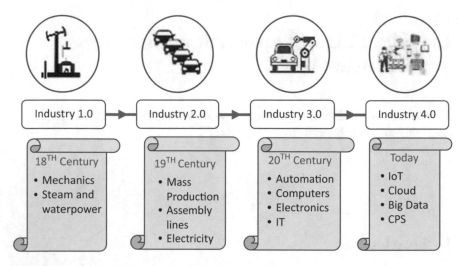

Fig. 3.1 Evolution cycle from Industry 1.0 to Industry 4.0

designed to decentralize production through shared facilities in industrial global systems and achieve personalization and resource efficiency [1]. This industrial revolution was first introduced in 2011 by the German Government [7, 8]. It has a profound impact on producers and consumers as it contributes over 25% of the Gross Domestic Product (GDP) and provides over seven million jobs [1].

The impact on producers is minimal since it uses marginal human interventions with computers automatically reconfiguring facilities to achieve the production goal [9]. In addition, manufacturers do not necessarily need to have their own factories and facilities anymore [1] because certain specialized companies provide their physical facilities to rent for production purposes. Furthermore, maintenance specialized companies can be hired by industrial owners; thus, maintaining their facilities and reducing additional costs due to their economic scale [3].

Similarly, Industry 4.0 has a great impact on consumers. It allows clients to get their individualized products [3], since manufactures can dynamically reconfigure manufacturing systems based on the collected customer needs in an online platform [10]. Hence, small and medium sized companies can benefit from Industry 4.0 methodologies and effectively provide other market opportunities [1, 3].

The German government had to revolutionize the industry to withstand an increasing global competition on product quality and production costs [1]. Existing manufacturing companies face tough challenges since customers are not willing to pay large price premiums for incremental quality improvements [1]. Hence, the industrial facility has moved to produced customized products with fast time to market [9]. In order to close the productivity and quality gab, several industries have moved their facilities to low wage aspiring countries. Thus, resolving the tension between economics of scale and scope as well as planning and value orientation [1].

Today, large investment companies, such as Amazon, Google, Apple and Facebook inspire to revive their investments in industrial fields grabbing a disproportionately large market share from today consolidated market leader [2]. Industry 4.0 uses a concept called "metered service" which highly flexible and can achieve a much higher resource efficiency [3]. To illustrate, a typical manufacturer must own several facilities to ensure production outcome during busy seasons. Then, the manufacturer can release unnecessary facilities to the cloud for other companies to be utilized during their off seasons [3]. Recent research shows great promise towards defining and decoding principles of Industry 4.0 [2]. This is done through a publication where governments plan to add a "super" tax incentive for investments in "Smart Factories" and outline the benefits of this new industrial revolution [2].

Even though current research in Industry 4.0 promises decentralized facilities, personalization and source efficiency [3], Industry 4.0 is a fairly a new concept with many unidentified terms related to CPS [11, 12].

The term 'Cyber Physical System' was first introduced by Helen Gill at the NSF in US [3] to inspire other researchers to study the interaction between physical systems and computing systems [13]. CPS include physical facilities with embedded devices that are controlled by external devices, including sensors, processors and actuators [4]. These systems have a great impact on computing procedures as they usually carry a feedback loop with physical facilities [3] to enhance the scalability of the system and improve its security and flexibility [14]. Additionally, CPS have a variety of applications in the medical, military, power, traffic and many other monitoring and control fields [13].

Industry 4.0 and CPS are two different concept even though they have a lot in common and used together in many cases. CPS not only carry applications in industrial fields, but other areas as well, such as healthcare, public transportation, and military [3]. Alternatively, Industry 4.0 serves the entire business cycle as shown in Fig. 3.2. It starts by gathering natural resources used to produced different customized components. Then, these components are assembled to deliver personalized products to customers [15].

Manufacturing industries have developed their physical facilities through acquiring more affordable sensors and better data acquisition systems. As a result, manufacturing systems usually produce a great amount of data, called Big Data [16], more than any other sector [17, 18]. According to [4], one machine can ultimately produce thousands of records, subsequently reaching several trillion records in a year. Also, data sizes range from a few dozen terabytes to many petabytes of data in a single data set [19]. Thus, the potential to reduce malfunction rates is affected by big data analytics tools and could ultimately improve production quality and capacity [4]. Furthermore, they have the potential to affect different sections of the manufacturing business management and supply chain [9].

In this paper, research regarding the connection between CPS and big data frameworks in Industry 4.0 is conducted to outline the key differences between them and help future researchers. The remainder of this chapter is organized as follows: Section 2 will present big data characteristics. Then, several industrial big data sources and applications are discussed in Sect. 3. Section 4 will bring more attention

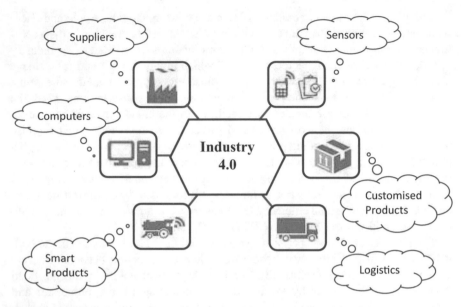

Fig. 3.2 A layout of Industry 4.0

to industrial big data challenges and issues. Section 5 will outline solutions and future remarks to handle big data-intensive applications. Finally, Sect. 6 concludes the chapter and discusses the future of big data research on CPS in Industry 4.0.

2 Big Data Characteristics

Manufacturing industries run their physical facilities through sensors and data acquisition systems generating extensive data to process, called Big Data [16]. There are several techniques to process large amounts of data, including capturing, transferring, storing, curing, analysing, visualizing, securing and ensuring privacy [4]. Data size variables are continuously changing due to large data sets and vary from Terabytes, Petabytes and Exabyte or Zettabyte [4]. There are many challenges that exist in the age of big data. To illustrate, GE company produces a personal care product which generates 5000 data samples every 33 ms. McKinsey institute reported that an effective use of industrial big data has the underlying benefits to transform economies and deliver new wave of production growth [9]. Hence, taking advantages of valuable industrial big data analytics will create competitions for today's enterprises and attract employees that have the critical skills on industrial big data [9].

Fig. 3.3 Big data characteristics

The industrial manufacturing stream characterizes big data into five categories, called the "five V's" [20], seen in Fig. 3.3. The most-widely used characteristics of Big Data are volume, velocity, and variety [21, 22].

According to the Central Limit Theorem, volume, which is related to the large amounts of data generated, is an important feature because more reliable data can be analyzed to produce accurate results [4]. Another important characteristic is velocity which detects how fast data is being generated and collected. This feature is very critical because data generated from social interactions, sensor monitors and business activities must be processed faster than its generation speed [4]. If the processing speed does not meet the minimum requirements, some data can be missed, thus making it challenging to accurately analyze and gain inside on the collected data. The last important characteristic of big data is variety which focuses on the different types of formats of data being generated from various sources. For example, certain animals are hard to locate in jungles through pictures, but through cameras combined with infrared photo analyzing techniques, animals are easier to capture due to their high body temperature when compared to the background [4]. Consequently, variety is very important as certain useful patterns can be observed and analyzed from different perspectives if they exit.

Other characteristics, which are not widely used, include veracity which determines the accuracy of data through inconsistencies and uncertainties [23]. Another feature is value which focuses on the ultimate gain and social impact that could be extracted from the data [24]. There are five other characteristics which have been gradually developed over time in Industry 4.0 by [20]. These characteristics include:

1. Validity: correctness of data.
2. Variability: dynamic behaviour
3. Volatility: tendency to change in time
4. Vulnerability: vulnerable to breach or attacks
5. Visualization: visualizing meaningful usage of data

Henceforth, different characteristics of big data require techniques that can handle and process large amounts data quickly. The must also be secure and robust to deal with heterogeneous data [4]. Large companies facilitate their growth through developing various data mining tools to aid them in better decision making [20]. Depending on the corporation's requirements, online big data analytics tools are vast and can vary from Hadoop, PiG, Hive, Cassandra, Spark, Kafka and many others.

While big data analytics tools are used more often in Industry 4.0 and other applications, more research is being conducted towards developing better big data analytics techniques and gain relevant information. Some of the main domains in which big data applications are revolutionized include, entertainment, insurance, education, automobiles and government. Since big data is utilized in many applications, the scope of big data will create numerous job opportunities in this field and a rising demand with huge salary aspects for individuals with professional big data analytics skills.

3   Industrial Big Data Sources and Applications

Industrial big data is generated by a wide variety of sources that need be distributed effectively to optimize industrial applications. This section analyzes some of the main industrial big data sources and their corresponding applications.

3.1   Industrial Big Data Sources

Generating reliable data analytics techniques will primarily rely on proper data collection devices. Such devices in Industry 4.0 include sensors, communication devices, logistics vehicles, factory buildings, humans, and many other manufacturing tracking systems [9]. The main distributing industrial big data sources are categorized by [9] into five main categories, including large-scale data devices, life-cycle production data, enterprise operation data, manufacturing value chain sources and finally collaboration data from external sources.

3.1.1 Large-Scale Data Devices

This section mainly involves CPS and their connection to physical sensors (IoT enabled devices), such as actuators, video cameras and RFID readers [9]. Ultimately, these devices will always be connected to the internet and the generated data will be collected, processed and analyzed either on-premises or through a remote facility such as a server farm or in the cloud. Once the data is analyzed, is can be used to help optimize machinery process and produce valuable decisions.

3.1.2 Life-Cycle Production Data

A life cycle analysis of a company involves data from all types of factory process, including production requirements, design, manufacturing, testing, sale maintenance and management [9]. The data is recorded, processed and analyzed to produce a production life cycle system that meet the demand of products. Current research focuses on eliminating external data collecting devices through embedding sensors around the product. Hence, generating a faster real time data management of the processes through making changes in production requirements, design, sales and work force.

3.1.3 Enterprise Operation Data

This section involves data used for operational business reporting, such as business management, organization structure, production, devices, marketing, quality control, procurement, inventory stocks and future goals and plans [9]. The industry can optimize its production lines through real-time monitoring of equipment and processes. Additionally, the industry can optimize the supply chain through procurement, storage, sales and efficient distribution of products. Finally, optimal production can be achieved through analyzing the sales and supplies data and dynamically adjust the production rhythm to meet the specified requirements and optimize energy consumption [9]. Additionally, Demand Response Management (DRM) models save money by offering a two-way communication between customers and suppliers, which in turn help utilize operations more efficiently [25].

3.1.4 Manufacturing Value Chain

The section includes other types of data involving customers, suppliers, and other partners. The current industrial global economical system brings enormous competition in production development, procurement, sales, services, and other internal and external logistic competitiveness factors [9]. Every part of the economical system carries an important role in developing each link of the manufacturing value chain. Hence, enterprise managers will regularly create strategic changes to enhance future decisions.

3.1.5 External Collaboration Data

External data involves data gathered from economy, industry, market, competitors and other external data sources. Since these types of data are external, they are susceptible to attacks from external sources [9]. Thus, organizations operating today must collaborate with their employees, customers and stakeholders to increase safety and encourage everyone to be responsible for the success of the organization [26]. Additionally, sharing external company information, skills, tools and other essentials influences everyone to make better decisions and in a timely manner [9].

3.2 Industrial Big Data Applications

The landscape of industrial big data is vast and includes different applications for different purposes. While big data analytics tools are used more often to analyze big data applications, more research is being conducted to revolutionize industrial big data applications. This section presents current major industrial applications and their big data processing techniques.

3.2.1 Smart Factory Visibility

Many manufacturing facilities usually have their devices and managing processes connected with IT and online operating systems. Thus, certain studies have introduced models that utilize Internet of Things (IoT) enabled smart factory visibility platforms to achieve real time production visualization and reflect on the production operations and behaviours [27, 28]. Another study presents a big data analytics platform that provides production line information to decision makers, displays performance data and status update and improves factory efficiency [9]. An additional referenced model of ubiquitous infrastructure was proposed for manufacturing information sharing and visualization [29]. Thus, with the development of IoT technologies in Industry 4.0, factories can manage their facilities in a timely manner and effectively collaborate with their production personnel [30].

3.2.2 Machine Fleet Management

Machine fleet refers to a large set of identical machines which are exposed to different working conditions for different tasks [9]. Current industries use predictive and prognostic methods to support similar machines without treating them as identical machines. Thus, contractors and equipment rental companies use Telematics, which is the integration of wireless communications, vehicle monitoring systems, and location devices to provide real-time spatial and performance data of the fleet machines [31]. Many machine fleet management platforms are simulated to integrate every instance within a plant and provide connectivity and information sharing across multiple locations and business processes [9]. This is done through automating workflows of different equipment and processes, with limited human intervention, to support machine fleet tasks and optimize production.

3.2.3 Proactive Maintenance

Many manufacturing facilities have implemented various preventive maintenance strategies to correct root causes of failure and avoid breakdowns of equipment through condition-based monitoring. According to [9], smaller companies, with low working capital, can implement low cost sensors, wireless connectivity and big data processing tools to make it cheaper and easier to collect actual performance data and monitor equipment health. This is done through using a data-driven algorithm which analyzes the information collected from a given machine and its ambient environment, and then process it back to the machine for adaptive control of effective and efficient production planning and in-time maintenance scheduling [9]. Due to significant downtime and frequent machine failures in current industries, [9] proposes a model that improves the system performance and achieves high reliability and maintenance availability through two main factors:

- Mitigation of production uncertainties to reduce unscheduled downtime and increase operational efficiency.
- Efficient utilization of the finite resources on the critical sections of the system by detecting its bottleneck components.

3.2.4 Service Innovation and Just in Time Smart Supply Chain

Just in time (JIT) supply chain manufacturing is an important concept that enhances competitiveness through service innovation and lead time reduction. Implementing JIT manufacturing process that provide full control of every part in the chain is very challenging due to many reasons including lack of required information sharing or communication between stakeholders and insufficient sound action or planning system [32]. A model is proposed by [9] to help manufacturers gain a better acquisition of the supply chain information, the flow of materials and manufacturing cycle times through integrating the production line and balance of plant equipment to suppliers. The model can also collect and feed delivery information into an Enterprise Resource Planning (ERP) system which can provide real time information regarding the availability of products and effectively update general product information [9]. Another case study proposes a framework that utilizes IoT technologies to collect real time data and facilitate dynamic JIT manufacturing [33]. This is done through adding functions that respond to the dynamic changes with customer orders, production progress, and availability of

required resources to allows manufacturers to maximize production outputs with
limited resources and proper planning [32].

4 Industrial Big Data Challenges and Issues

Industrial big data analytics bring about several challenges in Industry 4.0, including
industrial data access, integration, and sharing [34]. Furthermore, Big data are
often massive and defined using different representation methods and structural
specifications [9]. Thus, big data should be properly prepared for integration and
management, and the technical infrastructures must include appropriate information
infrastructure services to support big data analytics [9]. Challenges of big data
analytics in Industry 4.0 can be characterised into five different fields:

4.1 Lack of Largescale Spatiotemporal Database Representation

Big data is usually generated from manufacturing devices that are placed at a
specific geographic location with a time stamp. The time stamp of every device is
collected and processed to conduct statistical analysis on the data. Since manufacturing field produce large amounts of data, industries lack the appropriate infrastructure
services to support analysis of the data and perform data spatiotemporal integration
and fusion [9]. Hence, it will be very challenging to find cheaper approximation for
such manufacturing procedures.

4.2 Lack of Effective and Efficient Online Machine Learning Algorithms

Big data generated from industries that utilize IoT has different characteristics
than traditional big data. Based on data collection sources, conventional data
characteristics including heterogeneity, variety, unstructured feature, noise, and high
redundancy [9]. Detecting machine anomalies and monitoring production quality
requires instant answers in manufacturing industries and increasing the number of
machines to speed up the computation will result in high cost preventive measure
that are not effective and efficient in the long run. Hence, online large-scale
machine learning algorithms are currently applied in Industry 4.0 big data analytics
framework to improve big data analytics techniques. Additionally, traditional data
management techniques usually involve a single data source where industrial big

data management techniques have additional data sources to account for device status streaming, geospatial, and textual data [9].

4.3 Lack of Whole Processes Lifecycle Data Management Systems

Big data, generated from CPS in manufacturing industries, is usually produced at an unprecedented rate and scale which bring about various challenges in storage management system technologies. Industries with small storage management facilities cannot host huge data and thus data quality assurance techniques should be applied to help identify essential and irrelevant data [9].

4.4 Lack of Data Visualization Systems

Data visualization systems help convert massive amounts of raw data in graphical presentations to help in decision making and quickly reveal intuitive knowledge. Additionally, visualizing such a tremendous amount of information presents quantitative and qualitative information in some schematic form, indicating patterns, trends, anomalies, constancy, variation, in ways that cannot be presented in other forms like text and tables [35, 36]. Since Industry 4.0 systems are more challenging than conventional systems that reside in one location, these system must communicate with many devices and users simultaneously as well as send and receive data of different formats and at different frequencies [9]. While past studies focus mostly on geographic information capability systems, additional research is required to analyze massive heterogenous data that exhibit unique features that are difficult to visualize [37].

4.5 Lack in Data Confidentiality Mechanisms

As previously mentioned, Industry 4.0 relies on big data being shared with multiple online sources from different locations. Small industries cannot effectively analyze such huge datasets due to their limited income capacity. They are forced to rely on other enterprises and online tools to analyze their data and other sensitive information, which introduces potential safety risks [9]. Thus, small industries should be careful when dealing with a third party and develop proper preventive measures to protect their sensitive data [38].

5 Industrial Big Data Analytics: Solutions and Future Remarks

Big data and CPS in Industry 4.0 are considered highly distributed data sources which can ultimately cause several challenges, including data access, sharing and processing. Additionally, massive data allocated from various sources are often defined using large structural specifications and different representation methods [9]. Hence, industries usually handle big data challenges through proper integration and management as well as improvement of infrastructures to appropriately provide technical services to support big data analytics [9].

The correlation between industrial CPS and big data analytics can be demonstrated through two main categories. The first category will look after challenges of the system's infrastructure to ensure ultimate communication between facilities. The other category will focus on challenges of various data analytics techniques used to improve product personalization and resource efficiency. Figure 3.4 provides an outline of the main industrial challenges as well as current techniques used to handle industrial big data analytics of industrial CPS. The challenges and potential solution are highlighted in red and green, respectively.

5.1 System Infrastructures

The first main component of big data to be analyzed is the systems information infrastructure. As seen in Fig. 3.5, the three main solutions to solve challenges related to system infrastructures include data capturing, storing and distributing.

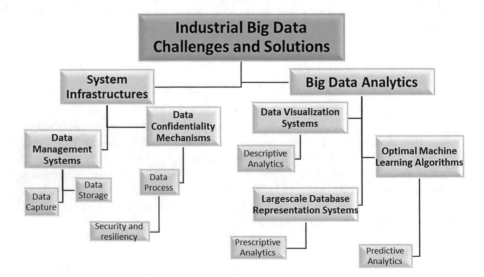

Fig. 3.4 An outline of Industrial challenges and solutions

Fig. 3.5 Big data landscape [40]

5.1.1 Data Capture

Current industrial system infrastructures produce a huge amount of data in a matter of seconds. Capturing accurate and reliable data is essential to gain consistent results and observe useful patterns. Existing capturing techniques have been recently developed to capture data in a reliable and cost-effective manner. These capturing techniques involve sensor data, system logs, camera images, radio-frequency identification (RFID) records, GPS data, Enterprise resource planning (ERP) data, and social media data [4].

High distributed data that are usually captured through the above-mentioned techniques bring about several challenges when it comes to capturing, accessing, sharing and analyzing the data. There are several key factors to consider when capturing accurate meaningful data. Initially, the process of collecting and transferring data to storing them on servers must be seamless and efficient [39]. Manual intervention can delay the efficiency of the process and result in missed warning signals being tracked on time [4]. Thus, maintenance preventive measures can be delayed and cause machine failure [39]. Another issue that could potentially arise from manual intervention is increasing the company's labor costs. According to [4], digital devices are more reliable and efficient to run routine processing tasks when compared to humans.

Secondly, generating reliable data analytics techniques will primarily rely on proper data collection devices [13] Choosing appropriate sensors to collect large amount of data based on the industry's infrastructure is important to continuously monitor the status of operating facilities [4, 9].

5.1.2 Data Storage

Industrial system infrastructures must ensure effective real-time communication between their facilities and CPS. Hence big data needs databases that can process any given data within a tolerable amount of time [4]. Industries have achieved that through storing large amounts of data in external database systems.

The landscape of external database systems is vast and includes different applications for different purposes. Figure 3.6 illustrates the landscape of various databases that are involved with big data and CPS in Industry 4.0.

The most widely used databases to consistently store and accurately handle and process big data include Cassandra, MongoDB and data warehouse [4]. The proposed databases are widely used in current industries and can handle various big data analyzing techniques when compared to rational external database systems [41]. Although rational database systems are constantly improving their accuracy and consistency, only the proposed systems will be discussed due to their high accuracy of analyzing monetary transaction data [4].

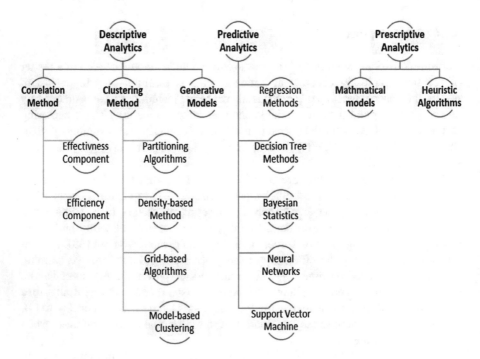

Fig. 3.6 Methods and techniques of big data analytics

Industrial big data analytics require strong computers or clusters to process them [4]. Generally, database systems save large amounts of data into tables for easy access. The first commonly used database system is Cassandra which is designed to save its values into a cluster database consisting of tables with rows and columns, unlike traditional database systems [42]. This makes it faster and more robust to retrieve data since the workload is being distributed over a cluster database instead of a single computer [4]. However, [43] indicates that such systems cannot fully guarantee the row level, when updating values that are in the same row at approximately the same time, due to certain attributes not being accurately updated. Therefore, Cassandra may be useful for applications with news feed and system logs but not be the main option for applications with inconsistent updates, such as stock trading and customer purchases and relationships [4].

Another commonly used database system is MongoDB where normalization of tables is critical to ensure the entity type and source [4]. To illustrate, MongoDB targets connected entity types, such as product information and customer reviews and saves them into one JSON-like document through secondary indexes [4], where other traditional systems create different documents for different tables. Consequently, MongoDB supports rich and expressive models and avoids high cost operations for objects with related properties since they can be nested in one another for multiple levels [44].

The final database system which is widely used by many industries are data warehouses. These systems are designed to save summarized information daily for further analysis [45–47]. For example, the total amount of sale records can reach billions for an individual company in a single year. Data warehouses avoid slow computational processes by adding daily total sales, which involve 365 worth of records, instead of adding billions of records at once [4]. This makes it much faster to calculate and attain information.

5.1.3   Data Process

As mentioned earlier, big data needs very strong computers with high storage space to accurately store and process data. Subsequently, most industries use clusters since they are efficient and more cost effective. There are several environmental settings in Industry 4.0 under which companies use clusters. The most common setting involves a large amount of data being retrieved from different computers that have a common location and use the same local area network. This type of setting is robust as it provides high speed network connection and prevent any delay in communication between computers. Thus, research shows that more attention is paid by industries to coordinate thousands of computers in one location [4].

The most widely used system in this field is the Hadoop-based industrial big data repository system which provides storage support and additional distributed database functionalities. The system assumes that hardware failures will occur only in a large cluster [48]. To explain further, if a cluster consists of 1000 computers, with a typical computer lasting 3 years before its first hardware failure, it can expect one hardware failure everyday. Hadoop systems are able to spread the data over a cluster and adjust the data when new computers are present [48]. Henceforth, upcoming research of data programming models should be directed towards data analytical algorithms and search for useful patterns instead of concerning about system failures.

Another environmental setting, in which clusters are being utilized, involves data gathered from computers in different locations. This environment is mostly present in international companies that have several branches in different countries. These settings provide network bandwidth challenges as the amount of data transferred needs to be reduced to achieve ultimate communication speed between computers [49]. To further illustrate, all raw data must be transferred to one computer to perform a simple calculation that involves information from global computers. This requires the system to have a large network bandwidth which is not very cost effective. A more effective solution is to perform the calculations needed in each computer, then transfer the results to a central server in which final calculations can be performed. This method makes it easier and faster to perform calculations and reduces large amounts of data being transferred. Another common challenge that exists in this environmental setting involves companies that use a lot of small cheap sensors to calculate certain functions. These sensors can quickly run out of battery and be rapidly overworked when sending daily information to the central server. Thus, [50] proposes a solution that utilizes one main powerful sensor to control other small sensors, summarize and analyze the data collected and send them to the central server. This solution provides consistent and accurate data and much more cost effective.

Another important environmental setting which involves processing big data is cloud computing. This environmental setting enables companies to share their system resources over the internet. Since the database is in the cloud, companies can minimize their IT infrastructures and leave management of IT to a third party could computing company [51]. Studies show that this technique has been utilized by Tao et al. [52] through combining current manufacturing models with clouding computing to improve service routines of cloud manufacturing. Additional research is proposed by Xu [53] to outline the key technologies for managing distributed resources encapsulated into cloud services.

5.2 Data Analytics Methods and Techniques

The second main component of big data and CPS in Industry 4.0 is data analytics. This section will focus on supporting functionalities and methods that help gain insight from data provided by the system infrastructures [4]. Such analytical methods can be divided into three main groups:

1. *Descriptive Analytics:* describes what happened to the data in the past [54, 55].

2. *Predictive Analytics:* predicts future results based on previous past assumptions [54, 55].
3. *Prescriptive Analytics:* prescribes preventive measuring techniques based on future predictions [54, 55].

5.2.1   Descriptive Analytics

There is a wide variety of methods used by CPS and Industry 4.0 to gain descriptive analytics from big data. Certain methods utilize Machine Learning and Data Mining algorithms to provide basic understanding of different data trends, correlation among attributes and outlier detection [3, 9, 56]. Such methods include descriptive statistical functions, such as mean, median and variance [4, 27]. Other methods which provide more consistent and accurate results, include correlation, clustering and generative models. However, these methods are relatively complicated and quite expensive.

Correlation Method

Since big data are usually presented in structured tables, correlation methods can easily analyze the rows and columns for changing attributes. There are many research papers conducted on various correlation techniques. Being a subtopic in statistics, correlation methods usually target attributes of big data that are changing at the same time [4]. Such methods include Chi-square [57] for categorical data, and Pearson correlation coefficient [58] for numeric data. To effectively understand correlation methods better, studies conducted on correlation are divided into two main components:

- *Effectiveness Component*

   In this section, each method will highlight different patterns base on impacts of random noise [4]. Current research propose alternative new methods to handle random noise, such as odds ratio, relative risk, likelihood ratio, lift, leverage, BCPNN, two-way support, added value, and putative causal dependency [4].

   Other research focuses on the causal analysis part of correlation, since the final analysis can be used to predict useful future patterns [59]. For example, if event A and B are correlated, certain patterns can be analyzed from event A based on event B. However, this relationship is not as useful when an intervention of a third event occurs. Thus, there should be a confounding factor called event C which can relate to both event A and B [60]. To illustrate, the medicine Advil is positively correlated with headaches. However, headaches are symptoms of many diseases and Advil cannot prevent all of them. Popular methods for detecting confounding factors include the Cochran-Mantel-Haenszel method, logistic regression model and partial correlation [4].

Furthermore, timestamps, which are a sequence of encoded information identifying when a certain event occurs, are very useful for causal analysis, since the cause event always happens before its effect [61]. Timestamps are effective in monitoring machine failure and providing preventive measures in Industry 4.0. Since different events require different intervention and maintenance techniques, correlation and causal analysis techniques can identify associated events with identical failure modes to effectively predict machine failure and provide maintenance plan improvement [4].

- *Efficiency component*

This section uses the co-occurrence function as a sub-optimal measure for correlation measurements. One of the most recognised algorithms is the Apriori algorithm proposed by [62] to search for the items frequency of co-occurring through utilizing downward closed properties [4]. For instance, the Apriori algorithm can analyze the exponential properties of a co-occurring event through Power Law Distribution methods which can mine frequent properties for Boolean association rules [4].

Other classical methods found in this field of research include FP-Tree [63], which uses an extended prefix-tree structure for storing compressed information, and ECLAT [64] which store transaction information in a vertical data layout for fast support counting [4]. However, these algorithms only utilize the co-occurrence function properties without comparing the actual properties against the expected ones. Hence, recent research, which utilizes the downward closed properties independently, include [65] who proposed a framework that decouple correlation functions to satisfy the downward-closed property [4].

Clustering Method

While correlation analysis looks for changing attributes, clustering methods target groups with similar records. Current research focuses on utilizing clustering algorithms to optimize costs and overall efficiency in Industry 4.0. For example, [66] used clustering techniques to group similar machines for fault detection. Clustering algorithms proposed in the past are many and can be categorized into four main groups.

- *Partitioning Algorithms*

Partitioning algorithms subdivide the data set into groups through moving objects into different clusters. Common algorithms of this group include K-means, K-modes, CLARANS, and K-medians [4]. While these algorithms are simple and can automatically assign items to clusters, they are sensitive to outliers since objects with extremely large value may substantially distort the distribution of data to the closest cluster center [4].

- *Density-based Clustering*

    DBSCAN is a partitioning method which has been proposed by [big data (Ester 1996)] to look for clusters of different shapes and sizes. Other common density-based algorithms include ST-DBSCAN, LDBSCAN, and OPTICS [3]. Although these methods are robust towards outlier detection and can discover random shaped clusters, they are expensive when used to process large amounts of data [37]. To illustrate, border values than can be reached from more than one cluster can be part of either cluster depending on how the data was processed. Advanced clustering techniques, such as gird-based algorithms can solve the issue by dividing the cluster space into girds [4, 67].

- *Grid-based Algorithms*

    Grid-based algorithms divide the whole featured space into grids and then merge those cells to their corresponding grid [4]. Since the objects are being nested into grids, the overall number of girds becomes much smaller and hence, these algorithms can run fast as clustering is performed on summaries and not individual objects. Current gird-based clustering methods include STING, OptiGrid, and DGB [4]. The clustering quality of these algorithms depends on the grid granularity, thus making them unsuitable for high dimensional data. Defining infinite number of gird cells is very difficult because the grid space is limited to a union of gird-cells with boundaries that are either vertical or horizontal [4].

- *Model-based Clustering:*

    Unlike the above-mentioned algorithms, model-based clustering techniques are based on formal models where detecting the most fitting parameter becomes easier with clear predefined clustering structures. Model-based methods focus on finding the best parameters suitable for a predetermined model. Current models include the statistical model which covers methods such as COBWEB and GMM [4]. Another widely used model is the neural network model which includes SOM and ART where SOM is based on reducing the mapping dimension and ART is an algorithm used to generate new neurons when current neurons present underlying patterns [3]. Hence, the above-mentioned models aid in reducing the dimensional space of big data with clear clustering structures to improve efficiency and performance.

Generative Models

Generative models focus on generating real life data through a user defined set of rules [4]. Current research in Industry 4.0 presents several manufacturing models [68] propose a model to improve the dynamic development of Computer Aided Design where [69] utilizes matrix factorization models to monitor air pollution in industrial zones. Real data can be approximated through defining a 'likelihood function' to analyze similarities between the generated data and real data. Models that utilize a likelihood function include Naïve Bayes, Latent Dirichlet Allocation,

Hidden Markov Models and Matrix factorization [4]. Thus, these models can reveal certain hidden parameter from real data records due to the proximation generated by utilizing the likelihood function.

5.2.2 Predictive Analytics

While descriptive analytics focus on analyzing events in the past, predictive analytics focus on utilizing the past patterns to predict the future. This process is possible under the assumption that what happened in the past will happen in a similar way in the future [4]. A research paper proposed by [70] utilizes neural networks and cheap sensors to predict machine status. Thus, helping low capital factories who cannot afford expensive sensor-embedded devices. Another paper applies acoustic signals on a gearbox to predict worn faces and broken tooth gears [71]. Predictive methods proposed in the past are numerous and can be categorized into five main groups.

- *Regression Methods*

Regression methods share a long history in statistics and can be used in descriptive and predictive models. The first model to utilize regression is the linear regression model proposed by [72] which predicts numeric target features and attributes. Logistic regression is a model proposed by [73] which utilizes a logistic function to model binary dependent variables. These models are linear and can produce wrong assumptions. Hence, other models, such as LOESS and LOWESS are proposed to fit non-linear models [3].

- *Decision Tree Methods*

Decision tree models consist of a tree-like structure with data records being allocated to each branch. It utilizes different functions to make records in each branch as pure as possible. These functions include information gain, gain ratio, and gini index [4]. As the number of records increase, the size of a decision tree can become quite large. Pruning is a technique in machine learning which reduces the size of a tree by removing sections that provide litter power to classify events [4], consequently improving the decision tree prediction performance.

- *Bayesian Statistics*

Bayesian statistics are statistical method that utilize Bayes' theorem to compute and update probabilities after obtaining new data [74]. These methods can achieve high prediction performance as long as the assumption of independency is correct. Other papers focus on solving the dependency issue in statistical modeling through a redefined Bayesian network that improves prediction performance [75].

- *Neural Networks*

A neural network is a construct of different networks which can be organized in layers. These layers are made of several interconnected nodes, including input nodes, hidden nodes, and output nodes [76]. These nodes are connected by weighted edges that are randomly assigned [4]. Each neural network includes a set of learning rules that modify the weights of the nodes according to the input pattern its presented with. Based on the distance between the predicted and actual value, neural networks can adjust the weights accordingly to achieve a more stable trained model [77].

- *Support Vector Machine Algorithm*

Support Vector Machine algorithms searches for a linear hyperplane in an N-dimensional space to distinctly classify data points of two different classes [78]. These methods utilize a linear hyperplane for separation, which requires long times to train when large data sets are present. Some studies use non-linear kernel functions to relocate the original feature space and map it to a higher dimension area that could be linearly separated [79].

5.2.3 Prescriptive Analytics

While predictive analytics focus on predicting future attributes, prescriptive analytics provide preventive measures in Industry 4.0 through optimization and programming techniques. Industries can use their products demands prediction analytics to calculate when certain products are need, the requirements of raw materials, production capacity, labor costs and other preventive measures [4].

Current research on industrial prescriptive analytics focuses on algorithms that can find an optimal plan with the lowest overall cost. A paper proposed by Maggio et al. [80] looks into different self-optimizing strategies to accomplish given targets in environments with changing requirements and needs. Another paper utilizes self-organized algorithms to reduce certain design costs in a distributed manner and enhance the industrial autonomy of CPS [81].

Due to the complicated nature of some industries, certain scholars focus on other prescriptive techniques to find the global optimal solution. Such techniques include typical heuristic algorithms, such as genetic algorithm, simulated annealing, hill climbing, tabu search, and colony optimization [4, 37].

6 Conclusion

Industrial revolutions in the past have been influenced by several technical innovations to withstand competition in global production capacity, quality and efficiency. Since industrial big data analytics and CPS are continuously developing, there exist several challenges. Manufacturing systems usually generate a large amount of data from various devices, systems and applications which can be applied to various processes to achieve personalization and improve robustness and efficiency.

In this chapter, research regarding the connection between Industry 4.0, CPS and industrial big data frameworks is conducted to outline the key differences between them. Also, Challenges including both data management and data analysis in Industry 4.0 are discussed to bring more attention to existing industrial issues and highlight the upcoming research path. Also, this survey will present new concepts, methodologies, and applications scenarios to reach a fully autonomous industry. Finally, this paper will propose potential effects of different manufacturing frameworks, business management models and service innovation in supply chain.

References

1. M. Brettel, N. Friederchsen, M. Keller, M. Rosenberg, How virtualization, decentralization and network building change the manufacturing landscape: An industry 4.0 perspective. World Acad. Sci. Eng. Technol. **8**(1), 37–44 (2014)
2. L. Bassi, in *Industry 4.0: Hope, Hype or Revolution?* IEEE 3rd International Forum on Research and Technologies for Society and Industry (RTSI), (2017), pp. 1–6
3. L.D. Xu, L. Duan, Big data for cyber physical systems in industry 4.0: A survey. Enterp. Inf. Syst. **13**(2), 148–169 (2019)
4. S. Yin, O. Kaynak, Big data for modern industry: Challenges and trends [point of view]. Proc. IEEE **103**(2), 143–146 (2015). https://doi.org/10.1109/JPROC.2015.2388958
5. Y. Lu, Cyber physical system (Cps)-based industry 4.0: A survey. J. Ind. Integr. Manag. **2**(3) (2017b). https://doi.org/10.1142/S2424862217500142
6. Y. Lu, Industry 4.0: A survey on Technologies, applications and open research issues. J. Ind. Inf. Integr. **6**, 1–10 (2017). https://doi.org/10.1016/j.jii.2017.04.005
7. H. Lasi, P. Fettke, G. Kemper, T. Feld, M. Hoffmann, Industry 4.0. Bus. Inf. Syst. Eng. **6**(4), 239–242 (2014). https://doi.org/10.1007/s12599-014-0334-4
8. S. Li, L.D. Xu, S. Zhao, 5G internet of things: A survey. J. Ind. Inf. Integr. **10**, 1–9 (2018). https://doi.org/10.1016/j.jii.2018.01.005
9. J. Wang, W. Zhang, Y. Shi, S. Duan, J. Liu, Industrial big data analytics: challenges, methodologies, and applications. IEEE Trans. Automat. Sci. Eng. 1–12 (2018)
10. S. Ganschar, M. Gerlach, T. Hammerle, S. Krause, in *Arbeit der Zukunft – Mensch und Produktionsarbeit Der Zukunft-Industrie 4.0*, 2013, ed. by D. Spath, pp. 50–56
11. H. Chen, Applications of cyber-physical system: A literature review. J. Ind. Integr. Manag. **2**(3), 2424–8622 (2017b). https://doi.org/10.1142/S2424862217500129
12. H. Chen, Theoretical foundations for cyber-physical systems: A literature review. J. Ind. Integr. Manag. **2**(3), 2424–8630 (2017). https://doi.org/10.1142/S2424862217500130
13. J. Lee, H. Ardakani, S. Yang, B. Bagheri, Industrial big data analytics and cyber-physical Systems for Future Maintenance & service innovation. Proc. CIRP **38**, 3–7 (2015). https://doi.org/10.1016/j.procir.2015.08.026
14. E. Lee, in *Cyber Physical Systems: Design Challenges*. Object Oriented Real-Time Distributed Computing (ISORC), (2008), pp. 363–369
15. L. Xu, Editorial: inaugural issue. Enterp. Inf. Syst. **1**(1), 1–2 (2007). https://doi.org/10.1080/17517570712331393320
16. J. Lee, E. Lapira, B. Bagheri, H. Kao, Recent advances and trends in predictive manufacturing systems in big data environment. Manuf. Lett. **1**(1), 38–41 (2013). https://doi.org/10.1016/j.mfglet.2013.09.005
17. M. Baily, J. Manyka, *Is Manufacturing 'Cool' Again* (McKinsey Global Institute, 2013), Retrieved 18 July 2019
18. Y. Chen, H. Chen, A. Gorkhali, Y. Lu, Y. Ma, L. Li, Big data analytics and big data science: A survey. J. Manag. Anal. **3**(2), 1–42 (2016). https://doi.org/10.1080/23270012.2016.1141332
19. *The rise of industrial big data*. (2012). GE Intelligent Platforms

20. *What is Big Data?* | *Big Data Definition* | *V's of Big Data.* (2018). Retrieved 7 18, 2019, from https://www.edureka.co/blog/what-is-big-data/
21. D. Laney, *3-D Data Management: Controlling Data Volume, Velocity and Variety* (META Group, 2001). Research Note
22. A. Mauro, M. Greco, M. Grimaldi, A formal definition of big data based on its essential features. Libr. Rev. **65**(3), 122–135 (2016). https://doi.org/10.1108/LR-06-2015-0061
23. M. Schroeck, R. Shockley, J. Smart, D. Romero-Morrales, P. Tufano, *Analytics: The Real-World Use of Big* (IBM Global Business Services, 2012). Retrieved from https://www-01.ibm.com/common/ssi/cgi-bin/ssialias?htmlfid=
24. J. Dijcks, *Oracle: Big Data for the Enterprise.* Oracle White Paper, (2012), Retrieved from http://www.oracle.com/us/products/
25. H. Karimipour, A. Rahimnezhad, H. Rouzba, Smart households demand response management with micro grid. arXiv **1**, –7 (2019c)
26. H. Karimipour, V. Dinavahi, Parallel domain decomposition based distributed state estimation for large-scale power systems. IEEE Trans. Ind. Appl. **52**(2), 1265–1269 (2016)
27. H. Karimipour, V. Dinavahi, Extended Kalman filter based massively parallel dynamic state estimation. IEEE Trans. Smart Grid **6**(3), 1539–1549 (2015)
28. Y. Zhong, X. Xu, L. Wang, IoT-enabled smart factory visibility and traceability using laser-scanners. Proc. Manuf. **10**, 1–14 (2017). https://doi.org/10.1016/j.promfg.2017.07.103
29. Y. Zhang, T. Qu, O. Ho, G. Huang, Real-time work-in-progress management for smart object-enabled ubiquitous shop-floor environment. Int. J. Comput. Integr. Manuf. **24**(5), 431–445 (2011). https://doi.org/10.1080/0951192X.2010.527374
30. A. Dehghantanha, A. Azmoodeh, K. Choo, Robust malware detection for internet of (battle-field) things devices using deep eigenspace learning. IEEE Trans. Sustain. Comput. **4**(1), 88–95 (2019a)
31. H. Said, T. Nicoletti, P. Perez, Utilizing telematics data to support effective equipment Fleet-management decisions: utilization rate and Hazard functions. J. Comput. Civ. Eng., 1–11 (2015). https://doi.org/10.1061/(ASCE)CP.1943-5487.0000444
32. Y. Xu, M. Chen, Improving just-in-time manufacturing operations by using internet of things based solutions. Procedia CIRP **56**, 326–331 (2016). https://doi.org/10.1016/j.procir.2016.10.030
33. A. Dehghantanha, T. Dargahi, S. Grooby, A bibliometric analysis of authentication and access control in IoT devices, in *Handbook of big data and IoT security*, (Springer, 2019b), pp. 25–51. https://doi.org/10.1007/978-3-030-10543-3_3
34. A. Dehghantanha, M. Conti, K.W. Franke, Internet of things security and forensics: Challenges and opportunities. Futur. Gener. Comput. Syst., 544–546 (2018a). https://doi.org/10.1016/j.future.2017.07.060
35. M. Friendly, The Golden age of statistical graphics. Stat. Sci. **23**(4), 502–535 (2008). https://doi.org/10.1214/08-STS268
36. K. Vassakis, E. Petrakis, I. Kopanakis, Big Data Analytics: Applications, Prospects and Challenges, in *Mobile Big Data*, (Emmanuel Petrakis's Lab, 2017). https://doi.org/10.1007/978-3-319-67925-9_1
37. H. Karimipour, A. Dehghantanha, J. Sakhnini, in *Smart Grid Cyber Attacks Detection Using Supervised Learning and Heuristic Feature Selection.* IEEE Int. Conf. on Smart Energy Grid Engineering (SEGE) (2019a), pp. 1–5
38. H. Karimipour, S. Mohammadi, V. Desai, Multivariate mutual information feature selection for intrusion detection. IEEE Canada Electr. Power Energy Conf. (EPEC), 1–6 (2018)
39. A. Vijayaraghavan, W. Sobel, A. Fox, D. Dornfeld, P. Warndorf, in *Improving Machine Tool Interoperability Using Standardized Interface Protocols: MT Connect.* International Symposium on Flexible Automation, (2008), pp. 1–6
40. GilPress. (2017, 10 1). *What's The Big Data?* (Venturebeat) Retrieved 08 13, 2019, from The Chatbots Landscape: https://whatsthebigdata.com/2017/10/01/the-chatbots-landscape/
41. P. Gölzer, P. Cato, M. Amberg, *Data Processing Requirements of Industry 4.0 - Use Cases for Big Data Applications* (Association for Information Systems (AISeL), 2015)

42. E. Hewitt, *Cassandra: The Definitive Guide* (O'Reilly Media, Inc., Sebastopol, 2011)
43. E. Anderson, X. Li, M. Shah, J. Tucek, J. Wylie, *What Consistency Does Your Key-Value Store Actually Provide?* (Hewlett-Packard Laboratories, 2009), pp. 1–6
44. K. Chodorow, S. Bradshaw, MongoDB: The Definitive Guide, in *Powerful and Scalable Data Storage*, 3rd edn., (O'Reilly Media, 2019), p. 425
45. H. Kagermann, J. Helbig, A. Hellinger, W. Wahlster, Recommendations for Implementing the Strategic Initiative INDUSTRIE 4.0, in *Securing the Future of German Manufacturing Industry*, (Forschungsunion, Acatech, 2013)
46. M. Santos, B. Martinho, C. Costa, Modelling and implementing big data warehouses for decision support. J. Manag. Anal. **4**(2), 111–129 (2016). https://doi.org/10.1080/23270012.2017.1304292
47. L. Xu, N. Liang, Q. Gao, An integrated approach for agricultural ecosystem management - IEEE journals & magazine. IEEE Trans. Syst. Man Cybern. Part C Appl. Rev. **38**(4), 590–599 (2008). https://doi.org/10.1109/TSMCC.2007.913894
48. K. Shvachko, H. Kuang, S. Radia, R. Chansler, in *The Hadoop Distributed File System*. IEEE 26th Symposium on Mass Storage Systems and Technologies (MSST), 2010, pp. 1–10. doi:https://doi.org/10.1109/MSST.2010.5496972
49. G. Jagannathan, R. Wright, in *Research Track Poster Privacy-Preserving Distributed k-Means Clustering over Arbitrarily Partitioned Data *. Proceeding of the Eleventh ACM SIGKDD International Conference on Knowledge Discovery in Data Mining (2005), pp. 593–599. https://doi.org/10.1145/1081870.1081942
50. Y. Yao, Q. Cao, A. Vasilakos, EDAL: An energy-efficient, delay-aware, and lifetime-balancing data collection protocol for heterogeneous wireless sensor networks. IEEE/ACM Trans. Networking **23**(3), 810–823 (2015). https://doi.org/10.1109/TNET.2014.2306592
51. A. Dehghantanha, O. Osanaiye, H. Cai, K.X. Choo, Ensemble-based multi-filter feature selection method for DDoS detection in cloud computing. EURASIP J. Wirel. Commun. Netw., 1–20 (2016). https://doi.org/10.1186/s13638-016-0623-3
52. F. Tao, L. Zhang, V. Venkatesh, Y. Luo, Y. Cheng, Cloud manufacturing: A computing and service-oriented manufacturing model. Proc. Inst. Mech. Eng. B J. Eng. **225**(10), 1969–1976 (2011)
53. X. Xu, From cloud computing to cloud manufacturing. Robot. Comput. Integr. Manuf. **28**(1), 75–86 (2012). https://doi.org/10.1016/j.rcim.2011.07.002
54. B. Daniel, Big data and analytics in higher education: Opportunities and challenges. Br. J. Educ. Technol. **46**(5), 904–920 (2015). https://doi.org/10.1111/bjet.2015.46.issue-5
55. D. Delen, H. Demirkan, Data, information and analytics as services. Decis. Support. Syst. **55**(1), 359–363 (2013). https://doi.org/10.1016/j.dss.2012.05.044
56. H.B. Karimipour, F. Derakhshan, in *A Layered Intrusion Detection System for Critical Infrastructure Using Machine Learning*. IEEE Int. Conf. on Smart Energy Grid Engineering (SEGE), (2019), pp. 1–5
57. W.P. Elderton, Tables for testing the goodness of fit of theory to observation. Biometrika **1**(2), 155–163 (1902)
58. K. Pearson, Note on regression and inheritance in the case of two parents. Proc. R. Soc. Lond. **58**, 240–242 (1895). https://doi.org/10.1098/rspl.1895.0041
59. A. Kramer, J. Green, J.T. Pollard, Causal analysis approaches in ingenuity pathway analysis | bioinformatics | Oxford Academic. Bioinformatics **30**(4), 523–530 (2014). https://doi.org/10.1093/bioinformatics/btt703
60. J. Pearl, *Simpson's paradox, confounding, and collapibility* (Cambridge University Press, Cambridge, 2000), pp. 173–200
61. S. Kleinberg, B. Mishra, The Temporal Logic of Causal Structures, in *Proceedings of the Twenty-Fifth Conference on Uncertainty in Artificial Intelligence*, (AUAI Press, 2009), pp. 303–312
62. R. Agrawal, R. Srikant, in *Fast Algorithms for Mining Association Rules*. Proceedings of 20th International Conference Very Large Data Bases, **15**(1215), 487–499 (1994)

63. J. Han, J. Pei, Y. Yin, Mining frequent patterns without candidate generation. ACM Sigmod Rec. **29**(2), 1–12 (2000)
64. M. Zaki, Scalable algorithms for association mining. IEEE Trans. Knowl. Data Eng. **12**(3), 372–390 (2000). https://doi.org/10.1109/69.846291
65. L. Duan, W. Street, Finding maximal fully-correlated itemsets in large databases. ICDM **9**, 770–775 (2009)
66. E.R. Lapira, Fault Detection in a Network of Similar Machines Using Clustering Approach. Doctoral Dissertation, University of Cincinnati, 2012
67. H. Karimipour, A. Dehghantanha, R. Parizi, K. Choo, H. Leung, A deep and scalable unsupervised machine learning system for cyber-attack detection in large-scale smart grids. IEEE Access **7** (2019b). https://doi.org/10.1109/ACCESS.2019.2920326
68. A. Jalowiechki, P. Klusek, W. Skarka, The methods of knowledge acquisition in the product lifecycle for a generative model's creation process. Proc. Manuf. **11**, 2219–2226 (2017). https://doi.org/10.1016/j.promfg.2017.07.369
69. L. Alleman, L. Lamaison, P. Esperanza, PM10 metal concentrations and source identification using positive matrix factorization and wind sectoring in a French industrial zone. Atmos. Res. **96**(4), 612–625 (2010). https://doi.org/10.1016/j.atmosres.2010.02.008
70. C.J. Kuo, D. Chen, L. Yang, H. Chen, Automatic machine status prediction in the era of industry 4.0: Case study of Machines in a Spring Factory. J. Syst. Archit. **81**, 44–53 (2017). https://doi.org/10.1016/j.sysarc.2017.10.007
71. B. Bagheri, H. Ahmadi, R. Labbafi, Implementing discrete wavelet transform and artificial neural networks for acoustic condition monitoring of gearbox. Elixir Mech **35**, 2909–2911 (2011)
72. J. Neter, M. Kutner, C. Nachtsheim, W. Wasserman, *Applied Linear Statistical Models*, 5th edn. (McGraw-Hill Irwin, New York, 1996), pp. 1–1415
73. D. Hosmer, S.S. Lemeshow, *Applied Logistic Regression*, 3rd edn. (Wiley, Hoboken, 2013)
74. P. Domingos, M. Pazzani, On the optimality of the simple Bayesian classifier under zero-one loss. Mach. Learn. **29**(2), 103–130 (1997). https://doi.org/10.1023/A:1007413511361
75. N. Friedman, D. Geiger, M. Goldszmidt, Bayesian network classifiers. Mach. Learn. **29**(2), 131–163 (1997). https://doi.org/10.1023/A:1007465528199
76. M. Hagan, D. Howard, M. Beale, O. De Jesus, *Neural Network Design*, 2nd edn. (Martin Hagan, 2014)
77. A. Dehghantanha, H. Haddad Pajouh, R. Khayami, K. Choo, A deep recurrent neural network based approach for internet of things malware threat hunting. Futur. Gener. Comput. Syst. **85**, 88–96 (2018b). https://doi.org/10.1016/j.future.2018.03.007
78. J. Suykens, J. Vandewalle, Least squares support vector machine classifiers. Neural. Process. Lett. **9**(3), 293–300 (1999). https://doi.org/10.1023/A:1018628609742
79. B. Boser, I. Guyon, V. Vapnik, in *A Training Algorithm for Optimal Margin Classifiers*. Proceedings of the Fifth Annual Workshop on Computational Learning Theory, (1992), pp. 144–152
80. M. Maggio, H. Hoffmann, A. Papadopoulos, Comparison of decision-making strategies for self-optimization in autonomic computing systems. ACM Trans. Auton. Adapt. Syst. **7**(4) (2012). https://doi.org/10.1145/2382570.2382572
81. P. Bogdan, in *A Cyber-Physical Systems Approach to Personalized Medicine: Challenges and Opportunities for NoC-Based Multicore Platforms*. Design, Automation & Test in Europe Conference & Exhibition (DATE), (2015), pp. 2553–2258. https://doi.org/10.7873/DATE.2015.1127

Chapter 4
A Privacy Protection Key Agreement Protocol Based on ECC for Smart Grid

Mostafa Farhdi Moghadam, Amirhossein Mohajerzdeh, Hadis Karimipour, Hamid Chitsaz, Roya Karimi, and Behzad Molavi

1 Introduction

Electrical distribution network today as an intelligent network, work with a more complex system structure compared to past electricity network and the needs of the twenty-first century make it more complicated and also unpredictable [1–5]. There are some shortages and disorders that is noteworthy like: Lack of an automatic analysis system, Weak field of view, Mechanical switches with low response speed and lack of situational awareness in the network [6, 7]. In the current situation, an intelligent electrical distribution network can be described as an electrical distribution network which uses ICT to meet communication needs and goals such as providing electricity in an appropriate, sustainable and sustainable manner and as a new model reliability of network management, performance and sustainability are significant [8]. In this network, which is also known as the next generation of electrical network it uses different smart devices in its structure which are used in different parts of the network, for example, smart devices at electrical stations, intelligent devices in the local network, RTU, PLC, smart network control system and other outdoor equipment. The smart network can be divided into three parts: control center, electrical substations and smart devices [9–11]. Due to the integration of the distribution system with the communication network,

M. Farhdi Moghadam · H. Chitsaz
Department of Computer, Vahdat Institute of Higher Education, Torbat-e-Jam, Iran

A. Mohajerzdeh · R. Karimi · B. Molavi
Department of Computer Engineering, Ferdowsi University of Mashhad, Mashhad, Iran
e-mail: Mohajerzadeh@um.ac.ir; Rkarimi@um.ac.ir

H. Karimipour (✉)
School of Engineering, University of Guelph, Guelph, ON, Canada
e-mail: hkarimi@uoguelph.ca; Canada-hkarimi@uoguelph.ca

© Springer Nature Switzerland AG 2020
K.-K. R. Choo, A. Dehghantanha (eds.), *Handbook of Big Data Privacy*,
https://doi.org/10.1007/978-3-030-38557-6_4

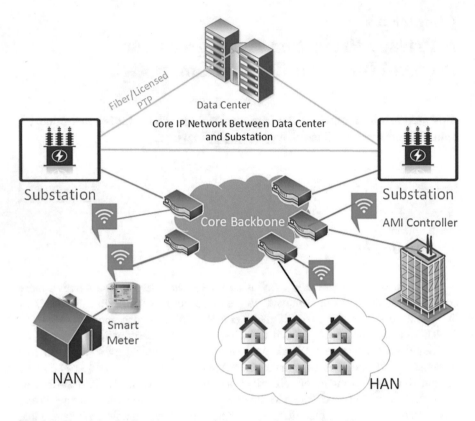

Fig. 4.1 Electricity distribution system and communication network architecture

it is expected that the electricity producer and information have the two-way communication [12, 13]. These networks can instantaneously monitor and control customers' consumption and produce power as much as they need. The intelligent network uses integrated solar energy and energy distribution systems to increase the efficiency and reliability of the electrical generation system [14–16]. However, in order to achieve this, it is necessary to use smart devices that can help identify and fix network vulnerabilities and weaknesses. The existence of vulnerability in the intelligent network is inevitable therefore, preventing vulnerabilities in such a network is much more important than the vulnerability in conventional networks. So that the vulnerability causes the attack to succeed and a successful attack by a network can put smart grids over large areas and cause greater financial losses [17]. In infrastructure electrical distribution intelligent network, the distribution system is one of the main components of the grid that is responsible for energy supply for consumers. This network uses two distribution posts, the main post and the secondary post [18]. Figure 4.1 shows the architecture and distribution electrical system in the intelligent electrical distribution network.

There are several components in the intelligent network that communicate through communication paths and sensors, such as distribution terminals, transmission systems, residential, commercial, and industrial locations. On the home network, power distribution is an instantaneous element of the electricity distribution system, and the amount of power consumed is provided to the consumer. At present, the communication infrastructure in the intelligent distribution network of IEC 61850 is used for communication between network components [19, 20]. This standard is based on Ethernet, and most of the intelligent network connections are Ethernet-dependent. IEC Standard 61850 provides standard communication protocols for communicating and connecting to hardware for the network, but it is not possible to cover network security [21, 22]. Intelligent network service providers based on information from smart devices in the network provides services to users [23]. In intelligent networks, various wired and wireless technologies are used to communicate between different network components [24]. These technologies are: power line carrier communication, industrial Ethernet, communications Fiber optics and other wireless networks that are used. The use of different technologies or the combination of different network models in the intelligent network communication system is common practice. The existence of different technologies allows communications for different parts of the network Smart has made it easy, but the consensus of these network communications with the vulnerability distribution system Creates security challenges for network [25]. Challenge security attacks such as the attack on the feasibility of further attacks, attacks MITM and phishing attacks by attackers [26–29]. In order to cover security issues in the smart network, it can use authentication, data encryption, access control, and other available methods. Also, authentication methods and key agreement schemes for smart watch have been considered in recent years. Despite the anticipated plans, most of them suffered from security breaches and did not fully meet security requirements [30, 31]. In other cases, the proposed methods, the anonymity and the unidentified entities Attention has been paid [30–34].

Another issue that should be considered with regard to intelligent network security schemes is their performance. As a result, the security of the network, especially privacy protection at lower cost in computing, is another challenge.

2   Related Work

Smart grid consists of two parts: computer network and power generation infrastructure. Since highly sensitive data are exchanged in this grid, the issue of providing security becomes critical. In recent years, several studies have been conducted on the security and its challenges. In 2014, Nicanfar et al., proposed an efficient authentication scheme for home area network using initial password, and reduced the number of secure password steps and exchanged packets. In addition, they presented an efficient key exchange protocol based on self-authentication cryptography with public key infrastructure [35]. In 2016, He et al., employed an ECC-based key distribution scheme (AKD) providing anonymity and mutual authentication between entities without the help of trusted third entity. The proposed AKD scheme, performs efficiently and better than its predecessor [36]. Privacy and anonymity of smart meters are very important in smart grid and then, different schemes have been proposed to meet these features. In 2016, Tsai et al., proposed a key distribution scheme for smart grid environment that utilized identity-based signature and identity-based encryption to generate key anonymously. In the proposed scheme, a smart meter can anonymously access the network services through service provider in middle. The access is performed using private key, without the interference of trusted third entity during authentication [37]. Despite all the efforts made, the scheme wasn't able to provide session key security and resist some security attacks [31]. To fix such issues, Odelu et al., exploited bilinear pairings to achieve mutual authentication and session key generation between smart meter and service provider entities [31]. Similarly, in spite of mutual authentication, this scheme was vulnerable to spoofing attack, and the smart meter was traceable by key generation center [38]. To address those issues, Chen et al., proposed the same bilinear pairings with Diffie-Hellman [38]. To prove the security of the proposed scheme, they used BAN logic and Random Oracle models. Nevertheless, the performance cost of the scheme is not negligible. Considering the requirements of smart grid and developing lightweight schemes, in 2018, Mahmood et al., presented a scheme providing an efficient ECC-based authentication for smart grid [34]. They exploited Burrows-Abadi-Needham (BAN) logic to prove the integrity and completeness of their scheme. Compared to schemes using public key cryptography, the ECC-based authentication ones have lower computational costs. Recently, Abbasinezhad-Mood and Nikooghadam proposed a key distribution scheme providing ECC-based privacy [39]. To show the security of their scheme, they utilized Random Oracle Model and implemented the cryptographic elements on two ARM chips. Moreover, Kumar et al., developed a key agreement and anonymous authentication scheme that includes parameters like ECC, symmetric cryptography, hash function and MAC [40]. Nonetheless, the timestamp they utilized in the scheme, may encounter the clock synchronization problem. Abbasinezhad-Mood and Nikooghadam proposed an anonymous password-authenticated key exchange protocol using extended Chebyshev chaotic maps for smart meters [41]. Their scheme solves the limitations of scheme of Sha et al., and provides the anonymity as well. Since the physical security is important too, Gope and Sikdar presented a novel privacy-aware authenticated key agreement scheme in which the physical security is considered in addition to communication security [41]. Duo to the wide range of security issues and challenges posed by the spread of smart grid, researchers also have proposed different schemes and security issues in 2019. Zhang et al., proposed a key exchange and lightweight anonymous authentication scheme for smart meter and service provider entities in smart grid [42]. They used Real-or-Random Oracle Model to evaluate their scheme. With respect to the widespread use of smart meters in smart grid and two-way communications between them, the authentication of smart meter is very important. Hence, Chen et al., proposed an authentication scheme based on bilinear map pairing, which is capable of providing more security features, e.g. complete privacy and message integrity [43]. Key generation security protocols play a significant role in maintaining secure communications over insecure channels. In this regard, due to various attacks and security challenges in smart grid, Abbasinezhad-Mood et al., developed a key exchange model that can resist Canetti and Krawczyk attacks. They utilized descriptive security analysis, an automatic formal verifier and exhaustive comparative efficiency analysis to prove their scheme [44]. All the proposed schemes reviewed here, attempt to provide communication security and privacy with low computational cost over authentication process in smart grid. However, in some schemes proposed, security requirements were not satisfied or the schemes were suffering from high computational costs due to heavy computation operations, e.g. bilinear map pairing in the process of performing the protocol. As a result, how to manage to achieve a good performance in authentication process and preserving privacy, still remains a challenge.

3   Contribution

The main contribution of our work summarized as follows:

Strong Authentication and Key Agreement Based on ECC Due to the importance of authentication of interlocking in the smart grid, the proposed method for authenticating entities is used as a strong method for authentication based on the elliptic curve and generates a separate session key for each session. It has the ability to prevent various attacks, which in the next attacks are specifically targeted.

Privacy Protection In the proposed schema, hash functions have been used to protect entity's identity in each session. The entity identity parameters are merged with other parameters and then they are hashed. Then the message that sent on the channel is protected by asymmetric encryption. In addition, no parameters related to the identity of the entities are sent to the channel. Also, in the proposed method, the authentication parameters were completely separate from the sessions with the previous sessions, so if an attacker can access to the messages under circumstances, he/she cannot determine which consecutive messages are related to which entity exists on the network. However, the adversary must first have to cross symmetric encryption in order to access the message. As a result, privacy and anonymity of entities in our plan are of high security.

Analyzed Security We analyze the proposed scheme to prove its security with manual and formal methods. We implement it with AVISPA tools and the result show that the proposed protocol is safe. In addition, different attacks are described and show how the proposed approach is safe against these attacks.

The rest of the chapter is organized as follows. Section 4 will describe the proposed scheme. The security and performance of the proposed scheme described in Sect. 5. Finally, conclusions are described in Sect. 6.

4 Proposed Key Agreement and Authentication Scheme

In this section we present our strong Authentication and key agreement scheme for entities in smart grid. The scheme consists of two phases: the registration and key agreement phase. The authentication is performed during the key production process. Table 4.1 shows the protocol symbols.

4.1 Registration Phase

In our scheme every smart meter or devices must be registered by the service provider in the first step. In this phase the entities (smart meter, Substation, ...) that they want to start a communication with data center must exchange Initial parameters such as: their ID, public keys. When the data center receives the parameters from the entities, generate a special certificate for the entities. There are different generation/authentication algorithms to generate certificates. The certificate is one the important parameters for authenticate the entities during the key generation process. Figure 4.2 show the registration phase.

Table 4.1 Symbols used in the proposed protocol

Symbol	Quantity
PU_{ent}	The Public Key of entity
K_{ent}	The Private Key of entity
PU_{dc}	The Public Key of Data Center
K_{dc}	The Private Key of Data Center
Cert	The certificate of substation
H	One-way hash function
E_{pudc}	Encrypt with data center public key
L_1	Concatenation operator
ID_x	Identity of Entity x
E_{puent}	Encrypt with entity public key
ΔT_i	The time of sending a packet
A	Random value
M, P, L_1	The values generated by the entity
SK	Session Key
$(.)'$	Regenerate the parameter by another entity
||	Concatenation operator
L_2	The values generated by the data center
Sign	The values generated by the entity and data center

Fig. 4.2 Registration phase

4.2   Key Agreement and Authentication Phase

In this phase the entity and data center communicate each other and send parameters to generate session key. Authentication between the entity and data center is done during the key generation process. The steps in this phase are as follows:

At the first step entity generate $Sign = K_{ent}.PU_{dc}$. The Sign parameter is one way that entity and data center can authenticate each other because on the other side of communication data center can compute the parameter Sign ($Sing = K_{dc}.PU_{ent}$). The Private key of entity and data center is used to generate the parameter Sign and its worth noting that without sending this parameter in the channel, it is possible the entity and data center authenticate each other.

Then entity attempt to generate the $P = H(Cert||ID_{ent}||sign)$. The second parameter that used for authentication process is P. In this parameter used the Cert that it is specially for the entity and Sign that generated by Private key of entity.

In the first step of Key agreement and Authentication phase, the entity after generating the Sign and P, choose A random number to generate parameter M.

$$M = H\left(Sign\,\|A\|\,P\right)$$

In the process of implementing our protocol, we need to make a difference between the keys of each session and the lack of dependence between them. To achieve this advantage, a random number has been used to generate the parameter M. Parameter M is one of the parameters used in generating the session key by the data center.

Next, $L_1 = H(M||P||sign)$ generated by the entity. This is another parameter used by the data center to authenticate the entity. Parameters Sign and P are used to generate the L_1 and this parameter just generated by the private parameter that only data center can compute them. For parameter Sign if any parameter except entity private key used on other side the result of multiplication of the private key of the data center and the device will not be the same. The value of the parameter Sign on both sides will be the same if the following process is established:

$$K_{ent}.PU_{dc} = Sign = K_{dc}.PU_{ent}$$

If any other entity attempts to communicate, the generated Sign will not be the same as the generated Sign on the data center side. Also needed to parameter Cert that it specially for the entity and other entity cannot access it.

At last of the first step, the entity encrypt the L_1, M, T_i with data center public key that it just decrypted by private key of data center.

The second step, Data center receive the encrypted message and in first action decrypt the message. When the message decrypted by Data center, it attempt to Check massage freshness by check the ΔT. In this step Data center authenticate the entity by computing the parameters Sign, P and L_1. First it compute $Sign' = K_{dc}.PU_{ent}$ if $Sign' = Sign$ then compute $P' = H(Cert||ID_{ent}||Sign)$. Next, Data center compute $L_1' = H(M||P||Sign)$ and check $L_1 = L_1'$. If the value of parameters are equal, the data center verifies the identity of the entity and then proceeds to generate the session key $SK = H(Sign||M||Cert)$. At the last Data center generate $L_2 = H(Sign'||P'||SK)$ for Authentication process on both sides and encrypt the L_2 and T_i by entity Public key. If the value of $Sign'$ and P' are not equal to Sign and P, the entity drops the connection.

The final step, entity receive the encrypted message that sent by Data center. First, decrypt the message by its Private key and check the ΔT to confirm freshness of the message. Then compute $SK' = H(Sign||M||Cert)$. Second compute $L_2' = H(Sign||P||SK')$ to authenticate the Data center and correctness of parameters. If $L_2' = L_2$. At the end, entity make sure of identity of data center and Accuracy of data then SK selected as session key. Figure 4.3 shows the key agreement and authentication phase.

5   Security and Performance Analyze of the Proposed Scheme

In this section, we analyzed the security of our proposed scheme. For prove the security of long-term parameters and security aspect the proposed scheme implemented by AVISPA tools. Also, Common attacks have been introduced and expressed how the proposed method resistant to these attacks.

5.1   Security Review of the Proposed Method Against All Types of Network Attacks

Reply Attack In the network, the reply attack is one the attacks that the intruder captures the valid data in communication and used them for malicious acts or fraudulently to repeated or delayed. To prevent this attack, we used time stamps to check the novelty of the message and a random number to make a difference in packets for each session. In each step of protocol, entities and data center check the time stamp, so attacker cannot perform this attack.

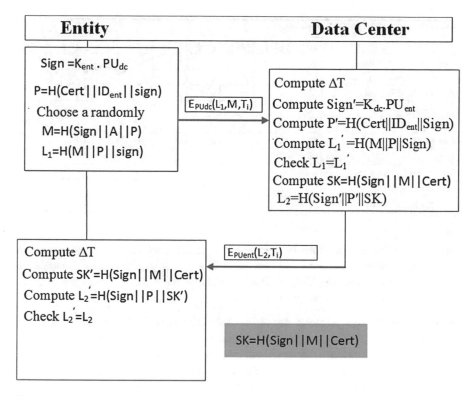

Entity	**Data Center**
Sign $=K_{ent} \cdot PU_{dc}$ $P=H(Cert\|\|ID_{ent}\|\|sign)$ Choose a randomly $M=H(Sign\|\|A\|\|P)$ $L_1=H(M\|\|P\|\|sign)$	Compute ΔT Compute $Sign'=K_{dc} \cdot PU_{ent}$ Compute $P'=H(Cert\|\|ID_{ent}\|\|Sign)$ Compute $L_1'=H(M\|\|P\|\|Sign)$ Check $L_1=L_1'$ Compute $SK=H(Sign\|\|M\|\|Cert)$ $L_2=H(Sign'\|\|P'\|\|SK)$

$E_{PUdc}(L_1, M, T_i)$

$E_{PUent}(L_2, T_i)$

Compute ΔT
Compute $SK'=H(Sign\|\|M\|\|Cert)$
Compute $L_2'=H(Sign\|\|P\|\|SK')$
Check $L_2'=L_2$

$SK=H(Sign\|\|M\|\|Cert)$

Fig. 4.3 Authentication and key agreement phase

Impersonation Attack In this attack, the intruder attempt to introduce himself as an authorized entity in network. He/she tries to communicate with other devices or entities. The proposed scheme to prevent this type of attacks, implement strong mutual authentication. In the protocol we consider three important parameters Sign, M and Carteret is a private parameter that generated by data center for each entity. Parameter Sign, this parameter depends on private key of both entities in communication and entities can computed it fully separate and using your private key. So if any attacker wants to generated the Sign must access to the private key of entities or data center. On the other hand, to generate the parameters P and M used the Sign and Cert, therefore, attacker first needed to two private parameters. To authenticate entity by the data center parameters Sign, P, L_1 computed by data center and in the next step it used this three parameters to authenticate itself to the entity. It is notable that any of this parameters (Cert, Sign and P) does not sent in channel.

Perfect Forward Secrecy It is important for each communication that the session keys be separated each other and if attacker can access to one session key. He/she cannot guess or calculate the other session keys. Perfect forward secrecy helps to the protocols to have secure communications by generating unique keys during the

Table 4.2 Security feature comparison

	[30]	[31]	[32]	[34]	[35]	[36]	[37]	[45]	Ours
Impersonation Attack	×	×	×	✓	×	✓	×	✓	✓
Mutual Authentication	✓	✓	✓	✓	✓	✓	✓	✓	✓
Session Key Security	×	✓	×	✓	✓	✓	×	✓	✓
Anonymity	×	✓	×	×	×	✓	✓	×	✓
Perfect Forward Secrecy	×	✓	×	×	✓	✓	✓	×	✓
Reply Attack	×	✓	✓	✓	✓	✓	✓	✓	✓
Man-In-The-Middle attack	×	×	✓	✓	✓	✓	×	✓	✓
Safe from DOS attack	-	×	×	✓	×	×	×	−	✓
NO Key Escrow Issue	✓	×	×	−	−	×	×	×	✓
Private Key Privacy	×	−	−	×	✓	−	−	−	✓

transferring the information. In our proposed scheme we used a random number to generate the parameter M and this parameter is one of the main parameters to generate the session key. This random number provide the different session key values in each session of communication.

Man-in-the-Middle Attacks In some cases, the hostile person changes information between sender and receiver. However, the two entities believe they are communicating directly with each other. In security and cryptography this type of attack called as man-in-the-middle attack. Our proposed scheme considered the strong authentication process. At the first step the attacker needed to private key of each entity to decrypt the message and if can access it, he/she reach to hash values that they are not usable. Also, two entities Authenticate each other in every steps with three parameters (Sign, P, L_1, L_2). Table 4.2 demonstrate the compassion of security feature of our proposed scheme with eight related schemes.

5.2 Result and Formal Analyze

In this section to prove safety of our proposed scheme against the passive and active attacks, we used the AVISPA software to analysis the security. This software is one of the trusted evaluation tools to verifying and analyzing the security protocols in network. This tool evaluate the capability of the protocols under variant attacks. AVISPA has an integrated automated security analysis and back-end servers, such as the On-the-Fly Modeler (OFMC) analyst and Constraint-Logic (Cl-AtSe) attacker. Due to the abilities of this software, we decided to verify the security of our protocol against the attacks and confidentiality of the private values among the relevant agents using the AVISPA tool [33]. Figure 4.4 illustrate the security result.

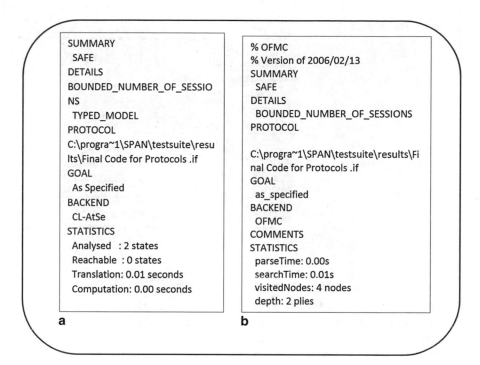

Fig. 4.4 AVISPA results. (**a**) ATSE (**b**) OFMC

Figure 4.4 shows the safety of our protocol against the deference type of passive and active attacks. The OFMC and CL-ATSE output show the confidentiality of the private parameters between the entity and data center is retained. Also show that the protocol is safe against active and non-active attacks. This analyzed result shows that the generated parameters during the performing the protocol are not available for attackers and they are safe.

5.3 Performance Analysis

In this section, we listed other existing authentication and key agreement protocols and compare them with each other. The two factor is considered communication steps and the number of message in transferring the protocol. The proposed protocol in some cases is far better than other and finally is more efficient than all listed protocols. It is needs fewer communication step and messages to reach the session key. Table 4.3 shows the performance of related protocols with the proposed method.

Table 4.3 Performance comparison

Protocol	Communications	Messages
Sha et al.'s [43]	2	5
Zhang et al.'s [42]	4	5
Abbasinezhad et al.'s [46]	5	18
Gope et al.'s [41]	4	9
Kumar et al.'s [40]	2	12
Abbasinezhad et al.'s [39]	3	5
Tsai and Lo [37]	3	5
He et al.'s [36]	3	5
Nicanfar et al.'s [35]	3	10
Mahmood et al.'s [34]	2	10
Nicanfar et al.'s [33]	9	9
Proposed scheme	2	2

6 Conclusion

In this paper, we proposed a strong Authentication and key agreement scheme that can provide privacy protection for the entities of smart grid communications. The proposed scheme can achieve mutual authentication and key agreement between the smart grid entities just in two steps of communication and with less number of messages in communication. Furthermore, two advantages such as intractability and perfect forward secrecy for entities of communication. This features can reach with low computation cost in communication steps and generated messages. As we show in security discussion, the proposed protocol is secure against the attacks and the result of performance analysis show that it lower that other protocols in messages and communication steps. At last, providing the security is a very difficult and every person has their ideas for security.

References

1. M. Chen, Y. Miao, Y. Hao, K. Hwang, Narrow band internet of things. IEEE Access **5**, 20557–20577 (2017)
2. M. Conti, A. Dehghantanha, K. Franke, S. Watson, Internet of things security and forensics: challenges and opportunitiesm. Futur. Gener. Comput. Syst. **78**, 544–546 (2018)
3. H. Karimipour, V. Dinavahi, Robust Massively parallel dynamic state estimation of power systems against cyber-attack. IEEE Access **6**, 2984–2995 (2017)
4. H. Karimipour, V. Dinavahi, Parallel relaxation based joint dynamic state estimation of large-scale power system. IET Gen. Trans. Dist. **10**(2), 452–459 (2016)
5. H.M. Ruzbahani, A. Rahimnejad, H. Karimipour, Smart households demand response management with micro grid, in *IEEE Innovative Smart Grid Technologies (ISGT 2019), Washington, DC* (2019), pp. 1–5
6. A. Dehghantanha, K. Franke, Privacy-respecting digital investigation, in *2014 Twelfth Annual International Conference on Privacy, Security and Trust* (2014), pp. 129–138

7. F. Ghalavand, B.M. Alizadeh, H. Karimipour, Micro grid islanding detection based on mathematical morphology. J. Energy **11**(10), 456–477 (2018)
8. R. Lu, X. Liang, X. Li, X. Lin, X. Shen, Eppa: An efficient and privacy-preserving aggregation scheme for secure smart grid communications. IEEE Trans. Parallel Distrib. Syst. **23**(9), 1621–1631 (2012)
9. H. Karimipour, V. Dinavahi, Extended Kalman filter based massively parallel dynamic state estimation. IEEE Trans. Smart Grid **6**(3), 1539–1549 (2015)
10. H. Karimipour, A. Dehghantanha, R.M. Parizi, R. Choo, H. Leung, A deep and scalable unsupervised machine learning system for cyber-attack detection in large-scale smart grids. IEEE Access **7**, 80778–80788 (2019)
11. H. Karimipour, V. Dinavahi, Parallel domain decomposition based distributed state estimation for large-scale power systems. IEEE Trans. Ind. Appl. **52**(2), 1265–1269 (2016)
12. N. Framework, *Roadmap for Smart Grid Interoperability Standards* (National Institute of Standards and Technology, 2010), p. 26
13. D.B. Rawat, C. Bajracharya, Cyber security for smart grid systems: Status, challenges and perspectives, in *IEEE SoutheastCon 2015* (2015), pp. 1–6
14. M. Damshenas, A. Dehghantanha, R. Mahmoud, A survey on malware propagation, analysis, and detection. Int. J. Cyber-Secur. Digital Forensics **2**(4), 10–30 (2013)
15. S. Hadayeghparast, A. S. Soltaninejad, H. Karimipour, Employing composite demand response model in microgrid energy management, in *IEEE International Conference on Smart Energy Grid Engineering (SEGE), Oshawa, Canada* (2019), pp. 1–5
16. S. Hadayeghparast, H. A. Shayanfar, H. Karimipour, Day-ahead scheduling of a virtual power plant in presence of an incentive-based demand response program, in *IEEE I&CPS Conference, Calgary, Canada*, (2019), pp. 1–5
17. P.-Y. Chen, S.-M. Cheng, K.-C. Chen, Smart attacks in smart grid communication networks. IEEE Commun. Mag. **50**(8), 24–29 (2012)
18. P. Lv, X. Wang, Y. Yang, M. Xu, Network virtualization for smart grid communications. IEEE Syst. J. **8**(2), 471–482 (2013)
19. Q. Song, W. Sheng, L. Kou, D. Zhao, Z. Wu, H. Fang, Smart substation integration technology and its application in distribution power grid. CSEE J. Power Energy Syst. **2**(4), 31–36 (2016)
20. E. Tebekaemi, D. Wijesekera, Designing an IEC 61850 based power distribution substation simulation/emulation testbed for cyber-physical security studies, in *Proceedings of the First International Conference on Cyber-Technologies and Cyber-Systems* (2016), pp. 41–49
21. C. Wester, M. Adamiak, J. Vico, IEC61850 protocol-practical applications in industrial facilities, in *2011 IEEE Industry Applications Society Annual Meeting* (2011), pp. 1–7
22. R. Tawde, A. Nivangune, M. Sankhe, Cyber security in smart grid SCADA automation systems, in *2015 IEEE International Conference on Innovations in Information, Embedded and Communication Systems (ICIIECS)* (2015), pp. 1–5
23. D. Li, Z. Aung, J. Williams, A. Sanchez, P3: Privacy preservation protocol for automatic appliance control application in smart grid. IEEE Internet Things J. **1**(5), 414–429 (2014)
24. R. Khan, K. Mclaughlin, D. Laverty, S. Sezer, Design and implementation of security gateway for synchrophasor based real-time control and monitoring in smart grid. IEEE Access **5**, 11626–11644 (2017)
25. X. Li, J. Niu, S. Kumari, F. Wu, K.-K.R. Choo, A robust biometrics based three-factor authentication scheme for global mobility networks in smart city. Futur. Gener. Comput. Syst. **83**, 607–618 (2018)
26. E. Modiri, A. Azmoodeh, A. Dehghantanha, H. Karimipour, Fuzzy pattern tree for edge attack detection and categorization. Elsevier J. Syst. Archit., 1–15 (2018)
27. S. Mohammadi, H. Mirvaziri, M.G. Ahsaee, H. Karimipour, Cyber intrusion detection by combined feature selection algorithm. Elsevier J. Inf. Secur. Appl. **44**, 80–88 (2018)
28. H. Karimipour, V. Dinavahi, On false data injection attack against dynamic state estimation on smart power grids, in *IEEE International Conference on Smart Energy Grid Engineering, Oshawa, Canada* (2017), pp. 1–7

29. W. Wang, Z. Lu, Cyber security in the smart grid: survey and challenges. Comput. Netw. **57**(5), 1344–1371 (2013)
30. D. Wu, C. Zhou, Fault-tolerant and scalable key management for smart grid. IEEE Trans. Smart Grid **2**(2), 375–381 (2011)
31. V. Odelu, A.K. Das, M. Wazid, M. Conti, Provably secure authenticated key agreement scheme for smart grid. IEEE Trans. Smart Grid **9**(3), 1900–1910 (2016)
32. J. Xia, Y. Wang, Secure key distribution for the smart grid. IEEE Trans. Smart Grid **3**(3), 1437–1443 (2012)
33. H. Nicanfar, P. Jokar, V.C. Leung, Smart grid authentication and key management for unicast and multicast communications, in *2011 IEEE PES Innovative Smart Grid Technologies* (2011), pp. 1–8
34. K. Mahmood, S.A. Chaudhry, H. Naqvi, S. Kumari, X. Li, A.K. Sangaiah, An elliptic curve cryptography based lightweight authentication scheme for smart grid communication. Futur. Gener. Comput. Syst. **81**, 557–565 (2018)
35. H. Nicanfar, P. Jokar, K. Beznosov, V.C. Leung, Efficient authentication and key management mechanisms for smart grid communications. IEEE Syst. J. **8**(2), 629–640 (2013)
36. D. He, H. Wang, M.K. Khan, L. Wang, Lightweight anonymous key distribution scheme for smart grid using elliptic curve cryptography. IET Commun. **10**(14), 1795–1802 (2016)
37. J.-L. Tsai, N.-W. Lo, Secure anonymous key distribution scheme for smart grid. IEEE Trans. Smart Grid **7**(2), 906–914 (2015)
38. Y. Chen, J.-F. Martínez, P. Castillejo, L. López, An anonymous authentication and key establish scheme for smart grid: FAuth. Energies **10**(9), 1354 (2017)
39. D. Abbasinezhad-Mood, M. Nikooghadam, An anonymous ECC-based self-certified key distribution scheme for the smart grid. IEEE Trans. Ind. Electron. **65**(10), 7996–8004 (2018)
40. P. Kumar, A. Gurtov, M. Sain, A. Martin, P.H. Ha, Lightweight authentication and key agreement for smart metering in smart energy networks. in IEEE Transactions on Smart Grid **10**(4), 4349–4359 (July 2019)
41. P. Gope, B. Sikdar, Privacy-aware authenticated key agreement scheme for secure smart grid communication. in IEEE Transactions on Smart Grid **10**(4), 3953–3962 (July 2019)
42. L. Zhang, L. Zhao, S. Yin, C.-H. Chi, R. Liu, Y. Zhang, A lightweight authentication scheme 403 with privacy protection for smart grid communications. Futur. Gener. Comput. Syst. **100**, 770–778 (2019)
43. Y. Chen, J.-F. Martínez, P. Castillejo, L. López, A bilinear map pairing based authentication scheme for smart grid communications: PAuth. IEEE Access **7**, 22633–22643 (2019)
44. D. Abbasinezhad-Mood, M. Nikooghadam, S.M. Mazinani, A. Babamohammadi, A. Ostad-Sharif, More efficient key establishment protocol for smart grid communications: design and experimental evaluation on ARM-based hardware. Ad Hoc Netw. **89**, 119–131 (2019)
45. K. Sha, N. Alatrash, Z. Wang, A secure and efficient framework to read isolated smart grid devices. IEEE Trans. Smart Grid **8**(6), 2519–2531 (2016)
46. D. Abbasinezhad-Mood, M. Nikooghadam, Efficient anonymous password-authenticated key exchange protocol to read isolated smart meters by utilization of extended Chebyshev chaotic maps. IEEE Trans. Ind. Inf. **14**(11), 4815–4828 (2018)

Chapter 5
Applications of Big Data Analytics and Machine Learning in the Internet of Things

Shamim Yousefi, Farnaz Derakhshan, and Hadis Karimipour

1 Introduction

Over the last decades, the software computing systems moved from the domain of the traditional desktops to the dynamic environments. The Internet of Things (IoT), also known as the Internet of Everything, is a novel technology paradigm in this realm, which is gaining significant attention from a wide range of industries [1]. The internet of things envisioned as the globally networked interconnection between the millions of smart sensors, machines, and everyday physical devices (things) interacted with each other to offer specific functionality, without human intervention [2–4]. To satisfy the requirements of the industries, IoT systems are facing some critical challenges that need to be dealt with to exploit the potential of IoT devices fully, including resource limitation (i.e., battery, bandwidth, memory, and computation), security (i.e., data confidentiality, trust, and privacy), and quality of services (throughput, and computational/transmission delay) [5–7].

To deal with IoT challenges, Machine Learning (ML) can be a promising solution. Machine learning is an artificial intelligence mechanism, which has acceptable performance in dynamic environments like IoT and does not need explicit programming [8]. Indeed, ML provides the potential of approaches for satisfying the requirement of reliable and efficient internet-based systems.

We found that so far several review paper on the applications of machine learning in the internet of things have been published [8–10]. However, we aim to prepare an up to date literature review for covering all significant issues on IoT by exploiting

S. Yousefi · F. Derakhshan
Department of Electrical and Computer Engineering, University of Tabriz, Tabriz, Iran
e-mail: sh.yousefi@tabrizu.ac.ir; derakhshan@tabrizu.ac.ir

H. Karimipour (✉)
School of Engineering, University of Guelph, Guelph, ON, Canada
e-mail: hkarimi@uoguelph.ca; Canada-hkarimi@uoguelph.ca

© Springer Nature Switzerland AG 2020
K.-K. R. Choo, A. Dehghantanha (eds.), *Handbook of Big Data Privacy*,
https://doi.org/10.1007/978-3-030-38557-6_5

ML mechanisms. The fundamental contributions of this chapter are summarized as follows:

- The literature on the machine learning applications in the internet of things is reviewed until most recent articles.
- The IoT systems, architecture, applications, and challenges are presented.
- Different machine learning mechanisms and their advantages/disadvantages to address various IoT applications are comprehended.
- A state-of-the-art review has been provided on ML-based data analysis, wireless communication, healthcare systems, industrial systems, and security approaches on the internet of things.
- Finally, possible challenges on the machine learning applications in IoT systems and some recommendations or research direction are presented.

The rest of this chapter is organized as follows: Sect. 2 presents an overview of IoT, consisting of the architecture, applications, and challenges in these systems. Section 3 describes machine learning on the internet of things, including different types of learning algorithms. The applications of ML in IoT and their challenges have been presented in Sect. 4. Section 5 shows an analysis of reviewed literature on ML-based applications in the internet of things. The challenges of machine learning mechanisms in IoT and some recommendations have been explained in Sect. 6. Finally, the chapter is concluded in Sect. 7.

2   Internet of Things

The internet of things has become one of the hottest software systems in the twenty-first century. The term IoT which masters entire world with its intelligent technologies and services refers the globally networked interconnection between smart physical devices, such as sensors, actuators, smartphones, and RFID tags that are scattered all over the monitoring area to communicate with each other and perform specific tasks without human intervention.

Kevin Ashton first introduced a concept called the *Internet of Things* in his researches in 1999 [11]. Since that time, IoT has become the heart of the technology-based world, which tries to communicate between human and smart devices offering different services. On the other, relying on the recent advances in multiple software and hardware technologies, IoT devices are equipped with sensing, identifying, processing, computing, and networking capabilities [12]. According to these abilities, the vision of IoT is couched on a broad scale of applications across various domains, including autonomous healthcare systems [13, 14], the smart world (cities, homes, offices, museums and gyms) [15, 16], intelligent energy systems [17], smart transportation and logistics [18, 19], industrial processing controllers [20], and intelligent agriculture [21, 22]. An overview of the IoT applications is illustrated in Fig. 5.1.

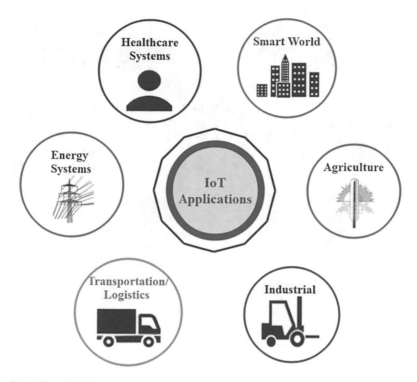

Fig. 5.1 IoT applications

These applications show that everything was dreaming in the past decades, is now a reality relying on advancements in IoT services. It is estimated that IoT systems will catch around 3.9–11.1 trillion U.S. dollar economic market by 2025 [23, 24]. Indeed, nearly 50 billion devices are going to be linked to the internet by 2020, and it will enhance exponentially through time [25]. Therefore, research and analysis on the internet of things, its architecture, the progress of IoT devices and their challenges are located at the center of the attention of the electrical and computer-since researchers in the last decades. The remainder of this section is organized as follows: Sect. 2.1 presents IoT architecture briefly, and Sect. 2.2 explains the significant challenges in the field of IoT systems.

2.1 IoT Architecture

The architecture of IoT, which starts with a software layer and ends in the hardware one, provides different platforms to offer services in various industries. The internet of things technology requires efficient communication protocols for connecting the power-constrained sensor nodes to the everyday physical objects. Different

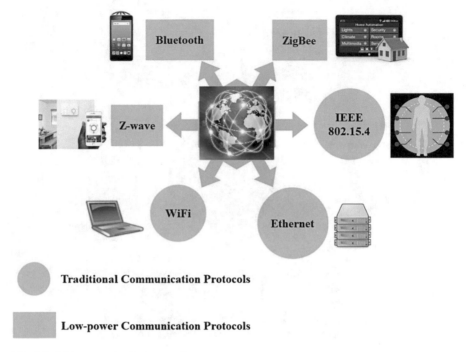

Fig. 5.2 IoT communication protocols

low-power communication protocols (i.e., ZigBee, Z-Wave, and Bluetooth) and traditional ones (i.e., Ethernet, IEEE 802.15.4, and Wi-Fi) are adopted in the layers of IoT architecture to send/receive the data [26, 27]. Figure 5.2 shows IoT communication protocols and the devices associated with them.

Due to the full range of communication protocols on the internet of things, high-tech companies such as Google Cloud, Microsoft Azure suite, Samsung Artik Cloud, and Amazon AWS expand their IoT-based platforms to offer certain services [28]. However, the standard architecture of IoT is composed of three layers: application, network, and perception ones.

Application Layer is at the top level of IoT systems. It provides the desired service of consumers through web-based or mobile programs [29]. Based on the recent technologically advances in this layer, IoT offers uncounted applications and services like smart home, city, health, transportation, etc. [30].

Network Layer is the second important one on the internet of things, who plays the role of the transmission/receiving medium of data using different protocols to connect IoT devices with intelligent services. The network layer contains local clouds/servers that process the data [31]. Nowadays, due to the ever-growing industries, IoT devices located in the physical layer are producing a massive amount of data continuously [13]. This big data should be processed, transmitted, or stored in the internet-based devices to satisfy the requirements of the smart services in this

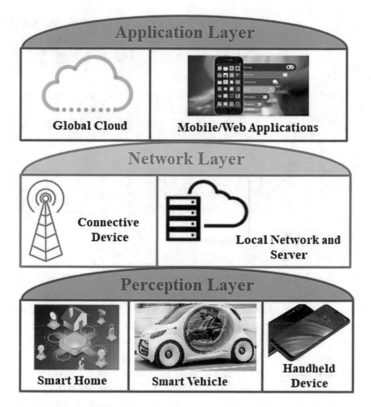

Fig. 5.3 Layers of a standard IoT architecture

layer [32]. Therefore, besides other typical methods, machine learning is extensively applied to analyze the big data in IoT devices [33].

Perception Layer is the lowest layer in IoT systems, which has two Physical (PHY) and Medium Access Control (MAC) sub-layers [34]. The physical sub-layer has a close relationship with hardware (i.e., IoT devices), which transmits/receives data using different communication protocols. Medium access control sub-layers also establish a link between IoT devices and the network layer using various protocols for big data transfers [35].

Figure 5.3 illustrates the layers of a standard IoT architecture.

2.2   IoT Challenges

The internet of things tries to bring everyday physical devices to close, connects the whole world, and provide low-power consumption, and high-performance services. However, it faces a different type of challenges, including resource limitation

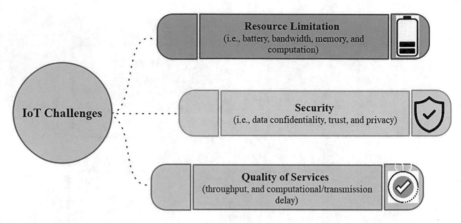

Fig. 5.4 The main IoT challenges

(i.e., battery, bandwidth, memory, and computation), security (i.e., data confidentiality, trust, and privacy), and quality of services (throughput, and computational/transmission delay). Figure 5.4 illustrates the various type of IoT challenges.

Resource limitation is the most crucial challenge, which limits the reliable and uninterrupted processing/communication in the internet of things [36]. In spite of significant developments in hardware and software technologies in the domain of IoT systems, the operational task of such networks still limited by the capacity of energy-constrained batteries. Furthermore, IoT devices have limited bandwidth, memory, and computation capabilities. In the heterogeneous networks of hundreds of wireless technologies and a large number of physical devices, resource limitation causes remarkable degradation to the quality of IoT systems [37].

Security is another significant challenge in almost all IoT applications. A fundamental principle about wireless communications proves that connection is perfect unless you expose poorly protected; i.e., personal information or the business data of the organizations should not be in public or semi-public [38, 39]. Although some approaches establish security in the internet of things, all these methods focus on basic privacy, including authentication, encryption, context removal, and data anonymity [40]. However, the security of vital data should be maintained while wireless communications. Besides, increasing security challenges appear with the invention of new technologies, for example, the integration of cloud computing, internet of things, and wireless sensor networks [41].

Quality of Services (QoS) refers to different technologies, which manages data traffic over the internet of things to minimize transmission delay, packet loss, and jitter. In today's technology-based world, big data collected by IoT devices should be transmitted and analyzed for suitable reactions to events in the shortest time. Although data analyzing speeds have enhanced rapidly, network bandwidth has not improved as acceptable [42]. On the others, supporting the transmission process of billions of data over geo-distributed IoT devices is hard to accomplish [43].

3 Machine Learning in the Internet of Things

Machine learning is an artificial intelligence-based mechanism, which trains IoT equipment using various algorithms to learn from their experience instead of explicit programming using human assistance or complicating mathematical equations [10, 44]. ML mechanisms can yield an acceptable performance in uncertain environments, such as the internet of things. Therefore, in the previous few decades, ML-based algorithms have been significantly expanded to deal with IoT challenges, including resource limitation, security, and quality of services [8, 45]. In this section, we review the machine learning mechanisms.

3.1 Machine Learning Mechanisms

Machine learning mechanisms consist of supervised learning, unsupervised learning, and reinforcement learning [10]. These algorithms could be applied to satisfy the requirements of IoT applications for acceptable services. In Fig. 5.5, ML-based mechanisms used in the IoT domain is illustrated.

3.1.1 Supervised Learning

Supervised learning is the most current machine learning mechanism that classifies the output based on the input, and a trained dataset (which is a called "learning

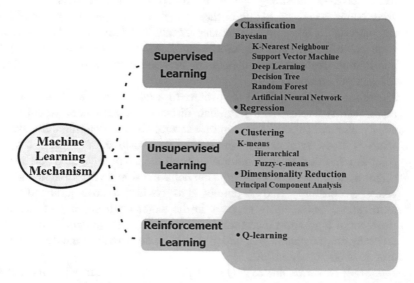

Fig. 5.5 Classification of ML-based algorithms

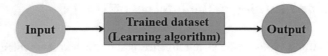

Fig. 5.6 Supervised learning

algorithm"). These algorithms find the relation between a set of input and datasets with labels (outputs) while training the system. Indeed, the main purpose of supervised learning algorithms is to generate the model to represent the relationships and dependency links between input and forecast objective outputs. The schematic presentation of supervised learning is shown in Fig. 5.6. Here we mention some of the well-known techniques for supervised learning.

1. *Classification* is one group of supervised learning algorithms. The output of these algorithms is a fixed discrete value/category, including (True or False) or (Yes or No). The classification contains various algorithms, such as logic-based (decision tree and random forest), perceptron-based (artificial neural network and deep learning), statistical learning (Bayesian/Naïve Bayes and support vector machine), and instance-based (k-nearest neighbor) algorithms.

   a. *Naïve Bayes (NB)* or the Bayesian theorem [46] is a widely-used machine learning algorithm, which requires the prior information to implement the Bayesian probability and predict the probable output. Indeed, NB is performed based on the probability of statistics theorem (Bayesian probability) to distribute learning and gets new outputs based on the present information using Bayesian probability. It should be noted that the result prediction is one of the major challenges in the internet of things; It successfully deploys using Naïve Bayes-based approaches in IoT [47]. The advantages of NB are understandable, less data requirement for classifications, applicable for multi-stage classification, and implementable. However, it depends on the prior information, features, and interactions between them, which is a challenge to reach the exact output.

   b. *K-Nearest Neighbor (KNN)* [48] refers to a nonparametric statistical algorithm, which exploits the Euclidian distance between data points as the main parameter to separate them into several classes, determine the average value of a new sample point and predict its classification. Indeed, if a data point is missed, then it is anticipated from the average value of the nearest neighbor. It is not an exact process but helps to estimate the possible lost data points. Accordingly, KNN is employed to provide monitoring, identification, localization, and security services in the smart environments of IoT [49]. However, a high consumed time to identify the missing data point and low accuracy are the challenges, which should be dealt with in the domain of K-nearest neighbor algorithm.

   c. *Support Vector Machine (SVM)* is a suitable machine learning algorithm for regression and classification analysis of data. This algorithm uses a plane, which is called "hyperplane", between two classes to maximize the distance of them. The main purpose of the hyperplane is to specify the classes with a minimum error at the maximum margin. For some scenarios, SVM exploits the kernel function to add new features for the hyperplane, when it becomes nonlinear after each analysis. This learning algorithm provides a high accuracy level, which makes it acceptable for classification, detection, and security application in the internet of things [50]. However, it is challengeable to employ the optimal kernel function in SVM [51].

d. *Deep Learning (DL)* [52] is a data learning representation algorithm, which is used for classification by providing multi-layer representations between the input and the output layers. The major purpose of this mechanism is to extract high-level features from the datasets, perform with or without labels, and train to solve the fulfill multi-objective challenges. So, deep learning is a useful algorithm to satisfy the requirements of various IoT applications, such as social network analysis, smart business, image processing, and pattern recognition [45]. However, a high amount of data should be trained in the scenario of a deep learning algorithm.

e. *Decision Tree (DT)* [53] is a natural machine learning algorithm which is categorized as a classification one. Each DT contains some branches as edges and leaves as nodes; it uses this structure to sort the desired samples based on the feature values. Since the decision tree algorithm has simple construction, easy implementation, and could handle a large number of samples, it is suitable for healthcare and privacy-centric services [54, 55]. However, this algorithm has some disadvantages, including a high space requirement to store the data and high complexity.

f. *Random Forest (RF)* [56] is a supervised machine learning algorithm with a set of trees, so that, each tree in the forest acts as a classifier. This algorithm consists of two main phases: (1) the creation of random forest classifier, and (2) prediction of results. RF predicts the missing values efficiently in the large and heterogeneous datasets. Besides, it will be the best appropriate approach to classify the hyperspectral data. Therefore, RF has been exploited to deal with various challenges in IoT systems, such as coverage and MAC protocol issues [57]. However, the sensitivity level of the random forest algorithm is less than other streamline ML-based classifiers due to the quality of training samples.

g. *Artificial Neural Network (ANN)* is an ML-based classification algorithm, which operates based on the neuron structure in the humans' brain to deal with the nonlinear problems in complex environments such as the internet of things. Indeed, it reduces the response time of the learning networks and subsequently enhances the performance of IoT systems. The main networks in the ANN are hierarchical and interconnected, which perform based on the three standard functional layers of the neuron: input, hidden, and output ones. However, the neural network has high complexity, and it is hard to implement it in distributed environments [9].

2. *Regression* [58] is a straightforward supervised learning algorithm, which predicts output values based on the input (a given set of features) with minimum errors. The variables of the regression models are quantitative or continuous. Due to simplicity and ease with implementation, regression is applied to the internet of things to analyze, monitor, and detect the events online [59]. However, all problems in our real world are not linear.

3.1.2 Unsupervised Learning

Unsupervised learning returns no output for the desired input variables. The input data of this group of machine learning algorithms are unlabeled; the system tries to extract the relationships from the data and classify dataset into different groups. Unsupervised learning mechanism also has been exploited to satisfy the requirements of IoT applications. It is divided into two sub-groups: clustering and dimensionality reduction. The schematic presentation of unsupervised learning is illustrated in Fig. 5.7.

1. *Clustering* is a group of unsupervised machine learning algorithms. These algorithms receive a dataset as the input, extract the similarities of its members, and classify the data into some clusters. The clustering algorithms categorized into various algorithms, such as k-means, hierarchical, and fuzzy-c-means.

   a. *K-means* [60] is a well-known unsupervised machine learning algorithm, which creates small clusters to group the samples of the desired dataset. First, the algorithm differentiates the member of the dataset into some clusters, where each cluster has a cluster-head. In this point, it selects a member from each cluster and relates it with the nearest cluster-head. This step is continued until every member of the dataset is contacted. Finally, the K-means redo its previous steps until it reaches the intended value [61]. Due to the actions of K-means, it is a simple algorithm to satisfy the requirements of the IoT

Fig. 5.7 Unsupervised learning

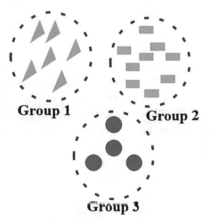

applications, when the labeled data is not available, including suitable area identification for human living and anomaly detection. However, the K-means algorithm is less effective than supervised ones [62].

b. *Hierarchical clustering* [63] groups similar data into clusters, which have a pre-determined bottom-up or top-down order. Bottom-up hierarchical clustering, which also named agglomerative clustering, assigns each observation to clusters based on density functions. In top-down hierarchical clustering which also called as divisive clustering, a large partition split recursively until a cluster is formed for each observation. Since the hierarchical clustering algorithm needs no prior data about the number of clusters, and its implementation process is easy, it is used to serve various services in the internet of things, such as data aggregation in mobile IoT systems, synchronization, and energy harvesting. However, unacceptable time-complexity of this clustering algorithm is the most apparent disadvantage [64].

c. *Fuzzy-C-Means (FCM)* or soft clustering [65] assigns the observation to some clusters, which are identified based on the similarity parameters, such as distance, intensity, and connectivity. The key objective of FCM is to find the optimal cluster centers. Therefore, it provides the optimal clusters in comparison to k-means for the overlapped systems. Accordingly, this algorithm used in various application of IoT, including smart world, localization, and mobile sink controlling [66]. However, fuzzy-c-means requires prior information about the number of clusters, have a high time-complexity, and it mainly depends on the number of clusters, iterations, dimensions, and data points.

2. *Dimensionality reduction* [67] is one of the statistics ML-based algorithms, which reduces the number of random variables based on the information theory, a set of principal variables, and under particular consideration. Dimensionality reduction algorithms are usually used for feature selection/extraction. Principal Component Analysis is a well-known dimensionality reduction algorithm in the IoT domain.

a. *Principal Component Analysis (PCA)* [68] or feature reduction algorithm decreases the complexity of the systems by converting a large dataset into smaller ones. This algorithm is usually combined with other machine learning mechanisms to select efficient features for high-frequency data analysis in vital applications, such as IoT-based healthcare systems.

3.1.3 Reinforcement Learning

Reinforcement Learning (RL) is a group of ML-based mechanisms, which continuously learn by interacting with the environment and collect information to perform specific actions. Therefore, it maximizes the performance of systems by determining the efficient information. The schematic presentation of RL is illustrated in Fig. 5.8. Q-learning is the best-known RL-based algorithm in the scenario of IoT applications.

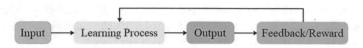

Fig. 5.8 Reinforcement learning

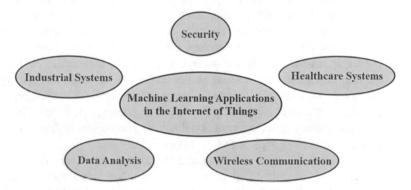

Fig. 5.9 Machine learning applications in the internet of things

1. *Q-learning* [69] is a model-free RL algorithm, which deals with the problems based on stochastic transitions and rewards, without adaptation. In this mechanism, each agent interacts with the environment of the system to reach a sequence of observations. The final objective of Q-learning is to find a policy, which tells an agent what action should be selected under a specific situation. Indeed, it finds an effective policy that maximizes the value of the reward. Q-learning guarantees the convergence even when approximation of function is exploited to estimate the value of actions. Therefore, it is a suitable solution for big data analyzing in smart IoT applications. However, Q-learning could make an overload of states, which diminish the outputs.

4   ML-Based Applications in IoT

Machine learning applications for IoT systems has become an emerging research field, which attracts the attention of researchers and developers. In this section, different ML-based applications in the internet of things have been presented in five categories: data analysis, wireless communication, healthcare systems, industrial systems, and security. Figure 5.9 illustrates the overall scheme of ML-based applications in IoT.

4.1   Data Analysis

Since the internet of things generates the increased volume of data in every location at any time, with different quality, and by various modalities, data science is considered a basic intelligent analysis approach to access new patterns from this big data (smart data) for smart IoT applications [10]. The smart data which is obtained from these analysis deals with the challenges posed by accuracy and volume of big data; accordingly provides operational information to make vital decisions.

To enhance the accuracy of data analysis, support vector machine and unsupervised classifiers have been combined to classify the big data streams on the Intel Lab dataset [70]. Since conventional classification mechanisms have an unbounded memory requirement, it is more accurate to organize the data using the combination of unsupervised classifier and a supervised one such as SVM on the internet of things.

In addition to increasing the accuracy of smart systems, analyzing public and private data could drive effective solutions for decision supporting in real-world applications. The main challenge in such scenarios is the dynamic selection of essential data and IoT sources for predictive analytics. Accordingly, Derguec et al. [71] presented an approach for the prediction of energy consumption of a building using essential data and IoT-based platform. Their solution consists of two main steps: data management for collection, and filtering information, and data analytics for source selection and prediction. The simulation results show that using the ANN for dynamic selection in IoT systems improve the accuracy and computational cost.

Since the supervised learning mechanisms such as random forest are fast, accurate, and scalable to the large datasets, they have been employed in various real-world applications, i.e., body poses recognition [72]. The fundamental purpose of this method is to determine the 3D positions of body joints on a single depth image, without the need for previous frame information. The complex pose estimation issue becomes a simple per-pixel classification problem by designing an intermediate representation, which random forest algorithm could estimate body part labels from the desired image invariant to body shape, pose, clothing, and other irrelevances. Other article developed an accurate big data analytics on the IoT-based healthcare systems using the random forest classifier and MapReduce process [73]. The data aggregated from patients are classified using the optimal attributes, Improved Dragonfly Algorithm (IDA), and random forest classifier. The implementation results show that the accuracy of the presented approach is better than the precision of other ML-based ones.

Kotenko et al. [74] proposed an artificial neural network-based architecture to forecast the states of IoT elements. Indeed, the presented mechanism is a combination of a probabilistic neural network and a multilayered perceptron for health data analyzing. To offer better IoT-based services over the online healthcare applications, other work presented a systematic approach for monitoring and diagnosing diabetes diseases. It suggested an artificial neural network-based data analyzing algorithm to diagnose the severity of the illness [75].

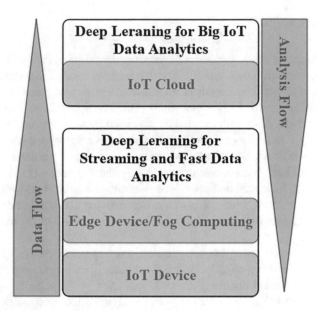

Fig. 5.10 Hierarchy of data generation in IoT [52]

In addition to health and smart building data analysis, other IoT applications, which appeared in different vertical domains, including transportation, agriculture, education, and smart city, need to an intelligent machine learning mechanism for prediction, pattern recognition, and data mining [52]. Deep learning is a classification approach has been exploited to provide IoT services. It should be noted that the terms of deep learning and the internet of things are among the top three strategic technologies of Gartner Symposium/ITxpo 2016 [76].

Figure 5.10 presents the hierarchy of data generation in IoT. There are three main sources of data in IoT: Clouds, Edge Device/Fog Computing, and IoT Devices. Machine learning algorithms play key roles in analyzing this massive amount of data; deep learning is employed to improve the data analysis methods for several applications related to IoT, such as image recognition [77, 78], physiological and psychological state detection [79–81], indoor localization [82, 83], and speech/voice recognition [84].

One of the other main issues in the big data analysis is to provide a strict quality of service. In [85], the quality of users' experience in edge computing to the internet of things has been addressed in terms of service response time. Authors presented a machine learning-based approaches for QoS improvement in IoT systems provide Pareto-efficiency, incentive compatibility, and computationally effectiveness.

The ever-growing wasted energy to satisfy the requirements of IoT applications generates many electricity consumption data. Clustering methods are essential data mining techniques to deal with such massive data. The classic privacy k-means algorithm efficiently deals with this problem [86]. However, its performance reduces when faces with the data distortion. To address this issue, other authors presented a privacy and availability data clustering mechanism exploiting k-means and differential privacy to minimize the outlier effect. This method, at the equal privacy level with the classic one, enhances the availability of clustering results [87]. At the same time, another paper designed an RFID IoT clustering analysis prototype system to tests the feasibility of the existing mechanisms [88].

4.2   Wireless Communication

As internet-based devices contribute to every aspect of modern lives, the requirement for wireless resources is increasing significantly. Based on Ericsson's mobility report 2018, there are 5.2 billion mobile devices all over the world, which generate more than 130 Exabyte wireless traffic each month [89]. Also, It is expected that the number of mobile devices increases to 50 billion by 2020, which will form a global internet of things [90]. To deal with this large volume of data, wireless communication technologies should coordinate with IoT devices in a distributed manner for spectrum usage optimization, overhead reduction, and efficient energy consumption. Machine learning mechanisms are introduced as a well-defined mathematical model to solve classification or regression challenges in IoT-based world [9].

Machine learning-based approaches are exploited to improve IoT data rate, throughput, bit error rate, and energy consumption. Indeed, adaptive rate control provides a useful structure to adapt the data rate on the channel conditions efficiently for maximizing the channel utilization. In [91], it is presented an adaptive rate control mechanism based on reinforcement learning to control the dynamic channel conditions. As the instantaneous channel gains could be estimated, they modeled the fading channel situation as an optimization problem forms to be solved in dynamic programming. To improve the transmission delay in IoT wireless communications, other paper described the necessity of congestion estimation in the internet of things and proposed a regression-based congestion classifier to model an adaptive data rate control mechanism [92]. The principal objective of this work is to avoid unnecessary data rate changes. Accordingly, the method predicts congestion status by ML-based way and determines whether a device changes data rate or not.

Furthermore, in [93], the authors provided a time-correlated region query approach for responding to continuous queries in the internet of things based on a grid cell. The paper firstly divides the monitoring environment into grid cells. Then, it develops a hierarchical clustering index tree for grid organization to minimize the energy consumption for messages transmission between IoT devices. To leverage the hierarchy of index tree, the authors presented a time-correlated region query mechanism for responding to continuous queries. The simulation results illustrate that responding to the queries by assembling the values of IoT devices could improve the energy consumption of the system.

Since sensor-based IoT devices often provide their required energy from low-power batteries, each layer of the network should be designed in such a way that minimizes the total energy consumption [94, 95]. Exploiting power control mechanisms reduces the energy consumption of IoT devices and consequently enhances the lifetime of the system [96]. To address the resource consumption and network lifetime issue, Yousefi et al. [36] presented an intelligent route planning for mobile agents on the internet of things by considering the distance of the devices from each other, the distance of the devices from the sink, residual energy of the devices and the priority of them as input parameters. The principal objective of this approach is to reach an advanced decision-making method, which enhances tradeoff between the performance metrics in IoT systems. In particular, the authors exploited reinforcement learning as an optimization approach to improve the decision-making process under uncertainty. Besides, considering the impact coefficient for parameters provides a tradeoff between the performance metrics in uncertain internet of things, including the energy consumption of the system, lifetime of IoT devices, data priority of the devices and reliability.

Vashishth et al. [97] presented an unsupervised machine learning-based mechanism for efficient route planning on the internet of things. The authors claim that infrequent connectivity, lack of network infrastructure, and random mobility of IoT devices make route planning as an increasingly complex problem. Therefore, using the ML-based soft clustering mechanisms to develop the proposed route planning combines the advantages of both context-aware and context-free approaches and consequently improves the delivery mobility, average hop count, network overhead ratio, and the number of messages dropped.

4.3 Healthcare Systems

Among the services provided by IoT technology, healthcare systems are particularly important ones. In IoT-based healthcare systems, data generated from devices attached to the elderlies or patients is made available to family and doctors for giving them the ability to monitor their vital signs from anywhere in 24 h a day [13]. The general architecture of IoT-based healthcare systems is illustrated in Fig. 5.11, which consist of three major elements: device (body area sensor network), fog (internet-connected smart gateways), and cloud layers.

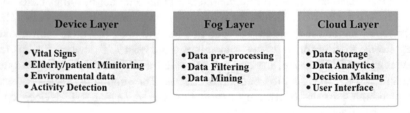

Fig. 5.11 The general architecture of IoT-based healthcare systems

Different applications offer services to the elderlies or patients through this platform. In many healthcare applications, wearable sensor-based IoT devices generate a massive volume of data continuously. To deal with health data, Kumar et al. [98] presented a scalable multi-tier architecture, which could organize and process the enormous amount of data: (1) The first tier collects wearable sensor data; (2) The second tier exploits Apache HBase to store sensed data in a cloud platform; and (3) The third tier provides a logistic regression-based model for heart disease prediction. Nguyen et al. [99] presented another multi-tier architecture for IoT health systems, which collects data from sensor-based devices, analyze it, and transform vital information into clinical feedback. The architecture consists of five layers: (1) sensing layer for collecting individual health data using wearable IoT devices or the sensors; (2) sending layer for transferring data to a cloud system using different communication mechanism; (3) processing layer for generating notifications and alerts after processing; (4) storing layer for storing processed data in clouded or servers; (5) mining and learning layer for converting data to decisions or predictions using machine learning algorithms. Other papers presented different multi-layer architectures for healthcare decision-making systems using deep learning, fuzzy logic, and reinforcement learning to improve the critical parameters in IoT systems, such as latency, energy consumption, and accuracy [100, 101].

Asthana et al. [102] proposed a recommendation system for individual wearable IoT devices. The sensor-based equipment collects health data of elderlies/patients, such as demographic features, health history, and previously collected data from IoT health devices. Since each disease has some attributes that need to be monitored, the recommendation system makes predictions about the conditions using the classification models like decision tree, and logistic regression. Finally, a mathematical optimization approach was employed to recommend the best solution for wearable IoT devices.

The first step towards smart healthcare systems is to continuously monitor an elderly/patient using wearable IoT-based devices for analyzing the possibility of health hazards, which may be deadly if not identified in time. To enhance the prediction process in healthcare systems, Walinjkar et al. [103] presented a prognostic method for real-time Electrocardiograph (ECG) analysis. The paper focussed on constantly monitoring of elderlies/patients' ECG data using a wearable 3-lead kit and performing real-time processing to identify arrhythmia to be able to predict heart risk. It first analyzes the real-time ECG data of IoT devices with K-NN algorithm for arrhythmia classification, which depends on the morphology of the electrocardiograph waveforms and the accuracy of ECG devices. Besides, a monitoring IoT network was set up for transferring the analysis results to the cloud system (National Health Services) in real-time. As a case study, a well-known Arrhythmia dataset (MIT-BIH, Physionet) was employed to test machine learning, classification, and prediction mechanisms. The simulation results illustrate that the ML-based healthcare system is accurate, de-noised, filtered, and real-time.

In the same way, a classifier integrated the decision trees and artificial neural network into an IoT-based healthcare system to process the data from breast cancer patients in an appropriate manner [104]. Since during mammogram screening, 16% of breast cancer detection is missed, some cases of this illness are not identified by radiologists. However, exploiting the image processing mechanisms improves the accuracy of the image segmentation process, solves breast cancer detection problem, and reduces the error in the classification of malignant cancers. The machine learning-based segmentation algorithm classifies the area between the breast and pectoral muscle for a reasonable feature estimation. It successfully predict the breast cancer in comparison with other well-kwon approaches, such as support vector machine, k-nearest neighbors, and Bayesian ones.

In today's IoT world, human presence detection is the first step to satisfy the requirements of several healthcare applications, including automation, problem detection, and person's pattern learning. Previous intrusion detection approaches usually have not an ideal performance in this area. Coordination between IoT devices for higher operation requires extra hardware or software for communicating and controlling them. Muzzley is a company, which creates a mobile application to register all devices of a person and manage them. Madeira et al. [105] proposed an IoT system to detect the human presence based on messages transmitted between devices and the Muzzley platform. For this, datasets generated by the Muzzley platform are exploited to create essential features for training and testing of the machine learning algorithms. In this point, the health system collects interaction data, including reading and writing, with the enormous diversities of IoT devices. Then it can predict the human presence using the decision tree and random forest algorithms.

Another paper exploited cloud computing and the internet of things to enhance the disease prediction process in smart cities [106]. In this approach, IoT devices are used to collect data from the monitoring environment and transfer it onto a cloud system. The paper focused on predicting healthcare services on the cloud system using a hybrid intelligent model based on linear regression and artificial neural network; linear regression is used to specify the critical factors, and artificial neural network is employed to prediction.

The modern health world has seen strong dependency between stress and heart disease. Also, stressful conditions have been proved to weaken humans' immune systems and lead to various cancers. This psychological challenge is tough to detect. However, when a person is stressed or nervous, his/her heartbeat is increased just like a heart attack situation. Smart stress detector is an IoT-based system which can identify the stress level of the humans using their heartbeat sensing. In this scenario, IoT devices locally sensed heartbeat information of a person and transmit it to a central server. Machine learning-based mechanisms are executed on this server to predict whether a person is stressed/nervous or not. Pandey [107] analyzed the reliable data of different persons' heartbeat for stress/nervousness prediction. For this purpose, a Wi-Fi-equipped board is designed to sense pulse waveform of persons' heartbeat. Then, the collected data is transferred to the central server. The central server predicts a person's stress level using an SVM-based algorithm or logistic regression. Kwapisz et al. [108] presented a user activity recognition mechanism using logistic regression on phone accelerometers. The approach first collects activity data from users' phones. Then, the system transforms it into user features, e.g., standard deviation, and average to classify the feature vectors into different activities using the logistic regression and multilayer perceptron. The results of analyzing data collected from 29 users show that the precision of multilayer classifier is better than standard logistic regression.

4.4   Industrial Systems

Smart industrial systems are the trend that has developed in a connected and sustainable world. To address the system challenges with the characteristics of smart connected, real-time monitoring, automation, and collaborative control, big data collected by IoT devices should be analyzed efficiently [109]. In the following, we mention some of the significant works in IoT based industrial systems:

Park et al. [110] presented a lossy compression mechanism for industrial data using artificial neural network algorithm. This approach uses some combining techniques for accurate data representation and prediction. Since vectorization of the technical data through the artificial neural network regression is inefficient on an hourly basis, the paper suggests a combinational method that exploits the data vectorization by dividing the whole data according to a specific range. Indeed, it compresses the data using a divide-and-conquer mechanism, splits the data into time units, and then applies neural regression to each of them. The comparison results of the presented method with various machine learning techniques show that the high accuracy of ANN-based one.

For efficiency of the compression mechanism, the divide-and-conquer method is exploited to handle the data based on the chunk size of it. Besides, machine learning mechanisms could improve the performance of smart meter operations. Due to the increasing number of smart meters on the internet of things, it is vital to predicting whether to transfer a technician to a customer location or not. To satisfy this requirement of IoT applications, different classification algorithms, including Bayesian, decision tree, and random forest, were tested [111]. The results illustrate that the random forest algorithm achieves the highest accuracy at a reasonable cost in comparison with other ML-base ones.

Patil et al. [112] proposed an internet of things for monitoring the environmental conditions of agriculture sites, including the temperature, humidity, and moisture to predict the grape diseases in its early stages. The collected data is transmitted to the server using ZigBee for extra analyzing based on reinforcement learning. The system is implemented in the real site to prove the accuracy of machine learning method.

Guo et al. [113] proposed an ML-based mechanism to detect the characterization of flowering dynamics of rice. The technique collects time-series of images from the rice fields to extract local feature points; this method employs SVM to classify the time-series of images, and specify the flowering part. Finally, visual words are generated as the object-recognition approach. The results illustrate that SVM

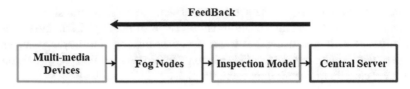

Fig. 5.12 Manufacture inspection system for the smart industry

performs well for counting the number of flowering panicles by the accuracy of over 80% when good training data are selected.

One of the most popular IoT application is to detect the defects of the products in the manufacturing environment. To address this issue, Li et al. [114] proposed an artificial neural network and deep learning-based classification mechanism to implement a robust and high-accuracy inspection system, which finds the defective products in the industrial area. The main objective of this work is to improve the performance of fog computing for big data processing in real-time. Since computation offloading is a vital element to enhance computing efficiency and provide a real-time wireless system, fog computing could be the right solution for defect detection. The presented manufacture inspection system is built from three modules: The fog-side and the server-side computing modules are responsible for calculating the deployed deep models, and the backend communication module exchanges the data and transfers command. The combination of these modules decreases the response time of the defect detection system and injected low traffic into the internet of things. As shown in Fig. 5.12, some IoT devices are deployed in some location of the manufacture to capture the multi-media data regarding the products. The sensed data will be uploaded to the fog nodes to analyze, detect the possible defects, and transmit the result packets to the central server. Finally, the central server aggregates all the useful data to provide recommendations and feedback on the current status.

For improving IoT technical data feature learning in such applications, an adaptive dropout deep computation model is presented with crowdsourcing to cloud in [69]. The model defined a distribution function to specify a dropout rate for each layer. Then, the selection algorithm based on the maximum entropy is used to select appropriate samples from the training set. In this point, supervised learning from multiple expert schemes is exploited to collect answers given by human workers and update the parameters.

Zhang et al. [115] presented an efficient deep learning mechanism based on the canonical polyadic decomposition for cloud workload prediction on the internet of things. The approach compresses the parameters by substituting the weight matrices to the canonical polyadic format. Then, the presented deep learning model is applied to the workload prediction after training the parameters. The experimental results on the PlanetLab datasets show that this ML-based approach has high accuracy and the potential to offer predictive services for industrial applications on the internet of things.

4.5 Security

The security issue in IoT services has become an emerging research field that attracts a lot of attention from the scientific community and addresses at other applications [116, 117]. Traditional authentication mechanisms used in the physical layer of IoT systems do not satisfy the security requirements in modern applications because of unwanted signals or fake alarms. However, ML-based approaches, like Q-learning, could minimize the authentication error and improve the overall performance of the systems [118]. Besides, an approach exploited some methods to specify the parameters of the logistics regression model for spoofing detection, overhead reduction, and secure authentication [119].

Aref et al. [120] employed a reinforcement learning mechanism and jamming signal information for selecting sub-band in a multi-agent environment. The principal objective of this method is to offer a low-complexity solution to avoid a jammer signal in the internet of things, which sweeps across over the spectrum band; it uses spectrum knowledge acquisition ability for location tracking of sweeping jammer and the signals of other wideband autonomous cognitive radios. Some additional papers used the combination of reinforcement learning and artificial neural network to avoid jamming signals of cognitive radios and expand an effective anti-jamming system [121, 122].

Furthermore, ANN is one of the well-known methods to enhance anti-DoS systems. Saied et al. [123] presented an ANN-based model for DDoS attack detection. In this scheme, only the real data packets got permission to transmit over the network (the fake packets are blocked). The authors argued that artificial neural network performed acceptably in detecting DDoS attack, where it was trained with updated datasets. Also, artificial neural network-based techniques were exploited to train the machines for anomaly detection in the internet of things [124]. Although using the ANN provides acceptable results in the field of IoT security, the system performance should be analyzed with more massive datasets in which more data have tampered with attacks.

To protect vital data through the internet of things and users' privacy, a principal component analysis-based intrusion detection system is developed for matching the characteristics of IoT systems and reducing dimensions of large datasets [125]. Besides, [126] focused on the FCM algorithm to enhance the segmentation accuracy in IoT systems. The paper exploited Graphics Process Unit (GPU) capabilities for reducing the execution times of the segmentation process and reaching the expected performance.

Pajouh et al. [127] presented a two-layer dimension reduction and two-tier classification model for anomaly-based intrusion detection in IoT systems. The principal objective of this approach is to detect "hard-to-detect" anomaly-based intrusions, such as user to root and remote to local attacks. It provides high detection rates using a multi-layer classification, low false-positive exploiting a refinement feature, accurate intrusion detection of security attacks without reducing the performance of the system, and low computational complexity employing dimension reduction in both layers. It should be noted that the paper applies the Bayesian and K-nearest neighbor algorithms to detect suspicious behaviors and deal with the user to root and remote to local attacks over IoT backbone network. The simulation results illustrate that the ML-based intrusion detection mechanism distinguishes between different attack types accurately.

Another article introduced learning-based Deep-Q-Networks to minimize the malware attacks in the healthcare applications of IoT [128]. Although the internet of things provides efficient protocols for health data management, several intermediate attacks could access this information and reduce the security, privacy, and reliability of the system. To solve these challenges, Deep-Q-Networks examined the health information in different layers using the Q-learning algorithm to reduce the intermediate attacks with minimum complexity.

Chatterjee et al. [129] proposed an artificial neural network-based approach for real-time authentication of wireless devices on IoT systems based on their original signatures automatically transmitted on a communicated signal, leading to an accurate analysis of the Physical Unclonable Functions (PUF) properties to improve the security level of the physical layer. This method employed the already-existing asymmetric IoT communication framework and stand-alone security feature for sufficient multifactor authentication. For this purpose, the conceptual development of radio-frequency PUF is proposed for an asymmetric internet of things. It consists of multiple low-power, low-cost, and preamble-less distributed transmitters, and a central hub as a receiver for intrinsic PUF-based authentication in IoT systems. The presented approach enables RF-PUF operation without any additional on-chip/off-chip circuitry hardware on the resource-constrained IoT devices and exploits a light-weight machine learning framework to accounts for both data and channel variability parallel; an artificial neural network is used as a learning engine for nonlinear multidimensional classification. The simulations show that using the supervised learning mechanisms which proves the practical feasibility of RF-PUF on the internet of thins, enhances the accuracy of wireless device authentication.

Recent improvements in power grids exploiting the IoT platform constructs a smart grid to handle the electricity smartly; accordingly, enhance the efficiency and security of the systems [130, 131]. IoT platform could prevent disasters in a smart grid and decrease economic losses. Due to these features, Karimipour et al. [132, 133] presented a real-time anomaly detection mechanism in smart grid environments to identify the patterns of changes in False Data Injection (FDI) attacks using the revealed features. A computationally efficient feature extraction model is generated using the Symbolic Dynamic Filtering (SDF) for causal interaction detection between the smart grids systems through Bad Data Detection (DBN). Indeed, DBN, mutual information, and machine learning methods are employed to detect unobservable cyberattacks. The authors have tried to identify dependencies between variables through assigning scalar energy to each of them, which consider as a measure of compatibility. The simulation results prove the high accuracy of the anomaly detection mechanism; it has low false alarm under different operation conditions because the method relies on the free energy to differentiate between the energy level and regular data sets besides using the pattern in the training ones.

5   Analysis

We review the literature, which exploiting the machine learning mechanisms to improve the quality of IoT services since 2010. Our studies show that this area grows increasingly every day. Figure 5.13 shows the dispersion of reviewed papers of the ML-based applications on the internet of things and their publication year. The numerical results illustrate that recently special attention has been paid to the integration of machine learning mechanisms and IoT for improving the quality of everyday human life, reducing the energy/other resource consumptions, and enhancing the security of systems.

Figure 5.14 illustrated statistical results on different machine learning mechanisms in IoT applications until 2019. The results show that reinforcement learning mechanisms like Q-learning, deep learning, and artificial neural networks were mostly used to improve the quality of IoT services in comparison with other Ml-based methods.

6   Challenges

In this section, we sum up the limitations of ML-based applications in the internet of things and provide some research directions to improve the performance of these integrated systems.

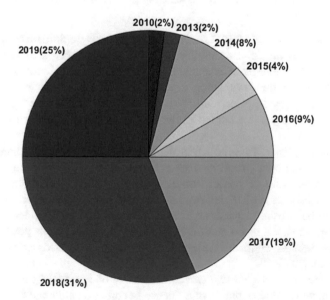

Fig. 5.13 Percentage of the most papers published about the application of machine learning in the IoT from 2010 to 2019

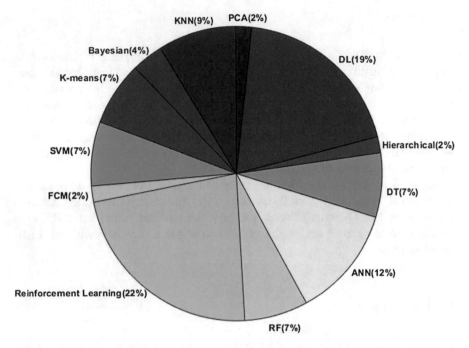

Fig. 5.14 Percentage of the paper published on various machine learning algorithms on IoT

There are several challenges about utilizing the machine learning mechanisms in IoT environments, including:

1. *Lack of standard datasets*: The main issue to developing machine learning mechanisms in the internet of things is the lack of access to standard real-world datasets, while more data is needed for achieving ideal accuracy, empirical validation and system evaluation in domains with ML-based services, such as the application of deep learning [52]. On the other, exploiting the private and copyrighted datasets is a burden in the field of personal data such as education and healthcare.

2. *Energy restrictions*: In spite of growing developments in IoT hardware and software technologies, most devices still have to provide their required energy for data processing or packet transmission from energy-constrained batteries. Besides, sensor-based IoT devices have limited computational capabilities, and they have been used in harsh and inaccessible natural environments for a long time [36]. Thus, the resource limitation of IoT devices such as power, memory, and processor is another challenge for executing high-complexity machine learning mechanisms.

3. *Lack of accurate analysis and correlation*: Most of IoT devices do not save any metadata, which makes pieces of evidence becomes a challenge for researchers. In the absence of aggregated data, correlation of evidence collected from different devices is almost impossible [134]. Beyond technical issues, privacy

is a significant challenge in the scenario of analyzing and correlating aggregated data, especially as sensor-based IoT devices are sensing personal information. Finally, the massive volume of aggregated data in heterogeneous IoT systems makes it impossible to provide an end-to-end analysis of residual evidence.

4. *False confidence*: False confidence in the domain of machine learning for predicting data, which is unrecognizable by humans, is known as another vital issue in IoT applications [52]. The malicious systems produce fooling data, and the classifiers such as artificial neural networks detect it as a familiar one.

Due to these challenges, some of the future works are presented to enhance the performance of machine learning mechanisms on the internet of things, including:

1. *Providing IoT standard datasets*: Obtaining standard free datasets would be a big step forward development of IoT systems based on the machine learning mechanisms. Since a remarkable part of big data in IoT systems is generated by mobile devices, exploiting efficient methods to provide standard datasets from this massive volume of data is a way to offer distributed learning framework in IoT domains, including smart city, traffic systems, and industrial environments.

2. *Presenting efficient data processing/aggregation methods*: It could be proposed more specialized approaches to reduce resource consumption in the internet of things, e.g., using the efficient data aggregation methods reduces the energy consumption of IoT systems, and exploiting sufficient data processing mechanisms improves the memory, processor, and energy consumption of IoT devices.

3. *Aggregating vital data*: Providing efficient approaches to memorize critical metadata, which is sensed by IoT devices could help the users for subsequent processing. However, the situation of complex systems cannot be analyzed by the IoT device data alone. Therefore, it is essential to IoT data would be fused with other sources for quick and accurate decision making, e.g., the pictures of a smart camera could be fused with contextual information such as users' daily habits to helps the system for performing best action.

4. *Security enhancement*: Presenting different techniques, guiding rules, protocols, and standards to improve the security, privacy, and trust level of IoT systems, which match the implementation of machine learning approaches could be a help for researchers and developers. Indeed, the success of each application in the IoT world significantly depends on the environment characteristics, e.g., openness, and heterogeneity, which security mechanisms employed in it.

7 Conclusion

In this chapter, we present a review of the applications of the machine learning mechanisms on the internet of things. First, the critical challenges behind IoT and the efficiency of using ML to solve them were discussed. Then, the approaches of ML-based mechanism in the internet of things were classified into five categories: data analysis, wireless communication, healthcare systems, industrial systems, and security. Practically, using the capability of the machine learning mechanisms in IoT systems could enhance the quality of real-world services, but in spite of all progress in IoT fields, lack of standard datasets, trust, and resource limitation are significant challenges in the ML-based applications. Therefore, it is necessary to improve the system security factors, resource consumption, and datasets for the next-generation applications of machine learning mechanisms in the internet of things.

References

1. S. Li, L. Da Xu, S. Zhao, 5G internet of things: a survey. J. Ind. Inf. Integr. **10**, 1–9 (2018)
2. J. Lin, W. Yu, N. Zhang, X. Yang, H. Zhang, W. Zhao, A survey on internet of things: architecture, enabling technologies, security and privacy, and applications. IEEE Internet Things J. **4**(5), 1125–1142 (2017)
3. A. Al-Fuqaha, M. Guizani, M. Mohammadi, M. Aledhari, M. Ayyash, Internet of things: a survey on enabling technologies, protocols, and applications. IEEE Commun. Surv. Tutor. **17**(4), 2347–2376 (2015)
4. S. Li, L. Da Xu, S. Zhao, The internet of things: a survey. Inf. Syst. Front. **17**(2), 243–259 (2015)
5. H.L.H. Karimipour, S. Geris, A. Dehghantanha, Intelligent anomaly detection for large-scale smart grids, in *2019 IEEE Canadian Conference of Electrical and Computer Engineering (CCECE)* (IEEE, 2019), pp. 1–4
6. Z. Li, W. Zhang, D. Qiao, Y. Peng, Lifetime balanced data aggregation for the internet of things. Comput. Electr. Eng. **58**, 244–264 (2017)
7. L. Li, S. Li, S. Zhao, QoS-aware scheduling of services-oriented internet of things. IEEE Trans. Ind. Inform. **10**(2), 1497–1505 (2014)
8. U.S. Shanthamallu, A. Spanias, C. Tepedelenlioglu, M. Stanley, A brief survey of machine learning methods and their sensor and IoT applications, in *2017 8th International Conference on Information, Intelligence, Systems & Applications (IISA)* (IEEE, 2017), pp. 1–8
9. H. HaddadPajouh, A. Dehghantanha, R. Khayami, K.K.R. Choo, A deep recurrent neural network based approach for internet of things malware threat hunting. Futur. Gener. Comput. Syst. **85**, 88–96 (2018)
10. M.S. Mahdavinejad, M. Rezvan, M. Barekatain, P. Adibi, P. Barnaghi, A.P. Sheth, Machine learning for internet of things data analysis: a survey. Digit. Commun. Netw. **4**(3), 161–175 (2018)
11. K. Ashton, That 'internet of things' thing. RFiD J. **22**(7), 1 (2011)
12. W. Li, H. Song, F. Zeng, Policy-based secure and trustworthy sensing for internet of things in smart cities. IEEE Internet Things J. **5**(2), 716–723 (2018)
13. F. Firouzi et al., Internet-of-things and big data for smarter healthcare: from device to architecture, applications and analytics. Futur. Gener. Comput. Syst. **78**, 583–586 (2018)
14. P.A. Laplante, N. Laplante, The internet of things in healthcare: potential applications and challenges. IT Prof. **18**(3), 2–4 (2016)
15. B.L. Risteska Stojkoska, K.V. Trivodaliev, A review of internet of things for smart home: challenges and solutions. J. Clean. Prod. **140**, 1454–1464 (2017)
16. A. Alkhamisi, M.S.H. Nazmudeen, S.M. Buhari, A cross-layer framework for sensor data aggregation for IoT applications in smart cities, in *2016 IEEE International Smart Cities Conference (ISC2)* (IEEE, 2016), pp. 1–6
17. W.T. Hartman, A. Hansen, E. Vasquez, S. El-Tawab, K. Altaii, Energy monitoring and control using internet of things (IoT) system, in *2018 Systems and Information Engineering Design Symposium (SIEDS)* (IEEE, 2018), pp. 13–18

18. P.M. Kumar, U. Devi G, G. Manogaran, R. Sundarasekar, N. Chilamkurti, R. Varatharajan, Ant colony optimization algorithm with internet of vehicles for intelligent traffic control system. Comput. Netw. **144**, 154–162 (2018)
19. K.-H.N. Bui, J.J. Jung, Internet of agents framework for connected vehicles: A case study on distributed traffic control system. J. Parallel Distrib. Comput. **116**, 89–95 (2018)
20. P.A. Pico Valencia, J.A. Holgado-Terriza, D. Herrera-Sánchez, J.L. Sampietro, Towards the internet of agents: An analysis of the internet of things from the intelligence and autonomy perspective. Ing. e Investig. **38**(1), 121–129 (2018)
21. S. Luthra, S.K. Mangla, D. Garg, A. Kumar, Internet of things (IoT) in agriculture supply chain management: a developing country perspective, in *Emerging Markets from a Multi-disciplinary Perspective. Advances in Theory and Practice of Emerging Markets*, ed. By Y. Dwivedi et al. (Springer, Cham, 2018), pp. 209–220
22. N. Khatri, A. Sharma, K.K. Khatri, G.D. Sharma, An IoT-based innovative real-time pH monitoring and control of municipal wastewater for agriculture and gardening, in *Proceedings of First International Conference on Smart System, Innovations and Computing. Smart Innovation, Systems and Technologies*, vol. 79 (Springer, Singapore, 2018), pp. 353–362
23. Statista, Technology & Telecommunication, Consumer Electronics (Source: IHS, 2019), https://www.statista.com/statistics/471264/iot-numberof-connected-devices-worldwide/
24. S. Smith, Internet of things' connected devices to almost triple to over 38 billion units by 2020 (2015), https://www.juniperresearch.com/press/press-releases/iot-connected-devices-to-triple-to-38-bn-by-2020
25. C.V. Forecast, *Cisco Visual Networking Index: Global Mobile Data Traffic Forecast Update, 2016–2021 White Paper* (Cisco Public Inf., 2017)
26. J. Granjal, E. Monteiro, J. Sa Silva, Security for the internet of things: A survey of existing protocols and open research issues. IEEE Commun. Surv. Tutor. **17**(3), 1294–1312 (2015)
27. J. Lloret, J. Tomas, A. Canovas, L. Parra, An integrated IoT architecture for smart metering. IEEE Commun. Mag. **54**(12), 50–57 (Dec. 2016)
28. J. Ju, M.-S. Kim, J.-H. Ahn, Prototyping business models for IoT service. Procedia Comput. Sci. **91**, 882–890 (2016)
29. T. Yashiro, S. Kobayashi, N. Koshizuka, K. Sakamura, An internet of things (IoT) architecture for embedded appliances, in *2013 IEEE Region 10 Humanitarian Technology Conference* (IEEE, 2013), pp. 314–319
30. M.A.A. da Cruz, J.J.P.C. Rodrigues, P. Lorenz, P. Solic, J. Al-Muhtadi, V.H.C. Albuquerque, A proposal for bridging application layer protocols to HTTP on IoT solutions. Futur. Gener. Comput. Syst. **97**, 145–152 (2019)
31. J. Ceron, K. Steding-Jessen, C. Hoepers, L. Granville, C. Margi, Improving IoT botnet investigation using an adaptive network layer. Sensors **19**(3), 727 (2019)
32. A. Azmoodeh, A. Dehghantanha, K.-K.R. Choo, Big data and internet of things security and forensics: challenges and opportunities, in *Handbook of Big Data and IoT Security* (Springer International Publishing, Cham, 2019), pp. 1–4
33. G. Manogaran, R. Varatharajan, D. Lopez, P.M. Kumar, R. Sundarasekar, C. Thota, A new architecture of internet of things and big data ecosystem for secured smart healthcare monitoring and alerting system. Futur. Gener. Comput. Syst. **82**, 375–387 (2018)
34. J. Zhang, S. Rajendran, Z. Sun, R. Woods, L. Hanzo, Physical layer security for the internet of things: authentication and key generation. IEEE Wirel. Commun. **26**(5), 92–98 (2019)
35. A. Kumar, M. Zhao, K.-J. Wong, Y.L. Guan, P.H.J. Chong, A comprehensive study of IoT and WSN MAC protocols: research issues, challenges and opportunities. IEEE Access **6**, 76228–76262 (2018)
36. S. Yousefi, F. Derakhshan, A. Bokani, Mobile agents for route planning in internet of things using markov decision process, in *2018 IEEE International Conference on Smart Energy Grid Engineering (SEGE)* (2018), pp. 303–307
37. H. Zhang, J. Li, B. Wen, Y. Xun, J. Liu, Connecting intelligent things in smart hospitals using NB-IoT. IEEE Internet Things J. **5**(3), 1550–1560 (Jun. 2018)

38. M. Ammar, G. Russello, B. Crispo, Internet of things: a survey on the security of IoT frameworks. J. Inf. Secur. Appl. **38**, 8–27 (2018)
39. S. Grooby, T. Dargahi, A. Dehghantanha, A bibliometric analysis of authentication and access control in IoT devices, in *Handbook of Big Data and IoT Security* (Springer International Publishing, Cham, 2019), pp. 25–51
40. M.A. Khan, K. Salah, IoT security: review, blockchain solutions, and open challenges. Futur. Gener. Comput. Syst. **82**, 395–411 (2018)
41. C. Stergiou, K.E. Psannis, B.-G. Kim, B. Gupta, Secure integration of IoT and cloud computing. Futur. Gener. Comput. Syst. **78**, 964–975 (2018)
42. E. Ahmad, M. Alaslani, F.R. Dogar, B. Shihada, Location-aware, context-driven QoS for IoT applications. IEEE Syst. J., 1–12 (2019). https://doi.org/10.1109/JSYST.2019.2893913
43. S. Najjar-Ghabel, S. Yousefi, L. Farzinvash, Reliable data gathering in the internet of things using artificial bee colony. Turk. J. Electr. Eng. Comput. Sci. **26**(4), 1710–1723 (2018)
44. M.R. Begli, F. Derakhshan, H. Karimipour, A layered intrusion detection system for critical infrastructure using machine learning, in *2019 IEEE 7th International Conference on Smart Energy Grid Engineering (SEGE)* (IEEE, 2019), pp. 1–5
45. H. Li, K. Ota, M. Dong, Learning IoT in edge: deep learning for the internet of things with edge computing. IEEE Netw. **32**(1), 96–101 (2018)
46. O. Osanaiye, H. Cai, K.K.R. Choo, A. Dehghantanha, Z. Xu, M. Dlodlo, Ensemble-based multi-filter feature selection method for DDoS detection in cloud computing. EURASIP J. Wirel. Commun. Netw. **2016**, 130 (2016)
47. Y. Chen, L. Lu, X. Yu, X. Li, Adaptive method for packet loss types in IoT: an naive Bayes distinguisher. Electronics **8**(2), 134 (2019)
48. G. Song, J. Rochas, L. El Beze, F. Huet, F. Magoules, K nearest neighbour joins for big data on MapReduce: a theoretical and experimental analysis. IEEE Trans. Knowl. Data Eng. **28**(9), 2376–2392 (Sep. 2016)
49. F. Alam, R. Mehmood, I. Katib, A. Albeshri, Analysis of eight data mining algorithms for smarter internet of things (IoT). Procedia Comput. Sci. **98**, 437–442 (2016)
50. Y. Alsouda, S. Pllana, A. Kurti, IoT-based urban noise identification using machine learning, in *Proceedings of the International Conference on Omni-Layer Intelligent Systems - COINS '19* (ACM, 2019), pp. 62–67
51. X. Kong, Z. Meng, N. Nojiri, Y. Iwahori, L. Meng, H. Tomiyama, A HOG-SVM based fall detection IoT system for elderly persons using deep sensor. Procedia Comput. Sci. **147**, 276–282 (2019)
52. A. Dehghantanha, K.R.C.A. Azmoodeh, Robust malware detection for internet of (battlefield) things devices using deep eigenspace learning. IEEE Trans. Sustain. Comput. **4**, 88–95 (2019)
53. I. Lee, K. Lee, The internet of things (IoT): Applications, investments, and challenges for enterprises. Bus. Horiz. **58**(4), 431–440 (2015)
54. A. Alabdulkarim, M. Al-Rodhaan, T. Ma, Y. Tian, PPSDT: A novel privacy-preserving single decision tree algorithm for clinical decision-support systems using IoT devices. Sensors **19**(1), 142 (2019)
55. S. Geris, H. Karimipour, A feature selection-based approach for joint cyber-attack detection and state estimation, in *IEEE Int. Conf. on Smart Energy Grid Engineering (SEGE)* (IEEE, 2019), pp. 1–5
56. M. Domb, E. Bonchek-Dokow, G. Leshem, Lightweight adaptive random-forest for IoT rule generation and execution. J. Inf. Secur. Appl. **34**, 218–224 (2017)
57. A.D. Shah, J.W. Bartlett, J. Carpenter, O. Nicholas, H. Hemingway, Comparison of random forest and parametric imputation models for imputing missing data using MICE: a CALIBER study. Am. J. Epidemiol. **179**(6), 764–774 (2014)
58. Z. Xuanxuan, Multivariate linear regression analysis on online image study for IoT. Cogn. Syst. Res. **52**, 312–316 (2018)

59. C. Ioannou, V. Vassiliou, An intrusion detection system for constrained WSN and IoT nodes based on binary logistic regression, in *Proceedings of the 21st ACM International Conference on Modeling, Analysis and Simulation of Wireless and Mobile Systems - MSWIM '18* (2018), pp. 259–263
60. H. Emami, F. Derakhshan, Integrating fuzzy K-means, particle swarm optimization, and imperialist competitive algorithm for data clustering. Arab. J. Sci. Eng. **40**(12), 3545–3554 (2015)
61. G. Han, H. Wang, M. Guizani, S. Chan, W. Zhang, KCLP: a k-means cluster-based location privacy protection scheme in WSNs for IoT. IEEE Wirel. Commun. **25**(6), 84–90 (2018)
62. J.L. Vermeulen, A. Hillebrand, R. Geraerts, A comparative study of k-nearest neighbour techniques in crowd simulation. Comput. Animat. Virtual Worlds **28**(3–4), e1775 (2017)
63. J.S. Kumar, M.A. Zaveri, Hierarchical clustering for dynamic and heterogeneous internet of things. Procedia Comput. Sci. **93**, 276–282 (2016)
64. V. Cohen-addad, V. Kanade, F. Mallmann-trenn, C. Mathieu, Hierarchical clustering. J. ACM **66**(4), 1–42 (2019)
65. F. Bu, An efficient fuzzy c-means approach based on canonical polyadic decomposition for clustering big data in IoT. Futur. Gener. Comput. Syst. **88**, 675–682 (2018)
66. K.A. Eldrandaly, M. Abdel-Basset, L. Abdel-Fatah, PTZ-surveillance coverage based on artificial intelligence for smart cities. Int. J. Inf. Manage. **49**, 520–532 (2019)
67. H.K.S. Mohammadi, V. Desai, Multivariate mutual information feature selection for intrusion detection, in *2018 20th International Conference on Advanced Communication Technology (ICACT)* (IEEE, 2018), pp. 1–6
68. Y. Aït-Sahalia, D. Xiu, Principal component analysis of high-frequency data. J. Am. Stat. Assoc. **114**(525), 287–303 (2019)
69. Q. Zhang, L.T. Yang, Z. Chen, P. Li, F. Bu, An adaptive dropout deep computation model for industrial IoT big data learning with crowdsourcing to cloud computing. IEEE Trans. Ind. Informatics **15**(4), 2330–2337 (2019)
70. M.A. Khan, A. Khan, M.N. Khan, and S. Anwar, A novel learning method to classify data streams in the internet of things, in *2014 National Software Engineering Conference* (2014), pp. 61–66
71. W. Derguech, E. Bruke, E. Curry, An autonomic approach to real-time predictive analytics using open data and internet of things," in *2014 IEEE 11th Intl Conf on Ubiquitous Intelligence and Computing and 2014 IEEE 11th Intl Conf on Autonomic and Trusted Computing and 2014 IEEE 14th Intl Conf on Scalable Computing and Communications and its Associated Workshops* (IEEE, 2014), pp. 204–211
72. J. Shotton et al., Real-time human pose recognition in parts from single depth images. Commun. ACM **56**(1), 116 (2013)
73. S.K. Lakshmanaprabu, K. Shankar, M. Ilayaraja, A.W. Nasir, V. Vijayakumar, N. Chilamkurti, Random forest for big data classification in the internet of things using optimal features. Int. J. Mach. Learn. Cybern. **10**, 2609–2618 (2019)
74. I. Kotenko, I. Saenko, F. Skorik, S. Bushuev, Neural network approach to forecast the state of the internet of things elements, in *2015 XVIII International Conference on Soft Computing and Measurements (SCM)* (IEEE, 2015), pp. 133–135
75. P.M. Kumar, S. Lokesh, R. Varatharajan, G. Chandra Babu, P. Parthasarathy, Cloud and IoT based disease prediction and diagnosis system for healthcare using fuzzy neural classifier. Futur. Gener. Comput. Syst. **86**, 527–534 (2018)
76. K. Panetta, Gartner's top 10 strategic technology trends for 2017, Smarter With Gartner (2016)
77. I. Mehmood et al., Efficient image recognition and retrieval on IoT-assisted energy-constrained platforms from big data repositories. IEEE Internet Things J. **6**(6), 9246–9255 (2019)
78. J. Su, V. Danilo Vasconcellos, S. Prasad, S. Daniele, Y. Feng, K. Sakurai, Lightweight classification of IoT malware based on image recognition, in *2018 IEEE 42nd Annual Computer Software and Applications Conference (COMPSAC)* (IEEE, 2018), pp. 664–669

79. C.-Y. Liao, R.-C. Chen, S.-K. Tai, Emotion stress detection using EEG signal and deep learning technologies, in *2018 IEEE International Conference on Applied System Invention (ICASI)* (IEEE, 2018), pp. 90–93

80. M. Alhussein, G. Muhammad, M.S. Hossain, S.U. Amin, Cognitive IoT-cloud integration for smart healthcare: case study for epileptic seizure detection and monitoring. Mob. Netw. Appl. **23**(6), 1624–1635 (2018)

81. M. Chen, Y. Zhang, M. Qiu, N. Guizani, Y. Hao, SPHA: smart personal health advisor based on deep analytics. IEEE Commun. Mag. **56**(3), 164–169 (2018)

82. M.I. AlHajri, N.T. Ali, R.M. Shubair, Indoor localization for IoT using adaptive feature selection: a cascaded machine learning approach. IEEE Antennas Wirel. Propag. Lett. **18**, 2306–2310 (2019)

83. B. Berruet, O. Baala, A. Caminada, V. Guillet, DelFin: a deep learning based CSI fingerprinting indoor localization in IoT context, in *2018 International Conference on Indoor Positioning and Indoor Navigation (IPIN)* (IEEE, 2018), pp. 1–8

84. J.H. Han et al., Machine learning-based self-powered acoustic sensor for speaker recognition. Nano Energy **53**, 658–665 (2018)

85. N. Sharghivand, F. Derakhshan, L. Mashayekhy, QoS-aware matching of edge computing services to internet of things, in *2018 IEEE 37th International Performance Computing and Communications Conference (IPCCC)* (IEEE, 2018), pp. 1–8

86. H. Hromic et al., Real time analysis of sensor data for the internet of things by means of clustering and event processing, in *2015 IEEE International Conference on Communications (ICC)* (IEEE, 2015), pp. 685–691

87. J. Xiong et al., Enhancing privacy and availability for data clustering in intelligent electrical service of IoT. IEEE Internet Things J. **6**(2), 1530–1540 (2019)

88. Z. Yu, Big data clustering analysis algorithm for internet of things based on K-means. Int. J. Distrib. Syst. Technol. **10**(1), 1–12 (2019)

89. I. Ericsson, Ericssoninterim mobility report (2018), https://www.ericsson.com/assets/local/mobility%2D%2Dr

90. C.V.N. Index, Global mobile data traffic forecast update 2017–2022, Cisco White Papers (2019)

91. X. Li, H. He, Y.-D. Yao, Reinforcement learning based adaptive rate control for delay-constrained communications over fading channels, in *The 2010 International Joint Conference on Neural Networks (IJCNN)* (IEEE, 2010), pp. 1–7

92. D.-Y. Kim, S. Kim, H. Hassan, J.H. Park, Adaptive data rate control in low power wide area networks for long range IoT services. J. Comput. Sci. **22**, 171–178 (2017)

93. J. Tang, Z. Zhou, J. Niu, Q. Wang, An energy efficient hierarchical clustering index tree for facilitating time-correlated region queries in the internet of things. J. Netw. Comput. Appl. **40**, 1–11 (Apr. 2014)

94. H.S. Aghdasi, S. Yousefi, Enhancing lifetime of visual sensor networks with a preprocessing-based multi-face detection method. Wirel. Netw. **24**(6), 1939–1951 (2018)

95. S. Najjar-Ghabel, S. Yousefi, Enhancing performance of face detection in visual sensor networks with a dynamic-based approach. Wirel. Pers. Commun. **97**(4), 6151–6166 (Dec. 2017)

96. F. Derakhshan, S. Yousefi, A review on the applications of multiagent systems in wireless sensor networks. Int. J. Distrib. Sens. Netw. **15**(5), 155014771985076 (2019)

97. V. Vashishth, A. Chhabra, D.K. Sharma, GMMR: A Gaussian mixture model based unsupervised machine learning approach for optimal routing in opportunistic IoT networks. Comput. Commun. **134**, 138–148 (Jan. 2019)

98. P.M. Kumar, U. Devi Gandhi, A novel three-tier internet of things architecture with machine learning algorithm for early detection of heart diseases. Comput. Electr. Eng. **65**, 222–235 (2018)

99. H.H. Nguyen, F. Mirza, M.A. Naeem, M. Nguyen, A review on IoT healthcare monitoring applications and a vision for transforming sensor data into real-time clinical feedback, in *2017 IEEE 21st International Conference on Computer Supported Cooperative Work in Design (CSCWD)* (IEEE, 2017), pp. 257–262

100. B. Farahani, M. Barzegari, F. S. Aliee, Towards collaborative machine learning driven healthcare internet of things, in *Proceedings of the International Conference on Omni-Layer Intelligent Systems - COINS '19* (IEEE, 2019), pp. 134–140

101. S. Shukla, M.F. Hassan, L.T. Jung, A. Awang, M.K. Khan, A 3-tier architecture for network latency reduction in healthcare internet-of-things using fog computing and machine learning, in *Proceedings of the 2019 8th International Conference on Software and Computer Applications - ICSCA '19* (IEEE, 2019), pp. 522–528

102. S. Asthana, A. Megahed, R. Strong, A recommendation system for proactive health monitoring using IoT and wearable technologies, in *2017 IEEE International Conference on AI & Mobile Services (AIMS)* (IEEE, 2017), pp. 14–21

103. A. Walinjkar, J. Woods, ECG classification and prognostic approach towards personalized healthcare, in *2017 International Conference On Social Media, Wearable And Web Analytics (Social Media)* (IEEE, 2017), pp. 1–8

104. A. Suresh, R. Udendhran, M. Balamurgan, R. Varatharajan, A novel internet of things framework integrated with real time monitoring for intelligent healthcare environment. J. Med. Syst. **43**(6), 165 (2019)

105. R. Madeira, L. Nunes, A machine learning approach for indirect human presence detection using IOT devices, in *2016 Eleventh International Conference on Digital Information Management (ICDIM)* (IEEE, 2016), pp. 145–150

106. A. Abdelaziz, A.S. Salama, A.M. Riad, A.N. Mahmoud, A machine learning model for predicting of chronic kidney disease based internet of things and cloud computing in smart cities, in *Security in Smart Cities: Models, Applications, and Challenges. Lecture Notes in Intelligent Transportation and Infrastructure*, ed. By A. Hassanien, M. Elhoseny, S. Ahmed, A. Singh (Springer, Cham, 2019), pp. 93–114

107. P.S. Pandey, Machine learning and IoT for prediction and detection of stress, in *2017 17th International Conference on Computational Science and Its Applications (ICCSA)* (IEEE, 2017), pp. 1–5

108. J.R. Kwapisz, G.M. Weiss, S.A. Moore, Activity recognition using cell phone accelerometers. ACM SIGKDD Explor. Newsl. **12**(2), 74 (2011)

109. J. Cheng, W. Chen, F. Tao, C.-L. Lin, Industrial IoT in 5G environment towards smart manufacturing. J. Ind. Inf. Integr. **10**, 10–19 (2018)

110. J. Park, H. Park, Y.-J. Choi, Data compression and prediction using machine learning for industrial IoT, in *2018 International Conference on Information Networking (ICOIN)* (2018), pp. 818–820

111. J. Siryani, B. Tanju, T.J. Eveleigh, A machine learning decision-support system improves the internet of things' smart meter operations. IEEE Internet Things J. **4**(4), 1056–1066 (2017)

112. S.S. Patil, S.A. Thorat, Early detection of grapes diseases using machine learning and IoT, in *2016 Second International Conference on Cognitive Computing and Information Processing (CCIP)* (IEEE, 2016), pp. 1–5

113. W. Guo, T. Fukatsu, S. Ninomiya, Automated characterization of flowering dynamics in rice using field-acquired time-series RGB images. Plant Methods **11**(1), 7 (2015)

114. L. Li, K. Ota, M. Dong, Deep learning for smart industry: efficient manufacture inspection system with fog computing. IEEE Trans. Ind. Inform. **14**(10), 4665–4673 (2018)

115. Q. Zhang, L.T. Yang, Z. Yan, Z. Chen, P. Li, An efficient deep learning model to predict cloud workload for industry informatics. IEEE Trans. Ind. Inform. **14**(7), 3170–3178 (2018)

116. S. Mohammadi, H. Mirvaziri, M. Ghazizadeh-Ahsaee, H. Karimipour, Cyber intrusion detection by combined feature selection algorithm. J. Inf. Secur. Appl. **44**, 80–88 (2019)

117. E.M. Dovom, A. Azmoodeh, A. Dehghantanha, D.E. Newton, R.M. Parizi, H. Karimipour, Fuzzy pattern tree for edge malware detection and categorization in IoT. J. Syst. Archit. **97**, 1–7 (2019)

118. E.M. Dovom, A. Azmoodeh, A. Dehghantanha, D.E. Newton, R.M. Parizi, H. Karimipour, Fuzzy pattern tree for edge malware detection and categorization in IoT. J. Syst. Archit. **97**, 1–7 (2019)

119. L. Xiao, X. Wan, Z. Han, PHY-layer authentication with multiple landmarks with reduced overhead. IEEE Trans. Wirel. Commun. **17**(3), 1676–1687 (2018)
120. M. A. Aref, S. K. Jayaweera, S. Machuzak, Multi-agent reinforcement learning based cognitive anti-jamming, in *2017 IEEE Wireless Communications and Networking Conference (WCNC)* (IEEE, 2017), pp. 1–6
121. S. Machuzak, S.K. Jayaweera, Reinforcement learning based anti-jamming with wideband autonomous cognitive radios, in *2016 IEEE/CIC International Conference on Communications in China (ICCC)* (IEEE, 2016), pp. 1–5
122. G. Han, L. Xiao, H. V. Poor, Two-dimensional anti-jamming communication based on deep reinforcement learning, in *2017 IEEE International Conference on Acoustics, Speech and Signal Processing (ICASSP)* (IEEE, 2017), pp. 2087–2091
123. A. Saied, R.E. Overill, T. Radzik, Detection of known and unknown DDoS attacks using artificial neural networks. Neurocomputing **172**, 385–393 (2016)
124. J. Sakhnini, H. Karimipour, A. Dehghantanha, Using machine learning to secure IoT systems, in *2016 14th Annual Conference on Privacy, Security and Trust (PST)* (IEEE, 2016), pp. 219–222
125. S. Zhao, W. Li, T. Zia, A.Y. Zomaya, A dimension reduction model and classifier for anomaly-based intrusion detection in internet of things, in *2017 IEEE 15th Intl Conf on Dependable, Autonomic and Secure Computing, 15th Intl Conf on Pervasive Intelligence and Computing, 3rd Intl Conf on Big Data Intelligence and Computing and Cyber Science and Technology Congress (DASC/PiCom/DataCom/CyberSciTech)* (IEEE, 2017), pp. 836–843
126. M.A. Alsmirat, Y. Jararweh, M. Al-Ayyoub, M.A. Shehab, B.B. Gupta, Accelerating compute intensive medical imaging segmentation algorithms using hybrid CPU-GPU implementations. Multimed. Tools Appl. **76**(3), 3537–3555 (2017)
127. H.H. Pajouh, R. Javidan, R. Khayami, A. Dehghantanha, K.-K.R. Choo, A two-layer dimension reduction and two-tier classification model for anomaly-based intrusion detection in IoT backbone networks. IEEE Trans. Emerg. Top. Comput. **7**(2), 314–323 (2019)
128. P. Mohamed Shakeel, S. Baskar, V.R. Sarma Dhulipala, S. Mishra, M.M. Jaber, Maintaining security and privacy in health care system using learning based deep-Q-networks. J. Med. Syst. **42**(10), 186 (2018)
129. B. Chatterjee, D. Das, S. Maity, S. Sen, RF-PUF: enhancing IoT security through authentication of wireless nodes using in-situ machine learning. IEEE Internet Things J. **6**(1), 388–398 (2019)
130. H. Karimipour, V. Dinavahi, Robust massively parallel dynamic state estimation of power systems against cyber-attack. IEEE Access **6**, 2984–2995 (2018)
131. J. Sakhnini, H. Karimipour, A. Dehghantanha, Smart grid cyber attacks detection using supervised learning and heuristic feature selection, arXiv Prepr. arXiv1907.03313 (2019)
132. H. Karimipour, A. Dehghantanha, R.M. Parizi, K.-K.R. Choo, H. Leung, A deep and scalable unsupervised machine learning system for cyber-attack detection in large-scale smart grids. IEEE Access **7**, 80778–80788 (2019)
133. V.D.H. Karimipour, On false data injection attack against dynamic state estimation on smart power grids, in *2017 IEEE International Conference on Smart Energy Grid Engineering (SEGE)* (IEEE, 2017)
134. M. Conti, A. Dehghantanha, K. Franke, S. Watson, Internet of things security and forensics: Challenges and opportunities. Futur. Gener. Comput. Syst. **78**, 544–546 (2018)

Chapter 6
A Comparison of State-of-the-Art Machine Learning Models for OpCode-Based IoT Malware Detection

William Peters, Ali Dehghantanha (iD), Reza M. Parizi, and Gautam Srivastava

1 Introduction

The Internet of Things (IoT) is a set of devices that are interconnected nodes that are sensing, processing, and communication data [1]. A wide range of applications have been introduced using IoT from healthcare [2–5], transportation [6, 7], smart grid [8, 9], urban management [10] and also agriculture [11]. It is predicted that well over 63 million IoT devices will be on the market by 2025 [12]. The IoT industry is expanding rapidly and could potentially generate $3.9 to $11.1 trillion by 2025 [13]. Evaluation Ericsson projects we see that by 2023, there will approximately 3.5 billion cellular IoT connections [14].

The widespread utilization and critical role of IoT networks have motivated cyber-criminals to devise detrimental and sophisticated attacks against IoT nodes and networks to misuse IoT's nodes and infrastructures [15, 16]. Mirai was one of the first malware to exploit IoTs on a large scale. Mirai organized a network of infected IoT devices (Botnet) to stage a Distributed Denial of Service (DDoS) attack [17]. Announcing Mirai's source code showed that it is very easy to create malicious IoT malware type attacks. For instance, BrickerBot which spreads by using the Mirai code and connects the infected device to a botnet removes the firmware and resets the device.

W. Peters (✉) · A. Dehghantanha
Cyber Science Lab, University of Guelph, Guelph, ON, Canada
e-mail: william@cybersciencelab.org; wpeters@uoguelph.ca; ali@cybersciencelab.org

R. M. Parizi
College of Computer and Software Engineering, Kennesaw State University, Marietta, GA, USA
e-mail: rparizi1@kennesaw.edu

G. Srivastava
Department of Mathematics and Computer Science, Brandon University, Brandon, MB, Canada
e-mail: srivastavag@brandonu.ca

© Springer Nature Switzerland AG 2020   109
K.-K. R. Choo, A. Dehghantanha (eds.), *Handbook of Big Data Privacy*,
https://doi.org/10.1007/978-3-030-38557-6_6

Machine Learning (ML) is a cutting-edge technology that has extensively leveraged to enhance the accuracy and robustness of detective and defensive systems in cybersecurity [18–20]. The ability of ML to learn complex patterns within complicated cyberattacks and its robustness to cope with unforeseen malicious attacks makes it a promising approach for detecting IoT's cyberattacks and protecting IoT networks against them. ML techniques have been widely leveraged in security [21–26], privacy [27] and forensic [28, 29] areas.

Typically, the following criteria are used to evaluate the utility of machine learning in malware detection [30–32]:

- **True Positive (TP)**: indicates that a malware is correctly identified as a malicious application.
- **True Negative (TN)**: indicates that a benign is detected as a non-malicious application correctly.
- **False Positive (FP)**: indicates that a benign is falsely detected as a malicious application.
- **False Negative (FN)**: indicates that a malware is not detected and labeled as a non-malicious application And the following metrics calculate the performance of an ML model:

Accuracy The percentage of correctly classified samples.

$$Accuracy = \frac{TP + TN}{TP + TN + FN + FP} \tag{6.1}$$

Precision The percent of predicted malware samples which were correct.

$$Precision = \frac{TP}{TP + FP} \tag{6.2}$$

Recall The percent of malware that were correctly identified.

$$Recall = \frac{TP}{TP + FN} \tag{6.3}$$

F1 Score Is a weighted average of *recall* and *precision*.

$$F1 - Score = \frac{2 * TP}{2 * TP + FP + FN} \tag{6.4}$$

In addition, *Cross-validation* is an ML technique to validate the extent that findings of an experiment can be generalized into an independent dataset [33, 34]. This chapter analyzes and reports findings for applying several different ML models on a collected dataset of IoT applications using extracted Operational Code (OpCode) of both malicious and benign samples.

The remainder of this chapter is divided into four sections. Section 2 reviews related literature and Sect. 3 gives information of used methodology. In subsequent, Sect. 4 presents experimental results, Sect. 5 discusses findings and Sect. 6 concludes this chapter.

2   Related Work

Malware detection approach is a topical category of cybersecurity divided into static and dynamic malware detection [35–37]. Dynamic methods employ run-time properties of samples such as system-calls, registry access, network traffic, and others to recognize its class. On the contrary, static methods statically inspect a program code to detect suspicious applications by using features such as Byte-Code, OpCode, control flow graph traversal, etc.

Darabian et al. [21] proposed an OpCode based static method using sequential pattern mining technique to recognize maximal frequent patterns withing executable samples and then inputted extracted feature for state-of-the-art supervised machine learning algorithms and achieved accuracy of 99% in the detection of unseen malware. In other related work, Pajouh et al. [38] utilized kernel base Support Vector Machine, and a novel weighting measure on samples' library calls to detect OSX malware and obtained accuracy of approximately 91% and false alarm rate of 3.9%. Dovom et al. [39] applied fuzzy and fast fuzzy pattern tree on a transmuted OpCodes to vector space and obtained an accuracy of higher than 90% for VX-Heaven, IoT and Kaggle datasets.

In order to dynamically detect intrusions, Pajouh et al. [40] proposed a layered architecture that included a dimension reduction and two-tier classification modules to detect malicious activities using dynamic behaviors of NSL-KDD dataset accurately. They achieved an overall accuracy of 84.86% as well as a detection rate of 70.15 and 42% for U2R and R2L attacks, respectively. Azmoodeh et al. [41] presented a grinding method to dynamically accept the power consumption signal of IoT application as input and grind it to sub-samples. Then, they classified sub-samples using KNN as a classifier and Dynamic Time Warping as distance measure and finally, aggregated sub-samples' class to identify crypto-ransomware [42, 43]. The method outperformed other classifiers and achieved accuracy of 90.67% to recognize malicious applications correctly.

Homayoun et al. [44] utilized frequent pattern mining approach on run-time activities of ransomware applications extracted by a virtual machine and could classify ransomware with an accuracy of 99.4% and area under curve 99%. In another related work, Homayoun et al. [45] leveraged network transactions as input and two deep structures where the first layer uses stacked autoencoders for feature extraction and the second layer uses Convolutional Neural Networks (CNN) in order to train a classifier for botnet detection. The method was applied on ISCX dataset and achieved 91% true positive rate with a false positive rate of only 13%.

3   Methodology

3.1   Dataset

In order to evaluate state-of-the-art ML techniques for IoT malware detection, an IoT dataset which includes 512 samples was used. The dataset consists of 268 benign samples and 244 malware samples. The last version of dataset as well as source code of this chapter are available on https://www.cybersciencelab.org/iot-malware-detection-dataset.

3.2   Dataset Preprocessing

Each dataset's sample includes a sequence of assembly OpCodes such ass ADD, MOV, SUB, PUSH, etc. First of all, a dictionary of unique OpCodes within all samples was generated. Then, so as to transmute the sequence of OpCodes to vector space, each sample was sequentially parsed and vector V was generated for each sample. Equation 6.5 describes vector V.

$$|V| = Number\ of\ Unique\ OpCodes \tag{6.5}$$

$$V_i = Total\ Number\ of\ OpCode_i\ in\ Sample$$

Finally, in each sample is normalized between [0, 1] (see Eq. 6.6).

$$V_i = V_i/\max(V) \tag{6.6}$$

3.3   Dataset Complexity

The preprocessed dataset includes 512 samples and each sample contains 378 features(number of unique OpCodes). In order to obtain a clear insight about the dataset, we have plotted the dataset in 2D plot using t-SNE [46] and PCA [47]

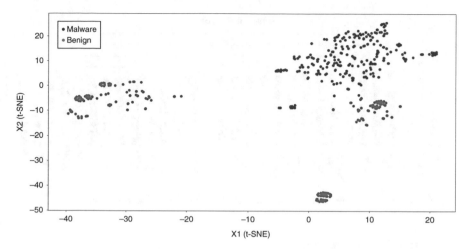

Fig. 6.1   Dataset visualization using t-SNE method

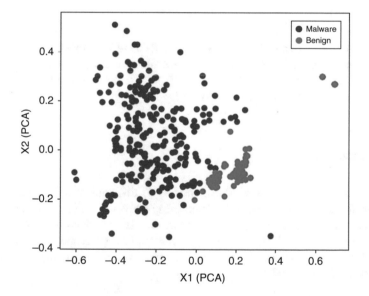

Fig. 6.2   Dataset visualization using PCA method

methods. Figures 6.1 and 6.2 illustrate 2D visualization of IoT dataset using t-SNE and PCA methods, respectively. Besides, to measure the effectiveness of each OpCode for classification, *Information Gain* of dataset was calculated. Figure 6.3 shows score of top 30 OpCode based on their information gain scores.

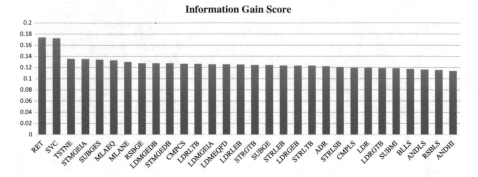

Fig. 6.3 Information gain score of OpCodes (30 OpCodes obtained highest score)

4 Experiment Results

4.1 Settings

All experiments were conducted on a PC with 8 GB of RAM and Core-i7(1.8 GHz) CPU. In addition, all source code was implemented using Python 3.7.1 and the library for ML task was *scikit-learn version 0.20.2*. In order to validate experiments, tenfold cross-validation technique was applied.

4.2 Accuracy

In order to evaluate accuracy of ML models to distinguish malware and benign samples, *Accuracy* metric was calculated using Eq. 6.1 and Fig. 6.4 gives information about performance of models. As can be clearly seen from Fig. 6.4, *RBF SVM* and *Naive Bayes* outperformed other algorithms and obtained maximum accuracy of 100%. Also, *Linear SVM* and *Random Forest* are less accurate models that obtained accuracy of 93.11 and 94.47%, respectively.

4.3 Precision

According to *Precision* performance measurement metric described in Eq. 6.2, precision of models were calculated. Figure 6.5 illustrates the performance of ML models based on the metric. *RBF SVM*, *Naive Bayes*, *AdaBoost*, *Random Forest* and *Decision Tree* achieved precision of 100% while those of *Neural Net* and *Linear SVM* were lowest and about 95.99 and 99.3%, respectively.

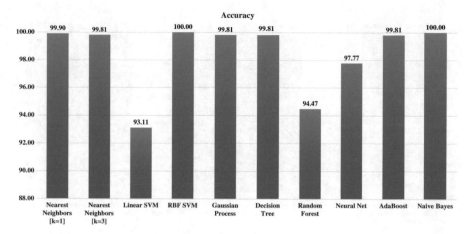

Fig. 6.4 Accuracy of machine learning models

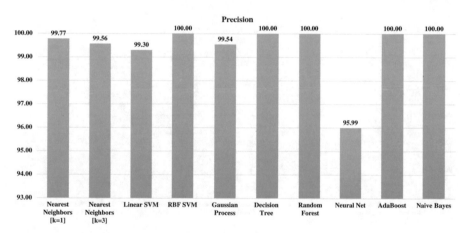

Fig. 6.5 Precision of machine learning models

4.4 Recall

In order to figure out *Recall* performance of models (Eq. 6.3), recall of all models were evaluated (See Fig. 6.6). As can be evident, *KNN(k = 1 and k = 3)*, *RBF SVM*, *Gaussian Process*, *Neural Net* and *Naive Bayes* achieved recall of 100% while *Random Forest* has obtained lowest recall (86.46%) and similarly the figure for *Linear SVM* is 86.66%.

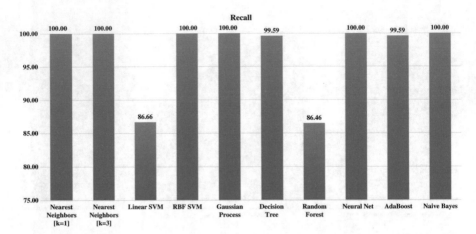

Fig. 6.6 Recall of machine learning models

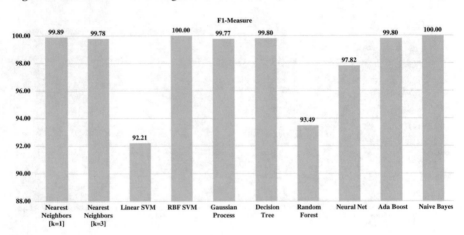

Fig. 6.7 F1 score of machine learning models

4.5   F1 Score

Finally, F1-measurement of ML models calculated using Eq. 6.4 and as can be seen from Fig. 6.7, *RBF SVM* and *Naive Bayes* obtained the 100% of F1-measure while the lowest ranked models are *Random Forest* and *Linear SVM* that only achieved 93.49 and 92.21% of the metric, respectively.

5 Discussion

In our experiments, the most successful ML models for IoT malware detection were *RBF SVM* and *Naive Bayes* based on their F1-measurement. The success of *Naive Bayes* model suggests that the normalized values of OpCodes can be assumed as an independent. Otherwise, the model would not have succeeded. Analyzing Figs. 6.1 and 6.2 explains the success of the *RBF SVM* model since, in both figures, the malware and benign applications are separate from each other. This divide allows for an *RBF SVM* to accurately separate and classify the data.

The least successful ML models were the *linear SVM* and *Random Forest*. Analyzing Figs. 6.1 and 6.2 show that a perfect linear divide between malware and benign applications does not exist which negatively affected the performance of the *linear SVM*. The *Random Forest* model's lack of success could be caused by the low information gain of the OpCodes. A *Random Forest* is made up of several small decision trees; however, the low information gain of individual OpCodes would reduce the accuracy of a smaller decision tree. When a random forest is composed of several small decision trees with low information gain decisions, it will perform sub-optimally, which could be what causes the low accuracy of the *Random Forest*. Both *Naive Bayes* and the *Random Forest* had low recalls as well.

The remaining models performed well with accuracies higher than 97% but not as well as *Naive Bayes* or *RBF SVM*. Most of the remaining models suffered from high false-positive rates leading to high recalls but low precisions. The *Neural Network* was the most extreme example of this disparity between precision and recall with a precision of 95.99%. An exception to this trend was the *Decision Tree*, which had a 100% precision but and a lower but still respectable recall of 99.59%.

6 Conclusion

With the advancement of the Internet of Things and significant prevalence of IoT networks to provide a wide range of high quality electronic services, cyber-criminals are endeavoring to misuse IoT network and devices to degrade its performance. Moreover, they also threaten the privacy of information that is being sensed, processed and communicated over the networks and there is an arms race between malware developers and security groups. In this chapter and so as to evaluate and compare state-of-the-art machine learning models, ten different models were applied to a dataset of malicious and benign IoT samples. Several experiments were conducted to analyze the dataset, distribution of samples, and score of each feature for classification tasks. Then, ML models were trained, and four performance measurement metrics were calculated. The overall evaluation demonstrates that RBF SVM and Naive Bayes outperform other models and can distinguish IoT malware and benign samples accurately.

References

1. M. Conti, A. Dehghantanha, K. Franke, S. Watson, Internet of things security and forensics: challenges and opportunities. Futur. Gener. Comput. Syst. **78**, 544–546 (2018)
2. S. Walker-Roberts, M. Hammoudeh, A. Dehghantanha, A systematic review of the availability and efficacy of countermeasures to internal threats in healthcare critical infrastructure. IEEE Access **6**, 25167–25177 (2018)
3. A.D. Dwivedi, G. Srivastava, S. Dhar, R. Singh, A decentralized privacy-preserving healthcare blockchain for IoT. Sensors **19**(2), 326 (2019). https://doi.org/10.3390/s19020326
4. A.D. Dwivedi, L. Malina, P. Dzurenda, G. Srivastava, Optimized blockchain model for internet of things based healthcare applications, in *42nd International Conference on Telecommunications and Signal Processing, TSP 2019*, Budapest, July 1–3 (2019), pp. 135–139. https://doi.org/10.1109/TSP.2019.8769060
5. R.M. Parizi, L. Guo, Y. Bian, A. Azmoodeh, A. Dehghantanha, K.R. Choo, CyberPDF: smart and secure coordinate-based automated health pdf data batch extraction. in *2018 IEEE/ACM International Conference on Connected Health: Applications, Systems and Engineering Technologies (CHASE)* (2018), pp. 106–111
6. G. Epiphaniou, P. Karadimas, D. Kbaier Ben Ismail, H. Al-Khateeb, A. Dehghantanha, K.R. Choo, Nonreciprocity compensation combined with turbo codes for secret key generation in vehicular Ad Hoc social IoT networks. IEEE Internet Things J. **5**(4), 2496–2505 (2018)
7. L. Malina, G. Srivastava, P. Dzurenda, J. Hajny, R. Fujdiak, A secure publish/subscribe protocol for internet of things, in *Proceedings of the 14th International Conference on Availability, Reliability and Security, ARES 2019*, Canterbury, August 26–29 (2019), pp. 75:1–75:10. https://doi.org/10.1145/3339252.3340503
8. J. Sakhnini, H. Karimipour, A. Dehghantanha, R. Parizi, G. Srivastava, Security aspects of internet of things aided smart grids: a bibliometric survey. Internet Things, 1–13 (2019). https://doi.org/10.1016/j.iot.2019.100111
9. H. Karimipour, A. Dehghantanha, R.M. Parizi, K.R. Choo, H. Leung, A deep and scalable unsupervised machine learning system for cyber-attack detection in large-scale smart grids. IEEE Access **7**, 80778–80788 (2019)
10. D. Wu, D.I. Arkhipov, E. Asmare, Z. Qin, J.A. McCann, Ubiflow: mobility management in urban-scale software defined IoT, in *2015 IEEE Conference on Computer Communications (INFOCOM)* (IEEE, Piscataway, 2015), pp. 208–216
11. A. Tzounis, N. Katsoulas, T. Bartzanas, C. Kittas, Internet of things in agriculture, recent advances and future challenges. Biosyst. Eng. **164**, 31–48 (2017)
12. P. Newman, *IoT Report: How Internet of Things Technology Growth is Reaching Mainstream Companies and Consumers* (Business Insider, New York, 2019)
13. J. Manyika, M. Chui, P. Bisson, J. Woetzel, R. Dobbs, J. Bughin, D. Aharon, The internet of things: mapping the value beyond the hype. Technical Report, McKinsey & Company (2015)
14. P. Cerwall, A. Lurdvall, P. Jonsson, S. Carson, R. Moller, R. Svenningsson, PerLindberg, K. Ohman, T. Sandin, L. Rangel, I. Sorlie, S. Elmgren, A. Karapntelakis, L. Wieweg, M. Halen, J. Esdtam, R. Queiros, F. Muller, L. Englund, R. Kirby, Ericsson mobility report. Technical Report, Ericsson (2018)
15. A. Azmoodeh, A. Dehghantanha, K.K.R. Choo, *Big Data and Internet of Things Security and Forensics: Challenges and Opportunities* (Springer International Publishing, Cham, 2019), pp. 1–4
16. P.N. Bahrami, A. Dehghantanha, T. Dargahi, R.M. Parizi, K.R. Choo, H.H.S. Javadi, Cyber kill chain-based taxonomy of advanced persistent threat actors: analogy of tactics, techniques, and procedures. J. Inf. Process. Syst. **15**, 865–889 (2019). https://doi.org/10.3745/JIPS.03.0126
17. C. Kolias, G. Kambourakis, A. Stavrou, J. Voas, DDos in the IoT: Mirai and other botnets. Computer **50**(7), 80–84 (2017)

18. N. Milosevic, A. Dehghantanha, K.K.R. Choo, Machine learning aided android malware classification. Comput. Electr. Eng. **61**, 266–274 (2017). https://doi.org/10.1016/j.compeleceng. 2017.02.013
19. O.M.K. Alhawi, J. Baldwin, A. Dehghantanha, *Leveraging Machine Learning Techniques for Windows Ransomware Network Traffic Detection* (Springer International Publishing, Cham, 2018), pp. 93–106.
20. R.M. Parizi, A. Dehghantanha, K.R. Choo, Towards better ocular recognition for secure real-world applications, in *2018 17th IEEE International Conference on Trust, Security and Privacy in Computing and Communications/12th IEEE International Conference on Big Data Science and Engineering* (TrustCom/BigDataSE) (2018), pp. 277–282. https://doi.org/ 10.1109/TrustCom/BigDataSE.2018.00050
21. H. Darabian, A. Dehghantanha, S. Hashemi, S. Homayoun, K.K.R. Choo, An opcode-based technique for polymorphic internet of things malware detection. Concurr. Comput. Pract. Exp. e5173 (2019)
22. S. Homayoun, A. Dehghantanha, M. Ahmadzadeh, S. Hashemi, R. Khayami, K.K.R. Choo, D.E. Newton, Drthis: deep ransomware threat hunting and intelligence system at the fog layer. Futur. Gener. Comput. Syst. **90**, 94–104 (2019)
23. A. Azmoodeh, A. Dehghantnha, K.K.R. Choo, Robust malware detection for internet of things devices using deep eigenspace learning. IEEE Trans. Sustain. Comput. **4**(1), 88–95 (2019)
24. M.R. Begli, F. Derakhshan, H. Karimipour, A layered intrusion detection system for critical infrastructure using machine learning, in *2019 IEEE International Conference on Smart Energy Grid Engineering (SEGE)* (2019)
25. S. Geris, H. Karimipour, A feature selection-based approach for joint cyber-attack detection and state estimation, in *2019 IEEE International Conference on Smart Energy Grid Engineering (SEGE)* (2019)
26. J. Sakhnini, A. Dehghantanha, H. Karimipour, Smart grid cyber attacks detection using supervised learning and heuristic feature selection, in *2019 IEEE International Conference on Smart Energy Grid Engineering (SEGE)* (2019)
27. I. Bilogrevic, K. Huguenin, B. Agir, M. Jadliwala, M. Gazaki, J.P. Hubaux, A machine-learning based approach to privacy-aware information-sharing in mobile social networks. Pervasive Mob. Comput. **25**, 125–142 (2016)
28. T. Mackey, J. Kalyanam, J. Klugman, E. Kuzmenko, R. Gupta, Solution to detect, classify, and report illicit online marketing and sales of controlled substances via twitter: using machine learning and web forensics to combat digital opioid access. J. Med. Internet Res. **20**(4), e10029 (2018)
29. K. Bolouri, A. Azmoodeh, A. Dehghantanha, M. Firouzmand, *Internet of Things Camera Identification Algorithm Based on Sensor Pattern Noise Using Color Filter Array and Wavelet Transform* (Springer International Publishing, Cham, 2019), pp. 211–223
30. H. Karimipour, S. Geris, A. Dehghantanha, H. Leung, Intelligent anomaly detection for large-scale smart grids, in *2019 IEEE Canadian Conference of Electrical and Computer Engineering (CCECE)* (2019)
31. S. Mohammadi, V. Desai, H. Karimipour, Multivariate mutual information-based feature selection for cyber intrusion detection, in *2018 IEEE Electrical Power and Energy Conference (EPEC)* (2018), pp. 1–6
32. R.M. Parizi, A. Dehghantanha, K.K.R. Choo, A. Singh, Empirical vulnerability analysis of automated smart contracts security testing on blockchains, in *Proceedings of the 28th Annual International Conference on Computer Science and Software Engineering, CASCON '18* (2018), pp. 103–113
33. R. Kohavi, et al., A study of cross-validation and bootstrap for accuracy estimation and model selection, in *IJCAI'95 Proceedings of the 14th International Joint Conference on Artificial Intelligence*, Montreal, vol. 14 (1995), pp. 1137–1145
34. S. Mohammadi, H. Mirvaziri, M. Ghazizadeh-Ahsaee, H. Karimipour, Cyber intrusion detection by combined feature selection algorithm. J. Inf. Secur. Appl. **44**, 80–88 (2019)

35. H. Hashemi, A. Azmoodeh, A. Hamzeh, S. Hashemi, Graph embedding as a new approach for unknown malware detection. J. Comput. Virol. Hacking Tech. **13**(3), 153–166 (2017)
36. M. Damshenas, A. Dehghantanha, R. Mahmoud, A survey on malware propagation, analysis, and detection. Int. J. Cyber Secur. Digit. Forensics **2**(4), 10–30 (2013)
37. F. Daryabar, A. Dehghantanha, N.I. Udzir, Investigation of bypassing malware defences and malware detections, in *2011 7th International Conference on Information Assurance and Security (IAS)* (2011). pp. 173–178. https://doi.org/10.1109/ISIAS.2011.6122815
38. H.H. Pajouh, A. Dehghantanha, R. Khayami, K.K.R. Choo, Intelligent OS X malware threat detection with code inspection. J. Comput. Virol. Hacking Tech. **14**(3), 213–223 (2018)
39. E.M. Dovom, A. Azmoodeh, A. Dehghantanha, D.E. Newton, R.M. Parizi, H. Karimipour, Fuzzy pattern tree for edge malware detection and categorization in IoT. J. Syst. Archit. **97**, 1–7 (2019). https://doi.org/10.1016/j.sysarc.2019.01.017
40. H.H. Pajouh, R. Javidan, R. Khayami, A. Dehghantanha, K.R. Choo, A two-layer dimension reduction and two-tier classification model for anomaly-based intrusion detection in IoT backbone networks. IEEE Trans. Emerg. Top. Comput. **7**(2), 314–323 (2019)
41. A. Azmoodeh, A. Dehghantanha, M. Conti, K.K.R. Choo, Detecting crypto-ransomware in IoT networks based on energy consumption footprint. J. Ambient. Intell. Humaniz. Comput. **9**(4), 1141–1152 (2018)
42. A.D. Dwivedi, P. Morawiecki, G. Srivastava, Differential cryptanalysis of round-reduced SPECK suitable for internet of things devices. IEEE Access **7**, 16476–16486 (2019). https://doi.org/10.1109/ACCESS.2019.2894337
43. S. Lou, G. Srivastava, S. Liu, A node density control learning method for the internet of things. Sensors **19**(15), 3428 (2019). https://doi.org/10.3390/s19153428
44. S. Homayoun, A. Dehghantanha, M. Ahmadzadeh, S. Hashemi, R. Khayami, Know abnormal, find evil: frequent pattern mining for ransomware threat hunting and intelligence. IEEE Trans. Emerg. Top. Comput. 1–1 (2017). https://doi.org/10.1109/TETC.2017.2756908
45. S. Homayoun, M. Ahmadzadeh, S. Hashemi, A. Dehghantanha, R. Khayami, *BoTShark: A Deep Learning Approach for Botnet Traffic Detection* (Springer International Publishing, Cham, 2018), pp. 137–153
46. L.v.d. Maaten, G. Hinton, Visualizing data using t-SNE. J. Mach. Learn. Res. **9**, 2579–2605 (2008)
47. S. Wold, K. Esbensen, P. Geladi, Principal component analysis. Chemom. Intell. Lab. Syst. **2**(1–3), 37–52 (1987)

Chapter 7
Artificial Intelligence and Security of Industrial Control Systems

Suby Singh, Hadis Karimipour, Hamed HaddadPajouh, and Ali Dehghantanha ⓘ

1 Introduction

Industrial Control Systems (ICS) is a standardized approach and an increasingly diverse and extensively connected set of technologies to command that automate and control significant portions of our connected society [1, 2]. This includes travelers commuting on rail systems, power moving through the electrical grid, oil flowing through pipelines, and systems controlling pharmaceutical and food manufacturing. ICS, which is a part of the Operations Technology (OT) environment in industrial enterprises, consists of mainly two parts. First part has combinations of components such as mechanical, electrical, hydraulic and pneumatic. They all act together to achieve an industrial objective e.g., manufacturing or transportation of matter or energy. This part of the system is referred to as process and is primarily concerned with producing the output at manufacturing and production departments. Second part of ICSs which can be considered larger than the first part, it is implemented by several types of control systems, including Supervisory Control and Data Acquisition (SCADA) systems, Distributed Control Systems (DCSs), and other smaller control system configurations such as programmable logic controllers (PLCs), intelligent electronic devices (IEDs), remote terminal units (RTUs) and other field devices [3–5]. These controllers are regularly applied to

S. Singh
University of Mumbai, Mumbai, India
e-mail: support@muonline.org.in

H. Karimipour
School of Engineering, University of Guelph, Guelph, ON, Canada
e-mail: hkarimi@uoguelph.ca; Canada-hkarimi@uoguelph.ca

H. HaddadPajouh (✉) · A. Dehghantanha
Cyber Science Lab, School of Computer Science, University of Guelph, Guelph, ON, Canada
e-mail: hamed@cybersciencelab.org; ali@cybersciencelab.org

© Springer Nature Switzerland AG 2020
K.-K. R. Choo, A. Dehghantanha (eds.), *Handbook of Big Data Privacy*,
https://doi.org/10.1007/978-3-030-38557-6_7

the systems that monitor, control and manage large production systems or critical infrastructure industries, such as electric power generators, transportation systems, dams, agriculture and chemical factories, water pipelines, petrochemical operations, oil and natural gas, food and beverage, pulp and paper, discrete manufacturing (e.g., aerospace, automotive, and durable goods) industries and others [6–8]. These control systems can be fully automated or may include a human in the process. Likewise, systems can be configured to operate in open-loop, closed-loop, and manual mode. In open-loop control systems, established settings are made to control the output and whole process is expected to faithfully follow its input command or set points regardless of the final result. In closed-loop control systems which are also known as the feedback control systems, an input has the effect of output (which can be considered as feedback) in such a way that desired objectives are maintained, whereas in manual mode, it requires humans to operate the whole system. Numerous control loops such as remote diagnostics and maintenance tools built using an array of network protocols and Human Machine Interfaces (HMIs) are used in a typical ICS system as shown in Fig. 7.1.

ICSs were originally designed to achieve the primary goal of infrastructure units such as increasing performance, reliability, and safety by reducing manual effort. Traditionally, physical isolation or a so-called air gap (i.e. security by obscurity) was a dominant way of achieving an ICS's security [9]. The fourth industrial revolution (Industry 4.0), a concept where cyber-physical systems such as the Internet of things are brought together, has started to find more resonance with OEMs [10], system integrators and asset owners. Many industrial and manufacturing firms have

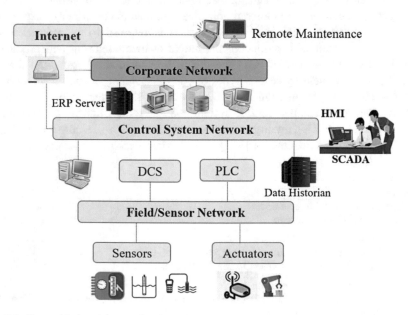

Fig. 7.1 General industrial control systems layout

felt the need of integrating wireless networks for sensors and controller systems to function effectively, and accordingly implemented this integration to upgrade internal processes, as ICS are allowing plants (from power plants to oil refineries, to manufacturing facilities of all types) to operate at higher efficiency and lower cost. Now, a lot of ICS information are routed to sophisticated applications across enterprises, through a wide area network; and this is where security by obscurity no longer offers valid security protection. Government plans to connect ICSs to the Internet for the projects such as smart grids and smart cities, which will significantly increase the risk of intrusion from malicious actors since ICSs are very crucial to the operation of critical infrastructures that are often highly interconnected and mutually dependent systems.

There have been tremendous developments in the field of communication technologies, hardware and software that have promoted the emergence of internet-based sensory devices [11, 12]. Great numbers of such Internet of Things (IoT) devices have been introduced to improve productivity and enhance system control, as a result of ICS modernization. According to various forecasts, it is expected that around 25–50 billion IoT devices would be connected to the Internet by 2020 [13]. Data monitoring, process controls, and communication with other systems have simplified with the use of related embedded technological IoT devices. One of the basics reasons for using these computing devices is to enhance human activities and experiences. However, as the technology becomes matured and number of these devices in ICS increases, amount of data generated also increases. A massive volume of data is published by these internet-connected physical devices, sensors and actuators. This data is characterized by velocity in terms of time and location; and variety in terms of different data formats and data quality. The amount of data generated is huge for ex. a single flight running between New York and London generates 0.98 GB of data/per day [14]. IoTs generated raw data can further be used to represent better real-time services to its users. Another use can be to enhance IoT framework performance to accomplish the tasks intelligently. In order to make use of this data, systems should be able to access and process raw data collected from different resources, located at different regions and mounted over the network; then analyze this data to extract information and knowledge useful to present realistic services to its users or possibly predict the future demand and upcoming threats. Apart from increased amount of data, as the internet-connected devices technology continues to boost the current network arena by providing easy connection and interaction between the physical and cyber worlds, it also increases the risk of cyber threats associated with it. Due to technological innovation and advancements of the Industrial IoT (IIoT) achieved in last 10 years, the industrial automations have directed themselves to become driven by a large amount of data. All the industrial data are being routed through the networks. This increases the inter-connectivity of networks, but may escalate threat scenarios. It becomes increasingly difficult to segregate and protect ICS platforms from both external and internal threats. Managing IoT devices in such a complex networked ICS environment can create major challenges in security because each device needs to be defended and secured properly [15–17].

Sophisticated attacks on ICS are on the rise, such as the Ivano-Frankivsk, Ukraine incident, just one of the multiple attacks that leveraged BlackEnergy malware. Also in 2015, Kemuri Water Company's ICS infrastructure in the US was attacked. In this attack, hackers had targeted company's computers after exploiting unpatched web vulnerabilities in its internet-facing customer payment portal. This attack had resulted in infiltrating the water utility's control system and changing the levels of chemicals being used to treat tap water. Device loss is also a major cause of data breach because one misplaced device may give cybercriminals the necessary access to penetrate and get into the target's network. Data generated from IoT devices can be useful in detecting such breaches by observing the anomalous patterns of the standard process. Thus, intelligent processing and analysis of this large data are the major factors to developing smart and secure IoT applications. Big data and Artificial Intelligence (AI) can play a big role to achieve this.

With the help of big data, companies can have the ability to visualize the quantities of data they collect, so that they can bring better improvements to products and processes. Cyber security approaches built along with the concept of big data techniques provide a run-time intelligence to monitor the packet's behavior over a network and also the network traffic itself, so that organizations can be safeguarded from external threats and attacks. Big data can be scaled up in size and speed predictably and straightforwardly way which provides business analytics reporting tools to grow organically. Speed is a critical parameter to the whole ICS process and big data may provide an advantage by adding a real-time view capability which can enable operational, engineering, and supervisory personnel to be more responsive and stay alerted in day-to-day situations. This reduces the response time in taking an appropriate action. The big data solution also increases the range and variety of data that can be analyzed all together. This can result in providing additional context and insights which could help in better decision-making process, optimization of process, and security awareness activities. Another concept, cognitive algorithms, an intelligence ability to do much as a human mind would do; which can undertake interpretation of data and previously discovered patterns to predict. If Cognitive IoT systems are built, they improve themselves by learning from feed data and previously generated patterns, while performing repetitive tasks by self-predicting the things; this makes the whole system to function under closed loop fashion, usually known as feedback system. Cognitive computing analyzes massive amounts of data and can act as prosthesis for human cognition when making certain decisions while responding to it in humanly manner. IoTs enabled with cognitive intelligence can play an important role in extracting the meaningful patterns from the IoT generated smart data. Also, AI technology not only potential to provide panacea for modern business problems or capable of helping enterprise and industrial companies make sense of mountains of data (including from IIoT devices), but also can help them boost the security of industrial control systems by providing an automated way to look over anomalies or vulnerabilities. The convergence of OT and IT is driven by industrial analytics applied to machine data for operational insights; this ultimately creates value for the fourth industrial revolution (Business 4.0). One proposed use case of AI systems, or to be more precise machine learning, is its use for detecting malware or anomalies on a network. If you have a baseline of how the network should operate and have sound machine learning algorithms and sufficient data access, this technology can be powerful in detecting network threats very quickly and over time, potentially reducing the number of false alarms for possibly suspicious code or network behavior. Thus, AI and big data have considerable potentials for ICS enhancement and its cyber security.

2   Architecture of ICS Networks

Industrial Control Systems (ICS) have transformed from traditional stand-alone isolated systems to interconnected systems. These modern ICS systems extensively use existing communication protocols and platforms. This transformation has resulted in increased productivity, reduced operational costs and improved organizational support model. To be benefitted from this new model, organizations have started to perform more and more integration, between not only common ICS applications but also have started integrating the typical business applications like Manufacturing Production Planning systems or Enterprise Resource Planning systems with the supervisory components of the ICS. This gradually increased the need for real-time information sharing, which caused the business operations of industrial networks to increase. It is widely recommended to segregate the ICS network from the corporate network while designing network architecture for an ICS deployment, so as to reduce the possibility of security threats as the nature of network traffic on these two networks is different. By saying different nature of traffic could mean that Internet access, FTP, email, and remote access. These are typically being allowed on the corporate network but should be blocked on the ICS network. Carrying ICS network traffic on the corporate network could be intercepted and subjected to Denial of Service or Man-in-the-Middle attacks. Having separate network policies for both corporate and ICS should help industries to guarantee that security and performance problems on the corporate or public network can not affect the ICS network. ICS systems generally have several different levels of networks, from enterprise level through to processes and control and then field level having sensors and actuators. These levels focus on functional hierarchy of different parts of critical infrastructure, be that an industrial operation, a power plant or a public facility. As shown in Fig. 7.2, Enterprise level can be considered as the general IT network of an organization, where the general-purpose IT systems such as Enterprise Resource Planning (ERP) and Manufacturing Execution Systems (MES) are connected and are functional at this level. Industrial Control System uses ERP, a business process management software and system of integrated applications, to manage the business functions and automate many back office tasks related to technology, services, and human resources. It also helps in providing business with a reliable and robust system and increased business efficiency. On the other hand, MES is an information system, and ICS uses this system because it provides a way to connect, monitor and control the complex manufacturing systems and data that flows in the factory. The

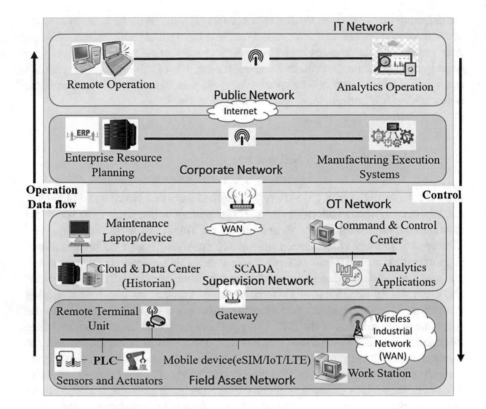

Fig. 7.2 Industrial connectivity

main objective of MES is to improve production output in an industry by ensuring an effective execution of the manufacturing operations. These are computerized *systems* used in *manufacturing*, to track and document the transformation of raw materials to finished goods.

Remote Operations provide the ability to remotely control, monitor, and manage ICS endpoints by enabling to perform changes remotely and investigate endpoint status in real time while reducing the need for on-site visits. This may involve a large physical distance between the site or the hub of the networks and person monitoring the system. Data among all these points need to be transmitted with the help of telephone cables, radio, satellite or wireless industrial network at the different levels of the ICS. As this mechanism allows data to flow on public network, it also poses a possible security risk. At factory process level, SCADA systems control the dispersed assets such as sensors and actuators, using a centralized data acquisition and supervisory control method, whereas production systems within a local area such as a factory are controlled by DCS using supervisory and regulatory control. In a SCADA network, the control level sends the coded information from higher level coordinating components to industrial machinery of an ICS and vice versa. This control level acts as the nerve center of the network, and it's how PLCs and sensors are associated with the broader network. The information carried though this level is generally transferred via wired networks, but could be broadcasted in wireless fashion in some cases, which may or may not be connected to the wider public internet. Data received at this level can be integrated with cloud computing technologies. Some of the main objectives of using cloud techniques is to save cost on processing vast amount of data, relax and get benefitted from the embedded security, ensure the uptime, and guarantee system redundancy which can be used in case of disaster. SCADA devices are also critical systems and require reliable redundancy, robust security, reduced operating costs, and maximum uptime. Thus, relocating SCADA devices to cloud technology can be preferred which can solve critical issues mainly related to uptime and redundancy in industrial control systems (ICS) environments. As discussed previously ICS environments have notoriously high uptime requirements which can be guaranteed with the use of cloud. Moreover, cloud computing for SCADA devices is also beneficial for providing access from any internet-connected location, featuring easy way to access the data. Also, in terms of scalability, cloud computing and big data allow new services and servers to be spun up in only a matter of minutes. Moving critical devices and/or services to cloud could help in setting up the baselines for uptime and redundancy while reducing the cost and protecting the system against cyber-attack by ensuring that data carried by ICS are firewalled and filtered. At the field Asset network level, information about the industrial process are collected by sensors and relayed to the PLC, which then broadcasts this information across the wider ICS. A number of different field sites or devices may be connected to a single control center (as a production line with a number of lathe machines, or a power plant with several reactors). Each PLC in the network is connected to a pertinent SCADA server, because of which sensors are monitored periodically, field sites or devices are repaired or reprogrammed whenever required, and developments in any faults are ascertained or notified in a reliable way with the help of alarms connected to it. The main control center is a critical component and it processes decisions by taking data into account, generated across the whole network. So, in the example of a railway station, multiple field sensors record when and which sections of railway are occupied by rail and when the trains are boarding. Then, this information is relayed to control centers, which then decides whether to allow trains to arrive at certain platforms and proceed with the announcements for the benefit of passengers.

Connection between the ICS and corporate network is required, but practical considerations, such as ICS installation cost and sustaining homogenous network infrastructure such as similar kind of network devices i.e. firewalls, often poses a significant security risk for possible cyber threats. This connection must be protected by boundary protection devices such as firewalls from different vendors or providing limited access to ICS information from outside environment of ICS. If the networks need be connected, it is strongly recommended that only minimal (single point if possible) connections should be allowed from corporate network, and even that connection should be through a DMZ (Demilitarized zone) and a firewall. A DMZ referred to as a screened subnet or perimeter network, is a separate subnetwork segment which connects directly to the firewall and exposes an organization's external-facing services to a larger network such as the Internet. It contains servers consisting of data or services from the ICS that needs to be accessed from the corporate network or untrusted network. Also, with any external connections, the minimum access should be allowed through the firewall to this network segment, opening only the ports required for specific communication. In this way, ICS networks and corporate networks should be kept segregated to maintain cyber security using different network architectures. Such several possible architectures have been discussed in below section along with the advantages and disadvantages of each.

2.1 Dual-Homed Computer

Dual-homed or dual network interface cards computers are capable of passing network traffic from one network to another. A computer having no proper security controls could pose additional threats and firewalls should be configured as dual-homed to traverse data from both the control and corporate networks to prevent these threats. Every connection between control network and corporate network must have a firewall, but this configuration lacks security improvement and should not be used to connect ICS and corporate networks [18].

2.2 Firewall Between Corporate and Control Network

As shown in Fig. 7.3 two-port firewall is used between the corporate and the control networks. This can help in achieving a noticeable security improvement, and if properly configured, a firewall significantly decreases the chance of a successful

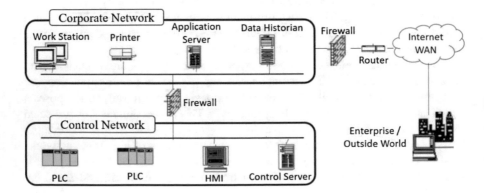

Fig. 7.3 Firewall between corporate and control network

execution of external attack on the control field level network. Alas, still the two issues exist with this ICS network architecture. First issue is related to data historian, if it is designed to be located on the corporate network, the firewall must allow the data historian residing at corporate level, to communicate with the control devices and services on the control network. This can lead to a packet originating from a corporate network's malicious program or incorrectly configured host (appearing to be the data historian itself) to be forwarded to individual PLCs/DCS residing at control field level network. And if the data historian is designed to reside on the control network, a firewall rule must exist that should allow all hosts from the enterprise or corporate level network to communicate with the historian, which again can lead to malicious packets to be injected. Another issue with this architecture i.e. having a simple firewall mechanism between the networks is that spoofed packets could be transmitted which can affect the control network by allowing covert data to be tunneled in allowed protocols. Overall, this architecture enables a significant improvement over a non-segregated network. But if not very carefully designed and monitored, use of firewall rules that allow direct links between the corporate network and the control network devices in this architecture can lead to possible security breaches [18].

2.3 Firewall and Router Between Corporate and Control Network

Figure 7.4 shows a slightly more sophisticated design of ICS network architecture with the use of a router/firewall combination. In this architecture, router offers basic packet filtering services while a firewall handles the more complex issues using either proxy techniques or stateful inspection. This design allows a faster router to manage the amplitude of the incoming packets, especially in the case of Denial

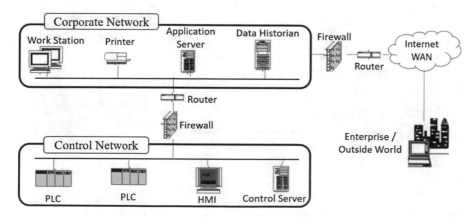

Fig. 7.4 Firewall and router between corporate and control network

of Service attacks, and reduce the load on firewall. This makes the architecture very popular in internet-facing systems. As an adversary must bypass two different devices, this design offers an improved defense-in-depth facility [18].

2.4 Firewall with DMZ Subnet Between Corporate and Control Network

Firewalls with the ability to establish a DMZ between the corporate and control networks can provide a significant improvement. Figure 7.5 shows that each DMZ can contain one or more critical components, such as data historian, wireless access point, or remote and third party access systems. Intermediate network segment can be created by DMZ capable firewalls, and these firewalls need to offer three or more interfaces, rather than just public and private interfaces. Among these interfaces, one can be connected to the corporate network, the second to the control network, and the remaining to the shared devices such as data historian server on the DMZ sub network. Corporate-accessible components are placed in the DMZ. Firewall rules should be set in such a way that communication between the control network and DMZ should be initiated by only control network devices. No direct communication paths must be formed from the corporate network to the control network; each path must effectively end in the DMZ. As Fig. 7.5 shows, an arbitrary corporate network packet can be blocked by firewall, from entering the control network. Firewall can also regulate network traffic from the other network zones including the control network. This architecture with little or no traffic passing directly between the corporate and the control networks and strict set of rules can provide a clear separation of ICS networks [18].

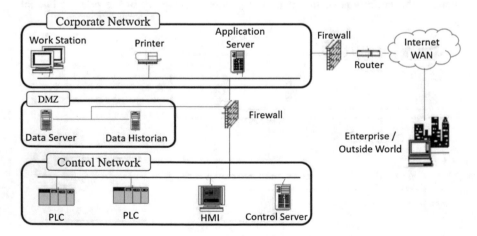

Fig. 7.5 Firewall with DMZ subnet between corporate and control network

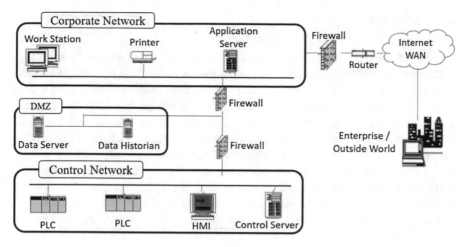

Fig. 7.6 Paired firewalls between corporate and control network

2.5 Paired Firewalls Between Corporate and Control Network

In this design, a pair of firewalls with a DMZ solution can be positioned between the corporate and ICS networks, as shown in Fig. 7.6. Shared servers such as the data historian are located between the firewalls in a DMZ-like sub network, sometimes this configuration is referred to as a Manufacturing Execution System (MES) layer [18].

In this architecture, the first firewall blocks arbitrary packets from establishing communication with the shared historians or the control network whereas the second firewall prevents an unwanted traffic from a compromised server from entering the control network. This prevents control network traffic from getting impacted by the compromised shared servers. Additionally, if firewalls from two different vendors are used, then this solution may offer an advantage. This also clearly separates the responsibility of the control and the IT group, as each group can manage a firewall device on its own. This architecture has some strong advantages for environments with stringent security requirements and where clear management separation is needed, but the primary disadvantage associated with this two-firewall architecture is increased cost and complex management.

3 ICS Protocols

ICS protocols may be serial, IP, or Ethernet-based versions. The security challenges and vulnerabilities are different for each variant. Following sections discuss some of the common industrial protocols and their respective security concerns.

3.1 Modbus

Modbus is one of the most commonly used protocols in industries such as utilities and manufacturing environments. Modbus protocol is available in multiple variants (for ex. serial, TCP/IP), and was originally programmed by Modicon, the first programmable logic controller (PLC) vendor and this protocol has been in use since the 1970s. Some older versions of Modbus communicate via broadcast. A common security challenge with Modbus is that it has no Default authentication process between communicating endpoints which means that only Modbus address and function call (code) are necessary for a message to reach its destination. This can allow an inappropriate source to send improper commands to its target destination. Upon receiving the improper command, the recipient can act on it accordingly, without realizing the actual intension behind it. In this way, an attacker can potentially impact recipient devices. Another security challenge with Modbus is that initiating application does not validate the message content. Instead, Modbus waits for the network stack to perform validation of the message content. This could lead to protocol abuse in the system [19].

3.2 DNP3 (Distributed Network Protocol)

DNP3, which provides serial communication between controllers and simple IEDs, is common in utilities and found in multiple deployment scenarios, industries, discrete and continuous process systems. Although DNP3 has placed great emphasis on the reliable delivery of messages, but there are many insecure implementations of DNP3 protocol. The ability to establish trust in the system's state is the missing security component in this protocol. It means that participants do not really verifies the messages and allow for unsolicited responses, which can cause an undesired response. This protocol does not guarantee the veracity of the information being presented.

3.3 ICCP (Inter-Control Center Communications Protocol)

ICCP, another common control protocol used in utilities, basically in North America, travels across the boundaries between different networks. Due to this, ICCP protocol carries an extra level of exposure and risk that can uncover an utility to cyber-attack. In difference to other protocols, ICCP was designed to work across a WAN. Despite having a role to work across WAN, initial implementations of ICCP could not deliver expected security measures and instead had several significant security gaps. One major vulnerability with ICCP is that system required no authentication for establishing communication. Another is that it did not provide encryption as a default condition across the protocols which could cause revealing connections to man-in-the-middle (MITM) and replay attacks.

3.4 OPC (OLE for Process Control)

OPC is a Microsoft interoperability methodology's OLE-based protocol. It is limited to operate at the higher levels of the control space in industrial control networks where devices have dependency on Windows-based platforms. Correspondingly, concerns around OPC rise with the operating system on which it operates, because many of the Windows based devices in the operational space are not fully patched, old, or at risk due to overabundance of well-known vulnerabilities. Attackers may take advantage of these well-known vulnerabilities. OPC is implemented in client/server fashion and another concern with OPC, particularly in this area is that OPC protocol is dependent on the Remote Procedure Call (RPC) protocol. This generates the need to have clear understanding and exposure of vulnerabilities associated with RPC, and also another need to identify the level of risk these vulnerabilities could bring to a particular network.

3.5 International Electro Technical Commission (IEC) Protocols

The IEC is a standard serial data transmission TCP/IP based network protocol. It was originally developed to provide vendor-agnostic solution for power utility systems. So that, it can facilitate the ability to exchange information between vendors and standardized communication protocols in a large heterogeneous network. This is broadly used for SCADA tele-control in Europe which are geographically dispersed control systems. Three types of messages were initially defined under this protocol:

1. MMS (Manufacturing Message Specification)
2. GOOSE (Generic Object Oriented Substation Event)
3. SV (Sampled Values).

Later, Web services were added as a fourth protocol, following is a short summary of each:

- MMS (61850-8.1): It is a client/server, TCP/IP based protocol which functions at Layer 3 i.e. Network layer and provides same functionality as other SCADA protocols, for ex. Modbus.
- GOOSE (61850-8.1): It is a Layer 2 i.e. Data Link layer protocol and functions through multicast over Ethernet. This message type is used with IEDs and allows

it to interchange information horizontally between bays and substations in order to interlock, measure, and trip the signals.

- SV (61850-9-2): Just like GOOSE, this message type is also a Layer 2 protocol and functions through multicast over Ethernet. It carries sample details such as voltage and current samples on the process bus. It can also function over the station bus. Both SV and GOOSE provide no reliable methods to ensure delivery of the data.

IEC has multiple known-security-challenges and vulnerabilities that could be exploited by skilled attackers who can then compromise a control system. In MMS, authentication is provided with clear-text passwords which can easily be exploited, whereas the other two messages types i.e. GOOSE or SV do not have any provision for authentication. It means that IES provides no verification for authenticity and integrity because no firmware is signed between client and server. GOOSE and SV have integrity of the message but that is limited, which makes proportionally easy for attackers to imitate a sender. Some of the versions of IEC provided little security capabilities with the introduction of certificate exchange for secure connection [19].

3.6 PROFIBUS

PROFIBUS (Process Field Bus) was first promoted in 1989 by BMBF, a German department of education and research. As the name only depicts, it is a standard Industrial computer network protocol which used for Fieldbus communication involving microprocessors in automation technology. This is typically used by Siemens. It sounds similar to PROFINET, a standard for data communication over Industrial Ethernet, but one should not get confused with these. PROFIBUS functions over client/server architecture by creating a hierarchy of two types of stations in a network. First is Active station which acts as master and the second one is passive station which acts as a slave and can never initiate communication on its own. Passive can only answer the Active's commands and at least one master present must be present in every PROFIBUS network.

3.7 Other Protocols

Before implementing any kind of controls or security measures, it is strongly recommended that a security practitioner must identify all aspects of the traffic traversing the network Understanding the most basic protocols including ARP, UDP, TCP, IP, and SNMP, transport mechanisms, and basic elements of any network are held into account. Few specialized environments where IoT networks need to contact the individual sensors, it may use other background control protocols such as Datagram Transport Layer Security (DTLS) and Constrained Application Protocol (CoAP). Such protocols have to be considered separately from a security perspective.

4 Constraints Faced by ICS Systems

Some of the potential security deficiencies with regards to network architectures in ICS systems have been observed in previous sections. ICS IT networks are different from ordinary IT networks and must deal with many different restrictions that don't generally apply to ordinary IT networks. This is because rather than only managing high throughput of information, ICS networks usually have to function more towards carrying out tasks reliably and punctually. It often has redundant systems so that when a component fails, other spare component shall be made available to carry out the processes continuously without any break. When failure occurs, ICS networks can't simply be rebooted just like a normal computer network. Safety of every field unit in ICS environments is responsibility of ICS network managers and sometimes they have to handle the scenarios where a network failure can cause a serious and instantaneous real-world repercussions or consequences such as a reactor meltdown or contamination of drinking water. Thus, risk management becomes a significant aspect of ICS network manager's job.

Inclusion of components that require direct physical connection with an Industrial process is another major difference that ICS possess than IT networks. These elements may include forces or high temperatures which can create challenging conditions for the components involved. ICS systems use software which may not be familiar to conventional IT managers. Also, these ICS software packages are developed by specialist firms and are proprietary, which makes upgrading these packages difficult. Another constraint is the irregular security patches for these software which is rarely the case with a well-run IT networks. Even while to change software, many ICS networks cannot easily be turned off and ICS managers must plan for any alterations well in advance. Any minor mistakes can lead to serious vulnerabilities, which in turn can cause security incidents. Following graph shows the trend line of ICS security related incidents reported in the years between 2009 and 2016, according to reports by the Industrial Control Systems Computer Emergency Readiness Team (ICS-CERT) (Fig. 7.7).

As we can observe from the trend line that the number of security-related incidents containing industrial control systems (ICSs) in the year 2012 was more than five times in the year 2010 (197 ICS security incidents were reported in 2012 as compared to 39 in 2010). This rising trend line in the incident count has acted a catalyst for the grown focal point on securing the industrial control systems. Earlier, ICSs were negligibly inclined towards traditional information technology (IT) systems in which proprietary control protocols were used by specialized hardware and software and had the resemblance of isolated ICS systems. Now, low-cost and widely available Internet Protocol (IP) based devices are taking place

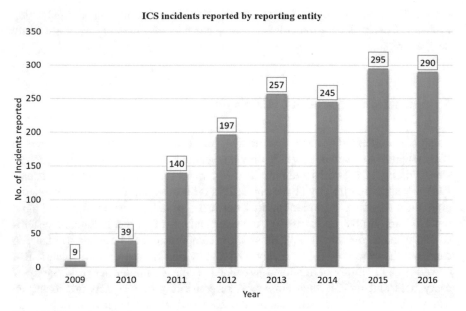

Fig. 7.7 Trend line of ICS incidents reported by reporting entity (source: ICS-CERT US)

of these proprietary solutions. This increases the probability of cyber security vulnerabilities and incidents due to Internet exposure. ICSs are acquiring IT solutions, so that it can provide remote access capabilities and corporate business systems connectivity. These facilities are designed and developed using industrial standard computers, operating systems (OS) and network protocols. This has made ICS to be more paralleled with IT systems. This integration provides ICS with IT capabilities such as controlling and monitoring the processes have become a lot easier while taking better decisions for future requirements. But along with these new capabilities, this integration also provides little or no isolation for ICS from the outside world. This creates a greater need to have these systems secured from remote and external threats. Increasing use of wireless networking causes ICS implementations to be at greater risk. Hostile governments, malicious intruders, terrorist groups, complexities, accidents, disgruntled employees, natural disasters, as well as malicious or accidental actions by insiders, are various sources which cause threats to control systems.

Most of the industries rely on security through obscurity i.e. using secrecy in an attempt to ensure security. These industrial control system stakeholders look at security as a low priority goal. Security through obscurity method has been in use consistently, but its success rate has differed across the three generations of industrial control systems. It greatly worked for first generation i.e. monolithic and second generation i.e. distributed industrial control systems. In these generations, proprietary software and closed-source components, standards and protocols were used with restricted or no connectivity to non-industrial-control systems. However, third generation which is the networked industrial control systems regularly use open technologies. It requires connection to and communication over other networks, potentially non-industrial-control-system. Increased awareness of industrial control system technologies, their use of standard protocols and openness to networking has advanced the susceptibility to attack. Most of industrial control systems are considered as critical infrastructures, making them attractive targets for attack [20].

Followings are the possible incidents, an ICS may face:

1. Flow of information through ICS networks can be blocked or delayed, and this could discontinue the ICS operation.
2. Damaging, disabling or shutting down the equipment can be caused by unauthorized changes to commands and instructions, or alarm thresholds. This could also create environmental impacts and endanger human life.
3. Incorrect information can be sent to system operators in order to hide unauthorized changes or to accelerate the operators to begin inappropriate actions. This could have various negative effects.
4. Inappropriately modified settings of ICS software or configuration or ICS software infected with malware could have various negative effects on ICS.
5. Human life can be put endangered due to interference with the operation of safety systems.

5 IT and OT Cyber Security Challenges

Operational Technology (OT) is a combination of hardware and software appliances which are responsible for detecting or promoting a change via direct monitoring and controlling of physical devices, processes and events in the enterprise. As discussed previously, industrial systems were solely based upon proprietary protocols and software for many years. Those systems were managed and monitored by human beings, manually. It provided no connection to the outside world for any reason. Because of their isolation from outside world, they did not provide any opportunities to hackers for any kind of threats as they had no network interface for causing an attack also no medium by which attackers could gain or destroy. Acquiring physical access to a terminal was the only way for attackers to exploit these systems, but this was not an easy task. Then in few years, even with limited integration of OT with IT could not raise the same kinds of vulnerabilities as ICS is facing today. Now with modernization, more industrial systems expect to deliver big and smart data analytics with the inclusion of online system. This technological integration helps them in adopting new capabilities and efficiencies which it provides to IT industries. This convergence provides organizations a single view point for industrial systems, all together with process management solutions. These systems make sure that accurate information in expected format is delivered to machines, sensors, switches, devices, and people at the right time. If configured properly, collaboration between

OT and IT provides new capabilities to remotely monitor and manage the devices. This advancement from closed to open systems has also lead to new security risks which need to be addressed and mitigated.

5.1 Reasons for Industrial Control Systems Being Targeted

Businesses and organizations are seeking for efficient control systems that can automatically manage their processes, so that they can sustain in today's market driven economy. ICS in plants or critical infrastructures has a significant role in operating a country. ICS with increased efficiency also introduces new risks for security. When such plants or critical infrastructures are attacked successfully, it can cause serious impact on any organization and provide attackers with much more to gain like intellectual property theft, shutting down the operations or damaging the equipment. This cost organizations in terms of financial loss and personnel's health and safety risks. Threat actors have different motives when an enterprise is targeted, some of which could be financial gain, political cause, or even a military objective. These attacks may be sponsored by competitors or may be directed by insiders with a malicious goal, and even hacktivists. For example, ICS attack that happened with 13 of DaimlerChrystler's car manufacturing plants in 2005 [21]. When the attack happened, these car plants went offline for nearly an hour which resulted in a production backlog and costing the company thousands of dollars. The main reason for the attack was Zotob PnP worm infections that affected a Windows Plug and Play service. The attack was not related to a group or individual; competitors could also hire cybercriminals and directed the attack because they have much to gain from the damage caused by such attack.

5.2 Implementation of ICS Attacks

The first step of building an attack against ICS is reconnaissance which means that attackers first start surveying the ICS environment. Then the next step is to develop different approaches and tactics that help attackers in gaining a foothold or entering in the target network. These tactics and strategies depend on targeted devices. Attackers make use of specific configurations of an ICS and all the possible vulnerabilities while launching a malware. After identifying and exploiting these vulnerabilities, attackers could carry out unexpected changes to certain operations and functions, and make adjustments to the existing controls and configurations. Different factors such as security of the system and intended attack impact determine the complexity of an attack being launched on ICS. For example, a denial-of-service is much easier than manipulating a service and removing its intended effects from the controllers because DoS attacks only cause disruption in the process

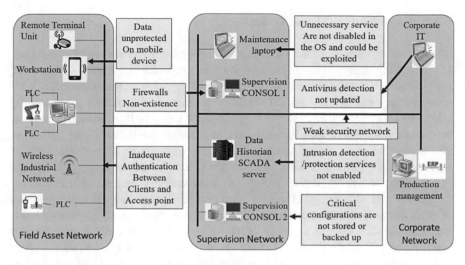

Fig. 7.8 Possible weaknesses in ICS network

of the target ICS. There are already a lot of methods for attackers to damage or disrupt an ICS process, but new strategies will continue to evolve with the devices that are introduced to every ICS environment. The following figure shows the possible weaknesses in an ICS network (Fig. 7.8).

5.3   Security Challenges for ICS

For most of the organizations, digital transformation synonymizes with the incorporation of IoT and OT devices and be a part of the hyper-connected world. And with the IoT devices adding up at a rapid pace, it becomes vital for the network security professionals to deeply understand the metrics that affect cybersecurity in the IoT ecosystem. Here are some of them:

5.3.1   Rapid Growth in the Amount of Data

As the volume of IoT connected devices increases, it is inevitable not to expect the drastic explosion of IoT data. This data is stored freely between the widespread physical and cloud-based networks. Availability of this enormous amount of data poses a high degree of challenges for the cyber security experts.

5.3.2   Gap Between OT and IT Team

Manufacturing operations are changing and becoming more and more connected. It's unlocking new levels of productivity and profit for the industry. Since OT professionals are expected to be the experts about what makes plants run, they must change too. And, indeed, OT teams are becoming more skilled at networking and plant connectivity, but many OT professionals do not have sufficient training or education in cyber security necessary to manage the nuances and pitfalls of combatting advanced ransomware or other kinds of evolving threats. Thus, plants find themselves in an awkward position, one where OT teams depend on IT staff that may not be local to the facility to ensure security and manage connected operations and also many IT teams often aren't familiar with the complexities of plant operations and manufacturing technologies. Because of disparate system and compounded by the physical or virtual gap, OT teams often have limited visibility into IT security policies. As OT teams make control system changes, they can accidentally violate IT security policies, potentially leading to an attack or to unplanned downtime.

5.3.3   Abrasion of Network Architecture

Standards and best practices either being misunderstood or the network interfaces being poorly managed are the biggest threat and challenge to network security. It is always a good security design practice to consider communication paths as insecure, rather than knowing what the actual communication paths are. It is very common that introduction of wireless communication in a standalone fashion, ad hoc updates and individual changes to hardware and machinery, are being considered as a solid design, but at the same time we may neglect its broader network impact, by not taking its impact to the original security design into considerations. This has led to underestimating the expanded and uncontrolled or poorly controlled OT network which can make systems security weak or inadequate [22].

5.3.4   Extensive Legacy Systems

Many operational systems are being treated as legacy systems due to the static nature and long lifecycles of components being used in industrial environments. It is not unusual to have bundle of aged mechanical equipment which are still operating alongside the modern intelligent electronic devices (IEDs), whereas in many scenarios, these legacy components have crossed the boundary of isolated network segments and have now been integrated with the IT operational environment. These pervasive legacy devices may have historical vulnerabilities or weaknesses, also may not be patched up or updated with the latest security trends. This is potentially dangerous from a security perspective because it is possible that patches are not even handy due to the epoch of the equipment. Their shared centralized compute resources and communication infrastructure are generally not built to be compliant with the modern standards. Communication methods and protocols of such devices could be generations old and interoperable with only the oldest operating objects in the communications path. These components may include routers, wireless Access points, servers, firewalls, switches, remote access systems, and network management or patch management tools, and may also have operable and exploitable vulnerabilities [22].

5.3.5   Less-Secured Operational Protocols

Most of the industrial control protocols were not designed with inherent strong security requirements, for ex. serial based protocol such as Modbus. These protocols were implemented under assumption that it will be used in secure network, and hence their operational environments were not designed with secured access control. Older variants of Industrial protocols such as SCADA, suffer from common security issues such as absence of authentication procedure between communicating endpoints, no protection or security measures being applied to data traversing over the link, and insufficient control measures to properly specify recipients or no mechanism provided to avoid default broadcast approaches. These protocols may not be as critical in an isolated self-contained systems or zones, but it requires special considerations while using in public network such as a WAN. Such industrial protocols may not be originated by private firms, and their operational methods and structure are easily available publicly because these are generally published for others to implement for the sake of interoperability. Thus, it comparatively becomes simple for these protocols to be compromised and then the malicious actors may use them to hack control systems for the purpose of either reconnaissance or attack, which could lead a normal functioning systems operation to an undesirable state [22].

5.3.6   Insufficient Security Knowledge

Traditionally, it has been observed that mostly investment in the industrial operations space is primarily for connectivity and increasing the computation speed, whereas little attention is paid to its security relating to the IT counterpart. Another relevant challenge is that industrial workforce has workers of higher age while new connection technologies being introduced in OT industrial environments require up-to-date skills. For example traditional serial based legacy technologies are being replaced with wireless, Ethernet and TCP/IP based technologies for connectivity. Extensive expansion and advancement of extended communications networks, has developed the need for having an industrial controls and security measures-aware workforce, otherwise it generates an equally serious gap in security awareness. This security knowledge gap in OT could be bridged by providing education for industrial security environments, particularly in the field of electrical utility, where some regulations such as IEC 62351 and NERC CIP (CIP 004) require duly training due to its criticality. Due philosophical differences between IT and OT environments; the process of upgrading industrial networks to the latest and most secure levels is a slow process [22].

5.3.7 Cryptojacking

Cryptojacking is a process by which the computing devices are secretly used to mine cryptocurrency. Now that IoT and OT devices are potentially less visible, they provide opportunities for the cryptojacking attacks by which these devices can be exploited to mine cryptocurrency. This poses a more significant threat for the networks that use IT for managing the operations. The success of cryptojacking efforts directly affect the efficiency of the overall system and cause it to slow down [23].

5.3.8 Headless Devices

Demand for IoT devices due to its efficiency has increased, so is the price of it, which resulted in vendors engineering these devices with only the bare essentials required to ensure functionality of these devices. These devices lack the controlling, monitoring and visibility (user interface) measures, making them inaccessible to patch or update. These devices may include conspicuous vulnerabilities and provide cybercriminals a way to inject AI-assisted attacks that can compromise IoT and OT devices. Swarm technology is one of such emerging techniques, which first transforms devices to malware proxies and then provides attackers with an ability to attack networks on a large scale [23].

5.3.9 Poor Network Visibility

Lack of visibility into the components or equipment functioning within an ICS network at any given time is one of the biggest vulnerabilities in OT environments. At any given point of time, thousands or more internet-connected devices can access a network from different locations, including the devices from remote offices connected via SD (Software-defined)-WAN, a new type of OT network. The main challenge, in this case, is that security is basically dependent on the ability of cybersecurity professionals to identify each device connected on the network. These professionals are also responsible for assigning ownership and policy, grouping the devices accordingly, and then actively monitoring and tracking those devices. Data generated by internet-connected devices and their applications must also be monitored even when they are highly mobile. Manual threat analysis, detection, and mitigation becomes extremely difficult in a large scale network and could lead unauthorized devices, rogue access points to operate secretly, but remain undetected in the network [23].

As connectivity on the plant floor increases, so does complexity and so do security concerns. Every new asset you put on the network, gets added to the list of devices which require monitoring and security consideration as they are just another risk which gets added to the system. In many plants, the increasing number of assets is making it difficult to see the security context and truly understand the network at any given moment. Organizations lack the ability to identify what even just normal network activity looks like. When abnormal conditions arise, that means they have no baseline for comparison making it difficult to identify threats.

Why can't they see the network? Since industrial control system (ICS) environments consist of many types of equipment operating with many different Industrial Internet of Things (IIoT) protocols, getting a centralized view is difficult, if not impossible. The greater scope of asset types and ages presents challenges that traditional IT environments don't encounter. At the same time, the manufacturing industry is becoming an increasingly alluring target for cybercriminals. Again, because of all those assets. Each one is a potential entry point. Many manufacturers are operating with aging assets and equipment. Having originated in a time far removed from today's threats, this equipment wasn't designed to guard against complex, high-tech cyber-attacks. And this leaves the IT/OT staff to pick up the slack (Cisco).

5.3.10 Multi-Vendor Environments

When an organization adopts the information systems, it gives rise to some challenges such as requiring regular system updates, change and patch management, or updates for all lower and middle level hardware used by information systems. This can involve the following types of hardware:

- Portable systems such as computers for operating and engineering staff
- Virtual servers or SCADA monitoring servers
- Network routing devices such as industrial routers
- Network switches
- Programmable Logic Controllers (PLC)
- Field devices of various levels of autonomy with digital or analog input/output and complexity

As the digital transformation efforts in industries have drastically increased the need for IoT and OT devices, different manufactures have been quick to margin their profit in it. This resulted in a myriad variety of IoT devices from numerous vendors being installed in network infrastructure. However, this has made harder for IT teams to secure, track, and account for each device due to the large number of multi-vendor devices being used in ICS environment. Upgrading industrial control systems is more time consuming than upgrading traditional IT systems. Industrial organizations have evolved with high-level information control systems using traditional IT based technologies [24]. These organizations needed to create an additional communication and information exchange path techniques, so that integration of these new information systems with existing industrial control systems could be done smoothly. But this approach can put the entire Confidentiality-Integrity-Availability (CIA) concept, and the safety of individual processes and related hardware, at risk.

Some of the additional cyber security challenges due to multi-vendor devices have been identified as below:

1. The risk of known and unknown vulnerabilities can be increased and exploited due to hardware devices and component software being implemented by different manufactures and these devices may be implemented with minimal security considerations. This can also increase the complexity of integrating Information systems.
2. Systems configured with compatible devices in newly designed information systems may be weak or highly vulnerable, because sometimes these devices lack the measures designed to ensure compliance with CIA requirements.
3. In the event of direct tampering with the control process, the safety measured deployed in a SCADA systems, including the field level devices may not perform well. These direct tampering can be caused by remote intruders or malicious use of access rights given to enterprise staff.
4. Around 10 or 15 years ago, air gap solution between the industrial network and other networks was an easy approach to implement, but now with the ever-growing dependence of modern supply, finance, and planning processes on business analytics and connectivity has made this air-gap methods impracticable [25].

6   Potential Impact of Cyberattacks on Industrial Systems

Target device's nature of operation and the motivation of cybercriminals define the impact of cyber-attacks on the industries using ICS equipment. Systems tampering may affect the output of actor's target and produce unpredictable and unwanted results. This may also cause change in functioning of Remote Terminal Units (RTU), Programmable Logic Controllers (PLC), and other controllers. A change in controller modules and controlling devices may lead to unexpected behavior of the system and damaged equipment or facilities. This process malfunction can disable the controls over a process or provide wrong information to operations which may lead to the execution of unwanted processes or perform unnecessary actions due to misinformation. Moreover, the malicious activity, injected code or the incident itself can be made unnoticed as wrong information may be passed. Post tampered safety controls, systems may fail to follow a systematic operation of fail safes and safeguards. This may lead to putting the lives of employees, staff, and possibly even the external clients at risk. For ex. in a manufacturing plant, a cyber-attacker may change the operations of storage tanks while processing raw material such as chemical reagents, and threatens to corrupt chemical products if a ransom is not paid. Another example of system tampering is, in the transport sector, cyber attackers may invade the control systems to shut off lighting in a tunnel and intervene with the running of traffic signals. Also, in Los Angeles during a strike in 2006, few disgruntled employees had caused traffic jams over many days, just by connecting to the city's network from their homes and reprogramming only four traffic lights. A latest example of ICS attacks comes from the energy sector, in which ISIS had attempted to hack the US energy grid, as informed by FBI publicly (Cyber Attacks 2017).

The following are some of the impacts of Cyber-attacks launched on industrial systems:

1. *Material or equipment damage/endanger human life*: Altering the normal settings of processes or installations could lead to physical damage, not only in the form of material or equipment but also human lives.
2. *Profits loss*: Sometimes production systems can not directly be targeted, so altering manufacturing settings of these production systems play a vital role. This can result in the output of nun-compliant products and cost considerable amount, and lead to a substantial loss of profits.
3. *Environmental impact*: Malfunctions in systems can lead to serious environmental issues, such as opening sluice gates to release polluting products openly, would promote significant pollution to industrial sites and its surrounding areas.
4. *Data theft*: Theft of confidential industrial data, such as loss of production statistics and secrets may be beneficial for competitors and a big loss for the companies at target.
5. *Non-compliance to regulatory risk management*: High monetary penalties are fined to the industries for being non-compliant with strict regulations of security. For ex. several hundreds of thousands of euros for the military spending law (LPM) in France.
6. *Criminal liability and civil reputation*: If services such as power and water distribution are made unavailable or defective products that could endanger consumers' lives are provided to the customer, not only it could lead to lawsuits for the damage it has caused but also adulterate the company's image in its customer's eyes for the future.

Industrial attacks may have serious impact on production systems, tools and processes and sometimes even on staff or general public. Enterprise managing teams and heads need to stop assuming that their infrastructures are impenetrable and untouchable. Instead, they must acquire safety measures to safeguard the security of their systems and installations.

7   IT and OT Security State

According to a survey held by Kaspersky, in the field of OT/ICS cybersecurity market (The state of Industrial Cybersecurity [26]), 58% of the companies surveyed consider that hiring ICS cybersecurity employees with the right skills is a major challenge. They consider this as a global cybersecurity challenge. This aspect is more critical because companies are integrating their OT/ICS systems with their IT systems and IoT ecosystems, which means that they are becoming more open to the outside world. Industrial workforce may not be fully aware of all security measures, as may be an IT team. Thus, to have a secured ICS space, IT department also needs to be involved throughout the entire implementation process of the ICS, rather than retrospectively involving them just after a cyber-attack occurs. The current problem is that the department set to benefit the most from the implementation of the new technology often focuses solely on deployment to see the results faster. However, this is when oversights occur and vulnerabilities materialize. For organizations to start understanding the problem with OT/ICS security, they will need to begin with looking closely at their network and involving IT in the conversation.

7.1   OT Threats Stats

According to Skybix Security's latest Vulnerability and threat trends report, there is an increased risk to the growing attack surface, typically brought about by the likes of the industrial internet of things (IIoT) and OT networks [27]. Attacks on OT have increased by 10% between 2017 and 2018. Taiwanese Semiconductor Manufacturing Co Ltd (TSMC), a chipmaker company was hit by a mutated WannaCry outbreak in 2018. It was a prime example of how a cybercriminal tool such as ransomware can create the perfect cyber-attack storm, wreaking havoc on a network and a company's bottom line. Stuxnet also caused similar damage in 2010. With the internet of things (IoT) technology, operational technology is a target because of its wide use and, as with IoT devices; OT devices are yet another endpoint. Hackers can use these devices to gain access to an otherwise secure and often valuable network and hamper it.

7.2   Looping in the IT Departments

An industry should first develop some kind of security framework. A lot of resources with IT skills are available now, but they lack experience in dealing with security breaches and may don't have security processes knowledge. This poses a lot of challenges for an industry. Traditional security components such as firewalls cannot simply manage the typical traffic produced by OT sensors and control these

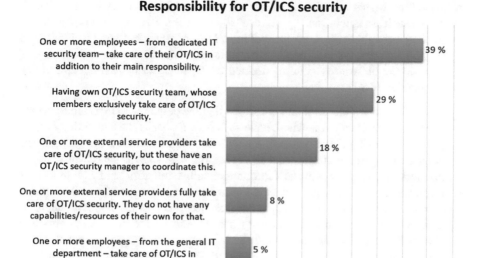

Fig. 7.9 Distribution of ICS security responsibilities with different departments [26]

devices. This makes IT department especially vital in remaining secured. Currently, Industrial production and resources department handle the responsibility for OT devices, but security of these devices from cyber threats should be handled by IT team. One of the main reasons for doing this is that these devices are connected to the internet. Efforts to secure industrial control systems (ICS) somewhere lags behind with the pace, as connectivity in the IIoT continues to accelerate. Despite these growing security concerns, internet-connected devices increasingly continue to get integrated with traditionally air-gapped OT because they improve operational processes, reduce costs and minimize downtime. But industrial organizations would remain soft targets for threat actors until security becomes a priority. Following bar graph shows the distribution of ICS security responsibilities with IT departments.

The graph in Fig. 7.9 shows that most of the organizations depend on IT people or department, making IT people necessarily to be looped in all the processes being carried out at Industrial sites. OT solutions highly depend on IT infrastructure and services, which increases the overlap of skills for managing the both OT solutions and IT services, and further justifies the need for having greater IT involvement. From the outset, employees should be duly educated and provided knowledge on security best practices just as with any digital transformation project, everything from regularly changing passwords, to being able to spot a phishing email. Securing multiple points of vulnerability has always been a major challenge for businesses and whether it's a company laptop, a phone, or a smart temperature gauge in a fish tank in an individual's home, the solution to securing different devices is never one-size-fits-all, it differs from device by device. Last year, the state of California passed a law setting higher security standards for net-connected devices making default password such as "admin" and "password" illegal to use. This same exemplar should be applied throughout the implementation roll-out of any operational technologies. Such best security policies need to be followed when it comes to securing IT devices. Some of security patterns defined by Open Security Architecture which can be applied ICS networks:

- Access Control: This mechanism assures that the person who is trying to access a system or application is who he/she says it is. It checks the authenticity of the person by making them to submit a unique identifier, such as a user ID, and the corresponding authenticating and secret information, such as a password.
- Network Security: It protects the confidentiality, integrity, and availability of information systems when connected to network, from external or even internal threats using a variety of security control devices, such as DMZ and firewalls.
- Log Management: This is a security control and let the critical systems and applications to generate and record the important security related events, these events can later be analyzed to assist in identifying threats to system and troubleshooting network or system related issues, and also help industries to be compliant with regulatory requirements.
- Remote Access: This lets users and vendors to seek access to the ICS environment for remote maintenance and support. This remote connection must secured with connection to private network and updated antivirus applications, also must not be permitted to connect to unwanted sites [28].

Apart from these measures, security awareness programs for staff, contractors and vendors with adequate and required access must be held. Security audits and assessments of control systems and their networks, including penetration tests, are also important and highly recommended in all sectors but less often implemented. Other technology-oriented measures should also be considered such as network monitoring, log analytics, IoT device behaviors analysis and vulnerability scanning techniques to make sure systems and applications are up to date, so that the known problems are fixed with this updates and patches. Vulnerability scans should be continuously performed without any fail, and should at least be done after every vulnerability database update. These measures can be implemented, and security related attacks can be avoided with the help of big data and Artificial Intelligence as mentioned in the beginning of this book chapter. In the future, we can expect more devices to become connected to the internet; and with this, IT teams will increasingly apply machine learning and artificial intelligence to keep them secure. Any changes in the implementation of OT must be shared with IT team. Also, any employees who share the responsibility of OT must adhere to the security policies and should be educated on basic security protocol. As the roll-out of OT continues to gather pace, the channel must do all that it can when it comes to helping to educate its customers and partners. In this way, educating every employee and department form the ground level on staying OT secure. In coming sections, we will discuss about how IT team can make use of big data and AI to prevent ICS cyber threats in detail in the next section.

8 Leveraging Big Data and Artificial Intelligence for Security

Experiencing increased number of IoT devices, the main challenge in Industrial environment originates from the vast amount of information being generated from these devices. In traditional systems, information was collected periodically like on monthly basis. Modern industrial systems present a new framework, in which information about different matters is gathered by all the interconnected nodes, at very frequent basis. For example, in smart grid infrastructure, devices gather information not only about consumption of the power but also other information such as peak loads, real-time prices, power quality issues, network status, etc. In this regard, one of the main challenges for computational intelligence is that managing such a huge amount of information intelligently. This is because valuable conclusions and inferences can be extracted from this data, to support the decision making processes. Complex Event Processing (CEP) techniques can be used to address this challenge effectively. The collection of information over the network of extensive logs is performed through a distributed file system (DFS). This is basically designed to safeguard the real-time requirements of industrial control systems and networks. Data analytics through big data computing algorithms can help in achieve this goal of finding conclusions. These analytics are designed with knowledge discovery from big data, predictive analytics, and descriptive statistics based on inference and probability theory. Distributed algorithms for very large graphs and matrices also help in deriving these analytics. Local cluster of computers runs these computing algorithms on cloud computing technique (Fig. 7.10).

Raw data plays no significant role unless it analyzed and is converted into knowledge. Then the knowledge extracted from data is beneficial for decision-makers while taking major decisions regarding architecture of the ICS network. With a Big

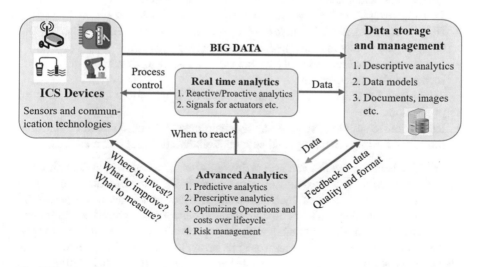

Fig. 7.10 Big data approach for ICS

Data point of view, this can lead to development of software-based analytics and decision tools which are suitable for industrial operations and management. Using these solutions, companies can observe the quantities of data they collect and then drive desirable improvements to processes and products. The foundation of any Big Data architecture is the data historian and infrastructure to feed real-time data to this historian. Big Data architecture and its implementation must ensure that the communication paths used by sensors are secured and sophisticated enough to allow forensic investigations for any security related incidents. Big Data architecture is determined by functional and network unit. More the information-based resources used, more the data will be produced and provide more advantages to an enterprise.

8.1   Advantages of Big Data

Big data solutions indicates the ability to aggregate disparate sources of data, disparate sources could be multi-vendor devices. This solution also provides ability to analyze this collected data to generate relevant patterns. End users can refer these patterns to make better decisions. This can also help in defining new baseline for competition and growth that creates a remarkable value for the world economy. Gathering information from multiple remote sites, systems, and sensors can be a challenge in designing big data solution. This implementation also requires considerable cost, engineering expertise, and time.

Big Data can be beneficial in achieving below goals:

- Information is made more transparent by providing visualization ability to the end users to visualize the insights that would not have been visible
- Quality and performance of the processes are increased
- Discover insights and utilize refined analytics to minimize risks
- Helps companies in taking investment decisions by implementing theories and analyzing its results in controlled experimental environments
- Increased automation and analytics help with real-time operations
- Increased risk management
- Minimized downtime also can result in 15% staffing reductions and 5% increased production.
- Revolutionize solutions such as supply chain management, demand forecasting, integrated business planning, and supplier collaboration and risk analytics.

Machine learning models can utilize this real-time data and help in detecting any unfamiliar activity. This provides owners and auditors with detection capabilities and visibility in any kind of incidents such as cyber-attack or even operational malfunction event. Every packet flowing through network is captured and examined by Capture and analysis. After analyzing every packet, a normal traffic patterns can be discovered, and any deviations from this normal traffic can be detected. There also exist the security challenges associated with Big Data, and once identified must be mitigated. These security challenges can be resolved by using security measures

Fig. 7.11 Distribution of organizations acquiring cloud services (source: [26])

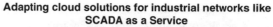

Adapting cloud solutions for industrial networks like SCADA as a Service

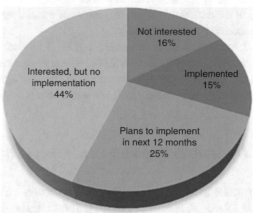

for automated data transfers, security solutions to keep up with the continuous evolution of non-relational database and ensuring data validation for trust i.e. origin and accuracy of the data. The following pie chart shows distribution of organizations acquiring cloud solutions for Industrial networks (Fig. 7.11).

8.2 Cloud and Edge Computing for Remote Operations

Both raw and processed data drive the implementation of all business processes and there is a need to compute this data as close to where the data originates as possible. Edge computing provides local processing of the data collected from different IoTs. This offers an opportunity for process industries to improve the end-to-end operational integrity for real-time remote operations [29]. The goal of remote operations is to avoid asset related issues and keep workers safe while persistently abide by industry, environmental, and other government regulations. Operating cost and downtime can be reduced by monitoring and controlling the assets at the edge, even it becomes feasible to dispatch repairs and replace equipment components before they fail.

8.3 Ability to Take Local Action

Remote operations, even in case of isolated locations, must be prepared and capable of taking local actions as necessary. An instant value secured from the data first processed at the edge, triggers IT/OT network managers to move edge data to the cloud. Data moved from edge to cloud can be widely accessed. It also provides the advantage of other integration services such as performing big data analytics to serve many applications. Edge computing can help remote sites to effectively work upon the data that matters to a location's real time situation and optimize the process based on the collected data.

Cloud techniques can also provide additional value in terms of leveraging a way to effectively train the machine learning algorithms which we deploy at the edge. Machines and systems can learn and become optimized from what is learned from other edge data, these machines and systems could be located at remote sites.

8.4   AI and Automation to Manage Cyber Security Threats

Artificial intelligence (AI) was first discovered in the late 1950s by Marvin Minsky. It is a method, tool or technique that imitates cognitive tasks that are associated with the human mind. Cognitive tasks could be learning, planning, problem solving, or reasoning. The importance of AI in cyber security can be related in two opposing directions. First side focuses that AI-controlled systems such as smart cities or smart grid, could also be a potential targets for cyber-attacks, this is because of their growing role in controlling complex and vital systems. On the flip side, second direction focuses that AI is a set of tools that can help identify cyber risk and cyber breaches.

Rapid growth in the number of IoT devices develops the need for a new security and data-processing architecture. Machines have much higher computational abilities than humans. They can process through the massive amount of data and use it to derive better decisions. AI can:

- Help in finding patterns, associations, and trends
- Disclose inefficiencies
- Become better by learning
- Execute plans
- Forecast future outcomes based on the historical trends
- Advise fact-based decisions
- Improve and automate complex analytical tasks
      Look at data in real-time, adjusting its behavior with minimal need for supervision

Machine learning is a type of AI that learns without being explicitly programmed. It allows computer processes to calibrate when exposed to new data. This is similar to data mining where databases are inspected by humans to produce new insight. Artificial intelligence (AI) and machine learning (ML) algorithms can be used to extract actionable insights from the immense amount of IoT data. These algorithms could be deployed at the edge such as flagging up and transmitting anomalous data patterns, or at the core such as analyzing medium or long-term trends. IoT data may come in great volumes, varieties and velocities, but the broad goal is to use data mining and AI/ML algorithms to discover patterns and generate insights in the most efficient manner possible.

IT professional and engineers have started to re-implement their security measures to include AI for integrating and automating security fabrics. This would secure IoT and OT devices, and also mitigate the common threats targeting them [23]. Artificial intelligence will eventually be used by every industry in the world. Here are a few ways that use AI to transform certain industries:

1. *Comprehensive Device Visibility over network*: AI can be integrated with network access module. Cyber security professional with the help of AI-assisted network access control, can have clear picture about every device connected to the network or accessing it at any point of time. Each device can be segmented, tracked, appropriately inventoried and secured with AI provided granular device visibility at machine speeds.
2. *Unified Threat Analysis and Threat hunting*: Due to digital transformation, organizations continuously put efforts in expanding their networks, both cloud based and physically connected devices. It becomes difficult for them to carry out threat analysis and mitigation activities for the increased network size, at a same rate as to keep up with the pace of modern cyber threats. AI provides a solution to this problem, by which latest threat analysis data can be collected by the IT team. AI would also help in identifying the vulnerabilities those exist within the ICS networks, and deploy those security solutions to mitigate the chances of having cyber-attacks. AI prediction technology makes itself intelligent by going through the millions of files and attack history, and learns from it. AI-based threat detection solutions prevent and protect network against future attacks. AI will repetitively walk through all the system data in search of recurring patterns, anomalous behavior and other outliers to present threat hunters for further investigation. SIEM utilizes AI to analyze network factors such as data, net flow, proxy, DNS, packets. User behavior analytics product will apply machine learning on user data to detect malware.
3. *Incident analysis and Investigation*: In the event of attack, AI will increasingly answer what happened to the asset (the attack's impact), who the attackers were, what were the past sequence in the attack chain on asset, what was attack's blast radius (including which other assets were part of the attack), and who was patient zero (where the attack originated). AI will mine past alerts, network and asset information, security logs and other relevant data to uncover clusters, associations and patterns to present human investigators in a concise manner.
4. *Automated Threat Anticipation*: A network breach can happen in just a fraction of seconds. The longer a network breach remains unnoticed or unattended, the more the damage can be spread. This is very significant across the healthcare, financial services, and critical infrastructure sectors because all required systems in these sectors need to be operational and available at all time. If these sectors are successfully attacked then it can cost excessive amount of money and even the lives of patients, citizens, or employees. Under these infrastructures, IoT and OT containment procedures can be automated by Artificial intelligence, which

can properly segment the infected devices or take such devices offline before they get a chance to spread affection to additional areas throughout the network.

5. *Incident Response*: AI techniques such as knowledge engineering and course based reasoning will be used to create playbooks that guide incident responders on what to do in the event of an incident. AI will review previous incidents and codified knowledge from experts, and it will continuously modify or create new branches in the main playbook as it learns from the new incidents.

6. *Reduced Energy Cost*: Companies in the energy sector can adopt AI intelligence to reduce operational costs and mitigate issues by increasing automation, optimizing asset management, improving operational performance, identifying efficiencies, and decreasing downtime.

For example, DeepMind is a technology based company. It was acquired by Google in 2014. It uses machine learning to solve everyday problems such as reducing energy usage. Then Google data centers also applied DeepMind's machine learning algorithms. As a result Google managed to reduce the amount of energy they consume for cooling, by up to 40%. These algorithms were designed to deal with complex data as every data center followed a unique architecture and environment. It required to build a custom-tuned model which is once used for one system may not be applicable to another. Hence, a common intelligence framework was required to have understanding of the data center's interactions andhistorical data from thousands of sensors within the data center such as power, temperatures, speed, pump, set points, etc. are collected and used it to train an orchestra of deep neural networks. With machine learning application to the problem, DeepMind researchers could significantly ameliorate the system's utility in less time.

8.5 Artificial Intelligence and Computational Intelligence for ICS

Different Artificial and Computational techniques which can be applied to different features of ICS are shown in Fig. 7.12. Managing a massive amount of data intelligently and extracting inferences from this vast information to better support the decision making process are done by Complex Event Processing (CEP) techniques. These techniques tend to look for relevant patterns by event filtering. These filtered events must logically-so powered that can provide clear understanding of on-going scenarios. CEP systems need to support the understanding of a process semantically, possibly by using the approaches of Qualitative Reasoning. For example, Smart Grid technologies, where these complex reasoning systems can be used to enhance the grid technologies. These systems are large-scale knowledge-based systems of common sense such as Scone, Cyc, or ConceptNet [30], which can provide advanced ability to help and power supervisory, control, and data acquisition process of SCADA systems. There also exists the problem of supplying the right amount of resources, at the right time and the right location. Active Demand Management tool

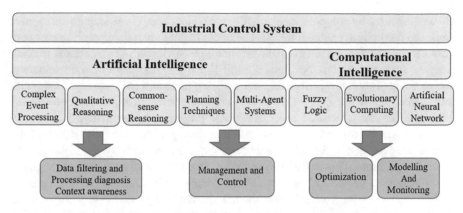

Fig. 7.12 Artificial intelligence and computational intelligence techniques

can assist in solving the allocating problems of resources which involves some sort of load balancing methods, and AI planning and knowledge-based techniques can contribute in this regard with great improvements. ICS can use the capabilities of AI not just to tackle the need for Information management, whereas, on the flip side, AI can also help ICS in dealing with several unpredictable and uncertain scenarios. For ex., ANN, the Active Network Management technology can intelligently automate the tasks such as fault detection, take a proper decision during fault occurred situation, and self-healing from these faults. Communication infrastructure is the primary requirement of this technology so that it can support SCADA systems, and intelligent distributed systems can play an important role in establishing such communication infrastructure. Distributed systems can help through communication approaches, algorithms, and consistent and replication (redundant data for disaster) techniques. Intelligent distributed systems such as Multi-Agent Systems (MAS) can assist in finding a suitable field of application in the ICS environment due to the heterogeneous essence of the problem.

Computational techniques such as Fuzzy logic or ANN can be used to solve dynamic and stochastic natured problems. Computational Intelligence techniques and AI are two main approaches while dealing with unpredictable or uncertain scenarios. Bothe approaches can be looked at as equivalent, but differ in a way they approach to solve a complex problem. Artificial intelligence technique uses some sort of goal-oriented approach, where finding association between the problems to be solved and the actions that can help in getting to the desired output can be a great help. This approach for complex problems is not much suitable for stochastic situations though. Such dynamic situations can be better resolved by computational intelligence techniques and approaches such as fuzzy logic, evolutionary computation, or artificial neural networks [31]. All these approaches focus on solutions rather than providing knowledge having a set of actions attached with a common goal. Traditional artificial intelligence techniques may find difficulties when several goals to be accomplished, are in conflict with each other. In contrary, such scenarios can be well-handled by computational intelligence techniques. These techniques support enriched methods to enable intelligent behavior under uncertain circumstances; they provide ability to anticipate germane information which can help in decision making support systems. ANNs, Artificial Neural Networks, comprise of interconnected nodes which are nothing but multiple processing units and each are associated with two values i.e. a weight and an input. ANNs are used in replication process of biological neural systems. Rather than being programmed explicitly, these neural networks can be trained to observe different data patterns. Initially, data and the targets are provided to the neural networks, making them to learn the identification of certain patterns. This technique requires a large amount of input data, enough for deriving correct behavioral patterns. Most relevant applications of ANN techniques is in energy systems such as while modeling solar energy and generating heat-up response, monitoring voltage stability, creating adaptive critic design, and predicting of the global solar irradiance or even for security issues.

8.6   Contribution of Intelligent Systems to Cyber Security

Two very familiar classes of AI techniques are knowledge-based systems and machine learning methods that contain valuable tools, which can be used cyber security. In knowledge-based systems, which are also referred to as expert systems, a massive amount of expert's knowledge is loaded to the computer memory [32]. In these systems, the learning part i.e. reasoning related to the knowledge is accounted by a programmed logics such as if-then or inference logic rules. Anti-span and antivirus software packages use implementations of expert systems in cyber security. In this regard, knowledge is obtained through a large amount of transactions methods that apply protocols, network traffic (e.g., VoIP, or email), and I/O interactions with operating system. All these parameters are analyzed systematically to protect systems from cyber breaches.

Machine-learning techniques are usually applied to the methods where learning factor is achieved by the computers themselves, usually by extracting germane and relevant patterns from the information. These methods are used in deriving predictions or smart recommendations, such as recommending users to buy certain products based on their historical search items. ML algorithms are matured automatically through experience with the data and give systems the ability to learn without being programmed explicitly. Cyber-security tasks such as spam filtering, monitoring, risk analysis, zero-day attack identification can be addressed by machine learning algorithms. Machine-learning methods are divided into two main classes and a hybrid of these two classes of ML methods. First class is unsupervised learning methods [33], where untagged data samples are uploaded to the system, to find relevant patterns. Some of the applications of unsupervised methods include anomaly detection in communication protocols [34], Fraud detection in financial systems, and identifying potential risk of software packages. These methods use anomaly detection and clustering technique to identify both positive and negative deviations from the expected behavior, which are then mapped into actions. For ex. blacklisted websites, risk assessment of software packages, or blocking suspicious users from internet connections.

The second class of machine-learning methods is supervised learning. In this class, tagged data samples (attached with desired output) are injected to the system, where it maps inputs to the correct outputs. For example, while generating a software's risk score in cyber security domain, descriptive features of software such as such as the communication paths, time, and the type of interaction with OS, etc. are taken into account and tagged as risky or non-risky. Then systems learn to predict high-risk software in advance [35]. Methods consisting neural networks with multiple processing levels form Deep- learning models, which are highly complex models. As discussed previously about ANNs, which require a large amount of data to derive certain patterns, in the same way data modelling methods also require a massive amount of data and high-speed processing units. These requirements can be made available with the development of big-data and cloud technologies. Deep- learning models, capable of addressing supervised learning methods and are found successful in signal processing, where a lot of tagged data is available. These techniques are also used for image processing, which provides computer vision, and for speech recognition, which can help in providing correct measure for user authorization. Deep learning is a type of machine learning and a central branch of AI, which can serve as an important tool in the cyber security. Deep leaning is useful in analytics activities, which require complex modeling of large data, often non-linear and establishing relations between inputs and outputs [36].

Machine learning and artificial intelligence are being applied increasingly in the energy sector in three essentially distinct areas. One is for predictive purposes such as weather forecasting, using past and current datasets to predict future patterns on varying time scales. Another is for management applications such as energy efficiency and demand response. The third, of a more detective nature, is for monitoring of data streams to pick out variances from determined 'normals' as indicative of a current or emerging problem. One application where this is being applied is asset monitoring and preventive maintenance. Another, which is attracting growing interest in cybersecurity, with one novel solution from Israeli company CyActive—subsequently acquired by PayPal—incorporating bio-mimicry to generate future malwares which can then be guarded against [37].

Andrew Tsonchev, Director of Technology at Darktrace says "Darktrace's machine learning and artificial intelligence-based solution is designed to cut through the challenges as well as to better support a disaster recovery". Darktrace considers the OT security problems as its priority and resolves those problems by extensive use of AI to identify and counteract cyber threats in critical infrastructure in real time [38]. Darktrace's Industrial Immune System, enriched by machine learning techniques, undertakes the normal 'pattern of life' for every device and ensures that cyber-attacks across OT and IT are stopped before they escalate into a crisis [23].

9   Impediments to Applying AI to Cyber Security

Automation delivers remarkable value to organizations in terms of carrying out repetitive and boring tasks such as analyzing large data samples, which usually are considered to waste valuable time and result in unengaged and unhappy employees. Nonetheless, Scientists opine that there should be some regulatory charges, maybe applied at the national and international level due to the impediments that might arise and need to be resolved while applying AI to solve cyber security issues. Some of such impediments have been identified and discussed as following:

1. Some of the challenges for OT and IT security protection in utilities include the mix of technologies of different ages or protocols, both open and proprietary, the large number of endpoints and the siloed approach to protection, having separate OT and IT security teams and those teams not always solely dedicated to security. Moreover, the protections must be of the same level, indicating that OT and IT is a complex task to protect technologically, and requires the right people in the right places.
2. Leading global companies are investing large amount of monetary values and resources in developing AI models for new applications, such as Google's self-driving cars, Apple's Siri, and Facebook's automated image tagging. Although, these models have delivered excellent results in accomplishing some specific tasks, its performance is not always assured, especially in non-continuity cases. Moreover, sometimes output from these models is by misunderstood cyber security analysts (Chief Information Officer) and decision makers because these models lack descriptive interpretation of the results.
3. False ICS Anomaly Detection: Power generation, substation and electric grid operators and many other critical infrastructure sectors typically use equipment from a heterogeneous assortment of vendors. This equipment runs thousands of real-time processes generating a huge volume of data. Increasing the interconnectedness and digitization of these systems is a pillar of improved operational efficiencies; however, it isn't risk free. Analyzing and monitoring this data to detect anomalies that might be caused by a cyber-attack is akin to searching for a needle, in thousands or even millions of haystacks. An ideal system should have a 100% detection rate with 0% false alarms. Organizations need to find a way to detect anomalies in their ICS environment as a foundation for reliable and resilient power delivery [39].
4. Many electric utilities have hundreds or even thousands of substations and they are critical for realizing the efficiency and adaptability vision of the smart grid. With the smart grid, information about consumption and operations needs to be sent back to a central point for analysis by energy management systems and substation automation systems, requiring two-way communication of data. To facilitate this, the communications networks of substations are being retooled to facilitate connectivity with multiple systems. The preferred networking technolo-

gies are based on Ethernet and TCP/IP, and adhere to the IEC 61850 standards. Modern substation systems need to support interoperability and deliver high reliability and availability. They also need to do this while addressing increasing concerns about cyber security [39].

5. Lack of knowledge, confidence: According to a survey, more than 25% of the companies surveyed informed that they did not have any current investment plans for Big Data and IoT, whereas some industries opined that they did not have justified knowledge to invest the costs in leveraging this technology. Over half of the companies cited that their organization is running fine without big data and cloud approach and they already have reliable and cost-effective measures and systems to ensure success and safety. Others reported that they lacked enough time, resources, and workforce. A challenge in exhausting the advantages provided with Big Data is not deploying a proper visualization tool which can capture all the available data to go through the iterative and multi-structured discovery methods that uncover information.

6. Passive monitoring devices solve an important part of the SCADA (supervisory control and data acquisition) security problem by automatically identifying industrial assets and providing comprehensive, real-time cyber security and visibility of industrial control networks. They should provide optimal performance while monitoring thousands of substations and assets across low bandwidth networks. However, delivering this functionality requires overcoming significant technical challenges. For starters, electric power generation systems and grids are characterized by large a geographic area, which similarly means a substantial amount of infrastructure. Asset tracking, including their real-time status, results in large volumes of data that needs to be mined to identify anomalous incidents. High-Performance Computing (HPC) is critical for on-line, scalable and distributed intrusion detection.

Increasing cyber threats, management fears, and government policies are driving using AI and ML techniques to improve the resiliency of their systems, with enhancements to their ICS cyber security programs. Five years ago, it was very difficult to have real-time visibility and cyber security of industrial control networks, which has changed now. The scale and complexity inherent in substation and power grid systems make identifying anomalous and harmful incidents complex, but that doesn't mean they can't be found. Just like the right equipment will eventually find the needle in the haystack, it is now possible to have comprehensive ICS cyber security that addresses the advancing threat environment in a manner that reduces cyber risks while improving operational excellence and reliability.

10 Case Study

10.1 An Intelligent System to Detect Unauthorized Internet of Things Devices

An AI-powered intelligent system is capable of detecting unauthorized and suspicious IoT devices. These systems can detect devices not only which are part of the ICS but also which are not part of the organizations. It maintains a white list of trustworthy IoT devices and provides a way to detect unauthorized IoT devices connected to their networks. Supervised machine-learning algorithms are applied in these systems to monitor the network traffic and precisely identify the IoT devices which are listed on the approved white list and will raise a security alert on finding any device that is not listed on the white list or found suspicious. The activity of identifying devices on network or within the organization can be looked at as a multiclass classification problem, in which two sets, one having the list of authorized devices D, typically a white list, and another structured set consists of traffic data, are mapped. Second set also has the assumption that each device Di in the set D has labeled dataset to represent its behavior. Then, the intelligent system observes the behavior of all the authorized devices on the white list, particularly with supervised learning method. It then induces a classifier C for unlabeled network traffic data post identifying a device on new stream. This intelligent system demonstrates how machine-learning and AI methods can be used for IoT security to solve cyber security threats.

10.2 ODIX Kiosk Solution

Use Case: Critical Infrastructure (Energy) US Power Plant

Challenge: US Power Plant's highly-secure critical infrastructure network is air-gapped, completely blocking access to external files, except via removable media. Yet one of the most severe threats to any organization is files inserted via removable media like USB drives, CDs, DVDs, and portable hard disks—and malware attacks take advantage of this vulnerability.

Solution: US Power Plant implemented the ODIX Kiosk solution. Ideal for critical infrastructure organizations with air-gapped networks, the ODIX Kiosk does not need to be connected to the organizational network. This configuration makes ODIX Kiosk a safe and secure solution for inserting files into such networks (Fig. 7.13).

After scanning files from removable media, the ODIX Kiosk stores them on a writable DVD. Then, the clean files can be safely inserted into the air-gapped system. A secure ICS/SCADA network Deployment assists the customer to meet NERC-SIP and NIST 800-53 requirements.

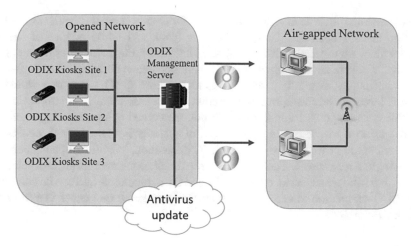

Fig. 7.13 ODIX Kiosks—ICS/SCADA network diagram (air gap) (source: Odix)

10.3   Real-World Example

At the last Black Hat Europe conference, security research firm CyberX demonstrated how data exfiltration was possible from a supposedly air-gapped ICS network. By delivering a payload of specific ladder logic code into Programmable Logic Controllers, the attack was programmed to send out copies of data through encoded radio signals which can be received by AM radios and analyzed by special-purpose software. As the communication channel is outside the TCP/IP stack, there is no encryption to safeguard the data once it's captured.

How does AI respond to this threat? In this case, Machine Learning can be used to craft an algorithm which establishes a "normal" state and monitors traffic and configurations to compare against that state. This baseline can include network traffic, equipment settings, and even the source code of PLCs. With its continuous heartbeat checks, the algorithm can detect when the system deviates from the baseline and immediately alert security staff of the change.

Another real-world example comes very recently from the ransomware attack on Atlanta's municipal infrastructure, which involved encrypting city files, blocking the city from processing court cases and warrants, and blocking access to online services. This is just the latest in a string of attacks on American cities. Previously, hackers gained access to Dallas's tornado warning system and set off sirens in the middle of the night. In the case of Atlanta, an AI cyber security layer would have been able to spot irregularities in system access and lockdown channels before the hackers could manipulate the permissions [40].

Where does AI fit into your existing ICS security program? You already have the ICS equipment sectioned off on its own VLAN(s), firewalled, monitored, and protected by IDS/IPS, SIEMs, and other security tools. Where does it make sense to insert AI/ML into the equation? The biggest advantage of implanting an AI solution is its real-time response and orchestration. AI tools don't need to wait for security staff to make a decision. They don't see a black and white picture of firewall rules which often miss malware traffic flying under the radar, masquerading as "normal" network signals. Machine algorithms can detect abnormal data exchanges and immediately respond to the threat, long before a SOC resource would be alerted. Some AI offerings can even monitor devices that don't communicate over TCP/IP, creating powerful visibility into non-networked equipment. A particularly interesting tool to protect industrial control systems is Cyberbit's ScadaShield, a layered solution to provide full-stack ICS detection, visibility, smart analytics, forensics, and response. ScadaShield performs continuous monitoring and detection across the entire attack surface for both IT and OT components and can be combined with SOC automation to trigger workflows that accelerate root cause identification and mitigation [40].

11   Conclusion

This Perspective explores that digital transformation efforts of organizations have sparked a trend towards IoT and OT adoption. Organizations in all sort of industries across the world continue to augment their on-going transformation efforts by adopting IoT and OT devices in great number. Nevertheless, cybercriminals are also into the competition and they are simultaneously expanding their capabilities to leverage new development and exploitation techniques to launch attacks faster and more sophisticated ways. Our focus was on highlighting the potential vulnerabilities and inequities that the use of IoT devices imposes on ICS environment in terms of security, and also explored that how AI and big data together can play a significant role in combating the security challenges associated with ICS. In our exploration of the security challenges, we identified that dealing with large amount of data generated by ICS devices, poor network architecture and protocols, and its visibility and lack of security knowledge are the major concerns which may provide attacker with an opportunity to exploit the smooth functioning of ICS industries, where Cyber security is a necessary component in this digital age.

In order to protect the triumph of digital transformation efforts of organizations, cyber security personnel should accept this challenge and stay ahead in game in to order to protect the new digital economy that driving this digital transformation. Cyber security actors can now adopt AI-assisted cyber security solutions that provide the efficient detection and response capabilities so that they keep pace with their competitors i.e. modern cybercriminals. With advancement in cutting edge technologies such as big data, cloud and AI, new vulnerabilities and exploits could easily be segmented, identified, and analyzed to avoid further attacks. Incident response systems could also be made more efficient by leveraging these techniques. These response systems must be able to identify the entry point of an attack, stop the attack as soon as it is identified, and patch the vulnerabilities so that similar attack should not occur in future. The application of artificial intelligence (AI) via the implementation of machine learning (ML) can help response systems to function in this expected way, when any system is attacked. This method is the fastest growing area of cyber security. ML-enhanced products produce results faster and more accurately than can be achieved by human operators; and this can result in cost savings through the need for fewer analyst employees. Artificial Intelligence can add values to the ICS security and with the advancements in AI, we can mitigate the problems being faced.

References

1. H. Karimipour, A. Dehghantanha, R.M. Parizi, R. Choo, H. Leung, A deep and scalable unsupervised machine learning system for cyber-attack detection in large-scale smart grids. IEEE Access **7**, 80778 (2019)
2. J. Sakhnini, A. Dehghantanha, H. Karimipour, Smart grid cyber attacks detection using supervised learning and heuristic feature selection, in *IEEE International Conference on Smart Energy Grid Engineering (SEGE)*, Oshawa, Canada (2019), pp. 1–5
3. A. Almalawi, X. Yu, Z. Tari, A. Fahad, I. Khalil, An unsupervised anomaly-based detection approach for integrity attacks on SCADA systems. Comput. Secur. **46**, 94–110 (2014)
4. H. Karimipour, V. Dinavahi, Accelerated parallel WLS state estimation for large-scale power systems on GPU, in *IEEE North American Power Symposium (NAPS)*, Manhatan, USA (2013), pp. 1–6
5. H. Karimipour, V. Dinavahi, Robust massively parallel dynamic state estimation of power systems against cyber-attack. IEEE Access **6**, 2984–2995 (2017)
6. H.M. Ruzbahani, A. Rahimnejad, H. Karimipour, Smart households demand response management with micro grid, in *IEEE Innovative Smart Grid Technologies (ISGT 2019)*, Washington, DC (2019), pp. 1–5
7. F. Ghalavand, B.M. Alizadeh, H. Karimipour, Micro grid islanding detection based on mathematical morphology. J. Energy **11**(10), 456–477 (2018)
8. S. Geris, H. Karimipour, A feature selection-based approach for joint cyber-attack detection and state estimation, in *IEEE International Conference on Smart Energy Grid Engineering (SEGE)*, Oshawa, Canada (2019), pp. 1–5
9. S. Vishwanath, Industrial control systems, PWC, India
10. L.D. Xu, E.L. Xu, L. Li, Industry 4.0: state of the art and future trends. Int. J. Prod. Res. **56**(8), 2941–2962 (2018)
11. E. Modiri, A. Azmoodeh, A. Dehghantanha, H. Karimipour, Fuzzy pattern tree for edge attack detection and categorization. J. Syst. Archit. **9**, 1–15 (2018)
12. H. Karimipour, S. Geris, A. Dehghantanha, H. Leung, Intelligent anomaly detection for large-scale smart grids, in *IEEE CCECE*, Edmonton, Canada (2019), pp. 1–4
13. M. Conti, A. Dehghantanha, K. Franke, S. Watson, Internet of things security and forensics: challenges and opportunities. **78**, 544–546 (2018)
14. S. Arun, in *IoT for oil & gas - the power of big data and ML (Cloud Next '18)*, VP data science and analytics (BHGE, 2018)
15. H. Karimipour, V. Dinavahi, On false data injection attack against dynamic state estimation on smart power grids, in *IEEE International Conference on Smart Energy Grid Engineering*, Oshawa, Canada (2017), pp. 1–7
16. M.R. Begli, F. Derakhshan, H. Karimipour, A layered intrusion detection system for critical infrastructure using machine learning, in *IEEE International Conference on Smart Energy Grid Engineering (SEGE)*, Oshawa, Canada (2019), pp. 1–5

17. S. Mohammadi, H. Mirvaziri, M.G. Ahsaee, H. Karimipour, Cyber intrusion detection by combined feature selection algorithm. J. Inf. Secur. Appl. **44**, 80–88 (2018)
18. K. Stouffer, V. Pillitteri, S. Lightman, M. Abrams, A. Hahn, Guide to industrial control systems (ICS) security, Revision 2, National Institute of Standards and Technology, May 2015
19. D. Hanes, G. Salgueiro, P. Grossetete, R. Barton, J. Henry, *IoT Fundamentals: Networking Technologies, Protocols, and Use Cases for the Internet of Things* (Cisco Press, Indianapolis, 2017)
20. W. Knowles, D. Princea, D. Hutchison, J.F.P. Dissob, K. Jonesb, A survey of cyber security management in industrial control systems. Int. J. Crit. Infrastruct. Prot. **9**, 52 (2015)
21. Sentryo, ICS architecture: everything you must know, Apr 2015
22. R. Barton, P. Grossetete, D. Hanes, J. Henry, G. Salgueiro, Securing IoT, Oct 2017
23. A. Lakhani, The role of artificial intelligence in IoT and OT security, Oct 2018
24. C. Shen, C. Liu, H. Tan, Z. Wang, D. Xu, X. Su, Hybrid-augmented device fingerprinting for intrusion detection in industrial control system networks. IEEE Wirel. Commun. **25**(6), 26–31 (2018)
25. Kaspersky lab ICS CERT, Threat landscape for industrial automation systems in the second half of 2016 (2016)
26. Kaspersky lab, The state of industrial cybersecurity 2018 (2018)
27. A. Azmoodeh, A. Dehghantanha, M. Conti, K.-K.R. Choo, Detecting crypto-ransomware in IoT networks based on energy consumption footprint. J. Ambient. Intell. Humaniz. Comput. **9**(4), 1141–1152 (2018)
28. L. Obregon, Secure architecture for industrial control systems, Sept 2015
29. H.H. Pajouh, R. Javidan, R. Khayami, A. Dehghantanha, K.R. Choo, A two-layer dimension reduction and two-tier classification model for anomaly-based intrusion detection in IoT backbone networks. IEEE Trans. Emerg. Top. Comput. **7**(2), 314–323 (2019)
30. M. Jose, X. del Toro-Garcia, J-C. Lopez-Lopez, in *Artificial Intelligence Techniques for Smart Grid Applications*, vol. XII, no. 4 (2011)
31. O.M. Alhawi, A. Akinbi, A. Dehghantanha, Evaluation and application of two fuzzing approaches for security testing of IoT applications, in *Handbook of Big Data and IoT Security* (Springer, Cham, 2019), pp. 301–327
32. A. Darejeh, H.H. Pajouh, A. Darejeh, in *An Investigation on the Use of Expert Systems in Developing Web-Based Fitness Exercise Plan Generator* (2014)
33. S.J. Pan, Q. Yang, A survey on transfer learning. IEEE Trans. Knowl. Data Eng. **22**(10), 1345–1359 (2009)
34. H.H. Pajouh, G. Dastghaibyfard, S. Hashemi, Two-tier network anomaly detection model: a machine learning approach. J. Intell. Inf. Syst. **48**(1), 61–74 (2017)
35. E.M. Dovom, A. Azmoodeh, A. Dehghantanha, D.E. Newton, R.M. Parizi, H. Karimipour, Fuzzy pattern tree for edge malware detection and categorization in IoT. J. Syst. Archit. **97**, 1–7 (2019)
36. H. HaddadPajouh, A. Dehghantanha, R. Khayami, K.K. Choo, A deep Recurrent Neural Network based approach for Internet of Things malware threat hunting. Futur. Gener. Comput. Syst. **85**, 88–96 (2018)
37. Y. Harel, I.B. Gala, Y. Elovicib, Cyber security and the role of intelligent systems in addressing its challenges (Tel Aviv Universitya, Ben-Gurion University of the Negevb, 2017)
38. A. Tsonchev, OT security and the next generation of industrial cyber-attacks, Jan 2018
39. E. Capdevielle, ICS anomaly detection: finding the right needle in the relevant electric haystack, Nov 2017
40. Y. Saydun, Artificial intelligence and ICS networks: filling security gaps in operations technology, Apr 2018

Chapter 8
Enhancing Network Security Via Machine Learning: Opportunities and Challenges

Mahdi Amrollahi, Shahrzad Hadayeghparast, Hadis Karimipour, Farnaz Derakhshan, and Gautam Srivastava

1 Introduction

Today, if you say that malware may hack into your Facebook account using your home toaster, one would be horrified and quickly cut off the toaster from power! The fact is that internet networking is capable of connecting all digital devices surrounding us; such as devices in our homes, workplaces, cars, and even in our bodies. In addition, the use of the Internet has grown dramatically in many activities of daily life. However, threats and Internet attacks have doubled with the use of the Internet. Therefore, using security tools in computer networks is essential.

Network security refers to the network protection against cyber-threats which may compromise network availability, abuse resources accessible by the network, or cause illegal access (Fig. 8.1). Businesses that are in cybersecurity threats, not only incur billions of dollars for the recovery of their systems but also experience negative effects on their reputation [1]. Consequently, one of the most important parts of network operations and management is network security. This is a fact that while security experts are trying to defend networks from attackers by different means, attackers are trying to find other ways to penetrate the network [2].

M. Amrollahi · S. Hadayeghparast · H. Karimipour (✉)
School of Engineering, University of Guelph, Guelph, ON, Canada
e-mail: mamrollahi@uoguelph.ca; shadayeg@uoguelph.ca; hkarimi@uoguelph.ca; Canada-hkarimi@uoguelph.ca

F. Derakhshan
Department of Electrical and Computer Engineering, University of Tabriz, Tabriz, Iran
e-mail: derakhshan@tabrizu.ac.ir

G. Srivastava
Department of Mathematics and Computer Science, Brandon University, Brandon, MB, Canada
e-mail: srivastavag@brandonu.ca

© Springer Nature Switzerland AG 2020
K.-K. R. Choo, A. Dehghantanha (eds.), *Handbook of Big Data Privacy*,
https://doi.org/10.1007/978-3-030-38557-6_8

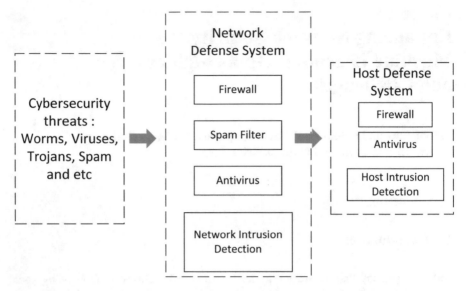

Fig. 8.1 Network security: threats, network defense, and host defense systems

Network security can be provided in different ways. Some examples of security processes are mentioned as follows [3]:

1. Network traffic encryption, most importantly the payload, for protecting the data transfer through the network.
2. Using authorization functions to restrict users from accessing different parts of the network and ban unauthorized users.
3. Adopting policies to give special rights to different users with different roles.
4. Using antiviruses and antimalware to protect systems as well as firewalls to protect or block unknown network traffic.

If login credential and keys can be accessed, the network is susceptible to various types of threats. Moreover, the mentioned set of patches and rules restrict the prevention capabilities of antiviruses and firewalls. Consequently, the second layer of defense for detecting signs of cyber-threats and quick reaction before any damage is necessary. The already mentioned systems are usually called Intrusion Detection/Prevention Systems (IDS/IPS). Intrusion detection systems are used to secure networks. These systems are classified according to the way in which intrusion detection operations are performed. One of the methods used to detect an intrusion is machine learning [4, 5].

Traditional detection techniques are inefficient when dealing with a huge amount of data because their analysis processes are complex and time-consuming. Hence, in order to reduce processing and training time, big data tools and techniques are utilized for the analysis and storage of data in intrusion detection systems. The two main methods used in the IDS (Intrusion Detection System) to detect attacks are Anomaly-based detection, which is dynamic as well as Signature-based detection which is static [6]. Signature-based detection schemes aim to acknowledge known attacks by utilizing the actual signatures of the attacks. It works well in identifying known attacks that have been pre-loaded in the IDS database. Thus, it is frequently viewed as considerably more exact at recognizing an intrusion attempt of known attacks [7]. However, the detection of new types of attacks is not possible since their signature is not provided. Therefore, the databases are often updated to improve detection effectiveness [8]. To overcome these problems, a dynamic scheme called anomaly-based detection which compares all known current activity against a predefined set of profiles is used to detect any behaviors that are deemed abnormal and identify patterns that may be considered intrusions. Due to the vast amount of malware with different behaviors, machine learning (ML) has created methods to overcome this dynamic range because ML covers a wide range of attack types such as spam, network intrusions, malware, false data injection, insider threats, and malicious domain names utilized by botnets [9–11].

This chapter gives a thorough literature review of new techniques for detection. We primarily focus on techniques that use ML approaches. Our chapter categorizes malware, spam and intrusion detection approaches into two focal groups: signature-based and anomaly-based detection under shallow and deep learning approaches. We summarize the significant contributions of this chapter as follows:

- Presenting an outline concerning identification approaches using ML and its challenges in the current era.
- Displaying a principled and classified review of the present ways to deal with machine learning instruments in the malware, spam and intrusion identification aspects.
- Investigating a structure of the significant strategies that are critical in the identification approach.
- Considering the significant factors of classification ML approaches in the detection and cybersecurity to deal with their problems in the futures.

The rest of this chapter is organized as follows. First, network security is explained in Sect. 2, followed by machine learning in Sect. 3 to provide the fundamental concepts and context. Then, in Sect. 4, different applications of machine learning in network security is discussed, from malware detection to various intrusion detection systems. After that, the chapter is ended up with a short summary, followed by opportunities and challenges section.

2 Network Security

System security can be defined as any action intended to ensure the ease of use of your system and information. It deals with both hardware and software technologies. Successful network security then manages access to the system. It aims at several different sorts of dangers, detects and prevents them from entering or spreading on your network. There are different types of network security, which can be summarized as follows [12–14]:

- Firewalls
- Behavioral analytics
- Data loss prevention
- Application security
- Access control
- Wireless security
- Intrusion prevention systems
- Network segmentation
- VPN and Web security
- Security information and event management
- Mobile device security

Many different layers of defense are brought together at the edge and in the network by network security (as shown in Fig. 8.2). Different controls and policies are adopted by each network security layer. While network resources are accessible for authorized users, malicious actors are prevented from conducting threats and exploits.

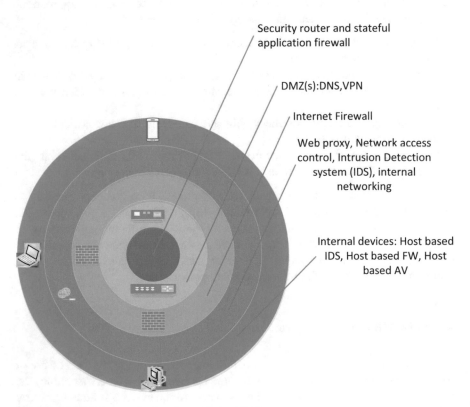

Fig. 8.2 Multiple layers of network security/architecture

Physical security is the first and fundamental stage of providing network security. It is a type of system security, guaranteeing that computer networks are safe from physical damages such as natural disasters, fire, and illegal access. Therefore, one network ensures that limitations of computer are met and followed by computers connecting to them. In addition, these types of systems contain alarm verification systems, and monitoring.

Perimeter protection is another type of system security. This kind of network security, as it can be easily understood from its name, separate the computer systems from physical computers and the rest of the world when you are online. Also, it may be virtual or physical. Firewalls and routers are some of the parts of perimeter protection network security. For the purpose of network protection against unauthorized access, there also exist application based firewalls. These kinds of network security provide protection and can block data from leaving or entering the network. Furthermore, protocols are implemented in perimeter protections in order to protect the entire network against unauthorized access.

Monitoring is the next kind of network security. In addition to blocking unauthorized data transfer to/from the computer, eyes on the whole network are needed. In the presence of monitoring, the entire computer system and network are being viewed so that unauthorized access to the system will be prohibited. However, monitoring tools are utilized by a large number of hackers when they hack into a system. This is a process where the hackers first observe the normal flow in the network before they hack and access the system and network as well.

Finally, the last item is training and user education. This part of network security deals with training and education of people, implementing network security protocols. This is not just due to the fact that they have a lot of information about computer systems. It means that they can maintain the safety of the network. It is noteworthy that there may be particular protocols implemented by people and if they do not have enough knowledge about them, they might not be able to deal with them. Due to the fact that it is how one will understand the limitations regarding the access to network security, this is a significant type of network security. Moreover, security protocols must be updated every so often. Consequently, informing people, who have access to the computer network, about these changes to guarantee its safety is essential.

3   Machine Learning

In this chapter, an introduction to machine learning and its algorithms will be presented. The algorithms of machine learning are classified into different categories, which will be briefly mentioned.

Fig. 8.3 Classification of
different learning

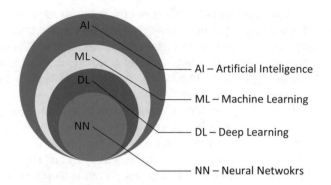

3.1 What Is Machine Learning?

The phrase machine learning was created by Arthur Samuel in the year 1959.
After this, the definition of machine learning was mentioned in the textbook of
Machine Learning by Tom M. Mitchell. This definition of machine learning field
is as follows:

> A computer program is said to learn from experience E with respect to some class of tasks
> T and performance measure P if its performance at tasks in T, as measured by P, improves
> with experience E [14].

Machine learning from above presents just a basic operational. Turing posed the
question in his paper titled *"Computing Machinery and Intelligence"*, that *"Can a
machine think?"*. This question was then replaced with a new question that is "Can
a machine do what we can do?". We see clearly this in Turing's proposal, it is
revealed that various characteristics that a thinking machine could have as well as
several implications if one of them is constructed.

In fact, Machine Learning (ML) is a subset of Artificial Intelligence (AI) (Fig.
8.3). Artificial means something that is non-natural or created by human and
Intelligence refers to the ability to think or understand. It is important to note that
AI is not a system, in fact, AI is developed in the system [15–17].

3.2 Machine Learning Algorithms

Machine learning algorithms vary from different aspects such as their approach,
the type of problem or task which they aim to solve, and the type of input and
output data. Moreover, different applications and views can result in different
classifications. Therefore, it is not possible to refer to a completely accepted
taxonomy from literature. Therefore, it is preferred to present an original taxonomy,
which can capture the differences among countless techniques that cyber detection
is applied to, as clearly illustrated in Fig. 8.4. Figure 8.4 is specific to security

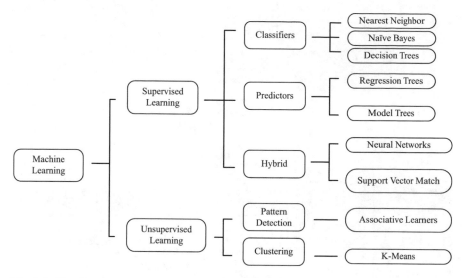

Fig. 8.4 Classification of ML algorithms for cybersecurity application

operators and not for all AI experts and application cases since it does not present ultimate classifications. One of the main differences between traditional ML, also known as shallow learning (SL), is the differences with more recent learning techniques such as Deep Learning (DL). For SL to work properly, an expert is needed to carry out tasks involving recognizing the characteristics of relevant data prior to performing SL algorithms. DL is based on a multi-layered representation of the input data. Also, by using process defined representations learning, DL is capable of carting out feature selection autonomously [18, 19].

3.2.1   Supervised Learning

Algorithms that are based on supervised learning are known to create models that are heavy in mathematics that focus on the inputs that the desired output of the algorithm. The data used for teaching the algorithm is known as training data. There is also the supervisory signal which can be defined as the one or more inputs in a training sample used to formulate the desired output. The training data is usually given in a matrix. Furthermore, training examples are given by an array or vector, which are often referred to as feature vectors. The main task of a supervised learning algorithm is to educate themselves about a given function, which can be adopted for the prediction of output connected with the new inputs, by iterative optimization of an objective function [20, 21]. The algorithm accurately specifies the output for inputs, which are not a part of the training data, by using an optimal function. An algorithm is said to have learned to carry out a task if it can increase accuracy of outputs/predictions. Supervised learning algorithms and how they work is shown in Fig. 8.5.

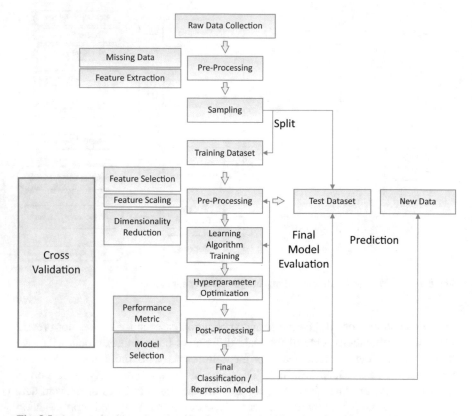

Fig. 8.5 A supervised learning algorithm/how supervised learning algorithms work?

In this method, each pattern has a Label, which is the desired output of that pattern. The purpose of this learning method is to map the patterns of input attributes to their corresponding labels. In fact, this works in phases. During the testing phase, the patterns whose labels are not specified are given to the system and the system is designed with the help of its learned function outputs or tags. Then, if the output of the discrete learning system is considered, the classification problem is called, and the function that maps the input to the output is called the classifier. Supervised learning algorithms consist of classification and regression. The utilization of regression algorithms is when any given output is any numerical value within some range, while we only use classification algorithms when outputs are limited to a finite value set. Similarity learning, which is part of supervised machine learning, is closely connected with classification and regression. However, it aims at learning from examples by through function known as similarity functions. Similarity functions measure the relation index between similar objects. Some common use cases include face verification, speaker verification, recommendation systems, and many others. In contrast, semi-supervised learning algorithms usually deal with problems where training data is missing training labels. In these cases, algorithms can still be used to increase quality level of a given model. Lastly, weakly supervised learning is used on data where the training labels are noisy, limited, or not very accurate. These labels are often cost-effective to obtain, which can result in much larger effective training sets [22].

3.2.2   Unsupervised Learning

We can define unsupervised learning algorithms as algorithms that:

1. Obtain in input data set
2. detect structures in the data such as clustering or grouping of data points.

   Therefore, we can say that the algorithms learn from the data, where the data here has not been labeled, categorized or classified. The algorithms try to determine common features in the data and react accordingly. Then, when new data is presented to the algorithm it reacts based on common features or lack of common features. Unsupervised learning can be applied to density estimation. We also see unsupervised learning in other applicable areas such as the summary and explanation of data features. In the well-known field of cluster analysis, we can cluster data using unsupervised learning based on the similarity or lack thereof in the data as presented. The assumptions made on the structure of the data varies in different clustering techniques, frequently specified by some similarity metric and assessed. Some examples include internal compactness, similarity in the same cluster, and separation or difference between clusters. We have also seen unsupervised learning used in graph connectivity and estimated density [23, 24].

4   Machine Learning in Network Security

Many areas for application of ML are present for network security such as Malware Detection and Classification, Domain Generation Algorithms (DGA) and Botnet Detection (BD), Network Intrusion Detection/Intrusion Detection System (IDS), Network Traffic Identification, SPAM and Phishing Identification/Detection, Insider Threat Detection (ITD) and False Data Injection Attack Detection [25–27].

   In Table 8.1, the most important ML algorithms, presented to solve the mentioned identified cybersecurity problems, are demonstrated. ML algorithms employed for each problem are shown in a specific cell. It is noteworthy that empty cells, to the best of the author's knowledge, indicate no proposal for that category of problems. According to Table 8.1, Supervised Learning (SL) algorithms can be adapted to all mentioned problems. Supervised Deep Learning (DL) algorithms can be widely used in the analysis of malware and not as much in the detection of intrusions. We often base spam detection solely on unsupervised deep learning algorithms. Also, DL algorithms are not adopted in DGA detection, although they are related to natural language processing. The overall number of algorithms based on SL is sig-

Table 8.1 Main ML algorithms for application on cybersecurity [27]

| | | Malware detection | SPAM detection | IDS | | |
				Network	Botnet	DGA
Deep learning	Supervised			RNN	RNN	
	Unsupervised	DBN SAE	DBN SAE	DBN SAE	–	–
Shallow learning	Supervised	RF NB SVM LR HMM KNN SNN	RF NB SVM LR KNN SNN	RF NB SVM LR HMM KNN SNN	RF NB SVM LR KNN SNN	RF HMM
	Unsupervised	Clustering Association	Clustering Association	Clustering Association	Clustering	Clustering

nificantly larger than those based on DL. We see that Deep Learning using massive neural networks are the current best approach compared to older SL algorithms. This hole between algorithm styles creates lots of research chances. Eventually, an important difference between supervised and unsupervised algorithms is that the first one is employed for classification purposes and can implement complete detectors, while the later approaches conduct ancillary activities. We have seen that unsupervised SL algorithms can be used for grouping data that have similar independent characteristics of classifications that are predefined as well as a farewell at the identification of useful features in situations where the data that needs to be analyzed has a high level of dimensionality.

Three fields where most cybersecurity and ML algorithms are adopted are Malware Detection, Spam and Phishing Detection and Intrusion Detection. We consider these next.

4.1   The Detection of Malware

There has been a significant increase in the frequency and diversity of malware attacks make a defense against them employing standard methods more difficult [28, 29]. ML provides the possibility of creating generalized models for autonomous detection and classification of malware. This can provide defense against light adversaries utilizing known malware and large adversaries utilizing new malware for attacks. There exist some methods to detect malware. DL detectors of adversarial applications on Android OS employing both dynamic and static feature analyses have been developed in [30]. Three sources namely sensitive Application Program Interfaces (APIs), static analysis of required permission, and dynamic behaviors were specifically utilized for obtaining features. Static features can come from the *installation* APK file and parsing the *AndroidManifest* XML and *classes* DEX files. This gives the needed authorization and the APIs utilized. The features that behave dynamically are from a dynamic analysis Droid Box data gathering. The features were then input to a DBN with two hidden layers. The results accomplished were 96.8% in precision, a 97.9% in TPR, and 4.3% in FPR. A two hidden layer DBN was shown to be successful after looking at many different configurations. The outcomes are better than those achieved using Naive Bayes, SVMs, random forests, and logistic regression that they tested. Dynamic features are likely to be more reliable compared to static features, which can be obscured without difficulty. Consequently, utilizing features like API calls, which are taken from running the software in a sandbox, is common. An example of this is Pascanu et al. [31], who developed a method for detecting malware employing RNN combined with multilayer perceptron (MLP) and logistic regression for classification. In order to forecast the next API call, the RNN is trained in an unsupervised manner. Max-pooling was performed systematically on the feature vector, and it was noticed that the output of the hidden layer corresponding to this RNN once fed into the classifier prevents it from reordering events temporal in nature.

CNNs and RNNs are used by Kolosnji et al. [32] for recognizing malware. By using one-hot encoding, the API call sequences are then turned into vectors binary in nature. The definition of one-hot encoding is to aim at storing data categorical in nature in a form that is easier for ML. The data is usually used to train the DL algorithm, which usually includes CNN and RNN. Accuracy close to 90%, recall also close to 90%, and also precision approximately 86% were shown for this model. A malware detector was developed by Tobiyama et al. [33] which experimented with API data regarding time series into an RNN to focus on feature extraction. After that, the extracted features are modified into image versions and a CNN is used for categorization of the features as either normal features or as malicious features. The RNN uses an LSTM, and a CNN using for the most part two distinct pooling layers and two distinct convolution layers. This is then proceeded by two connected layers. A DBN using the operational codes was then developed by Ding et al. [34] by preprocessing all Windows Portable Executable (PE) files, to then be able to extract the n-grams. Three of the layers are hidden in the DBN. The dataset included 3000 files benign in nature, 10,000 files unlabeled in nature, and 3000 malicious files. When the DBN model is pre-trained utilizing unlabeled data, it outperforms decision trees, SVMs, and k-nearest. The best performing DBN was accurate to approximately 97%. Furthermore, a detector, which does not need any feature selection or engineering, was built by McLaughlin et al. [35] by using opcodes from malware files. They used an embedded layer for opcode data raw in nature and then used a CNN with two distinct convolution layers, alongside one max-pooling layer, and also a connected layer. Lastly, they used a classification layer. The results differed with different datasets. They obtained accuracies of 98% and 80%, recall at 95% and 85%, precision at 99% and 27%, and an FI Score of 97% and 78% respectively. API calls were also used by hardy et al. [36] for developing a DL malware detector. For this purpose, they used auto encoders coupled with a sigmoid classification layer and the accuracy of 95.64% was attained.

4.2 SPAM and Phishing Detection

Spam and phishing detection consist of a great number of techniques with the purpose of decrease in time wastage and potential hazards caused by unwanted emails. Nowadays, a preferred way for attackers to establish initial penetration in a network is through a well-known technique of unsolicited emails, also known as phishing. The usual was that techniques known as phishing work is to include links to designated websites or malware within the emails. Due to the advanced evasion strategies adopted by attackers for bypassing traditional filters, spam and phishing detection becomes more and more difficult. The spam detection process can be improved by ML approaches.

Tzortzis and Likas study the classification of spam emails using DL in [37]. Feature extraction was performed by them using common words in emails and utilizing a deep belief network, also called a DBN. The accuracy of an SVM is known to be less than that of a DBN. The SVM was accurate to approximately 99%, 97%, and 96%. Comparatively the DBN was accurate to 99.4%, 97.5%, and 97.4% respectively. In [38], we have seen Mi et al. adopt auto-encoders. The authors used a total of five hidden layers as well as a final classification layer for spam detection. Comparative analysis was conducted between their method and other ML algorithms. Their methods were shown to be better than other existing methods, attaining accuracies higher than 95% on multiple data sets.

4.3 Intrusion Detection Systems (IDS)

Intrusion detection is a kind of security software developed for administrators in order to automatically alert them in case of information system compromise by security policy violations or malicious activities. On the other hand, an intrusion detection system, also known as an IDS, is a device primarily but also can be software that tries to detect policy violations or malicious activity by monitoring a network or systems. Malicious activity is reported to an administrator. The reports are usually through a SIEM system, short for security information and event management, which combines outputs from many resources and adopts techniques for alarm filtering that can differentiate false alarms from their malicious counterparts.

4.3.1 IDS vs. Intrusion Prevention Systems (IPS) and Firewalls

Firewalls restrict access between networks for preventing intrusion and do not indicate an attack from inside the network. In case of a suspected intrusion, an IDS describes it as well as signaling an alarm. Also, attacks originated from within a system are observed by IDSs. This is accomplished by recognizing

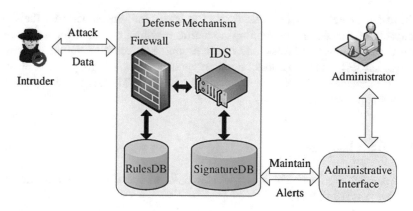

Fig. 8.6 Firewalls and IDS for cybersecurity

heuristics and patterns (commonly known as signatures) of common computer attacks, inspecting network communications, and taking action to alert operators. An intrusion prevention system is a system, which terminates connections and controls access like an application layer firewall. On the other hand, firewall is an access security gateway that allows or blocks the uplink and downlink network traffic, based on the predefined rules. Anti-virus software detects and removes computer viruses, worms and Trojans and malware. Rule violations in information systems or malicious and unauthorized activities are recognized by IDSs. Each carries out its own tasks for protection of central servers, network communication and edge devices (Fig. 8.6).

A number of systems might try on preventing intrusion attempts. However, it is not expected or required for monitoring systems. The main focus of Intrusion detection and prevention systems (IDPS) are recognizing incidents. From there, the information must be logged and reported. Moreover, IDPS is adopted by organizations for other aims like recognizing problems with security policies, deterring individuals from violating security policies, and documenting existing threats. Almost every organization has added IDPS to its security infrastructure as a necessary part. IDPS typically record data concerning observed events, alert security administers about significant observed events, and produce report. Also a possible IDPS response to threats that are detected may be to stop its success. Various techniques are adopted by IDPS such as changing the security environment (e.g. reconfiguring a firewall), stopping the attack by the IDPS itself, or changing the content of the attack.

The most important tasks of intrusion prevention systems include recognizing the malicious activity, log information concerning this activity, report it and try to block or stop it. Intrusion prevention systems are considered extensions of intrusion detection systems since both of them monitor network traffic and/or system activities for malicious activity. Intrusion prevention systems are placed in-line and are able to actively prevent or block detected intrusions in contrast to intrusion detection system that forms the basic differences between them. IPS is capable of functions like sending an alarm, resetting a connection or blocking from the offending IP address, and traffic dropping detected malicious packets. In addition, an IPS is able to correct cyclic redundancy check (CRC) errors, clean up unwanted transport and network layer options, alleviate TCP sequencing problems, defragment packet streams [39].

4.3.2   IDS Classification

The types of IDS vary from single machines to massive networks. Common classifications for IDS are

1. Network intrusion detection systems (NIDS)
2. Host-based intrusion detection systems (HIDS).

Systems which analyzes incoming network traffic is an example of a NIDS, while a system which monitors main operating system files is an example of a HIDS. IDS can also be classified based on the approach used. There are signature-based detection and anomaly-based detection. There is also reputation-based detection. Signature-based detection recognize bad patterns. Anamoly based detection detect bad traffic from normal good traffic on the network. Finally, reputation-based detection uses a scoring model to assign a reputation to network parties. A number of IDS players are capable of responding to detected intrusions. Intrusion prevention systems are typically described as systems with response capabilities. Generally IDS can be classified based on the employed detection method (signature or anomaly-based) or where detection happens (network or host) (Fig. 8.7).

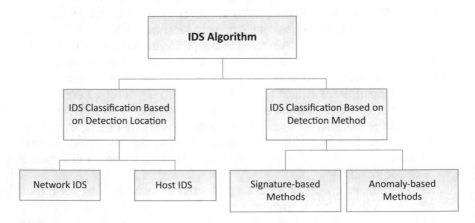

Fig. 8.7 Classification of IDS algorithms for cybersecurity application

4.3.3 IDS Classification Based on Detection Location

Network IDS, also known as NIDS, are placed at distinct points in a given network to monitor traffic. The traffic is then analyzed and compared to traffic of known attacks that are stored in a library. The alert is sent to the administrator when abnormal behavior is sensed or an attack is recognized. A good example of using NIDS is to install it on a subnet where firewalls are located to attempt to see if a hack occurred to the firewall. In an ideal scenario one would scan all traffic (incoming/outgoing). This, however may be network inefficient, causing a bottleneck for the network. Usually, OPNET and NetSim are used to simulated networks to detect network intrusions. Moreover, another capability of NIDS is comparing signatures to link similar packets and packets that are deemed harmful are dropped where their signature is a match in the library. There are two types when the design of the NIDS is classified based on the system interactivity property namely Online NIDS and offline NIDS, often called inline and tap mode, respectively. Online NIDS is known to deal with real-time data. In order to detect an attack, it performs an analysis of the Ethernet packets and uses a number of rules. Off-line NIDS deals with stored data and passes it through some processes to know whether or not it is an attack. We add here that NIDS can be made more effective when mixed with other technologies. Artificial Neural Network-based IDS are able to analyze enormous amount of data, in an intelligent manner, because of the self-organizing structure that gives INS IDS the opportunity of recognizing intrusion patterns more efficiently. Neural networks can assist IDS with predicting attacks. INN IDS are based on two layers. Layer 1 receives single values, while the input to the layer 2 is the first layer's output; the cycle repeats and leads to automatic recognition of new unexpected patterns in the network by the system. This system can achieve close to 100% rates for classification and detection [40].

HIDS which stands for host intrusion detection systems can run on individual hosts or devices on the network. Only inbound and outbound packets from the device are monitored by HIDS and will alert the administrator or user in case of detecting suspicious activity. A snapshot is taken of existing system files and matches it to the previous snapshot. The administer will receive an alert to investigate in case of modification or deletion of the critical system files.

4.3.4 IDS Classification Based on Detection Method

Signature-based IDS refers to the detection of attacks by searching specific patterns, such as known malicious instruction sequences adopted by malware, or byte sequences in network traffic. The origin of this terminology comes from anti-virus software in which the term "signature" is used for the detected patterns. Although detecting known attacks is easy for signature-based IDS, detecting new attacks with unavailable patterns is difficult. The signatures are released for its all products by a vendor in signature-based IDS. Therefore, on-time updating of the IDS with the signature is very critical. On the other hand, Misuse-based IDS includes monitoring the network and matching the network activities against the expected behavior of an attack.

The comprehensiveness of the attack signatures is the most important component of such a system. The signatures are typically given to misuse-IDS depend on expert knowledge. The source of this knowledge can either be extracted from data, or it can be human experts. However, manual inspection is made practically impossible because of the enormous volume of generated network traces. Furthermore, complex attacks with intermittent symptoms or capturing advanced persistent threats are not possible for attack signatures extracted by sequentially scanning network traces. Inserting noise in the data is a simple way which can be adopted by intruders for evading detection if the signatures depend on a stream of suspicious activities. According to the above discussion, ML becomes a suitable tool for misuse-based IDSs. The ability of ML to find patterns in big datasets is suitable for learning signatures of attacks from collected network traces. Consequently, seeing a large number of studies for misuse-detection relying on ML is not surprising. These works are summarized in Fig. 8.8. As expected, all existing studies use adopt supervised learning, and most of them perform offline detection. It is noteworthy that all studies in which normal and attack data is used in their training set are classified as misuse-detection and the resultant accuracy for each class is shown in Fig. 8.8. All data were collected from various sources such as [41].

One of the restrictions of the aforementioned research is its adoption offline. This prevents their practical use in online systems. A small number of studies investigated IDS. Re-training is required for most classifiers (e.g., image, text

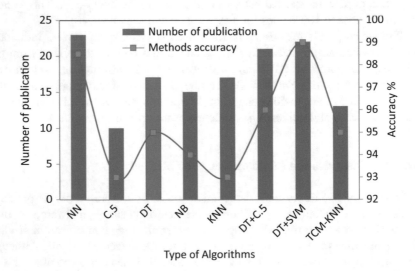

Fig. 8.8 The number of papers published in various ML-based misuse detection methods, and their accuracy (1998–2019)

recognition systems). However, the nature of cyber-threats leads to retraining for IDS carried out very often. Therefore, fast training time is important for adaptable IDS.

Denning proposed *anomaly detection* for intrusion detection systems in [42]. Anomaly detection is usually accomplished with thresholds and statistics for IDS, but can also be accomplished with soft computing, and inductive learning. Types of statistics proposed by 1999 included profiles of users, workstations, networks, remote hosts, groups of users, and programs based on frequencies, means, variances, covariances, and standard deviations. Anomaly-based intrusion detection systems are known to be historically used to detect unknown attacks. This is mostly due to the fast-moving threats from malware. The main method is to use ML to create a model of activity that can be deemed trustworthy. Then, the model is compared with new behaviour. This approach is known to enable the detection of previously unknown attacks. That being said, it is also known to suffer from many false positives.

An example of ML for anomaly-based detection can be seen as follows: if a student who usually logs in to the system around 9 am from a dormitory logs in at 6:30 am from an address in another country, the system would deem this as an anomaly. Anomaly detection focusses on a clear and present boundary between what is normal and what can be considered anomalous behaviours.

Anomaly detection can be split into flow feature or payload-based detection. On the other hand, it can also be divided into static, cognition and machine learning techniques, as seen in Fig. 8.9. We have also seen DL and RL added to the list of techniques in recent years [43–46].

Payload-based anomaly detection teaches themselves normal behaviour from packet payloads. From this, they can detect attacks inside the payloads, which sometimes can easily bypass system defenses. We discuss ML techniques that have been used to be used as a detection mechanism for anomalies using packet payloads or flow features here in the chapter. PAYL uses a method known as 1-g to model packet payloads. We have also seen the use of N-gram for text analysis as shown in [47]. The main idea is that of a sliding window of size n that scans the payload and counts the frequency of each n-gram. The mean and the standard deviation are also computed for each byte in the payload. PAYL generates a payload model for many attributes as the payload exhibits different characteristics for different services. After the models are generated, a distance measure known as the Mahalanobis distance is used to measure the deviation between incoming packets and the payload models. The larger distance coincides with the higher the likelihood that the newly arrived packet is abnormal (Fig. 8.10).

As an example, we have seen Zanero et al. initialize a two-tier architecture to be used for anomaly detection in their pivotal work in [48]. Tier 1 uses an unsupervised outliers detection algorithm that can classify packets. Tier 1 then provides a reduction of features as the result "compresses" classification for each packet into one byte of data. Tier 1 results are then fed into Tier 2 which is an algorithm for anomaly detection. In the first tier, packet header, as well as payload, are mentioned for detection of outliers. The authors compare three techniques

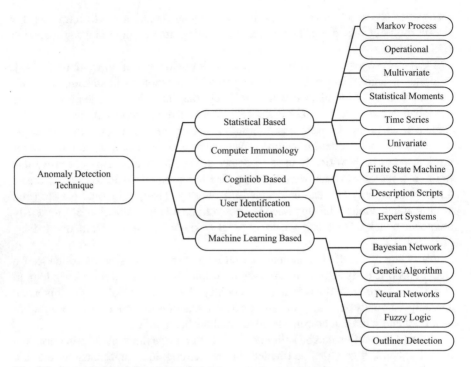

Fig. 8.9 Anomaly-based detection techniques

Fig. 8.10 Different between payload and flow-based approach

- SOM
- Principal Direction Divisive Partitioning (PDDP) algorithm
- k-Means

SOM was shown to outperform PDDP and k-Means. The factors for comparison were computational cost and classification accuracy. A preliminary prototype was evaluated in [49]. The authors show a 75% improvement in DR over an ID. We also have seen Gornitz et al. use semi-supervised Support Vector Data Description,

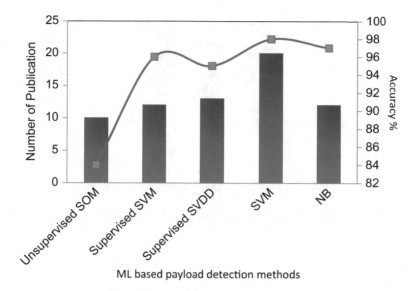

Fig. 8.11 The number of papers published on various ML for payload-based anomaly detection methods (2010–2019)

which is known as SVDD. They present an active learning technique to build an active SVDD (Active SVDD) model in [50]. Their model is first and foremost trains unlabeled examples and refines them by using labeled data. Their evaluation results are given in [51]. Summary of the most popular payload-based anomaly detection methods and their accuracy is listed in Fig. 8.11.

4.3.5   Deep and Reinforcement Learning-Based Anomaly Detection

During the last couple of years self-taught learning (STL) [52] techniques including deep Bayesian network (DBN) [53, 54], and recurrent neural network (RNN) [55] resulted in promising outcome for anomaly detection. In 2007, STL was introduced and is improved compared to semi-supervised learning. This technique uses data that is unlabeled from object class and improves the task of classification through learning of good feature representation. As an example, in [56], an encoder is mentioned to be used for dimensionality reduction. Their proposed model resulted in an accuracy of 92.10% with 1.58% false positive. In contrast, Tang et al. [57] used deep neural network (DNN) for anomaly detection that is flow-based by extracting features from the software-defined networking switches. The proposed DNN achieved an accuracy of 72%, precision of 79%, recall of 72%, and F-measure of 72% on the low end.

Reinforcement learning (RL) is an iterative algorithm that uses feedback from the environment to learn the correct sequence of actions to maximize a cumulative reward. In other words, it allows the machine to learn from the interaction with its

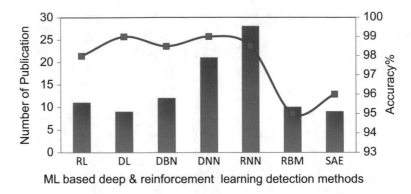

Fig. 8.12 The number of papers published on various ML for deep and reinforcement learning detection methods (2010–2019)

environment by performing actions to maximize the total feedback. RL algorithms do not know the exact mathematical model so are very useful when exact models are shown to be infeasible. RL is best suited for making cognitive choices, such as decision making, planning, and scheduling. We give a summary of most popular anomaly detection methods based on deep and reinforcement learning techniques along with their accuracy is depicted in Fig. 8.12 [58].

5   Summary

In this chapter. we survey the applications of ML for network security. We have focused on network-based intrusion detection techniques, algorithms, and schemes. We have been able to group work based on anomalies, hybrid networks IDSs, and misuse. The different ML techniques were presented and we also touched on some more recent applications of both DL and RL. In Fig. 8.13, there is clear illustration at the rate of publication in all fields is increasing when looking at the publications in ML-based methods on cybersecurity from 2010 to 2018. We also see a steady growth of publications. This clearly indicates the potential for researchers to contribute to this field. In Fig. 8.14, we present statistical results on different ML algorithms based on publications on the topic of cybersecurity until 2019. We still see that the research is increasing with time. We can conclude by stating that DL was mostly used cybersecurity technique compared to the other well known to learn methods. We hope that these figures can help future researchers in focussing their work in potential fields.

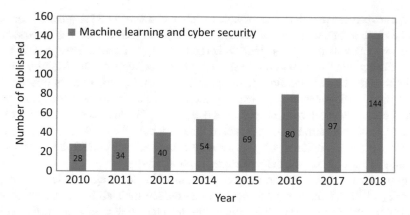

Fig. 8.13 The number of papers published on ML and cybersecurity from 2010 to 2018

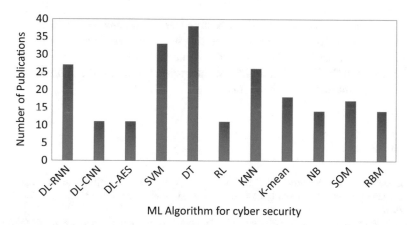

Fig. 8.14 A Statistic on papers published on most popular ML algorithms used in cybersecurity (2010–2019)

6   Opportunities and Challenges

The benefits of ML for IDS and Malware detection are clear. However, there is still much speculation about the application of machine learning techniques in this field.

There is still a big challenge with real-time Malware detection. We have seen considerable research showing the advances in design and systems that can automatically predicate the maliciousness of specific files, programs, and websites. Malware is a continuously growing area in terms of numbers and maliciousness. Web-based Malware detection is growing with the expansion of the Internet as well. With the availability of higher speeds and bandwidths for internet use, we potentially will see malware reach new heights in the coming years. The main issue that leads to difficulty in detection is the expansion of behaviors of different attacks. Polymorphic properties can cause IDSs to not be able to detect malware when required. Therefore, it takes time to find a pattern of the new malware and then detect it as an attack.

A major downside to these models is their accuracy. There is always an inherent risk of using any tool that is new, especially one that involves DL. Mainly, DL tool lacks a general understanding of the public. From this, when errors happen, it is often hard to diagnose what is causing the errors. For industry, cybersecurity has added costs involved with proper implementation. We also see that many of the models presented here focus on specific threat models. There is still a strong need for more flexible solutions. Ideally, a future could see multiple DL approaches and techniques running in parallel and acting synergistically.

In this chapter, we will end by saying that machine learning techniques in cybersecurity still have many downsides that can reduce their ability to be successful. Everything we have presented is vulnerable to adversarial attacks and often require constant re-training of the system. Deep learning itself is still in its early stages for cybersecurity implementation.

Our main takeaways here are that machine learning techniques can support better security. ML techniques can automate certain tasks however there are still positives and negatives of each model. The autonomous capabilities of some systems must not be taken lightly. We still need human supervision so that skilled attackers cannot infiltrate systems and leave them vulnerable.

References

1. D. Kiwia, A. Dehghantanha, K.K.R. Choo, J. Slaughter, A cyber kill chain based taxonomy of banking Trojans for evolutionary computational intelligence. J. Comput. Sci. **27**, 394–409 (2018)
2. H. Karimipour, S. Geris, A. Dehghantanha, H. Leung, *Intelligent Anomaly Detection for Large-Scale Smart Grids* (IEEE CCECE, Edmonton, 2019), pp. 1–4
3. F.N. Dezfouli, A. Dehghantanha, R. Mahmod, N.F.B.M. Sani, S.B. Shamsuddin, F. Daryabar, A survey on malware analysis and detection techniques. Int. J. Adv. Comput. Technol. **5**(14), 42 (2013)
4. N.B. Anuar, M. Papadaki, S. Furnell, N. Clarke, An investigation and survey of response options for Intrusion Response Systems (IRSs), in *2010 Information Security for South Africa* (IEEE, 2010 August), pp. 1–8
5. M. Baig, P. Zavarsky, R. Ruhl, D. Lindskog, *The Study of Evasion of Packed PE from Static Detection* (World Congress on. Internet Security (WorldCIS), 2012), pp. 99–104
6. M. Conti, T. Dargahi, A. Dehghantanha, Cyber threat intelligence: challenges and opportunities, in *Cyber Threat Intelligence* (Springer, Cham, 2018), pp. 1–6
7. C. Cepeda, D.L.C. Tien, P. Ordónez, Feature selection and improving classification performance for malware detection, in *2016 IEEE International Conferences on Big Data and Cloud Computing (BDCloud), Social Computing and Networking (SocialCom), Sustainable Computing and Communications (SustainCom) (BDCloud-SocialCom-SustainCom)* (IEEE, 2016 October), pp. 560–566
8. M. Damshenas, A. Dehghantanha, R. Mahmoud, A survey on malware propagation, analysis, and detection. Int. J. Cyber-Secur. Digit. Forensics **2**(4), 10–30 (2013)
9. S.R. Bragen, *Malware detection through opcode sequence analysis using machine learning*, Master's thesis (2015)

10. H. Karimipour, V. Dinavahi, On false data injection attack against dynamic state estimation on smart power grids. in *2017 IEEE International Conference on Smart Energy Grid Engineering (SEGE)* (IEEE, 2017), pp. 388–393
11. M.R. Begli, F. Derakhshan, H. Karimipour, A layered intrusion detection system for critical infrastructure using machine learning, in *IEEE Int. Conf. on Smart Energy Grid Engineering (SEGE)* (IEEE, 2019), pp. 1–5
12. E.M. Dovom, A. Azmoodeh, A. Dehghantanha, D.E. Newton, R.M. Parizi, H. Karimipour, Fuzzy pattern tree for edge malware detection and categorization in IoT. J. Syst. Archit. **97**, 1–7 (2019)
13. H. Haddad Pajouh, A. Dehghantanha, R. Khayami, K.K.R. Choo, A deep recurrent neural network based approach for internet of things malware threat hunting. Futur. Gener. Comput. Syst. **85**, 88–96 (2018)
14. E. Brynjolfsson, T. Mitchell, What can machine learning do? Workforce implications. Science **358**(6370), 1530–1534 (2017)
15. Z. Ghahramani, Probabilistic machine learning and artificial intelligence. Nature **521**(7553), 452–459 (2015)
16. A. Azmoodeh, A. Dehghantanha, K.K.R. Choo, Robust malware detection for internet of (battlefield) things devices using deep eigenspace learning. IEEE Trans. Sustain. Comput. **4**(1), 88–95 (2018)
17. O. Osanaiye, H. Cai, K.K.R. Choo, A. Dehghantanha, Z. Xu, M. Dlodlo, Ensemble-based multi-filter feature selection method for DDoS detection in cloud computing. EURASIP J. Wirel. Commun. Netw. **2016**(1), 130 (2016)
18. Y. Xin, L. Kong, Z. Liu, Y. Chen, Y. Li, H. Zhu, M. Gao, H. Hou, C. Wang, Machine learning and deep learning methods for cybersecurity. IEEE Access **6**, 35365–35381 (2018)
19. S. Dua, X. Du, *Data Mining and Machine Learning in Cybersecurity* (Auerbach Publications, Boca Raton, 2016)
20. R. Verma, M. Kantarcioglu, D. Marchette, E. Leiss, T. Solorio, Security analytics: essential data analytics knowledge for cybersecurity professionals and students. IEEE Secur. Priv. **13**(6), 60–65 (2015)
21. J. Sakhnini, A. Dehghantanha, H. Karimipour, Smart grid cyber attacks detection using supervised learning and heuristic feature selection, in *IEEE Int. Conf. on Smart Energy Grid Engineering (SEGE), Canada* (IEEE, 2019), pp. 1–5
22. H. Karimipour, A. Dehghantanha, R.M. Parizi, K.R. Choo, H. Leung, A deep and scalable unsupervised machine learning system for cyber-attack detection in large-scale smart grids. IEEE Access **7**, 80778–80788 (2019)
23. S. Omar, A. Ngadi, H.H. Jebur, Machine learning techniques for anomaly detection: An overview. Int. J. Comput. Appl. **79**(2), 33–41 (2013)
24. R. Sommer, V. Paxson, Outside the closed world: on using machine learning for network intrusion detection, in *2010 IEEE Symposium on Security and Privacy* (IEEE, 2010), pp. 305–316
25. C.F. Tsai, Y.F. Hsu, C.Y. Lin, W.Y. Lin, Intrusion detection by machine learning: A review. Expert Syst. Appl. **36**(10), 11994–12000 (2009)
26. G. Apruzzese, M. Colajanni, L. Ferretti, A. Guido, M. Marchetti, On the effectiveness of machine and deep learning for cyber security, in *2018 10th International Conference on Cyber Conflict (CyCon)* (IEEE, 2018), pp. 371–390
27. D.S. Berman, A.L. Buczak, J.S. Chavis, C.L. Corbett, A survey of deep learning methods for cyber security. Information **10**(4), 122 (2019)
28. C. Zhang, P. Patras, H. Haddadi, Deep learning in mobile and wireless networking: A survey. IEEE Commun. Surv. Tutor. **21**, 2224–2287 (2019)
29. Z. Yuan, Y. Lu, Z. Wang, Y. Xue, Droid-sec: deep learning in android malware detection, in *ACM SIGCOMM Computer Communication Review*, vol. 44, no. 4 (ACM, 2014), pp. 371–372
30. Z. Yuan, Y. Lu, Y. Xue, Droiddetector: Android malware characterization and detection using deep learning. Tsinghua Sci. Technol. **21**(1), 114–123 (2016)

31. R. Pascanu, J.W. Stokes, H. Sanossian, M. Marinescu, A. Thomas, Malware classification with recurrent networks, in *2015 IEEE International Conference on Acoustics, Speech and Signal Processing (ICASSP)* (IEEE, 2015 April), pp. 1916–1920
32. B. Kolosnjaji, A. Zarras, G. Webster, C. Eckert, Deep learning for classification of malware system call sequences, in *Australasian Joint Conference on Artificial Intelligence* (Springer, Cham, 2016 December), pp. 137–149
33. S. Tobiyama, Y. Yamaguchi, H. Shimada, T. Ikuse, T. Yagi, Malware detection with deep neural network using process behavior, in *2016 IEEE 40th Annual Computer Software and Applications Conference (COMPSAC)*, vol. 2 (IEEE, 2016 June), pp. 577–582
34. Y. Ding, S. Chen, J. Xu, Application of deep belief networks for opcode based malware detection, in *2016 International Joint Conference on Neural Networks (IJCNN)* (IEEE, 2016 July), pp. 3901–3908
35. N. McLaughlin, J. Martinez del Rincon, B. Kang, S. Yerima, P. Miller, S. Sezer, Y. Safaei, E. Trickel, Z. Zhao, A. Doupé, G. Joon Ahn, Deep android malware detection, in *Proceedings of the Seventh ACM on Conference on Data and Application Security and Privacy* (ACM, 2017 March), pp. 301–308
36. W. Hardy, L. Chen, S. Hou, Y. Ye, X. Li, DL4MD: a deep learning framework for intelligent malware detection, in *Proceedings of the International Conference on Data Mining (DMIN)*, (The Steering Committee of The World Congress in Computer Science, Computer Engineering and Applied Computing (WorldComp), 2016), p. 61
37. G. Tzortzis, A. Likas, Deep belief networks for spam filtering, in *19th IEEE International Conference on Tools with Artificial Intelligence (ICTAI 2007)*, vol. 2 (IEEE, 2007), pp. 306–309
38. G. Mi, Y. Gao, Y. Tan, Apply stacked auto-encoder to spam detection, in *International Conference in Swarm Intelligence* (Springer, Cham, 2015), pp. 3–15
39. O. Depren, M. Topallar, E. Anarim, M.K. Ciliz, An intelligent intrusion detection system (IDS) for anomaly and misuse detection in computer networks. Expert Syst. Appl. **29**(4), 713–722 (2005)
40. A.L. Buczak, E. Guven, A survey of data mining and machine learning methods for cyber security intrusion detection. IEEE Commun. Surv. Tutor. **18**(2), 1153–1176 (2015)
41. R. Boutaba, M.A. Salahuddin, N. Limam, S. Ayoubi, N. Shahriar, F. Estrada-Solano, O.M. Caicedo, A comprehensive survey on machine learning for networking: Evolution, applications and research opportunities. J. Int. Serv. Appl. **9**(1), 16 (2018)
42. D.E. Denning, An intrusion-detection model. IEEE Trans. Softw. Eng. **SE-13**(2), 222–232 (1987)
43. S. Mohammadi, H. Mirvaziri, M. Ghazizadeh-Ahsaee, H. Karimipour, Cyber intrusion detection by combined feature selection algorithm. J. Inf. Secur. Appl. **44**, 80–88 (2019)
44. H.H. Pajouh, R. Javidan, R. Khayami, D. Ali, K.K.R. Choo, A two-layer dimension reduction and two-tier classification model for anomaly-based intrusion detection in IoT backbone networks. IEEE Trans. Emerg. Top. Comput. **7**(2), 314–323 (2016)
45. S. Geris, H. Karimipour, A feature selection-based approach for joint cyber-attack detection and state estimation, in *IEEE Int. Conf. on Smart Energy Grid Engineering (SEGE)* (IEEE, 2019), pp. 1–5
46. S. Mohammadi, H. Mirvaziri, M. Ghazizadeh-Ahsaee, Multivariate correlation coefficient and mutual information-based feature selection in intrusion detection. Inf. Secur. J. Glob. Perspect. **26**(5), 229–239 (2017)
47. K. Wang, S.J. Stolfo, Anomalous payload-based network intrusion detection, in *International Workshop on Recent Advances in Intrusion Detection* (Springer, Berlin, 2004), pp. 203–222
48. S. Zanero, S.M. Savaresi, Unsupervised learning techniques for an intrusion detection system, in *Proceedings of the 2004 ACM symposium on Applied computing* (ACM, 2004), pp. 412–419
49. J. Beale, R. Deraison, H. Meer, R. Temmingh, C.V.D. Walt, *Nessus Network Auditing* (Syngress Publishing, Burlington, 2004)
50. N. Görnitz, M. Kloft, K. Rieck, U. Brefeld, Active learning for network intrusion detection, in *Proceedings of the 2nd ACM Workshop on Security and Artificial Intelligence* (ACM, 2009), pp. 47–54

51. L.L.C. Metasploit, The metasploit framework (2007), http://www.metasploit.com
52. A. Javaid, Q. Niyaz, W. Sun, M. Alam, A deep learning approach for network intrusion detection system, in *Proceedings of the 9th EAI International Conference on Bio-inspired Information and Communications Technologies (Formerly BIONETICS)* (ICST (Institute for Computer Sciences, Social-Informatics and Telecommunications Engineering), 2016), pp. 21–26
53. M.Z. Alom, V. Bontupalli, T.M. Taha, Intrusion detection using deep belief networks, in *2015 National Aerospace and Electronics Conference (NAECON)* (IEEE, 2015), pp. 339–344
54. Y. Li, R. Ma, R. Jiao, A hybrid malicious code detection method based on deep learning. Int. J. Secur. Appl. **9**(5), 205–216 (2015)
55. J. Kim, J. Kim, H.L.T. Thu, H. Kim, Long short term memory recurrent neural network classifier for intrusion detection, in *2016 International Conference on Platform Technology and Service (PlatCon)* (IEEE, 2016), pp. 1–5
56. R. Raina, A. Battle, H. Lee, B. Packer, A.Y. Ng, Self-taught learning: transfer learning from unlabeled data, in *Proceedings of the 24th International Conference on Machine learning* (ACM, 2007), pp. 759–766
57. T.A. Tang, L. Mhamdi, D. McLernon, S.A.R. Zaidi, M. Ghogho, Deep learning approach for network intrusion detection in software defined networking, in *2016 International Conference on Wireless Networks and Mobile Communications (WINCOM)*. (IEEE, 2016), pp. 258–263
58. J. Cannady, Next generation intrusion detection: autonomous reinforcement learning of network attacks, in *Proceedings of the 23rd National Information Systems Security Conference* (NIST, 2000), pp. 1–12

Chapter 9
Network Security and Privacy Evaluation Scheme for Cyber Physical Systems (CPS)

Mridula Sharma, Haytham Elmiligi, and Fayez Gebali

1 Introduction

Cyber Physical Systems (CPS) are the backbone of the modern Internet of Things (IoT) applications. CPS is the integration of three main subsystems namely physical/control subsystem, networking subsystem and cyber subsystem. The physical/control subsystem is the physical layer consists of sensors, actuators, RFID etc. The cyber subsystem does all the computations and decision making whereas, networking subsystems helps the other two subsystems communicate with each other. The physical subsystem has the ability to generate the data using devices for sensing and controlling, whereas, calculations and decision making is done at cyber layer to control the physical processes. Through the communication layer, data flows across the other two layers [1, 2]. The three subsystems interact with each other as shown in Fig. 9.1.

Cyber-physical systems are in the process of being widely integrated into various critical infrastructures. Many known examples of CPS include industrial control systems, smart grid systems, medical systems, smart cars, nuclear power plants, water and sewage systems, weather monitoring systems, agricultural and irrigation monitoring systems, etc. [1, 3, 4]. Smart grids are one area of applications of CPS. In smart grids, remote activities are monitored and controlled by specialized computing system called Industrial Control Systems (ICSs) or Supervisory Control And Data Acquisition (SCADA) systems. To keep a CPS secure, it is quite important to keep

M. Sharma (✉) · F. Gebali
Electrical and Computer Engineering, University of Victoria, Victoria, BC, Canada
e-mail: naina@uvic.ca; fayez@ece.uvic.ca

H. Elmiligi
Department of Computing Sciences, Thompson Rivers University, Kamloops, BC, Canada
e-mail: haytham@ieee.org

© Springer Nature Switzerland AG 2020
K.-K. R. Choo, A. Dehghantanha (eds.), *Handbook of Big Data Privacy*,
https://doi.org/10.1007/978-3-030-38557-6_9

Fig. 9.1 CPS structure
integrating physical layer,
communication layer and
computation layer

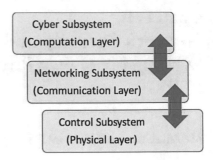

ICS/SCADA system safe and secure, so that we may prevent CPS from security
attack causing a physical hazard to the smart grid [5].

The physical subsystem of CPS consists of large number of sensors connected
together as a Wireless Sensor Network (WSN) to collect environmental data for a
variety of CPS. Any CPS may face many security challenges due to its widespread
use, inclusion of heterogeneous devices, its distribution area, limited capabilities of
the sensors etc. Few vulnerabilities of a CPS are: security protocols, establishing
trust between several subsystems, security of the physical layer as well as the
security of wireless protocols at this layer, etc. These are the common active attacks
on the CPS. There is another categories of attacks where the target is on the data
collection that can be used to leak sensitive information without anybody noticing
any change in the network. Known as passive attacks, these are the privacy attacks
in the network.

There is an ongoing need to address the security and privacy concerns at every
level of CPS right from the early stage of design to the final stage of deployment.
There are several well known cases of failure of CPS deployments as these are
vulnerable to intrusions.

1.1 Chapter Road-MAP

In this chapter, we are proposing a novel Network Security and Privacy Evaluation
Scheme (NSES) for CPS [6]. To do so, Sect. 2 will review some examples of CPS
attacks and the commonly used countermeasures to protect a network are explained
in Sect. 3. A thorough discussion of the prevailing security standards and other
standards proposed in the literature are discussed in Sect. 4. This is done to show
the rationale of developing the scheme followed by scheme explanation in Sect. 5.
The proposed scheme is based on the use of the countermeasures deployed in the
network. At the end of the chapter in Sect. 6, we will demonstrate the use of our
security scheme using different CPS examples.

2 CPS Attack Examples

This section discusses few examples of CPS attacks to understand the severity an the impact of such attacks on commercial platforms.

2.1 Stuxnet

Stuxnet targeted SCADA systems and caused substantial damage to nuclear centrifuges in Iran. Stuxnet, was discovered in June 2010, whereas known to be conceived back in 2005. In this attack, the cyber worm dubbed 'Stuxnet' and struck the Iranian nuclear facility at Natanz. Stuxnet targeted each of the three layers of a cyber-physical system. It used the cyber layer to distribute the malware and identify its targets, control layer (in this case, specific models of programmable logic controllers (PLCs) manufactured by Siemens) to control physical processes, and finally the physical layer, causing physical damage.

In action, the cyber worm of the Stuxnet alters the PLCs' programming, making the centrifuges spin very quickly and for too long, leading to the damage of the delicate equipment. At the same time, the PLCs of the systems tell the controller that everything is working fine, making it difficult to detect or diagnose what's going wrong until it's too late [7].

The worm infected over 200,000 computers and caused 1000 machines to physically degrade, and the effect spread through all across Iran and many other countries including India, Indonesia, China, Azerbaijan, South Korea, Malaysia, the United States, the United Kingdom, Australia, Finland and Germany. Stuxnet malware is comprised of three modules, a worm that executes all code related to the main payload of the attack; a link file to propagate the copies of the worm; and a rootkit component that may hide all malicious files and processes, so that the attack is not been detected.

Duqu, Flame, and Gauss are also similar attacks and are called as Cousins of Stuxnet [8].

2.2 Ukraine SCADA Attack

Ivano-Frankivsk region of Western Ukraine had a SCADA network, that controlled the power grid, allowed the attackers to hijack their credentials and gain crucial access to systems that controlled the breakers. By this attack, hackers caused the massive Ukraine power outage in December 2015, by sabotaging the control system and remotely opening the breakers.

This incident affected about 230,000 people and was regarded as the first high severity cyber-attack that caused power outage [9]. As studied in details, the skilled attackers planned their careful strategies over many months. In this period, first they studied the networks and found operator's credentials, and then launched synchronized assault in well-structured manner. They used social engineering and phishing in email to gain access.

It is claimed that the logging remotely into the SCADA network that controlled the grid was not secure and wasnt́ using two-factor authentication, which allowed the attackers to hijack their credentials and gain crucial access to systems that controlled the breakers.

2.3 Mirai Attack

The infamous Mirai attack brute-forced IoT devices using factory default usernames and passwords, and logged into them to infect these IoT devices with the Mirai malware. Discovered by MalwareMustDie!,[1] a white-hat security research group, in August 2016, this malware was created using ELF binaries and targets SSH or Telnet network protocols, so that it can exploit default and hardcoded credentials [10].

The malware hijacked nearly half a million internet connected devices, and resulted in the inaccessibility of several high-profile websites such as GitHub, Twitter, Reddit, Netflix, Airbnb and many others. The scale of the attack was unprecedented, and the exploitation of IoT devices to launch this DDoS attack may lead to more cyber-attacks in an even larger scale in the future.

By the end of November 2016, approximately 900,000 routers were infected and crashed due to failed TR-064 exploitation attempts by a variant of Mirai, which resulted in Internet connectivity problems for the users of these devices.

2.4 Maroochy Water Service Attack

A SCADA system breach occured on Maroochy Water Services on Queensland's Sunshine Coast in Australia. It was discovered in March 2000, when Maroochy Shire Council experienced problems with its new wastewater system [11]. The communications been sent to waste-water pumping stations by radio links were being lost, and as a result, pumps started mal-functioning. This case is also an important case that has been cited around the world as an example of the damage that could occur if SCADA systems are not secured.

This attack lead to severe disruptions of the plant, including disruption of proper pump operation, suppression of alarms, and even releasing of untreated sewage into local waterways. The attack caused 800,000 liters of raw sewage to spill out into local parks, rivers and even the grounds of a Hyatt Regency hotel. The

---

[1]http://www.malwaremustdie.org/, 2012, [Online; accessed 2019/07/07].

marine life died, the creek water turned black and the stench became unbearable for residents [12].

The detailed analysis of the incidents discussed above lead to several important points:

1. It is very important yet difficult to protect CPS against attacks
2. Radio communications commonly used in SCADA systems is insecure but should be monitored
3. SCADA devices and software should be secured to the extent possible using physical and logical controls
4. The security controls in SCADA should be used properly
5. SCADA systems must record all device accesses and commands, especially those involving connections to or from remote sites, and must follow sophisticated logging mechanisms.

In the next section, many possible countermeasures that may be deployed in the networks to make them secure are discussed.

3   Common Countermeasures to Protect Cyber Physical Systems

Security of any network is concerned with confidentiality, integrity, availability, non repudiation, authentication and safety. Typically, confidentiality and integrity have high priority on regular IT infrastructures, whereas, availability, privacy, integrity and safety dominate security concerns for CPS. In a regular IT infrastructure, where people use machine in networks, maintaining security is comparatively easier as we may develop standard human usage policies and performance requirements, whereas for CPS, it is very diverse and difficult to deploy. Since, the hardware requirements, policies and process requirements are very different and are very unique, therefore, a unique standard security solution for all CPSs is extremely difficult to develop. Since, CPSs are build using very diverse hardware, software and user policies, we need to understand and analyze these differences in order to manage expectations of future CPS security [13].

At the physical later of a CPS, the main security needs are availability, integrity and safety. We need to ensure that all the nodes are available and generating data. Besides that, data generated from each node reaches its target without been tampered in any way so that the data generated at the nodes is protected and is not misused. It is also important to ensure that the nodes are not tempered physically and are safe.

Let us compare the physical layer of a CPS with a house. The house security can be done through a three step process:

1. Install a physical lock on the main door. This lock is used to secure the house when we go out of the house. The keys are only with the authorized people i.e. home owners, and they can enter the door using those keys. They may give the

keys to their trusted friends or relatives only. Also the walls of the house are sound proof, so that the communication going on inside is also protected and is not heard outside.
2. Install motion sensors inside the house. These sensors can detect if somebody breaks in, and sends the message on our system or raise the alarm.
3. Install security locks in the inner rooms. All rooms in the house are locked so that the intruder cannot go further.

These three steps can represent three actions: prevention, detection and mitigation. In the following sub-sections, we will explain these scenarios in more details. We should point out that detection is the most challenging task and hence is the main focus of this chapter. Just to mention, no any single security countermeasure is fully effective against all threat scenarios, so we may use the collection of many.

3.1   Prevention

Prevention can be defined as the process in place that may/should not allow a new and unauthorized user to join the network or tamper the already connected devices. prevention requires careful analysis of the various targeted attacks. Prevention in a CPS needs to be done at all the three layers i.e. physical layer, communication layer as well as cyber layer. Our work mainly deals with the prevention at the physical layer only.

Prevention can be done using four main measures [14]:

3.1.1   Physical Protection

Some special lock and key arrangement to protect the hardware physically from the intentional tampering. The sensor nodes must be equipped with a certain physical hardware to enhance protection against various attacks. As an example, in order to protect against physical tampering of the sensors, one possible defense is to tamper-proof the node's physical package.

3.1.2   Firewall

An effective defense mechanism that acts as a gatekeeper over the communication traffic entering and exiting a network [15]. This may be done using some physical (extra hardware) security management or using cryptographic keys to ensure that only the authorized nodes can join the network. Even though, it is claimed that firewalls are quite impossible for the wireless networks, yet, it is possible to selectively control and block radio communication or using rule definition language [15, 16].

3.1.3 Access Control

Access Control is the enforced restrictions to the network to prevent unauthorized users to be able to access the network. It also protects the network by imposing restrictions on the access rights of the authorized users. Also implemented as user authentication, a tool to help identify and validate the identity of a particular user. Access control ensures that the new node needs to prove that it is not only has correct identity, also is truly new and authenticated to be admitted into the sensor network. [17]. This is possible using key establishment, which is a part of access control, that will help the new nodes to establish shared keys with its neighbors to ensure a secure communications with them.

3.1.4 Cryptography and Key-Exchanges

In order to ensure privacy in the network, the confidentiality of the data travelling through the network must be maintained. To do so, it is required to verify that the data is not be tampered while travelling. Encryption is the solution for this. Data is encrypted before sending, and is decrypted by the receiver to read it back. This may be achieved using key management. When a single key is used for both encryption and decryption, it is called Symmetric key and is a preferred method in WSN, as it consumes less battery power, memory and has minimum computation overhead. The other method is Asymmetric key cryptography, which uses two separate keys, one for encryption and another for decryption, and the two keys are interconnected with complex mathematical algorithm. This method, even though more reliable and safe, is rarely used in WSN as it has huge overhead on power, computation and memory [18, 19]. Cryptography and Key exchanges directly may not prevent an intrusion, but plays a big role in protecting the network by restricting the entry of an unauthorized user and also help in secure data transmission across different nodes and may protect data from tampering i.e. helps in maintaining privacy in the network.

3.2 Detection

In spite of all efforts of prevention, intrusion still may occur. Detection of one or several compromised nodes is extremely critical and difficult. We need to make our system to be able to detect an intrusion as early as possible. Intrusion detection systems (IDS) are the main tool used for this purpose [20–22]. An IDS can monitor the system activities and notifies as soon as a suspicious activity is found in the system. The IDS systems are prepared or trained to be able to detect attack signatures in terms of any changes in files, configurations or network activity. Role of the IDS is to monitor the entire system and hence should be strategically placed at a suitable position in the network. This is more of an art than a science. The main responsibility while using a IDS is to place it in a network at a suitable location from where it can monitor the entire network. This decision is taken keeping into account the threats, as well as intruder types, methods and processes [14].

3.2.1 Intrusion Detection System (IDS)

An Intrusion Detection System (IDS) can be defined as the process of identifying intrusions, that occur as a result of a security breach. The detection is then reported to the administrators, who can take any further action. IDS can identify attacks at run-time, but it is not defined to provide a response to the intrusion and hence cannot prevent any further disruptions of service [23, 24]. Known as the second line of defence, an IDS may perform the following actions:

- Monitors and analyzes the system and user activities
- Audits the vulnerabilities and system configuration
- May also assess the integrity of data files and critical systems
- Commonly analyze abnormal activities

It can be a software or hardware, or a combination system to automate the intrusion detection process [25].

IDS methodologies are classified as three major categories [26–28]:

1. Signature based intrusion detection—Only detects a specific signature of an attack. Also known as Rule-based IDS, they detect intrusions with the help of built-in signatures. The IDS belonging to this class can only detect well-known attacks with great accuracy because their signatures are already known, but it is unable to detect new attacks because of the absence of the their known signatures [29].
2. Anomaly based intrusion detection—Monitors the abnormal behavior of a network. The anomaly-based IDSs can detect intrusion by matching the traffic patterns or resource utilization's in the well known network. These IDS can detect both well-known attacks as well as new attacks, but the problem is of more false positive and false negative alarms i.e. detection even when no intrusion is there or not able to detect an intrusion [30, 31].
3. Hybrid intrusion detection—combination of both above. This IDS maintains the signature database as well as monitor the traffic for the changes that may occur to detect an intrusion. Composed of two detection modules; one for well-known attacks using signatures, and another, detecting the malicious patterns over the normal profile, these are more accurate in terms of attack detection with less number of false positives. The main drawback of the hybrid IDSs is more consumption of resources, therefore, they are generally not recommended for WSN's [32].

The main point to remember here is that IDSs are always passive in nature i.e. they can only detect intrusion, but cannot take any preventive action. Its role is to detect and raise an alarm.

3.3   Mitigation

Once the intrusion is detected, the possibility of a network to be able to take preventive actions can ensure the highest level of security. There are mainly two approaches of mitigation. First, as soon as an intrusion is detected with its location, the intruder is cut off from the network ensuring the intrusion is not spread across. Second approach is to pursue and prosecute the attacker. Whatever is the approach is, the main role is to take the response in timely manner. In the next section we will review the several tools used for prevention, detection as well as mitigation.

After an intrusion is identified and responded, the further need is to assess the damage done to the systems as well the need is to clean and recover the system to the original form. Another step is the post incident analysis and generating the reports that may be used for strengthening the information security cycle for future.

3.3.1   Intrusion Prevention System (IPS)

The Intrusion Prevention System (IPS) is an extension of IDS, having all IDS capabilities, and also could attempt to stop possible incidents. They only differ by one characteristic i.e. IPS can respond to a detected threat by attempting to prevent it from succeeding or spreading further. To do this, they may change the attacks content or may change the security environment by disabling the infected node. It is a pre-emptive control tool that can identify the potential threats first and then can respond to them very quickly.

Extending the role of IDS, an IPS can also:

- Send an alarm to the administrator
- Drop the malicious packets
- Block traffic from the source address
- Reset the connection

IPS methodologies can be classified as two major categories [26, 33]:

1. Network—This is a monitoring device, that can capture the entire network and analyze the traffic. The network IPS can detect any malicious activity in real time, and then take an immediate action. This can be done by deploying special sensors at some designated areas so that the entire network can be successfully monitored. To deploy network IPS, sometimes, additional hosts can be added with special monitoring capabilities in addition to the normal sensors. At the time of setting up the network, this is quite easy to deploy [33].
2. Host—by auditing log files, host file systems and resources, this IPS monitors operating system processes so that it can protect the critical system resources. Known as HIPS, it can be a combination of the best features of antivirus, behavioral analysis, signature filters, network firewalls, and application firewalls etc. The problem with this IPS is that it needs to run on every node in the network [33].

3.3.2   Secured Protocol

The protocol in any WSN allows the nodes to communicate. A secured protocol may protect the network by only authenticating and transferring the legitimate packets and defending the attack packets. Another role of the secure protocol is to detect an intrusion by monitoring the real-time behavior of their neighbors in order to detect malicious behavior. Re-routing by eliminating the malicious participants and to restore back the network functionality is also a task in secured protocol. Role of the secure protocol is to provide data confidentiality, two-party data authentication, integrity, and ensuring the freshness of data. Another role is providing authentication for data broadcast as well. Several secure protocols for WSN are SPINS, LEAP, RKP, TinySec, µTESLA etc.

4   Available Security Standards

To protect any network against the theft and misuse of confidential information as well as to protect it from the malicious attacks, several measures need to be taken. One of the methods is to define the security of the network at the time of setting up the network using the certified products. Certified products are the products that have passed some performance and quality assurance tests and meet the quality assurance criteria set by the certifying agencies. Using these products provides a confidence that the product will perform as the certified claims indicated. Although, security may not be assured by the use of certified products, a set of barriers may be used to protect the network. In this case, if one solution fails, others still can guard the network. In this section, we discuss three main certifying agencies namely Common Criteria, Federal Information Processing Standard and ETSI, which deals with certification of the products. Many researchers have also proposed some complex security measures to protect the network. In the later subsection, we will also discuss their contributions.

4.1   Common Criteria Security Standards (CC-EAL's)

Common Criteria is an international standard for computer security specifications. There are two key components of common criteria i.e. Protection Profiles (PP's) and Evaluation Assurance Levels (EAL's). The role of the Protection Profile is to define a standard set of security requirements for a specific type of product, e.g. a firewall. EAL are used to define the testing of the product. Scaled from 1–7, EAL's only assures the level of testing with one being the lowest-level evaluation and seven being the highest-level of evaluation. EAL are only numbers used to describes the rigor and depth of an evaluation testing for the security assurance requirements. This helps in certifying the development of an IT product across a certain level of strictness. These levels are considered as the security for applications in extremely high risk situations [34–36]. Each EAL level introduces a set of security assurance components (SARs) that must be included in the evaluation such that the EAL level is met. For the organizations to achieve a particular EAL level, they have to meet very specific assurance requirements, which may lead from design documentation and analysis to various testing, or implementation of extra hardware/software. For gaining high level of security, the organization may need to have more detailed documentation, analysis, and testing than the lower ones, which costs more money and time. The main benefit of this level number assignment is the indication of the security test level maintained by the organization. These security standard are applicable for an IT product or system, and is an international standard in effect since 1999. The EAL levels only state the level of security of the system at the time of testing and certifying. The Common Criteria evaluations are done solely on computer security systems and products.

In order to get the certified EAL level, the vendor needs to submit the product for validation to CC. The product is tested in the laboratory to verify the product's security features and then it is evaluated how well the product meets the specifications defined in the Protection Profile to grant an official certification of the product. The ultimate goal of a CC certification is just to assure customers about the products they are buying that it has been evaluated and the vendor's claims have been verified by a vendor-neutral third party. But, EAL levels does not ensures what the product must do. The EAL level itself is only one indicator on the security of a product and does not measure the security of the complete system or network, and specially not of the WSN.

4.2 Federal Information Processing Standard (FIPS)

Another commonly used security standard is FIPS i.e. Federal Information Processing Standard (FIPS) published by U.S. government computer security to approve cryptographic modules [37]. The main role of FIPS standards is to specify the best practices and security requirements for implementing crypto algorithms and encryption schemes. In order to handle important data, when cryptographic-based security systems are used, FIPS standards come into picture. FIPS defines specific methods for encryption and specific methods for generating encryption keys that can be used in these cases. These are the set of standards that only describe document processing, encryption algorithms and other information technology standards. Used within non-military government agencies, government contractors and the vendors working with the agencies, these standards include both hardware and software components. Covering many FIPS standards (140-2, 180-4 etc.), this specifically applies to the areas related to the secure design and implementation of a cryptographic modules like cryptographic module specification, cryptographic module ports and interfaces; their roles, services, and authentication etc. For example, FIPS (140) standard only defines the cryptographic algorithms that are approved by US Federal government to be used in their computer systems for the protection of sensitive data. Although, cryptography has a major contribution in maintaining security, but it alone does not ensure it all.

4.3   ETSI Security Standard for IoT

ETSI works for the establishment of the effective telecommunications systems to protect citizens on security issues in many fields like next generation networks, machine-to-machine communication, intelligent transport systems, quantum cryptography etc. The Cyber Security Technical Committee (TC CYBER) of ETSI is developing standards to protect the Internet and the communications. In a recently released standard ETSI TS 103 645, this committee has proposed a standard for cyber-security in the IoT, in order to establish a security baseline for internet connected consumer products [38]. They have tried bringing together widely considered good practices to maintain the security for internet-connected consumer devices. The document has a list of specifies high-level provisions for the security of consumer devices that are connected to network infrastructure, such as the Internet or home network, and their associated services. The list of recommended security provisions as listed in the document are: No universal default passwords, Implement a means to manage reports of vulnerabilities, Keep software updated, Securely store credentials and security-sensitive data, Communicate securely, Minimize exposed attack surfaces, Ensure software integrity, Ensure that personal data is protected, Make systems resilient to outages, Examine system telemetry data, Make it easy for consumers to delete personal data, Make installation and maintenance of devices easy, Validate input data etc.

In the next subsection, we discuss several security systems proposed in the literature.

4.4   Other Security Evaluation Standards

Till now, common certification standards are discussed that are used in industry. A lot of research is done to secure networks and several new schemes and measures are proposed from time to time. In this subsection, we will list some security systems proposed in the literature.

Alvaro, Tanya and Sastry proposed a security scheme for SCADA systems [39]. They proposed different countermeasures for different attacks by categorizing the attacks in three categories; (1) physical attacks from outsiders, (2) key compromise attacks and (3) insider attacks from somebody controlling a legitimate node. They first ranked the threats to calculate the score of the difficulty of accomplishing the attack. For their security scheme, they have considered extra hardware installation, physical access security, and required technical skills to enforce attacks. They did discuss various issues related to SCADA systems, but failed to provide any measure to provide security to the network.

Another framework that is used for modelling the security of CPS is based on traditional Byzantine model [40]. In this method, they considered only those cyber attacks that could lead to physical damages. Using state-based semi-Markov chain (SMC) model, they described the attacker and the system behaviour over time. They performed quantitative security analysis using metrics like mean time to security failures, steady state security, and steady state physical availability failures. This model does not consider deployment of any countermeasures in the network.

A game-theoretical model for cyber-physical security for wide area monitoring, protection and control applications (WAMPAC) is proposed, where authors considered the attacks as timing based attacks, integrity attacks and replay attacks [41]. They also considered security as three components: Wide-Area Monitoring (WAM), Wide-Area Control (WAC) and Wide-Area Protection (WAP). Their model works on various cyber attack scenarios based on the attack model, and the information sets available to the attacker and the defender.

Sensor data security estimator (SDSE), a new comprehensive security estimation module defined for WSNs [42]. This module is deployed on the base station and based on the cryptography algorithm, key management scheme and intrusion detection system, calculates the security level of the network. The main goal of this work is to calculate the security level (SL) of sensor data based on the three countermeasures and provide that to the WSN users.

A comprehensive value Q is defined as the security value of the whole network by analyzing the security value of network elements, and by adopting the Geometric mean method to determine this value [43]. A higher value of Q ensures that the network is secured. Common criteria EALs are used to calculate this value. Although their use of CCs CAP (Composed Assurance Package), which is an evaluation method to evaluate the composed information security where two or more IT products are used. Since CC is a well established standard and make this scheme more trustworthy but still the lack of consideration of deployed countermeasures does not make it practically very applicable.

A Three-Dimensional Model for Software Security Evaluation is proposed which provides a systematic way to analyze software security in three dimensions i.e. technology, management and engineering [44]. In technological dimension, CCs 7 security levels based on Evaluation Assurance Levels (EALs) are considered. For the management dimension, the management of software infrastructures, development documents and risks are considered and the engineering dimension is mainly focused on 5 stages of software development life-cycle.

A special threat framework proposed specifically for CPSs is based on the traditional Byzantine paradigm for cryptographic security [45]. In this scheme, the basic security features and requirements as specified are used to identify system vulnerabilities. The advantage of this framework is the use of formal analyses and security proofs that are done using existing cryptographic methodologies.

Using Trusted Platform Module (TPM), this scheme works for securing the data [46]. TPM is developed by the Trusted Computing Group[2] and works by generating the asymmetric key pair, their secure storage, generation of signatures and finally encryption and decryption of data. The scheme is tested and verified using Castalia simulator. The TPM needs to be deployed at every node in the network.

In Table 9.1, a summary of these security standards and systems is provided.

Although a lot of research has been done for defining security evaluations, but mainly these are for IT networks and systems. In the area of CPS, a standard scheme that can certify the security level of its physical layer, seems to be missing. To fulfill this gap, we have proposed a standard methodological Security Evaluation Scheme that may assess the level of security of the physical layer of CPS and may even provide recommendations to enhance the security level to the next level. The role of the Security Evaluation Scheme would be to provide a standard language for expressing security characteristics of any network and work towards establishing an objective basis for evaluating the security of a network in relation to these characteristics. The scheme may be used to express the required security characteristics of a network and then evaluate the deployment in context of the defined criteria. This scheme can also serve as frameworks based on their utility to both users and vendors in support of their security goals.

5   Network Security Evaluation Scheme (NSES) for CPS

Security requirement may vary from one CPS to another. This may be decided according to the importance of the CPS application and the information that is being obtained and/or exchanged. In the area of Cyber Physical Systems, this novel scheme can certify the security level of physical layer of the network and can recommend different security levels based on the security need of the specific domain of CPS.

5.1   Objective

Main objective of NSES is to maintain the required security level of physical layer of CPSs. Based on the basic security mechanism of prevention, detection and survivability [39], we have defined various levels. The minimum level of security is defined that may prevent any attack in the network as it will prevent a new insertion of a node. But even then an attack may occur. The next level will ensure an early

---

[2]https://trustedcomputinggroup.org/, 2019, [Online; accessed 2019/07/07].

Table 9.1 Security evaluation standards and systems

Evaluation standard	Description	Application domain
EAL	7 level security scheme defined by CC needing detailed documentation, analysis, and testing to get standards	IT products [34]
FIPS	Published by U.S. government computer security to approve cryptographic modules. four levels of security for potential applications and environments using cryptographic modules	Only for cryptographic modules [37]
ETSI security standard	Published by TC cyber to protect the internet and the communication. Has standards that increase privacy and security for organizations and citizens across Europe and worldwide	Businesses across different domains [38]
SMC based model	State-based semi-Markov chain (SMC) model to describe the attacker and the system behaviour over time. Only the cyber attacks that could lead to physical damages were considered	For any CPS [40]
Security scheme for SCADA	Taxonomy composed of the security properties of the sensor network, the threat model, and the security design space to protect SCADA systems. This aims to provide a holistic view of the security of Sensor Network by ranking the threats to calculate the difficulty level of an attack	Any commonly used CPS [39]
WAMPAC security	A game-theoretic framework to model CPS security covering various cyber attacks using attacker/defender model. Works by looking for the attacker strategies based on the defender actions. The defender progressively updates his strategy	Control systems [41]
Sensor data security estimator (SDSE)	Designed to estimate the sensor data security level based on security metrics by analyzing both attack prevention and detection mechanisms. The security evaluation module is at the base station that monitors the network by comparing the sent and returned messages	WSN [42]
CAP based security scheme	Using the Geometric mean method, this scheme determine the security value of the entire network. Also deals with the analysis and testing of the vulnerabilities in the network	Any network [43]
3-D model for security evaluation	Provides a systematic way to analyze software security in 3-D i.e. technology, management and engineering. The security evidences are collected from three points of view and are evaluated under a rule to calculate the value.	Software [44]
Security framework for CPS	Combines the cyber and physical aspects in terms of threat model and protect it according to the prevailing security policies. Identifies the features needs to be protected and apply the prevailing security policies	Cyber physical systems [45]
Security scheme for WSN using TPM	Used for WSN using the TPM deployed on every node. TPM works by generating the asymmetric key pair, their secure storage, generation of signatures and finally encryption and decryption of data	WSN [46]

detection of the attack. IPS on the next level will prevent it from expanding and breaking the entire network. Countermeasures deployed in the network may ensure a much secured and survived network.

5.2 Challenges

Main challenge for us was to design a security mechanism that can be used to prevent, detect and mitigate the attacks. Once the attacks at physical layer are classified, it becomes easier for system engineers to take different measures to protect the network from them. Different counter measures mechanism that can be followed are access control, key agreement, data encryption, secure routing protocol and trust management [1]. The proposed security evaluation scheme is defined based on these countermeasures in a network to ensure that any CPS network can achieve the level of security as required.

5.3 Advantages

This scheme has multiple levels of security based on the difficulty level of an intruder to get into the network. The applicability of the scheme is based on the knowledge about the processes controlled by the CPSs and the required level of security maintenance in the system. The main advantage of the scheme is to define a standard evaluation method to secure physical layer of CPS. For ease and standardization, every level has been given a specific color to depict the security level of a network. This will help developers to better streamline their security expectations for various CPS applications.

Benefit of our security evaluation scheme is both for the network engineers and the clients. The network engineers can always claim to have the security properly implemented and functioning in their network deployment based on the clients specifications. In future, verification of such claims and a stamp of approval by several clients will strengthen the network vendors reputation of setting up the networks as per the clients specifications. The clients gets the surety of the security maintained in their network as required as well as they have the recommendations from the network engineers to enhance their security specifications.

NSES is applicable to almost every IoT and CPS's physical layer. This scheme considers five countermeasures i.e. physical security, key management, cryptography and access control, IDS, IPS, and Secure protocol. For gaining high level of security in any network, network engineers may keep adding more countermeasures as recommended.

We would like to mention here that this scheme can further be extended for the entire CPS with some modifications and enhancements.

5.4 Security Level Codes with Description

The five levels of the security range from A to F. Starting from the highest level of security, we move to the minimum security needs of a network.

- **Security Level A: Fully Secured Network**—Defined as the highest level of security, 'A' certified networks can detect any kind of attack and take preventive actions automatically.
- **Security Level B: Highly Secured Network**—The network with 'B' level certification can detect attacks and do some basic level of prevention based on the tool used. This is done by raising alarm or inactivating the affected node so that to stop the invasion further.
- **Security Level C: Moderately Secure Network**—The network with 'C' level security can only detect the intrusion but cannot take any further action.
- **Security Level D: Above Basic Secure Network**—This level is only defined to ensure the Confidentiality, Integrity and Authentication (CIA) control in the network. The data exchange across the nodes is also protected using encryption/decryption to maintain privacy in the network.
- **Security Level E: Basic Secured Network**—Defined as a minimally secured networks, 'E' level networks has low level of security i.e. the nodes are physically secured and join the network using authenticated keys.

5.5 Deployed Countermeasures

- **Security Level A**—To ensure the highest level of security, this network has all the five major components i.e. Physical Security + Cryptography + IDS + IPS + Secure protocol in place. The Secure routing protocol ensures a correct and efficient route establishment between a pair of nodes. Any kind of attack can be traced and alarmed through this security level.
- **Security Level B**—This network has all the four components except the secure protocol in place i.e. Physical Security + Cryptography + IDS + IPS. Since an IDS can detect attacks but cannot prevent or respond. To ensure high level security, an immediate action must take place once the attack is detected. The IDS must raise an alarm to inform the controller that may take an action to stop the attack impact further. The Intrusion Prevention System will prevent the invalid node to invade further.
- **Security Level C**—This level has the network with Physical Security, Cryptography and IDS in place. It is said that the security-related solutions like authentication and key exchange can provide some security however they cannot eliminate most of the security attacks [47]. The implementation of IDS can enhance the security of network as it will ensure the authenticity of the data transmission over the network. Known as the second line of defence, this security measure can detect an intrusion into the network at an early stage. Most

Challenging attacks are because of node fabrication. An early detection of any attack is the objective of this security level.

- **Security Level D**—D level networks also secures the messages transmitting across the network to maintain privacy. This can be done by adding Cryptography and Key Exchange in addition to physical security. This will ensure the Confidentiality, Integrity and Authentication (CIA) control in the network.
- **Security Level E**—For the minimum level of security, the only have physical security of the nodes ensured by adding software firewall. This level ensures that the nodes are somewhat physically protected and can join the network by only using the authenticated key.

5.6   Color Codes

- Security Level A: Fully Secured Network—An olive green color indicates a fully secured network.
- Security Level B: Highly Secured Network—The green color is the indication of high degree secured network.
- Security Level C: Moderately Secure Network—The yellow color shows that network can detect the intrusion at an early stage.
- Security Level D: Above Basic Secure Network—Orange code is the indicator of a network that cannot detect an intrusion but may protect the message transfers using encryption.
- Security Level E: Basic Secured Network—Red color is the alarm that there is only a physical protection of nodes and new nodes can join using passKey.

The color scheme is defined in the Table 9.2.

Table 9.2 Color scheme of NSES

Level	Description
Security level A	A fully secured network
Security level B	Highly secured network
Security level C	Moderately secure network that can detect the intrusion at an early stage
Security level D	Above basic secure network where message transfer is secured in the network
Security level E	Basic secured network that only has physical protection and uses passkey to join the network

6 Case Studies

In order to illustrate the way this scheme can be used in real life Cyber Physical Systems, we would like to take a few examples. Since a CPS may range from smaller deployments like Body Area Networks (BAN) to larger one's like Environment Monitoring Systems, we are taking five different case studies and explain the applicability of this security scheme in that deployment.

6.1 Environment Monitoring System

There are several applications of the monitoring system i.e. agricultural, habitat, greenhouse, climate, forest monitoring etc. [48]. In such systems, reliability of the network is important in order to prevent packet loss.

6.1.1 Common Threats to the Network

The main threats to this type of networks are physical tampering or unauthorized access by the intruder i.e. preventing a node removal or insertion of an unauthorized node. Not only that, if there is an intrusion, the network should be able to prevent the spreading of the intrusion by either blocking the infected node or by re-configuring the network to re-route packets.

6.1.2 Required Security and Safety Specifications and Recommended Security Level of NSES

The security specifications for environment monitoring system should be that no unauthorized user is able to join the network. Also, the data transmission should be secure so that the message broadcast is also secure. Since the network is in large geographical area, we also need to monitor for any unauthorized activity happening in the network like node removal or an unauthorized node insertion or a node replacement with a faulty node. To meet this security need, the sensors must be physically protected. Also, there must be key exchange mechanism in place that restrict the new unauthorized nodes to join the network. In addition, deployment of IDS/IPS will detect any intrusion at an early stage. So for that purpose, the network should at least follow **Security Level B** as shown in Fig. 9.2. Just to note, Security Level B already covers the measures of Level C, D and E. This will ensure that the intrusion is detected and network is protected for spreading the attack.

Fig. 9.2 Security level of
environment monitoring
system

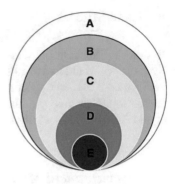

6.2 Body Area Network

CPeSC3 (Cyber Physical enhanced Secured wireless sensor networks integrated
Cloud Computing for u-life Care) is the use of WSN for health care [49]. In this
system, the sensed data is either human health data or data to be used for detection
of human activities for health care services. Here, the sensors are either attached
to the body of the patient or onto the walls in the home environment, and these
sensors can track the patients movement. This may collect the data about the patients
personal health or body movements. The recommendation is to have Image-based
authentication and activity-based access control mechanism to enhance security
and flexibility of users access [49]. The Key Management Techniques are most
relevant for data protection in MCPS [50]. Another similar example is of WBAN,
a communication network between the humans and computers through wearable
Devices [51]. They have also mainly stressed upon Cryptography, Key Management
and Trust Management. Secure routing in their work is also to ensure the end-to-end
communication verification purposes mainly. The recommendations in this work
are also of security and privacy in transferring data like human body signals, needs
Authentication, integrity, access control, non-repudiation and encryption features.

6.2.1 Common Threats to the Network

Physical tampering of the nodes or unauthorized access to modify the readings.
The need is that the patient's vital information must be stored and used with
confidence. Moreover, for the patients with a socially unaccepted disease, it is
even vital. Any failure or leakage of this type of patient's health information could
lead to humiliation, wrong treatments, relationship issues, or even job loss. In
case of negative perception of the health information can also invariably hinder
an individuals ability to get good treatment or coverage. Due to these reasons, it
is critically important to ensure the security and privacy of medical data of different
patients [52].

6.2.2   Required Security and Safety Specifications and Recommended Security Level of NSES

In this network, if we may just restrict unauthorized insertion as well may secure the message transmission, the network will work fine and will be maintaining the privacy of the data transmitting across. To match this need, the system administrators need to ensure that the network should have an above minimum security level, where the environment will be controlled physically and has cryptography deployed. The physical protection will protect the sensors so that they are not intentionally tampered externally and cryptography and key exchange barrier, will secure the message transmission. This will protect the patients data at the physical level as well only allow authenticated sensors and actuators. So, for that reason **Security Level D** will be appropriately suitable for this network as shown in Fig. 9.3. To be more critical patients, who are may be disabled or so, **Security Level C** may be more appropriately suitable.

6.3   Surveillance Control

The forest wildfire monitoring application is useful in remote areas. A Sybil attack is known to be a common attack on this network. A two-tier detection scheme is proposed by the authors [53]. Sybil attack is by the attacked nodes that transmit high false-negative alerts to an end user so that they may divert the attention to the less vulnerable geographical regions.

6.3.1   Common Threats to the System

Common threats here are nodes modification as well as the new node insertion.

Fig. 9.3 Security level of body area network (BAN)

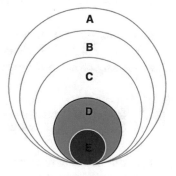

Fig. 9.4 Security level of
surveillance control systems

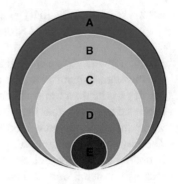

6.3.2 Required Security and Safety Specifications and Recommended Security Level of NSES

We need a full-proof security and safety of this network. So, the network must be protected at the **Security Level A** as shown in Fig. 9.4, so that any intruder can be identified as well as the protection alarm will ring. Moreover, through the secure protocol, the sybil nodes can immediately be identified and will be stopped from making an adverse effect on the network.

6.4 Smart-Home System

The current boom is the Internet connected household devices, such as light-bulbs, cameras, smoke-alarms, and door-locks, leading to a smart-home [54]. This helps in family safety, property protection, lighting/energy management, as well as pet monitoring. Garden irrigation system is also an added component.

6.4.1 Common Threats to the Network

The various devices in the smart home are from different vendors. This vast heterogeneity in devices makes overall attack vector very large and very challenging for a security professional to cover out the entire threat space.

6.4.2 Required Security and Safety Specifications and Recommended Security Level of NSES

As per our scheme, the sensors need to have some physical protection. Since the coverage in these networks in heterogeneous space and devices, it is important to define security through secure protocol in addition to key exchanges and IDS/IPS so

Fig. 9.5 Security level of
smart-home systems

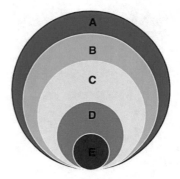

that any intrusion may be detected at an early stage. So for that purpose, the network
should follow **Security Level A** as per our scheme as shown in Fig. 9.5.

6.5 Smart Cars

Smart cars, or popularly known as intelligent cars, are the cars that are more
environment-friendly, fuel-efficient, safe by automatic monitoring of the road
threats. They also have enhanced entertainment and convenience features. The cars
have multiple computers networked together, known as Electronic Control Units
(ECUs). These ECUs mainly monitor and control various car functions. There are
sensors that keep sensing the road threats and accordingly control the car activities
like speeding or stopping [4].

6.5.1 Common Threats to the Network

As mentioned, the threat to the smart car is a hacker, who can attack a car's ECUs
(target) by exploiting weakness in the wireless interfaces (vector) so that it can cause
a collision or loss of control (consequence). If we may stop an external node to join
the local network that is collecting data and checking with the outside threats, we can
protect the car. So the plan may be to protect the car sensor network physically and
disable the unauthorized node to join the car network; then, it will ensure security
of the smart car.

6.5.2 Required Security and Safety Specifications and Recommended Security Level of NSES

As per our scheme, the sensors need to have some physical protection. Since the
coverage in these networks in heterogeneous space and devices, it is important to
define security through key exchanges so that no new node can join the network. So

Fig. 9.6 Security level of
smart-cars

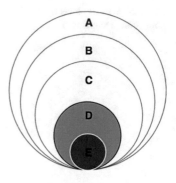

for that purpose, the network should follow **Security Level D** as per our scheme as
shown in Fig. 9.6.

7 Summary

Out of the three subsystems of CPS, namely, cyber subsystems, networking
subsystem and physical subsystems; physical subsystem is the one made up of
wireless sensors and actuators and is known as WSN. WSN is used to generate
data to send to cyber layer and also control physical layer using actuators.

To secure any network, several new and old security standards are widely
available. However, a scheme that defines the security level of a network as a
whole, is still needed. A novel security scheme that provides a holistic view of the
security of WSN for IoT/CPS applications is described in this chapter. Known as
NSES, this scheme is divided into 5 different security levels based on the deployed
countermeasures. The five levels of the security starts from the very basic security
level 'E' to the highest security level 'A', which is the fully secured network. Level
'A' covers all the levels from E to A with reference to the security countermeasures
deployed at every level.

Supported by a few CPS/IoT examples, the use of NSES is explained with a
particular focus on the security need of every network and the recommendations of
the security level from the NSES. These recommendations can be used by network
administrators at early design phases to define the security needs of the network and
then match them at the time of deployment.

The main advantage of NSES is that it can be used as a common platform by
the network users and network administrators to match their security needs with its
implementations.

References

1. Y. Ashibani, Q.H. Mahmoud, Cyber physical systems security: analysis, challenges and solutions. Comput. Secur. **68**, 81–97 (2017)
2. Z. Zhang, J. Porter, E. Eyisi, G. Karsai, X. Koutsoukos, J. Sztipanovits, Co-simulation framework for design of time-triggered cyber physical systems, in *Proceedings of the ACM/IEEE 4th International Conference on Cyber-Physical Systems*, Ser. ICCPS '13 (ACM, New York, 2013), pp. 119–128. Available: http://doi.acm.org.ezproxy.library.uvic.ca/10.1145/2502524.2502541
3. B. Berry, Do you know these key SCADA concepts SCADA tutorial: a quick, easy, comprehensive guide(white paper), DPS Telecom, Technical Report (2011)
4. A. Humayed, J. Lin, F. Li, B. Luo, Cyber-physical systems security—A survey, *CoRR* (2017). Available: http://arxiv.org/abs/1701.04525
5. S. Ali, T. Al Balushi, Z. Nadir, O.K. Hussain, *ICS/SCADA System Security for CPS* (Springer, Cham, 2018), pp. 89–113. Available: https://doi.org/10.1007/978-3-319-75880-05
6. M. Sharma, F. Gebali, H. Elmiligi, M. Rahman, Network security evaluation scheme(NSES) for WSN in cyber-physical systems, in *2018 IEEE 9th Annual Information Technology, Electronics and Mobile Communication Conference (IEMCON)*, (2018), pp. 1145–1151
7. J. Fruhlinger, What is stuxnet, who created it and how does it work? CSO, Technical Report, August 22, 2017. Available: https://www.csoonline.com/article/3218104/
8. B. Bencsáth, G. Pék, L. Buttyán, M. Félegyházi, The cousins of stuxnet: Duqu, flame, and gauss. Future Internet **4**(4), 971–1003 (2012). Available: https://www.mdpi.com/1999-5903/4/4/971
9. M.B. Farrell, J. Detsch, Hard lessons for Energy Department, power sector after Ukraine hack (2016). Available: http://link.galegroup.com/apps/doc/A452362153/CPI?u=uvictoria&sid=CPI&xid=02ff6650
10. Botnets, Mirai, in *NJ Cybersecurity & Communications Integration Cell(NJCCIC)* (2016). Available: https://www.cyber.nj.gov/threat-profiles/botnet-variants/mirai-botnet
11. J. Slay, M. Miller, Lessons learned from the maroochy water breach, in *International Federation for Information Processing Digital Library; Critical Infrastructure Protection*, vol. 253, (Springer, Boston,2007), pp. 73–82
12. M.D. Abrams, Malicious control system cyber security attack case study: Maroochy water services, australia, Technical Papers, August 2008. Available: https://www.mitre.org/publications/technical-papers/malicious-control-system-cyber-security-attack-case-study-maroochy-water-services-australia
13. E. Colbert, Security of cyber-physical systems, J. Cyber Sect. Inf. Syst. **5**(1), 41–47 (2017)
14. J. LaPiedra, The information security process: Prevention, detection and response, *GIAC Directory of Certified Professionals*, (SANS Institute, Bethesda, 2000–2002)
15. M.S. Hossain, V. Raghunathan, Aegis: a lightweight firewall for wireless sensor networks, in *Distributed Computing in Sensor Systems*, ed. by R. Rajaraman, T. Moscibroda, A. Dunkels, A. Scaglione (Springer, Berlin, 2010), pp. 258–272
16. M. Wilhelm, I. Martinovic, J. Schmitt, V. Lenders, Wifire: a firewall for wireless networks, in *Proceedings of the ACM SIGCOMM 2011 Conference on Applications, Technologies, Architectures, and Protocols for Computer Communications*, Toronto, August 15–19, 2011, (2011), pp. 456–457
17. Y. Zhou, Y. Zhang, Y. Fang, Access control in wireless sensor networks, in *Ad Hoc Networks*. Security Issues in Sensor and Ad Hoc Networks, vol. 5, No. 1, (Elsevier, Amsterdam, 2007), pp. 3–13. Available: http://www.sciencedirect.com/science/article/pii/S1570870506000497
18. S. Kumaran, N. Kailasanathan, S. Mohan, Review of asymmetric key cryptography in wireless sensor networks, Int. J. Eng. Tech. **8**, 859–862, (2016)
19. S. Kumaran, P. Ilango, Evolution of key management and variations of random pre key distribution in wireless sensor network: survey. Int. J. Appl. Eng. Res. **9**, 11 681–11 688, (2014)

20. S. Mohammadi, H. Mirvaziri, M. Ghazizadeh-Ahsaee, H. Karimipour, Cyber intrusion detection by combined feature selection algorithm, J. Inf. Sect. Appl. **44**, 80–88 (2019). Available: http://www.sciencedirect.com/science/article/pii/S2214212618304617
21. S. Mohammadi, V. Desai, H. Karimipour, Multivariate mutual information-based feature selection for cyber intrusion detection, in *2018 IEEE Electrical Power and Energy Conference (EPEC)* (IEEE, Piscataway, 2018), pp. 1–6
22. E. Modiri Dovom, A. Azmoodeh, A. Dehghantanha, D. Ellis Newton, R. Parizi, H. Karimipour, Fuzzy pattern tree for edge malware detection and categorization in IoT. J. Sys. Architect. **97**, 1–7, (2019)
23. I. Tomić, J.A. McCann, A survey of potential security issues in existing wireless sensor network protocols, IEEE Internet Things J. **4**(6), 1910–1923 (2017)
24. H. Karimipour, S. Geris, A. Dehghantanha, H. Leung, Intelligent anomaly detection for large-scale smart grids, in *IEEE Canadian Conference on Electrical and Computer Engineering (CCECE)*, Edmonton (2019)
25. H.J. Liao, C.H.R. Lin, Y.C. Lin, K.Y. Tung, Intrusion detection system: a comprehensive review. J. Netw. Comput. Appl. **36**(1), 16–24 (2013). Available: http://www.sciencedirect.com/science/article/pii/S1084804512001944
26. S. Duhan, P. Khandnor, Intrusion detection system in wireless sensor networks: a comprehensive review, in *2016 International Conference on Electrical, Electronics, and Optimization Techniques (ICEEOT)* (2016), pp. 2707–2713
27. N.A. Alrajeh, S. Khan, B. Shams, Intrusion detection systems in wireless sensor networks: a review. Int. J. Distrib. Sens. Netw. **9**(5), 167575 (2013)
28. H.H. Pajouh, R. Javidan, R. Khayami, A. Dehghantanha, K.R. Choo, A two-layer dimension reduction and two-tier classification model for anomaly-based intrusion detection in iot backbone networks. IEEE Trans. Emerg. Top. Comput. **7**(2), 314–323 (2019)
29. H. Karimipour, A. Dehghantanha, R. Parizi, R. Choo, H. Leung, A deep and scalable unsupervised machine learning system for cyber-attack detection in large-scale smart grids, in *IEEE Access* (IEEE, Piscataway, 2019)
30. S. Geris, H. Karimipour, A feature selection-based approach for joint cyber-attack detection and state estimation, in *IEEE International Conference on Smart Energy Grid Engineering (SEGE)*, Oshawa (2019)
31. M.R. Begli, F. Derakhshan, H. Karimipour, A layered intrusion detection system for critical infrastructure using machine learning, in *IEEE International Conference on Smart Energy Grid Engineering (SEGE)*, Oshawa (2019)
32. J. Sakhnini, A. Dehghantanha, H. Karimipour, Smart grid cyber attacks detection using supervised learning and heuristic feature selection, in *IEEE International Conference on Smart Energy Grid Engineering (SEGE)* (2019)
33. C. Paquet, *Implementing Cisco IOS Network Security (IINS): (CCNA Security Exam 640-553) (Authorized Self-Study Guide)*, ch. Network Security Using Cisco IOS IPS (Cisco Press, Indianapolis, 2009)
34. C.C. Portal, *Common Criteria for Information Technology Security Evaluation* (2012). www.commoncriteriaportal.org/files/ccfiles/CCPART3V3.1R4.pdf
35. K. Caplan, J.L. Sanders, Building an international security standard. IT Prof. **1**(2), 29–34 (1999)
36. Common Criteria (2018) . Available: www.commoncriteriaportal.org
37. U.S. Department of Commerce, *Security Requirements For Cryptographic Modules* (National Institute of Standards and Technology, Gaithersburg, 2001). Available: https://nvlpubs.nist.gov/nistpubs/FIPS/NIST.FIPS.140-2.pdf
38. ETSI, *CYBER; Cyber Security for Consumer Internet of Things*, (2019). Available: https://www.etsi.org
39. A.A. Cardenas, T. Roosta, S. Sastry, Rethinking security properties, threat models, and the design space in sensor networks: a case study in SCADA systems. Ad Hoc Netw. **7**(8), 1434–1447 (2009)

40. H. Orojloom M.A. Azgomi, A method for modeling and evaluation of the security of cyber-physical systems, in *2014 11th International ISC Conference on Information Security and Cryptology* (2014), pp. 131–136
41. A. Ashok, A. Hahn, M. Govindarasu, Cyber-physical security of wide-area monitoring, protection and control in a smart grid environmen. J. Adv. Res. **5**(4), 481–489 (2014). Cyber Security
42. A. Ramos, R.H. Filho, Sensor data security level estimation scheme for wireless sensor networks. Sensors **15**, 2104–2137 (2015)
43. X. Wu, J. Li, W. Yao, A network security evaluation model based on common criteria, in *2008 International Conference on Apperceiving Computing and Intelligence Analysis* (2008), pp. 416–420
44. Z. Han, X. Li, R. Feng, J. Hu, G. Xu, Z. Feng, A three-dimensional model for software security evaluation, in *2014 Theoretical Aspects of Software Engineering Conference* (2014), pp. 34–41
45. M. Burmester, E. Magkos, V. Chrissikopoulos, Modeling security in cyber physical systems. Int. J. Crit. Infrastruct. Prot. **5**(3), 118–126 (2012)
46. H. Fouchal, J. Blesa, E. Romero, A. Araujo, O. Nieto Taladrez, A security scheme for wireless sensor networks, in *2016 IEEE Global Communications Conference (GLOBECOM)* (2016), pp. 1–5
47. Y. Ping, J. Xinghao, W. Yue, L. Ning, Distributed intrusion detection for mobile ad hoc networks. J. Syst. Eng. Electron. **19**(4), 851–859 (2008)
48. M.F. Othman, K. Shazali, Wireless sensor network applications: a study in environment monitoring system. Procedia Eng. **41**, 1204–1210 (2012); International Symposium on Robotics and Intelligent Sensors 2012 (IRIS 2012)
49. J. Wang, H. Abid, S. Lee, F. Xia, Secured health care application architecture for cyber-physical systems (2012). ArXiv e-prints
50. O. Kocabas, T. Soyata, M.K. Aktas, Emerging security mechanisms for medical cyber physical systems. IEEE/ACM Trans. Comput. Biol. Bioinforma. **13**(3), 401–416 (2016)
51. S. Pathania, N. Bilandi, Security issues in wireless body area network. Int. J. Comput. Sci. Mob. Comput. **3**(4), 1171–1178 (2014)
52. S. Al-Janabi, I. Al-Shourbaji, M. Shojafar, S. Shamshirband, Survey of main challenges (security and privacy) in wireless body area networks for healthcare applications. Egypt. Inf. J. **18**(2), 113–122 (2017)
53. M.A. Jan, P. Nanda, X. He, R.P. Liu, A sybil attack detection scheme for a forest wildfire monitoring application. Futur. Gener. Comput. Syst. **80**, 613–626 (2018)
54. V. Sivaraman, D. Chan, D. Earl, R. Boreli, Smart-phones attacking smart-homes, in *Proceedings of the 9th ACM Conference on Security; Privacy in Wireless and Mobile Networks*, Ser. WiSec '16 (ACM, New York, 2016), pp. 195–200

Chapter 10
Anomaly Detection in Cyber-Physical Systems Using Machine Learning

Hossein Mohammadi Rouzbahani, Hadis Karimipour, Abolfazl Rahimnejad, Ali Dehghantanha (iD) **, and Gautam Srivastava**

1 Introduction

Cyber-Physical Systems are a result of an efficient combination of cyber systems and the physical world into an integrated structure for vital tasks which originated from advancements in digital electronics [1]. In these systems, physical components and computational resources are integrated through communication links for remote monitoring and control [2, 3].

The smart grid, as a cyber-physical system, emerged from the restructuring of traditional power networks [4]. These systems require smart tools not only for electrical flow, but also for better performance that has led to self-healing, adaptive protection, control, customer involvement, just to name a few [5–7].

Even though Cyber-Physical Systems develop system operator interaction with the consumer and other parties, many challenges have been created including security, reliability, stability, maintainability, safety, and predictability [8, 9]. Security is one of the most important challenges in cyber-physical systems due to the integration of many components which has made them vulnerable on both the physical and cyber sides. Malicious attacks have led to interrupt system operation or theft of arcane data which can be directed at the cyberinfrastructure or physical

H. Mohammadi Rouzbahani (✉) · H. Karimipour · A. Rahimnejad
School of Engineering, University of Guelph, Guelph, ON, Canada
e-mail: hmoham15@uoguelph.ca; hkarimi@uoguelph.ca; Canada-hkarimi@uoguelph.ca; arahimne@uoguelph.ca

A. Dehghantanha
Cyber Science Lab, School of Computer Science, University of Guelph, Guelph, ON, Canada
e-mail: ali@cybersciencelab.org

G. Srivastava
Department of Mathematics and Computer Science, Brandon University, Brandon, MB, Canada
e-mail: srivastavag@brandonu.ca

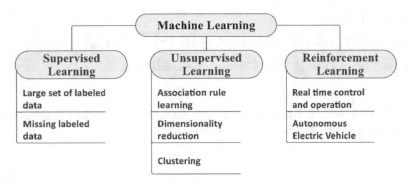

Fig. 10.1 Machine learning subsections in CPS security

components [8, 10–12]. Cyber-physical systems are facing a tsunami of generated data on different components which are too large and complex for real-time processing. Cloud computing techniques along with analytic methods such as machine learning (ML) can help generated information be secure whilst being processed, analyzed and stored [13, 14]. ML in the context of this chapter is referring to making predictions after learning from available data by a system. Figure 10.1 shows the application of ML in smart grid security.

There are many approaches such as ML to intrusion detection systems which are classified into supervised, unsupervised, and reinforcement learning and can build the requisite model based on training data [15]. In supervised ML, both normal and abnormal behaviors are provided to the model to learn trained labeled data. It is very difficult for attackers on cyber-physical systems to obtain labeled data [16, 17] while they do not need abnormal data in the training phase and it is a great advantage for unsupervised learning [2, 18, 19]. In reinforcement learning, there is no training data and as a result, the agent can learn from their own experience. In fact, it gathers the training examples by trial and error while it is attempting its tasks.

This chapter surveys ML methods for an anomaly attack detection framework for cyber-physical systems. Anomaly detection is defined as detecting patterns that do not fit into predictable behavior [20, 21]. Since the characteristics, structure, quantities, and patterns of research activities are understood by bibliometric analysis, the purpose of this chapter is to identify the state-of-the-art of anomaly attack detection in cyber-physical systems.

Web of Science is used as the search engine for this analysis. First, the related keywords are inputted for extracting publications. Then, we limit research time to the last 10 years. Finally, non-relevant and non-English publications were removed and the inquiry to collect the data for bibliometric analysis was as follows: (TS = ((anomaly detection OR outlier detection) AND (cyber-physical system OR cyber-physical system OR smart grid OR CPS cyber-physical systems))). As a result, in the primitive search, 389 publications were found which were reduced to 379 after the mentioned filters.

Results show that the greater number of the publications fall under computer science and engineering and most of them belong to the United States and China

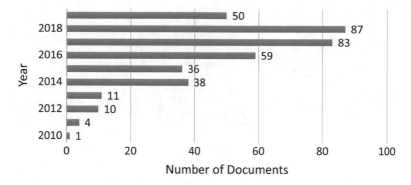

Fig. 10.2 The number of publications

(154 and 72 publications respectively). Iowa State University and the United States Department of Energy are the most productive institutions in this field of study, both being located in the United States.

Figure 10.2 shows 87 documents were published in 2018 while there was only one publication in 2010. Considering the fact that the study was conducted in August 2019, it is predictable to see the number of publications to be higher for 2019 compared to 2018.

The rest of this chapter is organized as follows. Section 2 presents an overall view of cyber-physical systems. Attack detection methods in CPS and anomaly detection are studied in Sects. 2 and 3 respectively. Section 4 provides a case study and Sect. 5 concludes the chapter.

2   Cyber-Physical Systems

According to the application of CPSs, these systems can be defined in different ways, such as deeply intertwined computation, communication, networking, advanced tools, and physical processes interacting with each other relying on IT systems, which are used to monitor and control the physical world [22, 23]. Figure 10.3 shows a holistic view of CPSs.

Different characterizations are presented for CPS which focus on different aspects of these systems including cyber capability, automation, dependability, networking, integration, complexity and reconfiguring [24] which we will briefly mention them [25].

Cyber-physical systems are the integrations of cyber capability and physical components which include distributed networks (i.e. Local Area Network, Bluetooth, Global System for Mobile Communications, etc.) and are severely limited by spatiality and real-time computation. Due to reliability and security necessities for CPS, there is a need to have adaptive capabilities with advanced feedback control technologies.

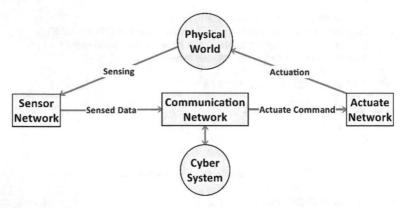

Fig. 10.3 Holistically view of CPSs

CPS Challenges	Attributes	Reason of Relation
Security	Availability	Denial of Service Issue
	Confidentiality	Privacy and Secret information
	Integrity	Trusted and Accurate Data
Dependability	Maintainability	Correct operation as always
	Availability	Readiness for operation
	Safety	Without harm
Reliability	Robustness	Stableness
	Predictability	Guaranteed behavior
	Maintainability	Able to keep operating
Sustainability	Adaptability	Evolving circumstances
	Resilience	Self-healing
	Reconfigurability	Dynamic tuning
	Efficiency	Well use of resources
Predictability	Accuracy	Quantitative outcome
	Compositionality	Behavior interface
Interoperability	Composability	Incorporating operating components
	Scalability	Scaling in size and throughput
	Heterogeneity	Combining different components

Fig. 10.4 CPS challenges

Since cyber-physical systems use distributed communication and smart tools and sensors, these systems are facing various challenges from different points of view which are presented in Fig. 10.4 [1]. However, in the rest of this part, we focus on security issues because CPSs are more vulnerable to cyber-physical malicious attacks [26–28].

Security solutions for cyber-physical systems are required and could be enhanced with Information Technology (IT) systems and techniques like cryptography, access

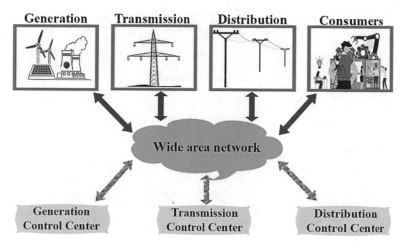

Fig. 10.5 Smart grid as a CPS

control, attack detection, or others. Lack of security in CPSs (e.g. nuclear power station or medical devices) could cause a worldwide threat or disaster.

Security is also one of the most important challenges in the smart grid due to the high dependency of these systems on cyber information yielding new security vulnerabilities [12, 26, 27, 29]. These systems with extensive communication capabilities are good examples of CPSs, which provide the required infrastructure for handling new challenges. Rising electrical energy demand and several technological developments have motivated the advancement of the smart grid. From this, it can be seen that a comprehensive approach is needed for the realization of this issue to quantify attack impacts and assess the effectiveness of countermeasures. The smart grid view as a cyber-physical system is shown in Fig. 10.5.

3 Attack Detection in CPSs

There are three main security properties for a Cyber-Physical system including confidentiality, integrity, and availability [30]. So, attacks are classified considering the security properties as shown in Fig. 10.6.

The most efficient way of defending against network-based attacks is Network Intrusion Detection Systems (NIDS). NIDS are used in almost all Cyber-physical systems. Anomaly-based NIDS and signature-based NIDS are the two main kinds of these detection procedures [31]. Signature-based systems use pattern recognition methods while anomaly-based systems configure a statistical model defining the standard network traffic and flag any abnormal behavior that diverges from the model [32]. It should be noted here that the database of previous attack signatures are preserved and compared with analyzed information for signature-based systems

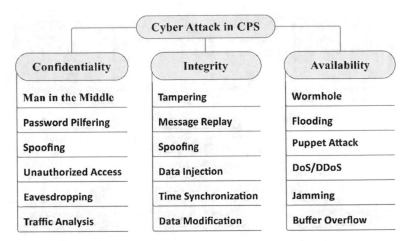

Fig. 10.6 Attack taxonomy for CPS

while in anomaly-based systems the database of general attacks a training phase is required, and it is a complex process due to the setting of a threshold level of detection. Since innovative attacks can be detected as soon as they take place, anomaly detection systems can detect zero-day attacks and it is a major advantage of this system in contrast to signature-based systems [33]. The rest of this section is focused on anomaly-based detection.

3.1 Anomaly Based Detection

The network's behavior is a very important factor and if it does not follow the predicted behavior which is learned by the specifications of the network managers, anomaly detection will commence. Given that various protocols are affected by the rule defining process, the ruleset can be recognized as the main drawback of anomaly detection. Rule definition becomes a difficult process when it is facing custom protocols. Network managers should be comprehensively familiar with the accepted network behavior because the malicious action goes unnoticed if it falls under the accepted behavior, while by defining the rules anomaly detection systems work properly [34]. Finally, anomaly detection is related to novel attacks without a signature which can be detected by anomaly-based method if it falls out of the usual traffic patterns [10]. This is a very big difference between anomaly and signature-based detection methods.

Anomaly detection could be matured upon a variety of general methods borrowed from various scientific fields including ML, statistics, artificial intelligence, clustering, pattern recognition, classification, system theory, signal processing, etc. Figure 10.7 shows a taxonomy for anomaly detection.

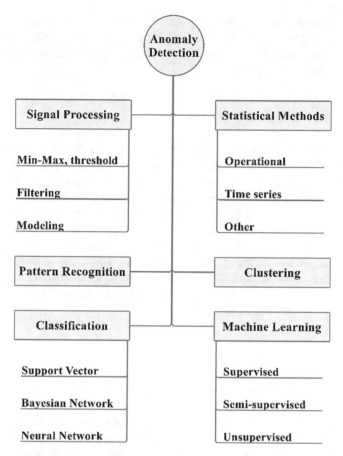

Fig. 10.7 Anomaly detection taxonomy

3.1.1   Statistical Methods

Anomaly detection methods have been advanced using statistical theories which are characterized and qualify the behavior of every component of the system. In these methods, the collected data should be given a probability distribution. The difference between current behavior and normal behavior is detected by using statistical properties such as mean, variance, etc. [35]. Corresponding to the currently observed and the previously trained profile are two different datasets during the anomaly detection which are used by statistical methods. There are many advantages for this method but the most important one is related to decreasing false detection rate because they can provide more accurate detection of malicious actions over a long duration. Given that the ability to learn from observation in statistical methods, detailed awareness about the standard activity of the system is not necessary [36, 37]. It should be noted here that these methods have some drawbacks. For example, the system can be attacked again by generating network traffic in such a way that looks similar to normal behavior. Another disadvantage is that if the system can be modeled in such a way that statistical methods cannot be used, it leaves the detection methods in a useless state [38].

3.1.2 Classification Based Methods

Each attack with a recognized outline and plan can be detected right away if it is dropped while the network administrator prepared details of the features to the detection system. That is why classification methods depend on administrators' substantial knowledge of the specifications of attacks [39]. If an attack signature has been provided previously by a network manager, the system is capable of detecting that because it can detect only what it knows is vulnerable to another new attack. Even if a new signature of attack is created and put into the system, the inflicted damages are not changeful and there are many losses likewise, the repair process is very expensive [40]. Finally, these methods are dependent on a standard traffic outline that makes the cognizance base and consider activities that stray from baseline outline as anomalous [41, 42].

3.1.3 Clustering Based Methods

One of the main subclasses of unsupervised ML is called classification. In this method, rules are found for grouping similar data examples without the need to labeled data [43]. There are many types of clustering methods but the two most important and functional ones are regular clustering and co-clustering [44, 45]. The difference between these methods is related to the method of clustering. In regular clustering, the rows of the data set are considered. In co-clustering the clusters are based on both rows and columns of the dataset simultaneously [46]. K-means is an example of regular clustering.

3.1.4 Signal Processing Approaches

Signal processing methods rely on time-series and spatial-temporal data [47, 48] which includes three sub-methods: Min-Max-Threshold, Filtering, and Modeling. The simplest form of anomaly detection is Min-Max-Threshold, where minimal, maximal or threshold values are defined from a series considered normal [49]. Filtering method compares a signal with a low-pass filtered version which gives an indication of an outlier value. Finally, the modeling method generates a model based on system identification techniques which are used to predict the next values.

3.1.5   Pattern Recognition

In this method, the difference between a normal and an abnormal state is made by the sequence of samples as the shape of the signal whereas the individual data alone is not important. Support vector machine, Neural networks, and Markov chains are trained in order to detect a difference between normal and abnormal shapes [50, 51].

3.1.6   Machine Learning

Machine learning aims to find patterns, make predictions, and make decisions based on historical information to perform a task [12]. Supervised, Unsupervised, Reinforcement and Semi-supervised learning are four types of ML. In supervised techniques, the rules are learned from different examples which are positive or negative and labeled data are used to find a model that explains the dataset. In unsupervised learning, a procedure cannot consider specified anomalies and the main objective is to find a pattern for unlabeled data. Finally, in semi-supervised learning, just the normal performance can be learned from positive examples so only a portion of data is labeled [16].

Machine learning approaches usually separate data into different categories: training and testing. Training data, which commonly is larger in size, is used for learning and providing a model for the system. Testing data, which is completely independent of the training, is used to assess the efficiency of the algorithm. In anomaly-based detection, the normal behavioral pattern is described and modeled by using a training set. Then, the model is applied to testing dataset in order to classify it as either normal or anomalous. In addition, some ML methods separate datasets into three categories instead of two, adding a validation dataset. The validation dataset is used to validate the testing dataset's accuracy when used as input to the given ML method. For illustration, the number of layers and nodes in Artificial Neural Network (ANN) can be varied and the best parameters are chosen that have less estimation of error and more efficient to be built depending on the performance on the validation dataset [12].

One important part of any anomaly detection method is evaluating the performance of ML algorithms. Classification accuracy is the most intuitive method in this evaluation, which measures the performance of the model by computing the ratio number of accurate predictions to the whole number of observations. The main drawback in this metric is that it works properly only when the dataset has equal values for false positives and false negatives [16, 18, 19].

F1 score is another metric in measuring the accuracy in uneven class distribution, which computes the balance between Precision and Recall. Precision is the ratio of correctly predicted positive observation compared to total positive observation, while Recall is the ratio of correct positive prediction to the total number of predictions in the same class (true positives and false negatives of the same class). As a result, F1-score can compute the performance by taking both false positives and false negatives into account. In multi-label ML algorithms, F1-score is usually used to evaluate the classification performance. Therefore, by maximizing the F1-score in multi-label classification, the performance of the algorithm can be considerably improved. Finally, ML is used in a wide range of cyber-physical systems due to the prediction and detection are the two most vital factors for these system operations. Anomaly detectors can be built based on ML algorithms, which could lead to secured cyber-physical systems [18, 19, 52].

4 Case Study

The use of ML techniques for the detection of anomalies can be exhibited through the following case study. Heuristic optimization algorithms are proposed as feature selection techniques to reduce the training time of the algorithms. Since one of the main concerns of the use of ML is computational efficiency, this case study aims to implement automated methods to reduce the dimensions of the data prior to training. This reduces the training and operating time of the ML algorithms for increased computational efficiency.

In this case study, ML classifiers are used to categorize the smart grid measurements as normal or malicious. A Support Vector Machine (SVM), K-Nearest Neighbor (KNN), and Naïve Bayesian (NB) classifier are implemented and compared in terms of classification accuracy. Each of the three classifiers is tested with three heuristic feature selection techniques, which are: Binary Cuckoo Search (BCS), Binary Particle Swarm Optimization (BPSO), and Genetic Algorithm (GA). These feature selection methods are optimization algorithms that find the ideal subset of features that produces the best accuracy. The classifiers are tested with each of the resultant subsets of features and evaluated based on its accuracy and F1 score.

Three different IEEE standard power systems are used in this experiment: The IEEE 14-bus system and the IEEE 118-bus system. The measurement data consists of power flow of branches and buses. For each power system, three sets of data were generated; a set of 1000 samples used for feature selection, a set of 40,000 samples used for training of the classification algorithms and a set of 10,000 samples used for testing and evaluation. Each set of data is divided in half into good and malicious data. The malicious data consists of measurements infected with a false data injection (FDI) attack.

Each of the classifiers, as well as the feature selection algorithms, consists of modifiable parameters that can affect the solution. As such, appropriate parameters must be chosen to ensure optimal solutions. For each of the classifiers, the parameters were chosen based on an accuracy test in which accuracy of the classifier was evaluated at varying parameters. Figure 10.8 shows the accuracy of the SVM with varying kernel coefficient (γ) and penalty parameter (C). Similarly, Fig. 10.9 shows the accuracy of the KNN with varying number of neighbors. These tests are performed on the smallest system, IEEE 14-bus system, due to their time-consuming nature. Based on these results, the parameters of the classifiers are chosen. The

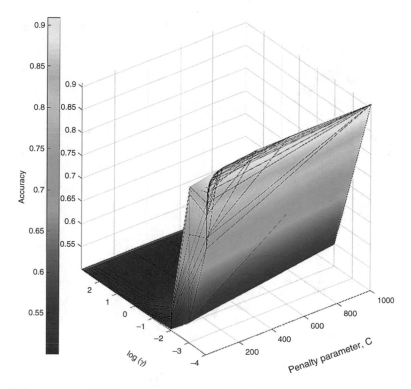

Fig. 10.8 Accuracy of SVM

penalty parameter and kernel coefficient of the SVM is chosen as 1000 and 0.0001 respectively, and the number of neighbors for the KNN algorithm is chosen to be 12. The Naïve Bayesian Classifier, however, was trained with the default smoothing rate of 1×10^{-9}.

Each machine learning classifier is tested with the subset of features produced by each of the feature selection algorithms. For each pair of classifier and feature selection algorithms, the classifier is used as the fitness of the solution for each of the heuristic feature selection techniques. The accuracy and F1-score of the classifiers are recorded for each of the resultant feature sets as well as without any feature selection. Furthermore, the runtime for each of the algorithms is recorded for analysis regarding computational efficiency.

The classification accuracy, F1-score, training time, and feature selection time are recorded for each combination of algorithms in Tables 10.1 and 10.2 for the IEEE 14-bus and IEEE 118-bus respectively. The results clearly demonstrate the trade-off between classification accuracy and runtime. The more simplistic classification algorithms like KNN and NB resulted in a much lower runtime; the associated feature selection time and training time is significantly lower than that of the SVM. The complex nature of the SVM algorithm results in a significantly longer feature selection time as well as training time. However, the resultant accuracy and

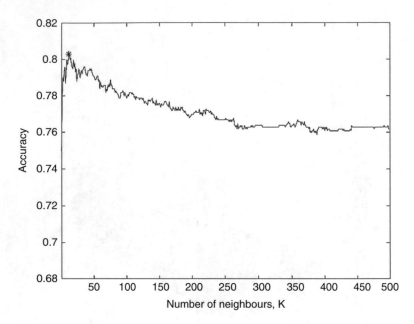

Fig. 10.9 Accuracy of KNN

Table 10.1 Results for the IEEE 14-bus system

Classifier	FSL	NF	CA (%)	F1-score (%)	FST	TT	TRT
SVM	None	34	88.89	88.85	0	1715.245	1715.245
SVM	BCS	10	90.16	90.07	109.855	522.311	632.17
SVM	BPSO	14	90.58	90.50	82.96	873.63	956.59
SVM	GA	8	89.64	89.53	1753.38	155.21	1908.59
KNN	None	34	73.33	73.10	0	0.0937	0.0937
KNN	BCS	21	74.23	74.03	19.59	0.0469	19.63
KNN	BPSO	5	75.62	75.53	15.05	0.0312	15.082
KNN	GA	11	75.06	74.97	265.78	0.0312	265.808
NB	None	34	77.73	77.20	0	0.0469	0.0469
NB	BCS	5	80.25	79.77	1.984	0.0156	2.000
NB	BPSO	5	81.00	80.56	1.509	0.0156	1.524
NB	GA	14	78.95	78.45	50.897	0.0156	50.91

FSL feature selection algorithm, *NF* number of features, *CA* classification accuracy, *FST* feature selection time, *TT* training time, *TRT* total runtime time

F1- score of the SVM algorithm is significantly higher. Furthermore, appropriate feature selection can significantly lower the overall runtime of the SVM, as can be seen from comparing SVM with no feature selection to that with BCS or BPSO for both power systems.

This case study demonstrates the effectiveness of ML techniques at classifying FDI attacks, which typically bypass the standard bad data detection systems.

Table 10.2 Results for the IEEE 118-bus system

Classifier	FSL	NF	CA (%)	F1-Score (%)	FST	TT	TRT
SVM	None	304	89.23	89.18	0	1584.34	1584.34
SVM	BCS	195	88.52	88.49	163.73	1172.16	1335.89
SVM	BPSO	185	87.50	87.47	154.04	1240.50	1394.55
SVM	GA	116	94.33	94.33	1816.94	1025.07	2842.01
KNN	None	304	76.07	74.95	0	0.7498	0.7498
KNN	BCS	189	75.90	74.83	68.308	0.4609	0.4609
KNN	BPSO	219	76.04	74.94	77.592	0.5166	0.5166
KNN	GA	125	78.43	77.67	776.94	0.2968	0.2968
NB	None	304	76.64	76.45	0	0.2656	0.2656
NB	BCS	91	79.17	78.97	6.341	0.0937	6.435
NB	BPSO	180	80.69	80.51	5.615	0.1718	5.786
NB	GA	146	81.11	80.93	106.53	0.1406	106.67

FSL feature selection algorithm, *NF* number of features, *CA* classification accuracy, *FST* feature selection time, *TT* training time, *TRT* total runtime time

Additionally, this study reveals the trade-off between computational time and performance. Furthermore, it was proven that heuristic feature selection can be successful at reducing the number of features and, as a result, reduce the training time of the classification algorithms. When combined with a computationally expensive classifier, heuristic feature selection can significantly reduce the overall runtime thus improving the computational efficiency of certain classifiers. This, however, was not exhibited in the more simplistic classifiers due to their much faster training time, which is reduced by less than the runtime of the feature selection algorithms. In realistic applications, with larger systems and larger data, the training time is expected to be significantly larger. As such, the reduction in runtime is expected to be much larger.

5 Conclusion

The main idea of cyber-physical systems is designing an integrated system instead of separate systems on cyber and physical systems. These systems could be a propitious paradigm for current and future engineered systems which are able to make an impressive impact on our interactions with physical components.

Security is one of the most important factors in CPSs because of the frequency of reported cyber-attacks. Although many detection methods have been proposed, new solutions are still expected against new threats and vulnerabilities. Many approaches are presented in this chapter for attack detection in CPSs such as anomaly detection by using ML including supervised, unsupervised, reinforcement, and semi-supervised methods. We also briefly introduce cyber-physical systems and security concerns about them. Then, detection methods were presented. Finally, a case study showing the effectiveness of different ML algorithms in classifying cyber-physical systems attack was given. Our results demonstrated that reducing the number of features can reduce the overall runtime of the program.

References

1. V. Gunes, S. Peter, T. Givargis, et al., A Survey on Concepts, Applications, and Challenges in Cyber-Physical Systems. Citeseer (2014). http://citeseerx.ist.psu.edu/viewdoc/download?doi=10.1.1.717.3807&rep=rep1&type=pdf
2. J. Goh, S. Adepu, M. Tan, et al., *Anomaly Detection in Cyber Physical Systems Using Recurrent Neural Networks* (2017). Ieeexplore.Ieee.Org. https://ieeexplore.ieee.org/abstract/document/7911887/
3. A. Jones, Z. Kong, C. Belta, Anomaly detection in cyber-physical systems: a formal methods approach, in *53rd IEEE Conference on Decision and Control* (2014). Ieeexplore.Ieee.Org. https://ieeexplore.ieee.org/abstract/document/7039487/
4. M. Cintuglu, O. Mohammed, K. Akkaya, A.S. Uluagac, *A Survey on Smart Grid Cyber-Physical System Testbeds* (2016). Ieeexplore.Ieee.Org. https://ieeexplore.ieee.org/abstract/document/7740849/
5. T. Agarwal, P. Niknejad, A. Rahimnejad, M.R. Barzegaran, L. Vanfretti, Cyber–physical microgrid components fault prognosis using electromagnetic sensors. IET Cyber-Phys Syst Theory Appl **4**(2), 173–178 (2019). https://doi.org/10.1049/iet-cps.2018.5043
6. H.M. Ruzbahani, H. Karimipour, Optimal incentive-based demand response management of smart households, in *2018 IEEE/IAS 54th Industrial and Commercial Power Systems Technical Conference (I&CPS)* (2018), pp. 1–7. https://doi.org/10.1109/ICPS.2018.8369971
7. H.M. Ruzbahani, A. Rahimnejad, H. Karimipour, Smart households demand response management with micro grid, in *2019 IEEE Power & Energy Society Innovative Smart Grid Technologies Conference (ISGT)* (2019), pp. 1–5. https://doi.org/10.1109/ISGT.2019.8791595
8. C.K. Keerthi, M.A. Jabbar, B. Seetharamulu, Cyber Physical Systems (CPS): security issues, challenges and solutions, in *2017 IEEE International Conference on Computational Intelligence and Computing Research (ICCIC)* (2017), pp. 1–4. https://doi.org/10.1109/ICCIC.2017.8524312
9. A. Rahimneiad, I. Al-Omari, R. Barzegaran, H. Karimipour, Hybrid harmonic estimation based on least square method and bacterial foraging optimization, in *2018 IEEE Electrical Power and Energy Conference (EPEC)* (2018), pp. 1–6. https://doi.org/10.1109/EPEC.2018.8598450
10. A. Azmoodeh, A. Dehghantanha, K.-K.R. Choo, Robust malware detection for internet of (battlefield) things devices using deep Eigenspace learning. IEEE Trans Sustain Comput **4**(1), 88–95 (2019). https://doi.org/10.1109/TSUSC.2018.2809665
11. A. Azmoodeh, A. Dehghantanha, R.M. Parizi, H. Karimipour, E. Modiri, D.E. Newton, Fuzzy pattern tree for edge malware detection and categorization in IoT zero trust distributed computing view project naive-Bayesian-based model for interoperability among heterogeneous Systems in Intelligent Buildings View project fuzzy pattern tree for edge malware detection and categorization in IoT. J. Syst. Archit. **97**, 1–7 (2019). https://doi.org/10.1016/j.sysarc.2019.01.017
12. H. Karimipour, A. Dehghantanha, R.M. Parizi, K.-K.R. Choo, H. Leung, A deep and scalable unsupervised machine learning system for cyber-attack detection in large-scale smart grids. IEEE Access **7**, 80778 (2019). https://doi.org/10.1109/ACCESS.2019.2920326
13. R. Altawy, A.M. Youssef, Security tradeoffs in cyber physical systems: a case study survey on implantable medical devices. IEEE Access **4**, 959–979 (2016). https://doi.org/10.1109/ACCESS.2016.2521727

14. C.-W. Tsai, C.-F. Lai, M.-C. Chiang, L.T. Yang, Data mining for internet of things: a survey. IEEE Commun. Surv. Tutorials **16**(1), 77–97 (2014). https://doi.org/10.1109/SURV.2013.103013.00206

15. J. Sakhnini, H. Karimipour, A. Dehghantanha, *Smart Grid Cyber Attacks Detection Using Supervised Learning and Heuristic Feature Selection* (2019). http://arxiv.org/abs/1907.03313

16. O.M.K. Alhawi, J. Baldwin, A. Dehghantanha, Leveraging machine learning techniques for windows ransomware network traffic detection, in *Cyber Threat Intelligence*, (Springer, Cham, 2018), p. 70. https://doi.org/10.1007/978-3-319-73951-9_5

17. N. Milosevic, A. Dehghantanha, K.-K.R. Choo, Machine learning aided android malware classification. Comput. Elect. Eng. **61**, 266–274 (2017). https://doi.org/10.1016/J.COMPELECENG.2017.02.013

18. A. Shalaginov, S. Banin, et al., *Machine Learning Aided Static Malware Analysis: A Survey and Tutorial* (Springer, Berlin, 2018). https://link.springer.com/chapter/10.1007/978-3-319-73951-9_2

19. A. Shalaginov, S. Banin, A. Dehghantanha, K. Franke, *Machine Learning Aided Static Malware Analysis: A Survey and Tutorial* (2018). https://doi.org/10.1007/978-3-319-73951-9_2

20. V. Chandola, A. Banerjee, V. Kumar, Anomaly detection. ACM Comput. Surv. **41**(3), 1–58 (2009). https://doi.org/10.1145/1541880.1541882

21. S. Mohammadi, H. Mirvaziri, M. Ghazizadeh-Ahsaee, H. Karimipour, Cyber intrusion detection by combined feature selection algorithm. J. Inform. Secur. Appl. **44**, 80–88 (2019). https://doi.org/10.1016/J.JISA.2018.11.007

22. M. Conti, S. Das, C. Bisdikian, M. Kumar, et al., Looking ahead in pervasive computing: challenges and opportunities in the era of cyber–physical convergence. Pervasive Mob. Comput. **8**, 2–21 (2012). https://www.sciencedirect.com/science/article/pii/S1574119211001271

23. I. Horvath, B.H. Gerritsen, *Cyber-Physical Systems: Concepts, Technologies and Implementation Principles* (2012). Researchgate.Net. https://www.researchgate.net/profile/Imre_Horvath/publication/229441298_CYBER-PHYSICAL_SYSTEMS_CONCEPTS_TECHNOLOGIES_AND_IMPLEMENTATION_PRINCIPLES/links/0912f500e60008cd01000000.pdf

24. L. Miclea, et al., *About Dependability in Cyber-Physical Systems* (2011). *Ieeexplore.Ieee.Org*. https://ieeexplore.ieee.org/abstract/document/6116428/

25. J. Shi, J. Wan, H. Yan, H. Suo, A survey of cyber-physical systems, in *2011 International Conference on Wireless Communications and Signal Processing (WCSP)* (2011), pp. 1–6. https://doi.org/10.1109/WCSP.2011.6096958

26. F. Ghalavand, B. Alizade, H. Gaber, H. Karimipour, Microgrid islanding detection based on mathematical morphology. Energies **11**(10), 2696 (2018). https://doi.org/10.3390/en11102696

27. F. Ghalavand, B. Alizade, H. Gaber, H. Karimipour, F. Ghalavand, B.A.M. Alizade, et al., Microgrid islanding detection based on mathematical morphology. Energies **11**(10), 2696 (2018). https://doi.org/10.3390/en11102696

28. H. Karimipour, V. Dinavahi, On false data injection attack against dynamic state estimation on smart power grids, in *2017 IEEE International Conference on Smart Energy Grid Engineering (SEGE)* (2017), pp. 388–393. https://doi.org/10.1109/SEGE.2017.8052831

29. H. Karimipour, V. Dinavahi, Robust massively parallel dynamic state estimation of power systems against cyber-attack. IEEE Access **6**, 2984–2995 (2018). https://doi.org/10.1109/ACCESS.2017.2786584

30. S. Geris, H. Karimipour, A feature selection-based approach for joint cyber-attack detection and state estimation, in *IEEE International Conference on Smart Energy Grid Engineering (SEGE)* (2019), pp. 1–5. https://www.scpslab.org/publications.html

31. S. Mohammadi, V. Desai, H. Karimipour, Multivariate mutual information feature selection for intrusion detection, in *IEEE Canada Electrical Power and Energy Conference (EPEC)* (2018), pp. 1–6. https://www.scpslab.org/publications.html

32. H. Karimipour, S. Geris, A. Dehghantanha, Anomaly detection for large-scale smart grids (2019), pp. 1–4. https://www.scpslab.org/publications.html
33. M.R. Begli, F. Derakhshan, H. Karimipour, A layered intrusion detection system for critical infrastructure using machine learning, in *A Layered Intrusion Detection System for Critical Infrastructure Using Machine Learning* (2019), pp. 1–5. https://www.scpslab.org/publications.html
34. H. Pajouh, R. Javidan, et al., *A Two-Layer Dimension Reduction and Two-Tier Classification Model for Anomaly-Based Intrusion Detection in IoT Backbone Networks* (2016). *Ieeexplore.Ieee.Org*. https://ieeexplore.ieee.org/abstract/document/7762123/
35. G. Sebestyen, A. Hangan, et al., *A Taxonomy and Platform for Anomaly Detection* (2018). *Ieeexplore.Ieee.Org*. https://ieeexplore.ieee.org/abstract/document/8402710/
36. A. Patcha, J.-M. Park, An overview of anomaly detection techniques: existing solutions and latest technological trends. Comput. Netw. **51**(12), 3448–3470 (2007). https://doi.org/10.1016/J.COMNET.2007.02.001
37. N. Ye, Q. Chen, An anomaly detection technique based on a chi-square statistic for detecting intrusions into information systems. Qual. Reliab. Eng. Int. **17**(2), 105–112 (2001). https://doi.org/10.1002/qre.392
38. P. García-Teodoro, J. Díaz-Verdejo, G. Maciá-Fernández, E. Vázquez, Anomaly-based network intrusion detection: techniques, systems and challenges. Comput. Secur. **28**(1–2), 18–28 (2009). https://doi.org/10.1016/J.COSE.2008.08.003
39. C.-I. Chang, S.-S. Chiang, Anomaly detection and classification for hyperspectral imagery. IEEE Trans. Geosci. Remote Sens. **40**(6), 1314–1325 (2002). https://doi.org/10.1109/TGRS.2002.800280
40. M. Ahmed, A. Mahmood, J. Hu, A survey of network anomaly detection techniques. J. Network Comput. Appl. **60**, 19–31 (2016). https://www.sciencedirect.com/science/article/pii/S1084804515002891
41. W. Lee, X. Dong, Information-theoretic measures for anomaly detection, in *Proceedings 2001 IEEE Symposium on Security and Privacy. S&P 2001* (2000), pp. 130–143. https://doi.org/10.1109/SECPRI.2001.924294
42. I. Steinwart, D. Hush, C. Scovel, A classification framework for anomaly detection. J. Mach. Learn. Res. **6**(Feb), 211–232 (2005). http://www.jmlr.org/papers/v6/steinwart05a.html
43. V. Estivil-Castro, ACM Digital Library, Proceedings of the twenty-eighth australasian conference on computer science, Newcastle, Australia, in *Proceedings of the Twenty-eighth Australasian Conference on Computer Science*, vol 38 (2005). https://dl.acm.org/citation.cfm?id=1082198
44. L. Portnoy, *Intrusion Detection with Unlabeled Data Using Clustering* (2000). https://doi.org/10.7916/D8MP5904
45. F. Zhouyu, W. Hu, T. Tan, Similarity based vehicle trajectory clustering and anomaly detection, in *IEEE International Conference on Image Processing 2005* (2005), pp. II–602. https://doi.org/10.1109/ICIP.2005.1530127
46. M. Ahmed, A. N. Mahmood, & M. J. Maher (2015). *Heart Disease Diagnosis Using Co-clustering*. https://doi.org/10.1007/978-3-319-16868-5_6
47. S. Agrawal, J. Agrawal, Survey on anomaly detection using data mining techniques. Proc. Comput. Sci. **60**, 708–713 (2015). https://www.sciencedirect.com/science/article/pii/S1877050915023479
48. M. Gupta, J. Gao, et al., *Outlier Detection for Temporal Data: A Survey* (2013). *Ieeexplore.Ieee.Org*. https://ieeexplore.ieee.org/abstract/document/6684530/
49. N. Laptev, S. Amizadeh, et al., *Generic and Scalable Framework for Automated Time-Series Anomaly Detection* (2015). *Dl.Acm.Org*. https://dl.acm.org/citation.cfm?id=2788611
50. S.-W. Joo, R. Chellappa, Attribute grammar-based event recognition and anomaly detection, in *2006 Conference on Computer Vision and Pattern Recognition Workshop* (*CVPRW'06*) (2016), p. 107. https://doi.org/10.1109/CVPRW.2006.32

51. L. Lankewicz, M. Benard, Real-time anomaly detection using a nonparametric pattern recognition approach, in *Proceedings Seventh Annual Computer Security Applications Conference* (n.d.), pp. 80–89. https://doi.org/10.1109/CSAC.1991.213016

52. M. Kakavand, M. Dabbagh, et al., *Application of Machine Learning Algorithms for Android Malware Detection* (2018). Researchgate.Net. https://www.researchgate.net/profile/Mohammad_Dabbagh3/publication/331216763_Application_of_Machine_Learning_Algorithms_for_Android_Malware_Detection/links/5c74adcb92851c69504146a9/Application-of-Machine-Learning-Algorithms-for-Android-Malware-Detection.pdf

Chapter 11
Big Data Application for Security of Renewable Energy Resources

Hossein Mohammadi Rouzbahani, Hadis Karimipour, and Gautam Srivastava

1 Introduction

Modern power grids have seen substantial technological advancements during the past century [1]. Traditional electric power systems consist of four sub-systems from power stations as the first section to the end-users as the latest one. Intermediate subsections include transmission and distribution systems [2]. The Renewable Energy Sources (RES) have helped to keep these systems updated while, smart monitoring, security, control, load management, and demand response techniques have also been added to power systems [3, 4]. These new advanced features help the system achieve better performance [5].

Modern electric power systems are facing a series of challenges which is causing their decision-making process to become more difficult [5]. These challenges can be divided into two main categories: permanent and emerging ones through the expansion of the network and the use of new technologies [6]. Stability, reliability, load growth, expenses, environmental concerns, and security are some of the key issues in power systems [7]. While these issues themselves are interdependent they still affect each other.

Application of smart appliances, electric vehicles, and house monitoring systems will grow the global electricity demand by an unprecedented 30% by the year 2035. To handle the load increases, transmission, and generation expansions are required [8]. Demand utilizing inverter-based technologies, including applications

H. Mohammadi Rouzbahani (✉) · H. Karimipour
School of Engineering, University of Guelph, Guelph, ON, Canada
e-mail: hmoham15@uoguelph.ca; hkarimi@uoguelph.ca; Canada-hkarimi@uoguelph.ca

G. Srivastava
Department of Mathematics and Computer Science, Brandon University, Brandon, MB, Canada
e-mail: srivastavag@brandonu.ca

© Springer Nature Switzerland AG 2020
K.-K. R. Choo, A. Dehghantanha (eds.), *Handbook of Big Data Privacy*,
https://doi.org/10.1007/978-3-030-38557-6_11

of RES and the large-scale growth of energy efficiency would intensify the need for network control. An increased need for regulation, ramping, and reserves are needed for overcoming issues as a result of the successful integration of variable energy resources [9]. The demand for energy resource development and demand for response impose additional changes to the distribution system. These changes result in power flows to perform in two directions where traditionally power flowed in only one direction [3]. This issue has been the subject of many researchers due to electrical power systems moving towards the next-generation [10]. The central controllers of the smart grid through two way communication have continuous interaction with local actuators [11]. This type of communication is used to respond digitally to the changing demand. The smart grid solutions aim at the calculation of optimum generation-transmission-distribution algorithms and storing power system data. RES can be considered as a potential solution for environmental concerns as well as efficient generation and distribution [12].

The dominance of large-scale centralized power stations is changing due to the expansion of RES. Therefore, traditional centralized control strategy is becoming less effective as a result of unidirectional power flow [13]. In addition, real-time data processing is required to deal with the formed mass data generated via integrating smart communication, automation and electric network control [14]. This large volume of data requires real-time management and storage of historical information for an evidence-based decision making based on specific cases [15]. Smart meter communications with other devices generate detailed data which is required for automated decision support and reliable information. Although the data itself has great value, the analysis and application of the data is a complex process which can threaten security and privacy.

In dealing with challenges of big data in RES, novel and advanced methods are required for gathering, managing, and intelligent interpretation compared to conventional methods [16]. Renewable energy production and consumption patterns have been impacted by big data. Big data analytics enables rapid failure detection and restoration as well as faster demand response. Also, customers will have more control over their consumption as a result of more reliable and economical energy supply.

The outline of security in RES is provided in Sect. 2. Next, the application of big data to support the RES in the smart grid is presented in Sect. 3. We continue this chapter with the relationship between big data and RES security illustrated in Sect. 4. Finally, Sect. 5 concludes this chapter.

2 Security in Renewable Energy Sources

Over the last decade, the portion of RES (i.e. wind, solar, biomass, hydro, and geothermal energy) in total energy consumption has significantly increased. Figure 11.1 shows the worldwide growth of renewable energy consumption and the capacity over the past few years [17]. Based on the International Energy

Total Renewable Energy Capacity and Production 2012 - 2018
Source: The International Renewable Energy Agency

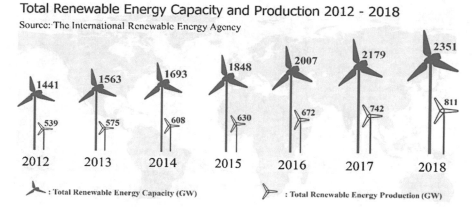

Fig. 11.1 Total renewable energy capacity

Agency (IEA), the most optimistic scenario is that the renewable share of electricity generation will increase to 39% by 2050 from 18.3% as recent as 2002. The new generation of energy systems including RES is specially designed to tolerate heavy power generation which delivers energy to its distant consumers through a two-way structure. For the efficient operation of these systems, smart decentralized integrated communication, smart metering, monitoring and controlling [18] will be necessary for these systems [19].

This new generation of tools and specifically RES will play a key role in the preventing of global warming by reducing global CO2 emissions [17]. Although RES has great benefits, there are many challenges which must be addressed. The most important challenges are related to policy, technical details, economics, human resources, and cybersecurity [20]. While security is one of the most significant concerns in the new generation of power systems, this factor to support RES has been less investigated [21]. Integrity, privacy, and availability of service are three main points for security. Moreover, there are security threats due to mutual communications between consumers and also between consumers and utilities, at both the physical and logical layers. There has been lots of research interest in this security issue [22, 23]. While data confidentiality can be mentioned as a vulnerability at the logical layer, the physical layer is facing many threats including sabotage, theft, and vandalism [24, 25].

2.1   Potential Risks and Vulnerability

There is a range of vulnerabilities in RES including a reduction in demand as a result of lack of availability of services initiated by cyber-attacks [26]. The scope of an attack is broad and covers many areas from physical breaches and social engineering attacks to brute force server and Distributed Denial of Service

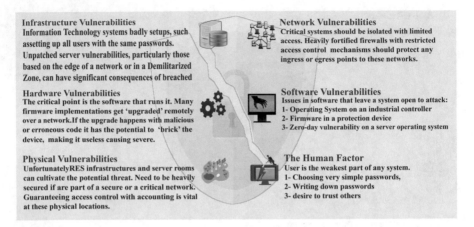

Fig. 11.2 Different types of vulnerabilities

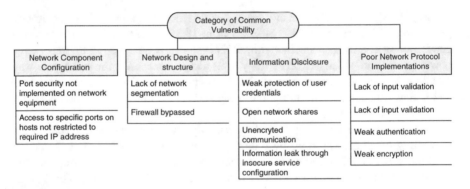

Fig. 11.3 Vulnerabilities assessment of RES

(DDoS) attacks. These types of attacks can focus on specific vulnerabilities or be general in nature like DoS attacks. Figure 11.2 shows some of the key attacks to consider [27].

Vulnerabilities regarding data network securities which are also possible for the smart grid technology are given in Fig. 11.3 which is categorized by Control System Security Program (CSSP) [28, 29].

An attacker can breach into the network, take over controlling the system to disrupt operation in unforeseeable actions due to system vulnerabilities [30]. Thus, to determine securities requirements, all likely vulnerabilities for Supervisory Control And Data Acquisition (SCADA) and the smart grid should be considered. Many approaches and solutions are discussed in the literature to moderate vulnerabilities [31]. The vulnerabilities related to network design in the smart grid infrastructure requires more attention. The distributed structure of these system has led to many chances for an attacker to interrupt the system.

Some significant cases of possible security risks due to increase's accessibility and expansion of networks are presented by the National Institute of Standards and Technology (NIST) [32]:

- Manifold complexity may have led to unintended errors and facing attackers.
- Networks with more interaction with others, present common vulnerabilities.
- Chance of DOS attacks has been increased due to more interconnections.
- Two-way communication and massive data gathering may lead to a breach of data confidentiality and consumer privacy.

2.2   Possible Threats and Cyber Attackers

Threats are not only limited to cyber threats but also include social engineering, physical, and environmental threats that can contain unauthorized access to these layers where an attacker breaks into the system and debilitates hypercritical facilities. Environmental threats include natural disasters and extreme weather conditions while in social engineering, techniques are used to get information from employees to get access to internal networks. Finally, in cyber threats, weaknesses in security are analyzed and discovered to gain access to systems using software [33]. This subsection focuses on cyber threats as the smart grid is a cyber-physical system (CPS). The three leading causes of cyber threats are manipulation, sabotage, and espionage which can happen consciously or unconsciously. The Application Centric Infrastructure (ACI) principles in the system are intentionally harmed by conscious attacks such as hackers, cyber and organized crimes, anti-governments and terrorists. Also, customers may attack energy infrastructure through smart meters for energy theft, fraud, sabotage, and vandalism [34].

There are different types of cyber attackers such as non-malicious attackers, terrorists, consumers, internal employees and rivals [35]. Non-malicious attackers use intellectual concepts trying to decrypt the security system as a puzzle while terrorists aim to shut down the system or restore critical information. Consumers and internal employees are two types of attacker driven by retaliation or perhaps lack of training. Finally, for saber-rattling, personal benefits or interrupting the resources of a counterpart, rivals may attack each other.

Unconscious attacks are non-intentional attacks which are committed by users who are uneducated in cybersecurity. Conscious attackers usually manipulate these users.

2.3   Security Goals and Requirements

The three high-level security objectives are cited in this section based on the NIST comprehensive guideline for cybersecurity [30].

1. *Confidentiality*: To keep authorized limitations on data access and revelation to shield proprietary information and personal privacy, in particular, to protect information from unauthorized access.
2. *Integrity*: To protect against inappropriate modification of data or demolition to ensure data authenticity. A loss of this factor can further enforce incorrect decision regarding load management.
3. *Availability*: The most vital objective of the smart grid is to guarantee apropos and reliable approachability to and use of information where a loss of availability may further undermine the electrical energy delivery.

In addition, this guideline recommends specific requirements, including CPS. The cybersecurity portion entails security issues and requirements for information and network systems; the physical security part defines details related to environment protection and physical equipment as well as jobholder and staff security rules. Cybersecurity requirements are presented as follows [30, 36].

- *Attack detection and resilience operations*: Smart system structures open telecommunication over an extensive distributed network which makes it impossible to ensure every node to be invulnerable to cyber-attacks [37]. Thus, consistent profiling, testing, and comparison are required by the communication network. It is necessary to recognize and find irregular events due to attacks via monitoring the system traffic. Furthermore, a self-healing ability is needed for the network to operate during attacks [10].
- *Identification, authentication and access control*: The key process of verifying the identity of a device or user is known as identification and authentication which is a prerequisite to allowing access to resources in any system. The objective is to confirm only allowed staffs who are exactly identified can access the resources. For every node, a basic cryptographic algorithm is vital to secure these requirements such as symmetric and asymmetric cryptographic primitives.
- *Secure and efficient communication protocols*: In two-way communications, message delivery imposes both time-criticality and security which usually contradict each other. Since, smart networks are not constantly provided with secure, physically protected and high-bandwidth communication channels, optimum trading is essential to delivering high-performance interactions and data security in the communications protocols and structures.

2.4 Attack Taxonomy and Classification

Attacks are classified considering the security objectives including confidentiality, integrity, and availability (CIA) as mentioned in the previous subsection. Table 11.1 shows a taxonomy of cyber-attacks which can block CIA directly or indirectly. Generally, all of the attacks can be created by malware (i.e. virus, spyware, trojan, etc.) [25, 38–40] and intrusions [24]. Developers can intentionally implant the last three types of malware into software to initiate attacks at a future time.

Table 11.1 Cyber-attack taxonomy in RES

Confidentiality	Integrity	Availability
Man in the middle	Tampering, wormholes	Wormholes
Password pilfering	Message replay	Flooding
Spoofing	Spoofing	Puppet attack
Unauthorized access	Data injection	DoS/DDoS
Traffic analysis	Time synchronization	Jamming
Eavesdropping	Data modification	Buffer overflow

Even though attackers use various methodologies, they usually follow an overall outline. In this subsection, we present examples for each level of the cyber-attacks.

- Reconnaissance can happen by sending a tsunami of phishing electronic mails to staffs of a corporation or scanning of IP addresses visible to attackers. Organization of information from phishing scams might result in enumeration which can be considered the research element of an attack.
- Vulnerability assessment is a component of an attack and a process of checking exposed devices or services for identified vulnerabilities. Systems with a web-interface will give details which can expose them to vulnerabilities that could be simple (e.g. looking up the default login information for a particular control system model) or complex (e.g. seeking for weaknesses in the security of physical components over time).

In the exploitation stage, the cyber-attack breaches system defenses. Some examples include malware being placed onto a machine and changing the settings by logging into a control system.

In the following section, we present general and more detailed categorizations for different types of attacks [41, 42]. The general category contains two types of security attacks including passive (e.g. eavesdropping attacks and traffic analysis) and active attacks which are carried out by third parties intentionally or unintentionally.

In a passive attack, the attacker learns the system architecture, configuration, and typical behavior by obtaining transmitted data. The focus for preventing these types of attacks should be on prevention as the detection of these attacks is difficult due to no change in the data. These attacks violate the confidentiality principle.

Active Attacks aim to disturb the operation of the system and result in the violation of availability, integrity, or partial confidentiality principles. These attacks are performed by altering the dispatched information or by adding retouched and managed data. An attacker can use malware to smash the smart appliance and smart meters or vital resources in the system by altering/deleting sensitive data.

For unauthorized access, we mention here that in any given network if a security mechanism to check the authenticity of logins is not used, an attacker can easily access the network. This can lead to the exploitation of network resources as well as long term issues such as undetectability of future login breaches. In the replay category of attacks, an attacker sends false messages or retransmits the same message several times. In DoS attacks the response from servers is delayed for authorized users and it has the possibility of vulnerabilities as the smart grid logs IP addresses and can also block message packet transmission over the network. Therefore, valid transmissions may become blocked unnecessarily. Finally, in traffic analysis attacks, a cyber-attack would simply analyze the pattern in which data packets are directed as well as the network traffic. Next, crucial data such as energy usage and price, and system structure becomes available to the attacker.

3 Application of Big Data in RES

There is no clear description of the application of big data in RES at present. However, there is an agreement among available descriptions, and it can be defined depending on the data analytics concepts and the hardware requirements used to process massive data. Big data is an evolving technical issue presented by a large volume of data, complicated structures, and several categories and for effective data mining there is need for unique framework and methods [43]. To deal with challenges related to handling and processing big data from different components of RES, various technologies have been introduced which covers the big data term. These technologies provide value by excavating the intelligence from data that can change the energy production and consumption pattern [44].

3.1 Big Data Characteristics

There is a universal model to explain big data characteristics which is known as the 5-V model which includes *Volume*, *Velocity*, *Variety*, *Veracity*, and *Value*. A short description of each is provided below [45].

In this model, volume refers to the huge amount of data which makes datasets large for storing and analyzing using customary database technology. RES applications in the smart grid provide huge amounts of data by using smart tools such as smart meters and sensors. Storing data in connected distributed locations and bringing them together by software is a possible solution to this problem. Velocity refers to the speed of generating and moving data. For example, when one million smart meters are installed in a network and sampling happens every 15 min, just higher than 35 billion records get generated which is equivalent to 2920 terabytes in quantification [46]. Variety is the types of data we can use, and we need to handle unstructured data and bring them together with big data technology. These different types include video or voice recordings, social network chat, pictures, etc. Veracity covers the messiness or reliability of data where the accuracy is less reliable with huge quantity of data are involved. In power system operation, security and efficiency rely on the data assessment and state estimation. However, failures in tools or errors in data transmission might impact measurements in the smart grid. Finally, value refers to the capability of deriving valuable data from big data and extracting a well understanding of the value. The density of valuable information in big data is not correlated to the quantity of data, meaning if the amount of data is large, the value density will be lower.

3.2 Big Data Analytics

Data analysis or data mining is a computational process and is the most important stage of a big data analytics which discovers valuable information and potential relations between variables with different concepts to support the decision-making process. These concepts are listed in Fig. 11.4.

There are different categories and algorithms in data analytics as shown in Fig. 11.5. The most frequently used categories are supervised and unsupervised learning as shown in Fig. 11.5 along with other categories (i.e. correlation and dimensionally reduced). The analytics model for supervised learning algorithms can be trained based. This can happen using the given data to determine the relationship between data characteristics and the matching categories while, for those without labels, the possible clusters among all the items are identified by the different design of analytics model [23, 36].

Data is collected from various sources and stored as a huge number of datasets ready for analytics which plays a vital role to make the system more beneficial, gainful, and lastly smarter. Various types of analytics in the smart grid are presented in Fig. 11.6. Signal analytics and event analytics focus on signal processing and events respectively. Furthermore, state analytics help with having a perspective for the state of the network. We add here that engineering operations aim at the grid

Data Analysis Concepts

Statistics
Mathematics methods can discover potential relations based on some hypothesis

Machine learning
A technique for learning the law in the data with the help of computers automatically

Data mining
Computing data for discovering valuable information in large data sets

Artificial intelligence
The simulation of human intelligence processes by machines, especially computer systems

Deep learning
A branch of machine learning based on complex structure of neural networks

Pattern recognition
A branch of machine learning that focuses on the regularities in data

Fig. 11.4 Data analysis concepts

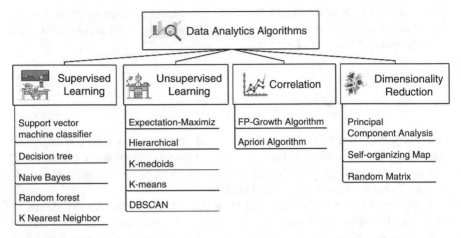

Fig. 11.5 Data analytics categories and algorithms

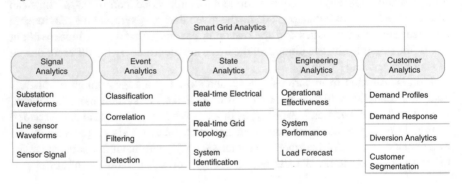

Fig. 11.6 Smart grids analytics

operating side. Finally, customer data can be processed through customer analytics. There are two procedures to process big data including batch and stream processing. In batch processing, the data is processed without high requirements on response time in a period of time. Stream processing requires a very low response delay, it is used for real-time applications [47].

Next, we present some of the related research that has used big data in renewable energy where the common purpose of all works has been cost minimization. Paro and Fadigas [48] proposed a methodology for efficiency assessment of biomass energy which can be applied in the distributed network. MacGillivray et al. [49] and Wool et al. [50] focused on marine energy. MacGillivray et al. presented a simple learning model to describe a series of learning investments which makes marine energy technologies become more cost-competitive while the latter looked at the tribological design of three green marine energy systems (i.e. tidal, offshore wind, and wave machines). Additionally, Kaldellis [51] presents an independent wind energy system sizing by using recorded data of wind speed for remote consumers. Kaldellis used the proposed system to address the electrical energy demand necessities to improve these consumers welfare.

4   Big Data and Security of the Renewable Energy Sources

To understand the state-of-the-art applications of big data for RES security, we have conducted a bibliometric analysis which will be presented here. It is vital to identify related keywords, top-tier researchers, organization, institutes, country, and collaboration amongst them as well as hot topics. This bibliometric analysis is based on relevant publications in the Web of Science from 2010 to 2019. The retrieval time was dated July 18, 2019. After using Web of Science as the database, we identified related keywords for extracting publications. There is some equivalent work done for Big Data in [52, 53] which we use to search the database. The inquiry to gather data in this bibliometric analysis was as follows:

- (TS = ((Big Data OR Massive Data OR Data Lake OR Massive Information OR Big Information OR Semi-Structured Data OR Semi-structured Data OR Unstructured Data) AND ((Security OR Cybersecurity OR cyber-physical security OR security and privacy) AND (Renewable Energy Sources OR Renewable Energy OR Solar energy OR Wind energy OR Hydroelectric energy OR Geothermal energy OR Biomass Energy OR smart grids)))

As a result of this bibliometric analysis, we detected a total of 228 publications, from which we filtered non-relevant and non-English databases. From this filtering process, 215 publications were left for analysis purposes. The number of publications in different years is shown in Fig. 11.7. The number of publications has a peak

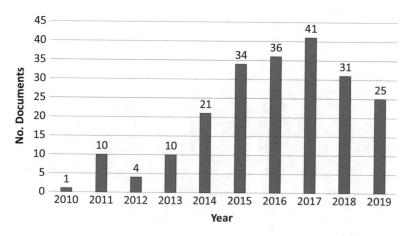

Fig. 11.7 The number of publications in the last decade

occurring in 2017. Since the study was conducted in the middle of July 2019, it is expected to see the number of publications to be higher for 2019.

The majority of publications are related to engineering and computer science. In terms of productivity, China and the United States are the lead countries in the number of publications. Table 11.2 lists the findings for authors who published three or more documents on the related topics. As Table 11.2 demonstrates, the majority of the authors are from the United States, with authors from Canada and China also contributing.

Finally, a total of 6176 keywords and 652 titles were extracted from the filtered 215 publications between 2010 and 2019. To provide an in-depth analysis, Fig. 11.8 demonstrates a word map based on keywords and title analysis of the publications. The keywords are divided into two clusters where the green cluster highlighted keywords related to "big data", "renewable energy", "security", "energy security". The red cluster contains keywords such as "network", "smart grid", "system", "network".

Table 11.2 Author information

Author	Publication (No)	Publication (%)	Country
Zhou, KL	4	1.86	China
Kim, YJ	3	1.39	United States
Zhang, YC	3	1.39	United States
Choi, BJ	3	1.39	Canada
Thottan, M	3	1.39	United States
Du, XJ	3	1.39	United States
Yang, SL	3	1.39	China

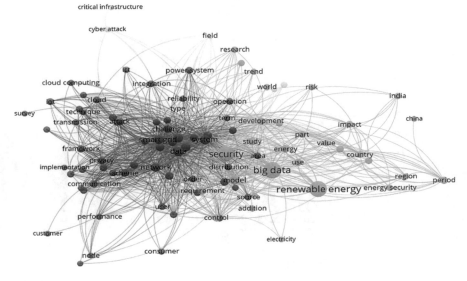

Fig. 11.8 Keyword map

Potential vulnerabilities in RES infrastructures are related to having devices integrated via communication networks. Moreover, to reduce investment cost in areas such as hardware and energy, the electrical companies run their applications using virtual technologies as shown in [54]. These virtual technologies have some security limitations. One major security issue is related to shared platforms between multiple users. There is another challenge which causes low latency problems in real-time applications originating from network bandwidth and requires highly scalable, available, and fault-tolerant connections.

Next, we discuss the main security vulnerabilities and requirements in privacy, integrity, authentication and third-party protection from a big data perspective.

4.1   Privacy

Privacy of information is an important issue for energy management systems [55, 56]. The data collected from smart meters containing consumer consumption information which can picture customer's behavior and habits is a certain kind of privacy that should be protected. The development of data mining and social engineering technology can be boosted through some financial or political incentives [57]. One of the well-known security problems with big data applied in power systems is connected to the end user's privacy where many approaches have been proposed to answer this problem. For example, a distributed incremental data aggregation method is presented by Li et al. [58] using neighborhood gateways. Kalogridis et al. [59] proposed using battery storage to hide consumption data. Rastogi and Nath [60] introduced an algorithm for time-series data which suggests proper utility with no trusted server.

4.2   Integrity

Integrity focuses on preventing unauthorized access (persons or systems) to modify information. In the smart grid domain, integrity avoids changes via message delay, reply and injection and focuses on data for instance product and control guidelines and sensor values. Liu et al. [61] study the possibility of integrity-targeting attacks which is definitely actual and sophisticated.

Ruj and Pal [62] presented a model to attack nodes by eliminating them with possibility comparative to the node's degree meaning a node with a lower degree will be deleted with less possibility.

Yuan et al. [63] identified that the inordinate generation dispatch and energy routing would raise the cost of system operation. Tan et al. [64] employed a control theory to control the real-time Locational Marginal Prices (LMP) exactly when an attack is taking place. Their method analyzes the attack effect on pricing stability using control theory. Further, Jia et al. [65] proposed an analysis framework to quantify the data quality impact on real-time LMP. Esmalifalak et al. [66] characterized the relationship between attackers and defenders by implementing a novel tactic.

4.3 Authentication

Authentication means validating a user's identity and mapping it to the existing authentication table in the system [16, 67]. In most security solutions, authentication is used to differentiate legal and illegal identity. Hamlyn et al. [68] present a security management and network authentication method by designing a new security structure to cover actions and requests in multiple security fields. Based on the Diffie-Hellman key launch protocol, Fouda et al. [69] presented a light-weight message authentication mechanism which lets distributed smart meters to make mutual authentication.

4.4 Third-Party Protection

Power systems after being attacked would potentially result in initiating different type of attacks on the grid or a third party. This will damage the owner's character, or perhaps compensation to a third party due to damage.

Trusted Third Party (TTP) could be a useful strategy for Personally Identifiable Information (PII) in the security of electrical systems since the third party is not mentioned in authentication roster. To analyze identity data on untrusted hosts, Ranchal et al. [70] used a predicate encryption outline and multi-party calculating. Also, Ben-Or et al. [71] used secret input from all parties to define a multi-party computing protocol.

5 Conclusion

In this chapter, we have surveyed the state-of-the-art application of big data for RES security. Using RES is transitioning towards deployment of advanced tools, specifically smart communication devices and metering. This, in turn, will generate big data in terms of volume, velocity, and variety. The big data generated by RES requires novel data analytics methods (i.e. machine learning, deep learning, data mining, artificial intelligence, and pattern recognition) for data extraction and appropriate management. Big data knowledge has been considered as the main factor for smart network structure and becomes more common in technology and different industries.

Even though there is a lot of benefits in big data application, this has also brought a lot of data security threats to the system. However, concurrently big data application has made security and privacy much easier. In this chapter, we have also given an in-depth look at big data analytics and security. As a crucial part of the big data, the security in using RES was demonstrated in different aspects including integrity, authentication, privacy, and third-party protection.

References

1. H.M. Ruzbahani, H. Karimipour, Optimal incentive-based demand response management of smart households, in *2018 IEEE/IAS 54th Industrial and Commercial Power Systems Technical Conference (I&CPS)* (2018), pp. 1–7
2. A. Askarzadeh, Solving electrical power system problems by harmony search: a review. Artif. Intell. Rev. **47**(2), 217–251 (2017)
3. M. Henderson, D. Novosel, M.L. Crow, *Electric Power Grid Modernization Trends, Challenges, and Opportunities* (2017). ieeeorg-stg.ieee.org
4. A. Rahimnejad, H.M. Rouzbahani, H. Karimipour, *Smart Households Demand Response Management with Micro Grid*. preprint arXiv (2019). arxiv.org, pp. 1–5
5. V. Dinavahi, H. Karimipour, Parallel relaxation-based joint dynamic state estimation of large-scale power systems. IET Gener. Transm. Distrib. **10**(2), 452–459 (2016)
6. F. Kratima, F. Gherbi, F. Lakdja, Applications of cooperative game theory in power system allocation problems. Leonardo J. Sci., 12 (2013). *193.226.7.140*
7. M.J. Estahbanati, Hybrid probabilistic-harmony search algorithm methodology in generation scheduling problem. J. Exp. Theor. Artif. Intell. **26**(2), 283–296 (2014)
8. L. Abdallah, T. El-Shennawy, *Reducing Carbon Dioxide Emissions from Electricity Sector Using Smart Electric Grid Applications* (2013). hindawi.com
9. H. Karimipour, V. Dinavahi, Extended Kalman filter-based parallel dynamic state estimation. IEEE Trans. Smart Grid **6**(3), 1539–1549 (2015)
10. S. Mohammadi, H. Mirvaziri, M. Ghazizadeh-Ahsaee, H. Karimipour, Cyber intrusion detection by combined feature selection algorithm. J. Inf. Secur. Appl. **44**, 80–88 (2019)
11. H. Karimipour, V. Dinavahi, *On False Data Injection Attack Against Dynamic State Estimation on Smart Power Grids* (2017). ieeexplore.ieee.org
12. H. Karimipour, V. Dinavahi, On false data injection attack against dynamic state estimation on smart power grids, in *2017 IEEE International Conference on Smart Energy Grid Engineering (SEGE)* (2017), pp. 388–393
13. H. Karimipour, V. Dinavahi, Accelerated parallel WLS state estimation for large-scale power systems on GPU, in *2013 North American Power Symposium (NAPS)* (2013), pp. 1–6
14. H. Karimipour, V. Dinavahi, On detailed synchronous generator modeling for massively parallel dynamic state estimation, in *2014 North American Power Symposium (NAPS)* (2014), pp. 1–6
15. Y. Zhang, T. Huang, E.F. Bompard, Big data analytics in smart grids: a review. Energy Inform **1**(1), 8 (2018)
16. A. Azmoodeh, A. Dehghantanha, K.-K.R. Choo, Big data and internet of things security and forensics: challenges and opportunities, in *Handbook of Big Data and IoT Security*, (Springer, Cham, 2019), pp. 1–4
17. Renewable Energy Statistics, 2018. */publications/2018/Jul/Renewable-Energy-Statistics-2018*
18. Y. Yan, Y. Qian, H. Sharif, D. Tipper, A survey on smart grid communication infrastructures: motivations, requirements and challenges. IEEE Commun. Surv. Tutorials **15**(1), 5–20 (2013)
19. M. Zahran, *Smart Grid Technology, Vision, Management and Control. WSEAS Transactions on Systems* (2013). researchgate.net

20. S. Geris, H. Karimipour, A feature selection-based approach for joint cyber-attack detection and state estimation, in *IEEE Int. Conf. on Smart Energy Grid Engineering (SEGE)* (2019), pp. 1–5
21. M.R. Begli, F. Derakhshan, H. Karimipour, A layered intrusion detection system for critical infrastructure using machine learning, in *IEEE Int. Conf. on Smart Energy Grid Engineering (SEGE)* (2019), pp. 1–5
22. H. Karimipour, V. Dinavahi, Robust massively parallel dynamic state estimation of power systems against cyber-attack. IEEE Access **6**, 2984–2995 (2018)
23. H. Karimipour, A. Dehghantanha, R.M.M. Parizi, K.-K.R.R. Choo, H. Leung, A deep and scalable unsupervised machine learning system for cyber-attack detection in large-scale smart grids. IEEE Access **7**, 1–1 (2019)
24. H.H. Pajouh, R. Javidan, R. Khayami, A. Dehghantanha, K.-K.R. Choo, A two-layer dimension reduction and two-tier classification model for anomaly-based intrusion detection in IoT backbone networks. IEEE Trans. Emerg. Top. Comput. **7**(2), 314–323 (2019)
25. A. Azmoodeh, A. Dehghantanha, M. Conti, K.K.R. Choo, Detecting crypto-ransomware in IoT networks based on energy consumption footprint. J. Ambient. Intell. Humaniz. Comput. **9**(4), 1141–1152 (2018)
26. S. Clements, H. Kirkham, *Cyber-Security Considerations for the Smart Grid* (2010). ieeexplore.ieee.org
27. F. Sabena, A. Dehghantanha, A.P. Seddon, A review of vulnerabilities in identity management using biometrics, in *2010 Second International Conference on Future Networks* (2010), pp. 42–49
28. S. Sagiroglu, A. Ozbilen, I. Colak, Vulnerabilities and measures on smart grid application in renewable energy, in *2012 International Conference on Renewable Energy Research and Applications (ICRERA)* (2012), pp. 1–4
29. D.R. McKinnel, T. Dargahi, A. Dehghantanha, K.-K.R. Choo, A systematic literature review and meta-analysis on artificial intelligence in penetration testing and vulnerability assessment. Comput. Electr. Eng. **75**, 175–188 (2019)
30. A. Metke, R. Ekl, *Security Technology for Smart Grid Networks* (2010). ieeexplore.ieee.org
31. A. Ozbilen, I. Colak, S. Sagiroglu, *A Survey on SCADA/Distributed Control System Current Security Development and Studies* (2010)
32. Guidelines for smart grid cyber security, Gaithersburg, MD (2010)
33. A. Azmoodeh, A. Dehghantanha, R.M. Parizi, H. Karimipour, E. Modiri, D.E. Newton, Fuzzy pattern tree for edge malware detection and categorization in IoT zero trust distributed computing view project naive-Bayesian-based model for interoperability among heterogeneous systems in intelligent buildings view project fuzzy pattern tree for. Art. J. Syst. Archit. (2019)
34. F. Daryabar, A. Dehghantanha, N. I. Udzir, S. bin Shamsuddin, Towards secure model for SCADA systems, in *Proceedings Title: 2012 International Conference on Cyber Security, Cyber Warfare and Digital Forensic (CyberSec)* (2012), pp. 60–64
35. T. Flick, J. Morehouse, *Securing the Smart Grid: Next Generation Power Grid Security* (2010)
36. J. Sakhnini, H. Karimipour, and A. Dehghantanha, *Smart Grid Cyber Attacks Detection using Supervised Learning and Heuristic Feature Selection. arXiv Prepr. arXiv1907.*03313 (2019)
37. A. Azmoodeh, A. Dehghantanha, K.-K.R. Choo, Robust malware detection for internet of (battlefield) things devices using deep Eigenspace learning. IEEE Trans. Sustain. Comput. **4**(1), 88–95 (2019)
38. K. Shaerpour, A. Dehghantanha, R. Mahmod, Trends in android malware detection. J. Digit. Forensics Secur. Law (2013)
39. A. Shalaginov, S. Banin, et al., *Machine Learning Aided Static Malware Analysis: A Survey and Tutorial* (Springer, Berlin, 2018)
40. I.A. Saeed, A. Selamat, A.M.A. Abuagoub, A survey on malware and malware detection systems. Int. J. Comput. Appl. **67**(16), 25–31 (2013)

41. X. Wang, P. Yi, Security framework for wireless communications in smart distribution grid. IEEE Trans. Smart Grid **2**(4), 809–818 (2011)
42. M. Gunduz, R. Das, Analysis of cyber-attacks on smart grid applications, in *2018 International Conference on Artificial Intelligence and Data Processing (IDAP)* (2018). ieeexplore.ieee.org
43. P. Zikopoulos, C. Eaton, *Understanding Big Data: Analytics for Enterprise Class Hadoop and Streaming Data* (2011).
44. G. Escobedo, N. Jacome, G. Arroyo-Figueroa, Big data & analytics to support the renewable energy integration of smart grids—case study: power solar generation, in *Proceedings of the 2nd International Conference on Internet of Things, Big Data and Security*, 2017, pp. 267–275
45. T. Zhu, S. Xiao, Q. Zhang, Y. Gu, P. Yi, Y. Li, Emergent technologies in big data sensing: a survey. Int. J. Distrib. Sens. Networks **2015**, 1–13 (2015)
46. S. Sagiroglu, R. Terzi, Y. Canbay, I. Colak, Big data issues in smart grid systems, in *2016 IEEE International Conference on Renewable Energy Research and Applications (ICRERA)* (2016), pp. 1007–1012
47. H. Daki, A. El Hannani, A. Aqqal, A. Haidine, A. Dahbi, Big data management in smart grid: concepts, requirements and implementation. J. Big Data **4**(1), 13 (2017)
48. A. Paro, E. Fadigas, *A Methodology for Biomass Cogeneration Plants Overall Energy Efficiency Calculation and Measurement—A Basis for Generators Real Time Efficiency Data Disclosure* (2011). ieeexplore.ieee.org
49. A. MacGillivray, H. Jeffrey, M. Winskel, I. Bryden, Innovation and cost reduction for marine renewable energy: a learning investment sensitivity analysis. Technol. Forecast. Soc. Change **87**, 108–124 (2014)
50. R.J.K. Wood, A.S. Bahaj, S.R. Turnock, L. Wang, M. Evans, Tribological design constraints of marine renewable energy systems. Philos. Trans. R. Soc. A Math. Phys. Eng. Sci. **368**(1929), 4807–4827 (2010)
51. J. Kaldellis, Optimum autonomous wind–power system sizing for remote consumers, using long-term wind speed data. Appl. Energy **71**(3), 215–233 (2002)
52. C. Kacfah Emani, N. Cullot, C. Nicolle, Understandable big data: a survey. Comput. Sci. Rev. **17**, 70–81 (2015)
53. M. Chen, S. Mao, Y. Liu, Big data: a survey. Mob. Networks Appl. **19**(2), 171–209 (2014)
54. B. Fang et al., *The Contributions of Cloud Technologies to Smart Grid* (Elsevier, Amsterdam)
55. S. Watson, A. Dehghantanha, Digital forensics: the missing piece of the internet of things promise. Comput. Fraud Secur. **2016**(6), 5–8 (2016)
56. A. Aminnezhad, A. Dehghantanha, A survey on privacy issues in digital forensics. Int. J. Cyber-Security Digit. Forensics **1**(4), 311–323 (2012)
57. P. McDaniel, S. McLaughlin, *Security and Privacy Challenges in the Smart Grid* (2009). ieeexplore.ieee.org
58. F. Li, B. Luo, P. Liu, *Secure Information Aggregation for Smart Grids Using Homomorphic Encryption* (2010). ieeexplore.ieee.org
59. G. Kalogridis, C. Efthymiou, S. Z. Denic, T. A. Lewis, R. Cepeda, Privacy for smart meters: towards undetectable appliance load signatures, in *2010 First IEEE International Conference on Smart Grid Communications*, 2010, pp. 232–237
60. V. Rastogi, S. Nath, *Differentially Private Aggregation of Distributed Time-Series with Transformation and Encryption* (2010). dl.acm.org
61. L. Xie, Y. Mo, B. Sinopoli, *False Data Injection Attacks In Electricity Markets* (2010). ieeexplore.ieee.org
62. S. Ruj, A. Pal, *Analyzing Cascading Failures in Smart Grids Under Random and Targeted Attacks* (2014). ieeexplore.ieee.org
63. Y. Yuan, Z. Li, K. Ren, *Quantitative Analysis of Load Redistribution Attacks in Power Systems* (2012). ieeexplore.ieee.org
64. R. Tan, V. B. Krishna, et al., *Impact of Integrity Attacks on Real-Time Pricing in Smart Grids* (2013). dl.acm.org
65. L. Jia, J. Kim, R. Thomas, L. Tong, *Impact of Data Quality on Real-Time Locational Marginal Price* (2013). ieeexplore.ieee.org

66. M. Esmalifalak, G. Shi, Z. Han, L. Song, Bad data injection attack and defense in electricity market using game theory study. IEEE Trans. Smart Grid **4**(1), 160–169 (2013)
67. G. Epiphaniou, M. Walshe, H. Al-Khateeb, M. Hammoudeh, V. Katos, A. Dehghantanha, Non-interactive zero knowledge proofs for the authentication of iot devices in reduced connectivity environments. Ad Hoc Networks **95**, 101988 (2019)
68. A. Hamlyn, H. Cheung, T. Mander, L. Wang, C. Yang, and R. Cheung, Network security management and authentication of actions for smart grids operations, in *2007 IEEE Canada Electrical Power Conference*, 2007, pp. 31–36
69. M. M. Fouda, Z. M. Fadlullah, N. Kato, R. Lu, X. Shen, Towards a light-weight message authentication mechanism tailored for Smart Grid communications, in *2011 IEEE Conference on Computer Communications Workshops (INFOCOM WKSHPS)* (2011), pp. 1018–1023
70. R. Ranchal et al., Protection of identity information in cloud computing without trusted third party, in *2010 29th IEEE Symposium on Reliable Distributed Systems* (2010), pp. 368–372
71. M. Ben-Or, A. Wigderson, A. Wigderson, Completeness theorems for non-cryptographic fault-tolerant distributed computation, in *Proceedings of the Twentieth Annual ACM Symposium on Theory of Computing—STOC '88* (1988), pp. 1–10

Chapter 12
Big-Data and Cyber-Physical Systems in Healthcare: Challenges and Opportunities

Jesus Castillo Cabello, Hadis Karimipour, Amir Namavar Jahromi, Ali Dehghantanha ⓘ **, and Reza M. Parizi**

1 Introduction

The term "Cyber-Physical Systems" (CPS) was coined by Helen Gill in 2006 [1]. A system has to integrate networking, computation and physical processes in order to be considered a CPS. Understanding the physical and computational components of systems are not enough to perceive the CPS, but also, it is necessary to understand the interaction between its underlying areas. CPS provides the foundation of critical infrastructure and will bring advances in areas like personalized healthcare, emergency response, traffic flow management, and electric power generation and distribution [2].

CPS are physical systems with a computing and communication center that monitors, coordinates and integrate the operations of said system. CPS enables the organizations to live monitor networks, patients, and systems. Also, CPS transform communication protocols around us. Demands from sectors like aerospace, building and environmental control, critical infrastructure, process control, factory automation, and healthcare have given helped CPS technology to gain popularity [3].

The potential benefits of CPS are enabled by several trends like low-cost sensors, abundant internet bandwith, and wireless communication. However, this large scale and transformation of systems brings new challenges like lacking a technology base to build a proper large-scale safety-critical CPS or lacking a solution for

J. C. Cabello · H. Karimipour · A. N. Jahromi · A. Dehghantanha
Smart Cyber-Physical System Lab, University of Guelph, Guelph, ON, Canada
e-mail: jesuscc@uoguelph.ca; hkarimi@uoguelph.ca; Canada-hkarimi@uoguelph.ca; anamavar@uoguelph.ca; ali@cybersciencelab.org

R. M. Parizi (✉)
College of Computer and Software Engineering, Kennesaw State University, Marietta, GA, USA
e-mail: rparizi1@kennesaw.edu

© Springer Nature Switzerland AG 2020
K.-K. R. Choo, A. Dehghantanha (eds.), *Handbook of Big Data Privacy*,
https://doi.org/10.1007/978-3-030-38557-6_12

measurement tampering and cyber-attacks in systems that allow internal two-way communication [3, 4].

Using the current cyber-physical systems, the rate of data generation has been growing up in the last few years. Every 18 months,the data volume increases more than double in size [5]. This growth generates challenges in data management and analysis, as well as the opportunity of using data to achieve valuable information. However, this rate of growth has left conventional data structures unable to handle new datasets effectively [5]. To handle the challenge of big datasets, researchers defined the term of *big-data* and build techniques to handle it. The NIST *big-data interoperability* Framework defines big-data as:

> Big-data consists of extensive datasets primarily in the characteristics of volume, variety, velocity, and/or variability that require a scalable architecture for efficient storage, manipulation, and analysis [5].

Big-data brings significant opportunities and transformative potentials for various sectors; it also presents new challenges when trying to exploit the vast growing volumes of data. Advanced data analysis techniques, and efficient data mining and machine learning methods are essential to explore data, explain the relationships between features, monitor the changes, and predict future observations from big-data. However, big-data analysis presents challenges, including the data volume, velocity, value, veracity, variety (five V's of big-data; see Fig. 10), also the need for scalability, and performance with real-time responsiveness. These challenges get harder in fields like social networks navigation,, biomedicine, finance, and astronomy [6].

Big-data has accelerated the evolution of the hardware and software of systems architectures. Also, it handles the development of analytical techniques like statistical analysis, visualization, data mining, and machine learning. This areas are usually dealt with by proposing new techniques, or by strengthening the existing ones, another approach is experimenting with the combination of different algorithms [6].

The effective use of big-data in the industrial sector has the potential to transform economies, and create new means of achieving productive growth [7]. This possibility is present in other areas too. There are studies on challenges, data sources, techniques, technologies, as well as the future directions in the field of big-data analytics in healthcare [8]; automatization, augmentation, and integration of systems in areas likeenergy efficiency, smart cities, autonomous vehicles, and smart manufacturing [9]. In the last 20 years, information technology has played an essential role healthcare. The availability, traceability, and liquidity of data has improved in the health sector [10]. Healthcare data from cyber-physical systems (CPS) can be efficiently managed with the assistance of cloud computing and big data.

In the healthcare industry, cloud and big-data have become the trend in healthcare innovation. Big-data analytics provides benefits in healthcare areas like infrastructure, operations, organization of the healthcare system, management, and strategic approach [11]. However, there are also downsides, for example, cloud computing systems make it difficult for users to know when the devices are collecting data, therefore endangering the user's privacy [12]. The job of a doctor is transforming into a decision support role for the patients, this is due to the increasing reliance of medicine on the analysis of patient data. Medical knowledge is growing thanks to the assimilation of technologies like 3-D printing, cloud computing, gene sequencing, and wireless sensors to the health sector. Furthermore, joining big-data with healthcare can yield the following benefits [13].

- Services based on patient needs: Discovering symptoms of disease at earlier stages, minimizing drug doses and using genetic makeups to administer medicine are benefits derived of big data applications. The benefits of implementing this measures are lower readmission rate, and faster relief of the patients.
- Earlier detection of spreading diseases: Live analysis can be used to predict the spread of viral diseases before and epidemic outbreak occurs. Obtaining and analyzing the social logs of the patients in particular region can give an early warning so healthcare professionals can take preventive action.
- Supervise the hospital's condition: Periodical check-ups on the hospitals condition makes it easier to detect unfit hospitals and to take appropriate measures.
- Upgrade the treatment techniques: Individualized patient treatment and regular checkups on the patient's response to medication allow faster relief and proactive care for patients. Medics can make better treatment decisions by leveraging the data of the patients that presented the same conditions.

The remaining of the chapter is organized as follows. In section two, the methodology of this research is described. Section three explains the usage of cyber-physical systems and big-data in the healthcare sector that followed by the characteristics of big-data in section four. In section five, the architecture of the cyber-physical system in the healthcare area is described. Section six introduces machine learning and its applications in the healthcare area. In section seven, challenges of using big-data to develop models are explained that is followed by the opportunities described in section eight.

2 Methodology

Figure 12.1 shows the method that was followed to conduct this research. In the first phase, the research questions and protocol were defined. The search for articles was conducted in Web of Science and IEEE Xplore Library. The search query that was used was: "(Big Data) and (Cyber-Physical Systems)" that comprises all the books, articles and conference papers from 2009 to 2019. The research questions are:

- What are the publication trends of big-data and CPS in the healthcare context?
- How is big-data and CPS applied in healthcare?
- What are the strengths and weakness of big-data and CPS in healthcare?
- What are some of the unresolved problems/challenges of big-data and CPS in healthcare?

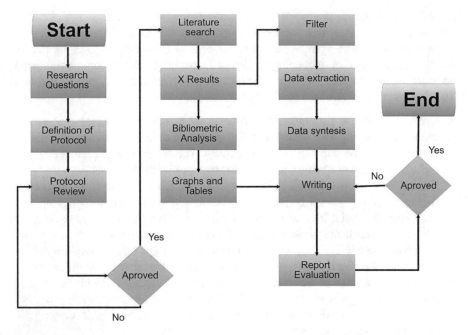

Fig. 12.1 Flowchart of methodology

3 Cyber-Pysical Systems and Big-Data in Healthcare

3.1 Applications

Figure 12.2 shows the escalation in the use of big-data in healthcare sector from 2010 to 2018. Big-data publications in the healthcare sector were increased eight times in 2018 compared to 2013. The total number of papers also grew almost 21 times in the last 5 years, based on the number of google scholar publications retrieved by the query of "Applications of Big Data" and "Healthcare".

The applications of big-data in healthcare industry revolutionize the medical industry by providing better health and information to patients [14]. In the following paragraphs, we will provide some examples of applications of big-data in the healthcare industry.

- **Cross-domain sensing:** Sensing information can be used to identify an individual patient. Reference [15] talks about an authentication mechanism that can validate if two nodes are part of the same BSN using the hearthbeat timing as input. Patients having small sensors (EMG (electromyography), SpO2, accelerometer, and ECG) attached to them can improve future healthcare treatments [15].
- **Decision/actuation system:** There are six roles in a recommendation system for doctors and nurses: Actuator Entity (AE), Surveillance Center (SC), Home Manager (HM), Sensing Entity (SE), Local Responder (LR), and Locality Manager (LM) [15].

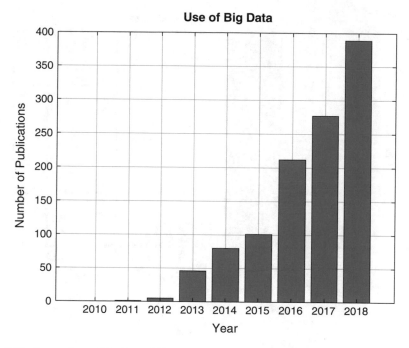

Fig. 12.2   Comparison of big-data publications in healthcare from 2010 to 2018

- **Real-time anomaly detection:** Real-time anomaly detection is becoming more critical for older people who are living alone. This capability assists doctors and nurses to make wiser decisions by detecting anomalies in patients at more convenient times [16].

    Figure 12.3 shows the most popular big-data Tools that are in use today. The y-axis represents the number of papers published in the Web of Science database from 2010 to 2019. The queries used are: "Data integration" and "Healthcare"; "Machine Learning" and "Healthcare"; "Searching and Processing" and "Healthcare"; "Stream Data" and "Healthcare"; "Visual Data" and "Healthcare". Seventy nine percentage of the publications are related to machine learning, and the second place is data integration with 10% of the publications.

4   Big-Data Characteristics

The term Big Data refers to growing data sets that can be classified in structured, unstructured and semi-structured data. The complicated constitution of Big Data generates demand for powerful technologies and advanced algorithms. For example, domain decomposition techniques are used to solve complex systems [17].

    The sources of data can be summarized in three types. The first type is the structured data type. This data has a defined format, data type, and structure. Some

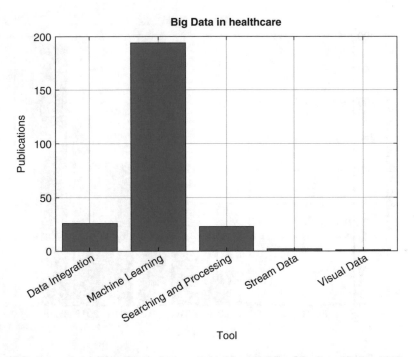

Fig. 12.3 Comparison of big-data tools usage in healthcare publications from 2010 to 2018

examples of this data are laboratory results, symptoms and diagnosis information, and drug and billing information. The second type is the semi-structured data, it has been standardized with little structure but it describes itself via metadata. Data from sensors is a good example of this type of data. The last category is the unstructured data, it has no structure. Medical prescriptions written by hand, discharge summaries, biomedical literature, and clinical letters are good examples of this category of data [18]. Parizi et al. have made some steps in this area, they proposed a Coordinate Based Information Extraction System (CBIES) this is a tool capable of extracting PDF batch data in an automatic way. This tool has the potential to release health organizations from duplicate efforts and may reduce labor costs by extracting patients informations from their documents automatically [19].

The Vs of big-data are important characteristics. However, there is no consensus on how many Vs there are. The Vs range from 3Vs to 9Vs [20].We present the five more common Vs that define big-data.

- Volume: The total digital data created, replicated, and consumed is growing at faster rates. In 2015 digital data was 8 ZB, and will reach 40 ZB by 2020 [6]. This enormous increase in data is generated by the plethora of devices and applications that create data continuously.
- Velocity: Wall-mart creates over 2.5 PB of data hourly from its clients' purchases. In order to extract useful information and relevant insights, data should be processed as quickly as possible [6].

- Variety: Big-data is created from various sources and in different formats (photos, videos, documents, comments, logs, etc). As a result of this big data sets can contain structured data and/or unstructured data, public and/or private, local and/or remote, complete and/or incomplete, etc [6].
- Veracity: Garbage in, garbage out. Without accuracy data is meaningless and useless, veracity is accuracy, truthfulness, and meaningfulness. Answering the question: "how do we know that the operation is successful and accurate?" is no easy task [20].
- Value: Big Data is preoccupies itself with the discovery of hidden value from stored data. Data in itself has no value, what gives the data value is being able to uncover a useful information or relationship from the data. Therefore Big Data is a platform that transforms unworthy data into something valuable [20].

Big-data is appropriate for some applications, including Internet of Things (IoT), smart grid, public utilities, transportation and logistics, e-health, and public monitoring. The role of Big Data in the healthcare sector is to serve predictive methods and machine learning algorithms so that viable solutions, like personal treatment plans, can be discovered and implemented. Big data characteristics have been redefined in the healthcare context into three characteristics: Silo, Security, and Variety. Silo is a database that holds public healthcare data. The security characteristic suggests extra care is needed to protect health-care data. The variety characteristic keeps the same connotation about the form of the data (structured, unstructured and semi-structured) [18] (Fig. 12.4).

4.1 Stakeholders and Big-Data Sources in Healthcare

4.1.1 Patients

Patients desire a vast spectrum of healthcare services with personalized recommendations and reasonable cost. Big-data sources can be a powerful tools that enable the patients by allowing them to connect with other patients to gain knowledge on side-effects, drug information, and other relevant information on their sickness and treatment while also enhancing their privacy [18]. Telemedicine becomes a viable option for patients who are incapable to go to hospitals. An archive could be created, using this technology, by capturing and streaming important health signs such as heart rate, temperature, and blood pressure into a central storage unit.

4.1.2 Medical Practitioners

Using of data from wearables for healthcare applications can provide advantages like facilitating physicians to keep record of the use of drugs and oversee the patient's health whenever he feels the need to do so. Classification methods for diseases, laboratory results, clinical notes, medical imaging data, and sensor devices

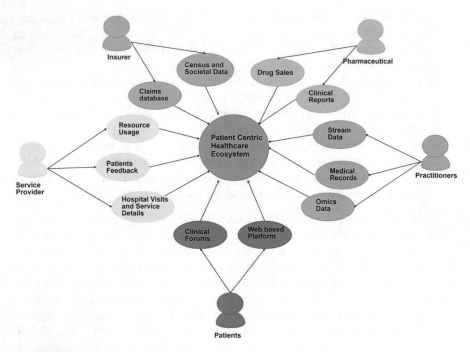

Fig. 12.4 Patienent-centric heatlhcare ecosystem from the big-data perspective

are all big-data generators in the healthcare system. This big-data sources improve public health vigilance and offer quicker response, and adequate diagnosis of disease patterns when they are considered when building the Clinical Disease Repository (CDR) [18].

4.1.3 Hospital Operators

Improvement of descriptive models based on data produced after treatment (phone calls, email, and text messages) eases the improvement of the offered services. Hospital operators depend greatly on big-data sources in order to administer the patient's experiences while optimizing resource usage. Data scientists develop predictive and prescriptive models in order to measure and understand how patient satisfaction is affected by the services provided [18].

4.1.4 Pharma and Clinical Researchers

Pharmaceutical enterprises can benchmark the performance of drugs in development with smaller trials by doing an adequate study of health data. Building predictive models to understand the biological and drug processes with great success rate on adequate medicine designs are a consequence of using clinical big-data in the building processes of said drug [18].

4.1.5   Healthcare Insurers

Mobile IoT is in a can revolutionize the healthcare system. IoT allows new business models to arise while changing work processes, it also improves productivity and customer experiences. The combined use of big-data and IoT improves the success of insurers by introducing new and innovative business models by studying the patients behavior [18].

4.2   Big-Data Frameworks in Healthcare

In scientific applications, like Body Area Networks (BANs), were the health conditions of a patient are important we must use a multitude of linked sensors over the patient's body to gather data like blood, pulse, blood pressure, breath, glucose, insulin, and body temperature must be deployed. However, the original MapReduce (will be introduced in next sub-section) model does not support transmitting and analyzing a stream of health data. Several expansions have been made to the usual MapReduce model to permit iterative computing. Two such expansions are the Hadoop system and Twister. Hadoop was conceived to deal with big-data which was already at hand in the distributed file system. However, resource wastage may occur in network bandwidth and processor resources due to the need to reload and reprocess data on each iteration because processed data may stay constant over distinct iterations. Unlike Hadoop and existing MapReduce expansions, Spark gives ground for dynamic queries and iterative computing. Spark is effective in repetitive use-cases that demand several processes on huge in-memory datasets thanks to RDD caching [21].

Hadoop and Spark are the most common frameworks used in healthcare applications [21].

4.2.1   Apache Hadoop

Hadoop is an Apache project started by Doug Cuttin and Mike Cafarella in 2008 [21]. Hadoop has two key elements, one which manages data storage (Hadoop Distributed File System) and an implementation of the MapReduce model (Hadoop MapReduce).

Hadoop Distributed File System (HDFS)
The HDFS presents a scalable distributed file system for storing huge files reliably and efficiently. HDFS is based on the Google File System (GFS), its architecture is a master/slave one and is open-source. The *name node* is the master node while

a number of data nodes function as slaves. Setting aside and distributing physical space were large files can be stored is a responsibility of the name node. The files are provided by the HDFS client. The name node searches those files in its indexing system and forwards the files' location to the client. Finally, the name node sends the relevant metadata (filename, file location, etc.) of the stored files to the HDFS client. The secondary name node serves as a backup node in the event of a name node failure and it will take control over immediately. In order to do so successfully it must record the state of the name node regularly [21].

MapReduce Programming Model

MapReduce was conceived by Google to handle with parallel processing of vast amounts of data. This programming model has two key functions: Map and Reduce. A single key–value pair is used as input in the Map function and creates several intermediate key–value pairs. After being organized those values are transferred to the Reduce function, along with the corresponding intermediate key. The purpose of the Reduce function is creating a small set of values that contains the merged information of the intermediate key and the original set of values. The principal steps of Map Reduce are:

- Data reading: The input is divided into a number fixed-size subsets and processed by the Map function.
- Map phase: Map function generates a set of intermediate key–value pairs.
- Combine phase: All intermediate key–value pairs related with the corresponding intermediate key are grouped.
- Partitioning phase: The outcomes of the last phase are distributed over the disrinct Reduce functions.
- Reduce phase: The key–value pairs having the same key are merged by the Reduce function. Then, this function calculates the final result [21] (Fig. 12.5).

4.2.2 Apache Spark

Originally conceived at UC Berkeley in 2009 as a way to ease the efficient analytics of heterogeneous data. Spark is employed by enerprises like Yahoo, Baidu, and Tencent. Resilient Distributed Datasets (RDDs) is an important term in the Spark architecture. RDD is an immutable collection of objects dispersed over a Spark cluster.Transformations and actions are the two types of operations we are able to use in RDDs. A transformations generates a new RDD from previously existing ones by employing functions like map, filter, union, and join. Actions are the final product of RDD calculations. Figure 12.6 shows the architecture of this framework [21]. Like the HDFS architecture the Spark cluster takes inspiration from a master/slave architecture and it has three important elements:

- Driver Program: It preserves the Spark context (an object), manages the Spark context, and supervises running applications. Its role is comparable to one of a slave node.

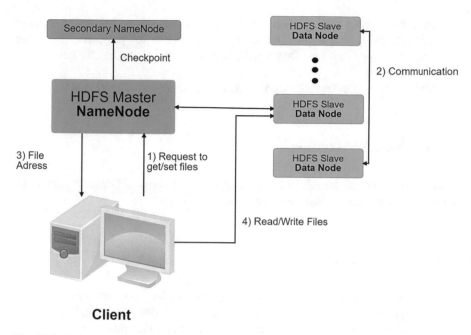

Fig. 12.5 Hadoop distributed file system (HDFS) architecture

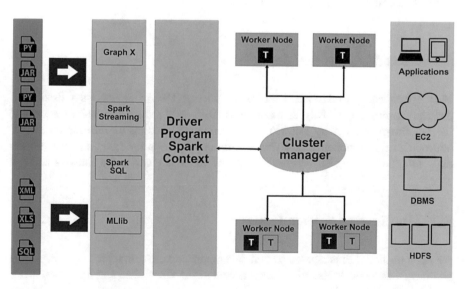

Fig. 12.6 Spark architecture

- Cluster Manager: All resources in the cluster are controlled and monitored by this cluster. It also provides their state to the driver program. The driver program assigns the workflow application to workers, this cluster coordinates the workflow.
- Worker Nodes: One operation correspond to a single worker node [21].

5   Health-CPS Architecture

The architecture of Health-CPSs is comprised of three different layers (data collection, data management, and application service).

5.1   Data Collection Layer

The important elements of this layer are data nodes and adapters, it allows the management of multi-source heterogeneous data (sources include hospitals, Internet, or user-generated content) in a unified system access interface. Crude input with different makeup and frameworks can be prepared so that the transfer of data to the data management layer is protected.

5.2   Data Management Layer

This layer is comprised of a distributed file storage (DFS) element and a distributed parallel computing (DPC) element. The DFS will boost the effectiveness of the healthcare system by allowing the adequate recording of information. DPC contributes the complementary processing and analysis methods, those methods expect the data to be well-timed and that preference is given to the analysis task.

5.3   Application Service Layer

An open unified API is created so that developers can provide relevant personalized healthcare services. It also gives users access to the visual data and the results from the analysis (Fig. 12.7).

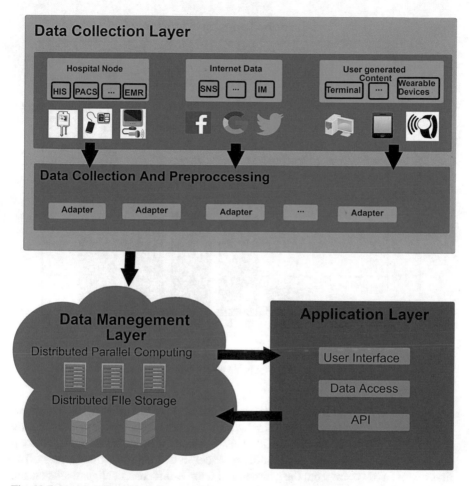

Fig. 12.7 Health-CPS architecture

6   Machine Learning

Figure 12.8 shows the number of machine learning publications in the healthcare sector from the Web of Science database by year. As illustrated in this figure, the number of papers was increased nine times from 2014 to 2018. In this section, some machine learning applications in healthcare area will be introduced.

In big scale data focused applications the MapReduce architecture is one of the most practical ones. It allows the development of of distributed data-intensive applications in the cloud [22]. Recently, machine learning is popular in big-data problems and applying machine learning approaches to resolve big-data problems becomes an attractive research theme. Due to the challenges presented by biomedical data, machine learning algorithms will hold an essential job in big-data handling [22].

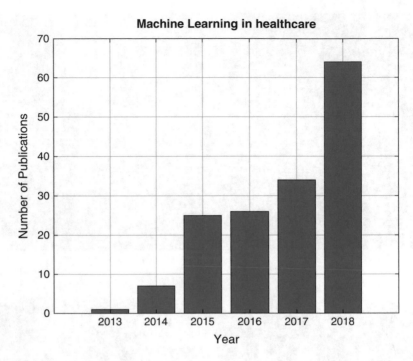

Fig. 12.8 Comparison of machine learning publications in healthcare from 2013 to 2018

An expandable and precise classification method for the geometries of protein-ligand binding was proposed by Estrada et al. [23]. The technique is useful for drug design applications in the real-world. This technique was implemented in Hadoop and it uses the MapReduce programming model. It encompasses three phases. The first returns a 3D point from the geometry of a three-dimensional ligand adaptation. The second phase creates an octree by allotting an octant identifier to each one of the points, finally the densest octant is determined. According to the results, the technique is well suited for clustering docking consequences. The duration of the time series and a low level of parallelism are some of the limitations of this method [22].

Moreover, an optimized two phase entity recognition method suitable for big-data applications exists. This method takes advantage of conditional random fields and MapReduce. This method betters the performance of optimization model by employing a conditional random. All real entities are specified on the first level, also, entity detection takes place. Then, the label of the semantic class of the entity is identified. The results obtained by this method illustrated small training times and strong performance, but it also presents poor trainig efficiency depending on the sample size. This technique could influence current biological big-data processing methods [22].

Zhu-Hong Youa et al. [24] suggested a MapReduce-based parallel Support Vector Machine (SVM) model that uses protein sequences as input for predicting Protein-

Protein Interactions (PPI). The proposed model extracted the regional sequential characteristics from protein sequences. Then the MapReduce framework trained SVM classifiers to improve the training time and accuracy. After that new training set was created from the union of the support vectors of two classifiers. This process went on until am individual classifier left. The results demonstrated that the parallel algorithms could handle large-scale PPIs datasets and perform appropriately when using velocity and accuracy as evaluation metrics. This method was used for large-scale PPI forecasting. Despite the benefits, there was a high overhead of training process caused by sharing of training data between different nodes [22].

Huaming Chen et al. [25] formulated a simple shallow neural network as a supervised machine learning algorithm on gene expression data. The Monte Carlo algorithm was used to govern the structure. The supervised model demonstrated a shallow neural network model with a batch of parameters, and narrowed its computational process into several parts. This batch was processed easily and reached the optimal goal. Over learning was minimized using function design. This neural network suffers from an inadequate number of dataset samples.

Moreover, a procedure more precise for health related datasets has been proposed. The individual's health criterion required extra attention, given that the patient's disease status is affected by the patient's metabolism. This methodology employed a decision tree forest for assorting the individuals. To test this method, the clinical measurements and patterns of individuals were assessed by classifying the pathologic community [22, 26].

The presented mechanisms are useful to solve the big-data challenges while lowering computational time. In addition, these mechanisms provide accuracy, performance and scalability, while averting the problem of single point failures. One common downside of these mechanisms is their high execution times. Having to retrain the model, during the whole building process, for each kind of drug is another disadvantage of these techniques. Moreover, the data-labeling process is very time, labor, and budget-consuming [22] (Fig. 12.9).

7 Challenges

There are two main challenges when using big-data. The first challenge is the selection of the big-data platform to develop the model for a certain application. The selected platform must contain all necessary tools to handle big-data, including the machine learning libraries. Also, some solutions are needed to aggregate data from divergent sources. Since no single algorithm provides a fit-all solution to healthcare data, so ensemble learning is an important technique in healthcare area. Ensemble learning is defined as the use of multiple machine learning models to solve a single problem that can provide better and more reliable results than using a single model [8]. Nature of the big-data is the second challenge of handling big-data problems. This challenge arises with five characteristics of big-data, regardless of the area. Figure 12.10 summarizes these characteristics [20].

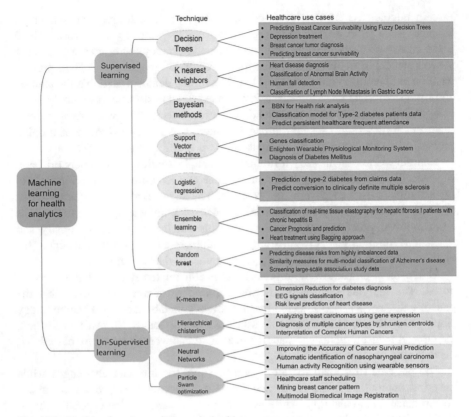

Fig. 12.9 Machine learning techniques in healthcare area

In this section, challenges of using big-data are introduced, including challenges of implementation of big-data in an organization, safety, security, privacy, sustainability, data cleaning, big-data aggregation, imbalanced system capacities, imbalanced datasets, big-data machine learning, and quality of service.

7.1 Challenges on Implementation of Big-Data in an Organization

Big-data practitioners, must determine the strategic and business value of big-data analytics in place of solely concentrating on a technological understanding of the implementation of big-data. Despite that, 77% of companies do not have clear and well defined strategies for implementing big-data analytics into their organization. This is especially true for healthcare industries were healthcare transformation is still in its early stages. Appropriate strategies are needed so healthcare organizations can harness benefits from big-data analytics in an efficient and effective way [11].

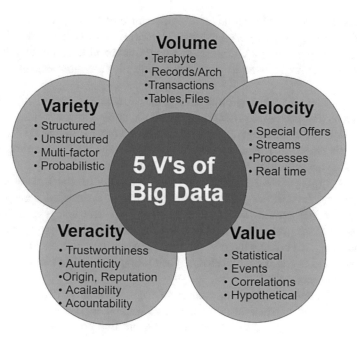

Fig. 12.10   Five V's of big-data

To implement big-data in an organization successfully, nine challenges should be solved.

- **Big-data governance:** Data governance is an expansion of IT governance, it focuses on using enterprise-wide data generate business value and opportunities. Big-data analytics can backfire on a company as healthcare organizations with insufficient IT governance might incur in substantial financial burden by making poor IT investment decisions [11].
- **Information-sharing culture:** If an information-sharing culture is not promoted within the organization, data collection and delivery will be impaired. Adverse impacts can involve the effectiveness of the analytical and predictive capabilities. Resistance to new information management systems might be diminished by this culture thus speeding the full implementation of big-data in the organization This will also improve the quality of data, the accuracy of analysis and the accuracy of prediction [11].
- **Training key personnel:** Incorrect interpretation of the reports could mislead the organizations judgment and augment the probability of taking questionable decisions. Equipping managers and employees with appropriate professional capabilities (critical thinking and correct interpretation of the results) is crucial for the correct usage of big data analytics [11].
- **Incorporating cloud computing:** Almost all hospitals are small and Medium-Sized Enterprises (SMEs) and often struggle with cost and data storage, analysis,

and bottom line. Public cloud is a significant cost savings option with many security and privacy-preserving issues. However, a private cloud solves these problems by providing a more secure environment and keeping the critical data in-house. Despite the benefits of private clouds, they are more expansive than the public ones.

- **Business ideas from big-data analytics:** New ideas can change business operations that increases productivity and build competitive advantages. specific reporting and identification of market trends grant companies the ability speed up new business ideas. Managers should also encourage staffs to leverage outputs such as reports, alerting, KPIs, and interactive visualizations [11].
- **Lack of appropriate IT infrastructure:** Dealing with the lack of IT infrastructure and transitioning from printed records to distributed data processing are key for the successful implementation of big data analysis in healthcare. Adding to those problems the resistance to modernizing processes, resistance to technologies that change the way the healthcare system operates and the demand of high initial investment, makes it difficult to implement Big Data technology in the medical sector [27].
- **Real time analysis:** A plain, comfortable and transparent Big Data analytics system that can be used in real-time cases is needed [28]. However, concerns with the use of Big Data analytics in healthcare like processing of information without human supervision that might lead to false conclusions remain.
- **Data Management:** The major technical challenges in Big Data analytics, with respect to data management, encompass fragmented data, limitations of observational data, validation, data structure, data standardization, data inaccuracy, data veracity, data reliability, semantic interoperability, network bandwidth, scalability, and cost, integration of structured, semi-structured and unstructured data from different sources, missing data and false-positive associations [27].

7.2 Safety

Safety, as established, by ISO 60601, is the action of preventing the emergence of hazards in the physical environment. ISO 60601 can be used on CPSs in a non-medical context by extending the definition of threats. Faulty operation of the computing unit and thermal effects are some examples of this threats [29]. Safety demands a deep awareness of the physical state of the surroundings and characteristics of the computing unit. We can classify the interaction safety hazards into three kinds of cyber-physical interactions.

- Computing unit to computing unit interactions: Cyber-physical interactions of computing units could interfere with each other's operation in dangerous ways. A good example of this are the problems caused by headphones in peacemakers.
- Computing units to physical environment interactions: This interactions of the computing units with the environment may create adverse effects.

- Physical environment to computing unit interactions: The physical activity of the enviroment may create obstacles to the operation of the computing unit, for example, tissue expansion into or around the implanted sensors can impede sensing and communication [29].

7.3 Security

The security of a CPS is can be as the capacity to ensure that system's capabilities can only be accessed when authorized. The healthcare industry continues to be one of the most susceptible to publicly disclosed data breaches [30]. So, the growth of malware in volume and complexity adds danger to this vulnerability [31]. Traditional security methods are no longer capable to fully defend the network against advanced intrusion attacks [32]. However, there are several publication focused on intrusion detection techniques [4, 32–38]. There are other challenges regarding the use of CPS in healthcare.

- **Mission-critical nature:** A security breach of the cyber or the physical component of a CPS can have deep consequences due to the frequent use of CPS in mission-critical applications. This is why CPS are popular objectives for cyber attacks. One example of this attacks is the attack targets pacemakers, is not only revealed the patient's electrocardiogram data but forced the peacemaker to actuate an improper pulse [30].
- **Information detail and sensitivity:** CPSs contain sensitive information about important physical processes. This information can be exploited to facilitate loss of privacy, abuse, and discrimination [30].
- **Ability to actuate:** Allowing unauthorized parties to use the CPS's ability to effect changes in the environment can be harmful to the environment itself [30].
- **Ubiquity:** Spetial attention has to be paid to CPSs' protection measures so that automated and efficient service management is possible and, also, extended into the area [30]. A compromised insider can easily access information stored in a compromised node [37]. This is why individual sensors in a large-scale network are the main target of security compromises.

7.4 Privacy

Privacy is the right of individuals to decide when, how and how much information is shared to others. The objective of privacy protocols is preventing others from reviewing a person's personal and sensitive information [39]. Two important elements in healthcare are patient privacy and confidentiality. The emergence of advanced persistent threats, targeted attacks against information systems, whose main purpose is to smuggle recoverable data by the attacker have created a challenge for organizations to address these different complementary and critical problems [30]. K-anonymity and two-phase top-down specialization (TDS) are techniques developed to deal with this problem, however, both of those are still vulnerable to correlation attack [30].

Data sharing between various agents to obtain intuitions from data can increase the need for privacy [40]. Informed consent and privacy are key areas of concern in the medical industry. The dearth of data standards and protocols are some of the control problems that faced big-data analytics must sort out in healthcare. Implementing (big) data governance developing an information-sharing culture, employing security measures, Training key personnel. Incorporating cloud computing into the organization's Big Data analytics are strategies useful for curbing the aforementioned issues [27].

Current cyber-physical systems do not support the control rights over our data asserted by EU and US legislation. The individual who is being studied has insufficient control and insight of what is being collected and how it is used [41].

7.5   Sustainabilty

The battery or the AC mains usually provide the energy needed in CPS components like sensors or servers. The traditional energy supply model for CPS has to change due to the changes in supply technologies, pushing toward alternative green sources of energy, and the new role of the customer and his increasing impact are that shapes the electricity system architecture [29, 42]. The cyber-physical energy supply creates some problems when trying to achieve a sustainable design of CPSs [29] and security of the network [43]. There are two main concerns in the sustainability sector. The first one is the intermittent energy supply. The intermittent nature of green energy sources creates problems when trying to secure the energy demand of the computing units of CPSs. Supply and demand, usually, are not naturally synchronized. The sustainable CPS design must match the power from energy sources with the total demand of the system and it also must minimize energy misuse. Load characteristics must be taken into account when calculating the optimum operational voltage and current to maximize the system's energetic performance [29].

7.6   Data Cleaning

Making sure that the data sources are trustworthy and the data is of sufficient quality is of utmost importance to achieve reliable analysis results. Data sources may be erroneous, noisy or incomplete, this complicates the management, processing and cleaning of big-data and makes the reliability question harder to answer [6].

7.7 Big-Data Aggregation

Analyzing the organizations generated data is not enough, also, there are some external source of data that should be considered in most of big-data applications. This heightens the importance of the synchronization of external data generators with the internal frameworks of the institution. Merging internal data and external sources is imperative for an adequate implementation of Big-Data [6].

7.8 Imbalanced Systems Capacities

The CPU and disk drive performance are doubled every 18 months according to Moore's Law, but, the I/O operations are not subject to this law. So, imbalanced system capacities makes the data access slow which in turn affects the performance and the scalability of big-data applications. Imbalanced system capacity may slow down the system performance and affect other devices capabilities (sensors, disks, and memories) over a network [6].

7.9 Imbalanced Big-Data

Traditional learning techniques are not suitable for imbalanced datasets. Classes with different distributions result from real world applications. The first type of class, known as the minority class, is underrepresented with a negligible number of instances. The second, called majority class, have an abundant number of instances. The minority classes are important in fields such as medical diagnosis, software defect detection, finance, drug discovery, and bioinformatics. If the model design was inspired on global search that does not consider the number of instances, the minority class would be neglected during the model construction due to the privileged given to global rules. The disregard for underrepresented classes is important because they may hold the important cases to identify. Handling multi-class tasks, is more difficult than dealing with two-class ones. Real world problems are harder to manage given that usually problem domains present more than two classes and uneven distributions. To faced the mentioned challenges, two categories of solutions have raised. The first category consists of extending multiple binary classification algorithms so that they can solve multi-class classification problems (decision trees, Naive Bayes,discriminant analysis, k-nearest neighbors, support vector machines, and neural networks). The second category of solutions is called Decomposition and Ensemble Methods (DEM). DEM breaks down a multiclass classification problem into several sets of binary classification problems. Binary Classifiers (BCs) can solve this type of sets [6].

7.10 Big-Data Machine Learning

7.10.1 Data Stream Learning

Applications like banking transactions, sensors networks, blog posts, stock management, and network traffic generate vast datasets. Discovering patterns and finding buried valuable information in huge datasets and streams of data is made possible thanks to data mining. Nonetheless, commonly used data mining methods such as clustering, classification, and association mining are less efficient, scalable, and accurate when used on big datasets in a changing environment. The speed, variability, and size of streams does not allow permanent storage and posterior analysis. Researchers require new methods so analytical techniques are optimized, data instances are processed in a timely manner and with low resources usage and to accurate real-time results are provided. Additionally, incoming variable data streams present unpredictable changes (changing the distribution of instances for example). Because the model is trained by past instances this change have an influence of accuracy of the classification model. Several data mining techniques have been modified so that the algorithm is able to cope with the changing algorithm and the drift can be detected. Experiments on data streams demonstrate that modifications to the latent concept have consequences on the performance of the classifier. Thus, analytical methods capable of adapting and detecting concept drift are needed [6].

7.10.2 Deep Learning

Deep learning is an active area of research in ML and pattern recognition. Commonly used machine learning techniques and feature engineering algorithms have trouble processing raw data. Deep learning, on the other side, solves analytical and learning problems inherent to large datasets. Deep Learning can also draw out complex data representations from unsupervised and uncategorized raw data. Due to its hierarchical learning feature, deep Learning can be easily used to simplify the analysis of large data volume into a fitting internal representation so that the learning subsystem can classify or determine patterns. Even though big-data has advantages it must still surpass significant challenges related to deep learning [6]:

- Vast volumes of big-data: the training phase is a complicated matter. The challenge relies on parallelizing the iterative computations of the learning algorithms. Efficient and scalable parallel algorithms are still needed to better the training of deep models.
- Heterogeneity: Heterogeneity concerns itself with high dimensionality (attributes), different outputs, and huge numbers of inputs.
- Noisy labels, and non-stationary distribution: Analytical researchers must face old challenges like missing labels, data incompleteness, and noisy labels due to the different sources of big-data.

- High velocity: high velocity, data is often non-stationary which means that its distributuin is not constant over time. Data are processed in real time at an astonishing speed.

Deep learning solutions lack maturity and require further research to improve the results. Further considerations should be taken on how to optimize deep learning algorithms so that streaming data, high dimensionality, and model scalability issues are dealt with. Furthermore, some researches are required to better criteria selection for extracting good data representations, data abstractions' formulation, data tagging, semantic indexing, distributed computing, information retrieval, and domain adaptation [6].

7.10.3   Incremental and Ensemble Learning

Incremental learning and ensemble learning are two, widely used, dynamic learning strategies. These two methods are commonly used when working with data streams and big-data. They tackle challenges, such as data availability, and limited resources. They are employed in applications such as user profiling and stock trend prediction. Employing incremental learning enables the model to provide faster classification times while processing fresh data. By comparing these algorithms, it is noticed that incremental algorithms have faster execution times, but not all classification algorithms are compatible with incremental learning. Using an incremental algorithm when there is a lack of concept drift or smooth concept drift is present is recommended. Also, incremental algorithms can be used when the data stream is simple or presents a high level of real-time processing. Flexibility and adaptability to concept drift are the strong points of ensemble algorithms. furthermore, most classification algorithms can be implemented in ensemble algorithms. Ensemble algorithms are favored when high accuracy is important or when the concept drift is big or sudden. Regarding data streams ensemble learning constitutes a better choice if the stream is complicated or presents an unknown distribution [6]. Ensemble algorithms are favored when high accuracy is important or when the concept drift is big or sudden. Regarding data streams ensemble learning constitutes a better choice if the stream is complicated or presents an unknown distribution [6].

7.10.4   Granular Computing

Granular Computing (GrC), initially called information granularity, was first introduced in 1997. GrC encompasses a variety of theories, methodologies, and techniques that use "granules" to solve complex problems. A granule, in the most basic leves, is made up of basic elements like subsets, classes, objects, clusters, and elements of a universe. This granules can be grouped together by their differences, similarity and functionality to generate bigger granules. Granules can be categorized into different levels depending on complexity, abstract and size [44]. GrC has gained popularity applications in big-data domains. It possesses advantages for intelligent data analysis, pattern recognition, machine learning, and uncertain reasoning. Users must understand big-data at different granularity levels aided by distributed systems. Data analysis and different perspective results are also needed. Comprehension and analysis of the complexity of various big datasets is enabled by GrC's tools for multiple granularity and multiple viewing of data analysis.

Furthermore, GrC techniques can function as processing tools for real-world intelligent systems. GrC allows the model to tackle changing attributes and objects in streams over time. The integration of GrC and computational intelligence has become a prominent research area that aims to advance decision-making models so complex big-data problems can be solved. GrC can be put into action by a plethora of technologies such as rough sets, random sets, fuzzy sets, etc. Fuzzy sets allow us to explore and represent the set-members relationship by using a continuum degree of belonging and they help us to depict and handle information at distinct levels of granularity. Moreover, fuzzy set methods are embedded in all stages of the big-data value chain, from handling raw data to data annotation and representation. Thanks to the structure supports for lar datasets matrices are being used, more and more, for rough data analysis and approximations. In order to handle evolving data streams, the model is updated and rather than recalculating the entire relation matrix the computations are made on small relation matrices (sub-matrices). Therefore, GrC methods can boost big-data techniques while dealing with the big-data challenges like 5Vs, preprocessing data, or reframing the problem at certain granular problem. Finally, we must not forget that the main job of GrC and fuzzy techniques is to provide tools for representing and abstracting knowledge [6].

7.11   Quality of Service

The current mechanisms for Quality of Service (QoS) have major limitations in the provision and support of Service Level Agreements (SLAs) in IoT and clouds. These mechanisms must be revised so that the challenges posed by remote health care chain applications are met. This challenge is accentuated by the shortage of standardized end-to-end approaches for QoS assurance. There are other requirements needed such as detect/notify events within 5 min of occurrence that must be also guaranteed [45]. The ability to collect and monitor data from all the big-data processing frameworks while allowing administrators to easily track and understand application-level QoS without the understanding of the whole platform is an obstacle to the widespread use of big-data in the healtcare sector [45].

Figure 12.11 shows a summary of this section.

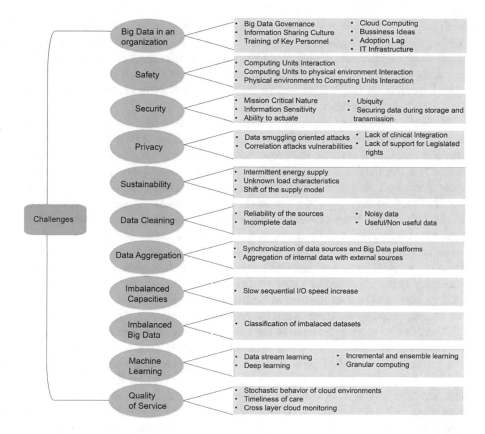

Fig. 12.11 Challenges for big-data in healthcare

8   Opportunities

Despite the progress has been made, there are still areas of improvement in the research. An important open problem in big-data in healthcare sector is the lack of five-star algorithms for environmentally coupled CPS workload. The ability to control the physical environment demands a precise characterization of the cyber–physical interactions during the workload scheduling [29]. In order to gain cloud computation power and achieve high scalability, an anonymization algorithm to speed up anonymization of big-data streams is needed. Even though an algorithm has been proposed there are still many work left to be done in the design and implementation of a distributed cloud-based framework [30]. An efficient algorithm capable of solving all particular cases of the Non-deterministic Polynomial time-hard (NP-hard) problem does not exist. Optimization problems in the bioinformatics domain require methods that capable of handling that level of complexity [22].

The heterogeneous data fusion and the open platform data access and analysis is another problem to be solved. The lack of universal standards and systems makes it difficult to integrate heterogeneous data and the relevant managements [46]. Virtual Reality (VR) research integrates multiple technologies such as computer simulation, multimedia technology and sensing. Integration of VR technology with physiological signals has not been achieved. The combination of smart clothing signal monitoring and virtual reality technology will support the emergence of broader ranges of applications [47].

A single system that considers all challenges (reliability, scalability, security, and ease to use) in healthcare big-data does not exist. Most of the methods in the research assess and evaluate the proposed components via recreation. For the next research stage, these methods should become viable in real case scenarios so that their elasticity to supervise instances autonomously can be exploited. Self-caring services may become a possibility in the future if home diagnosis is developed. Understanding the level of self-efficacy and its relationship to performance hold promise as future research lines due to the ever present concern of data security.

In addition, modeling pipelines is important in the healthcare analytics area. Developing pipelines, like treatment comparison, risk stratification, and patient similarity is the objective of future work. Furthermore, special attention must be paid on how the big-data handler in healthcare and manager systems can maintain the models remotely the models can be maintained remotely [22].

There is also work to be done in the CPS dimension. For example, future trends for passive RFID (Radio Frequency Identification) tag antenna-based sensors can be categorized into three directions. The first issue is networking and standardization. Future work can be done in the array or tag-tag coupling for boosting coverage, integration with UWB technology, creating a standard for integration of sensing capability, Wireless Integrated Sensing Platforms (WISPs) evolution for reduced power consumption and more external sensors in the systems, and integration with narrow-band IoT. The second direction is how to further the ubiquity and adaptability of the sensors. For example, integration with chip-embeddable sensors, analog memory with function materials, automatic impedance matching and digitalization of RSSI, and wearable electronics. The last direction focuses on how to make the sensors more reliable and straightforward: Software-Defined Radio (SDR) for clear and cheap readers, harsh environment monitoring, and a chipless antenna with a changable programming system [46].

Examining the impact of big-data analytics capabilities on healthcare organization with a quantitative analysis method based on primary data could shed different lights. Reference [11] notes the need for more scientific, quantitative studies, and better analytic methods, such as deep machine learning algorithm capable of detecting instances of interest in vast volumes of unstructured data, and capable of discovering connections on the data without needing coding the instructions. This is crucial analytical and decision support capabilities. Future scientific studies should develop efficient unstructured data analysis algorithms and applications as primary technological developments [11].

Also, there is a lack of theory in the current cyber defense architecture. The effectiveness of security measures varies significantly and the insider threat cannot be mitigated by one solution. Most security measures require breaches to occur before an analysis of malicious activity can prevent it. This reactive approach is not effective in the protection of the healthcare system and infrastructure [48]. Artificial intelligence, machine learning, and advanced data mining techniques are needed due to the increase in the number of cyber-attacks that require detection, analysis, and defense in almost real-time [49].

Finally, the published work notes the importance of the future employment of big-data. However, documentation of a real-world implementation of big-data in healthcare was not found. The qualitative approach is usually employed by studies to demonstrate the advantages and disadvantages of the implementation of big-data in healthcare applications. The qualitative studies are needed to demonstrate the practical benefits and facilitate the wide-scale adoption of technology. Finally, [27] notes that most of the papers included in the review are from developed countries. Data analytics in developing countries will allow the delivery of better quality care.

References

1. E.A. Lee, S.A. Seshia, *Introduction to Embedded Systems. A Cyber-Physical Systems Approach*, 2nd edn. (MIT Press, Cambridge, 2017)
2. E.R. Griffor, C. Greer, D.A. Wollman, M.J. Burns, Framework for cyber-physical systems: volume 1, overview. Tech. Rep., National Institute of Standards and Technology, Gaithersburg (2017)
3. R. Rajkumar, I. Lee, L. Sha, J. Stankovic, Cyber-physical systems: the next computing revolution, in *Design Automation Conference* (2010), pp. 731–736
4. J. Sakhnini, H. Karimipour, A. Dehghantanha, Smart grid cyber attacks detection using supervised learning and heuristic feature selection, in *IEEE SEGE 2019* (2019)
5. W.L. Chang, NIST big data interoperability framework: volume 1, definitions, special publication (NIST SP)-1500–1, (2015)
6. A. Oussous, F.Z. Benjelloun, A. Ait Lahcen, S. Belfkih, Big data technologies: a survey. J. King Saud Univ. Comput. Inf. Sci. **30**(4), 431–448 (2018)
7. J. Zhang, W. Shi, Y. Duan, S. Liu, Industrial big data analytics, in *2015 IEEE/ACM 1st International Workshop on Big Data Software Engineering* (2015), pp. 1–3
8. G. Harerimana, B. Jang, J.W. Kim, H.K. Park, Health big data analytics: a technology survey. IEEE Access **6**, 65661–65678 (2018)
9. D.W. McKee, S.J. Clement, J. Almutairi, J. Xu, Survey of advances and challenges in intelligent autonomy for distributed cyber-physical systems. CAAI Trans. Intell. Technol. **3**(2), 75–82 (2018)
10. Y. Zhang, M. Qiu, S. Member, C.-W. Tsai, Health-CPS: healthcare cyber-physical system assisted by cloud and big data. IEEE Syst. J. **11**(1), 1–8 (2015)
11. Y. Wang, L.A. Kung, T.A. Byrd, Big data analytics: understanding its capabilities and potential benefits for healthcare organizations. Technol. Forecast. Soc. Chang. **126**, 3–13 (2018)
12. A. Dehghantanha, R. Mahmod, N. Udzir, Z. Ahmad Zulkarnain, User-centered privacy and trust model in cloud computing systems, in *Computer and Network Technology* (2010), pp. 326–332
13. J. Archenaa, E.A. Anita, A survey of big data analytics in healthcare and government. Proc. Comput. Sci. **50**, 408–413 (2015)
14. P. Kaur, M. Sharma, M. Mittal, Big data and machine learning based secure healthcare framework. Proc. Comput. Sci. **132**, 1049–1059 (2018)

15. F.J. Wu, Y.F. Kao, Y.C. Tseng, From wireless sensor networks towards cyber physical systems. Pervasive Mob. Comput. **7**(4), 397–413 (2011)
16. R.A. Ariyaluran Habeeb, F. Nasaruddin, A. Gani, I.A. Targio Hashem, E. Ahmed, M. Imran, Real-time big data processing for anomaly detection: a survey. Int. J. Inf. Manag. **45**, 289–307 (2019)
17. H. Karimipour, S. Member, V. Dinavahi, S. Member, Parallel domain-decomposition-based distributed state estimation for large-scale power systems. IEEE Trans. Ind. Appl. **52**(2), 1265–1269 (2016)
18. V. Palanisamy, R. Thirunavukarasu, Implications of big data analytics in developing healthcare frameworks - a review. J. King Saud Univ. Comput. Inf. Sci. **31**, 415–425 (2019)
19. R.M. Parizi, L. Guo, Y. Bian, A. Azmoodeh, A. Dehghantanha, K.R. Choo, Cyberpdf: smart and secure coordinate-based automated health pdf data batch extraction, in *2018 IEEE/ACM International Conference on Connected Health: Applications, Systems and Engineering Technologies (CHASE)* (2018), pp. 106–111
20. R. Patgiri, A. Ahmed, Big data: The v's of the game changer paradigm, in *2016 IEEE 18th International Conference on High Performance Computing and Communications; IEEE 14th International Conference on Smart City; IEEE 2nd International Conference on Data Science and Systems (HPCC/SmartCity/DSS)* (2016), pp. 17–24
21. W. Inoubli, S. Aridhi, H. Mezni, M. Maddouri, E. Mephu Nguifo, An experimental survey on big data frameworks. Futur. Gener. Comput. Syst. **86**, 546–564 (2018)
22. A. Pashazadeh, N.J. Navimipour, Big data handling mechanisms in the healthcare applications: a comprehensive and systematic literature review. J. Biomed. Inform. **82**, 47–62 (2018)
23. T. Estrada, B. Zhang, P. Cicotti, R.S. Armen, M. Taufer, A scalable and accurate method for classifying protein–ligand binding geometries using a MapReduce approach. Comput. Biol. Med. **42**, 758–771 (2012)
24. Z.-H. You, J.-Z. Yu, L. Zhu, S. Li, Z.-K. Wen, A MapReduce based parallel SVM for large-scale predicting protein–protein interactions. Neurocomputing **145**, 37–43 (2014)
25. H. Chen, H. Zhao, J. Shen, R. Zhou, Q. Zhou, Supervised machine learning model for high dimensional gene data in colon cancer detection, in *2015 IEEE International Congress on Big Data* (2015), pp. 134–141
26. M. Priya, P.R. Kumar, A novel intelligent approach for predicting atherosclerotic individuals from big data for healthcare. Int. J. Protein Res. **53**(24), 7517–7532 (2015)
27. N. Mehta, A. Pandit, Concurrence of big data analytics and healthcare: a systematic review. Int. J. Med. Inform. **114**, 57–65 (2018)
28. W. Raghupathi, V. Raghupathi, Big data analytics in healthcare: promise and potential. Health Inf. Sci. Syst. **2**, 3 (2014)
29. B.A. Banerjee, K.K. Venkatasubramanian, T. Mukherjee, S.K.S. Gupta, Ensuring safety, security, and cyber - physical systems. Proc. IEEE **100**(1), 283–299 (2012)
30. K. Abouelmehdi, A. Beni-Hssane, H. Khaloufi, M. Saadi, Big data security and privacy in healthcare: a review. Proc. Comput. Sci. **113**, 73–80 (2017)
31. P.G. Shinde, P. Motwani, P. Shinde, Survey on malware detection techniques. Int. J. Mod. Trends Eng. Res. 74–79 (2015)
32. S. Mohammadi, V. Desai, H. Karimipour, Multivariate mutual information-based feature selection for cyber intrusion detection, in *2018 IEEE Electrical Power and Energy Conference (EPEC 2018)* (2018)
33. E.M. Dovom, A. Azmoodeh, A. Dehghantanha, D.E. Newton, R.M. Parizi, H. Karimipour, Fuzzy pattern tree for edge malware detection and categorization in IoT. J. Syst. Archit. **97**, 1–7 (2019)
34. B. MohammadReza, F. Derakhshan, H. Karimipour, A layered intrusion detection system for critical infrastructure using machine learning, in *IEEE International Conference on Smart Energy Grid Engineering, Oshawa* (2019), pp. 1–5
35. S. Geris, H. Karimipour, A feature selection-based approach for joint cyber-attack detection and state estimation, in *IEEE International Conference on Smart Energy Grid Engineering (SEGE), Oshawa* (2019), pp. 1–5

36. S. Mohammadi, H. Mirvaziri, M. Ghazizadeh-Ahsaee, H. Karimipour, Cyber intrusion detection by combined feature selection algorithm. J. Inf. Secur. Appl. **44**, 80–88 (2019)
37. H. Karimipour, A. Dehghantanha, R.M. Parizi, K.R. Choo, H. Leung, A deep and scalable unsupervised machine learning system for cyber-attack detection in large-scale smart grids. IEEE Access **7**, 80778–80788 (2019)
38. H. Karimipour, V. Dinavahi, Robust massively parallel dynamic state estimation of power systems against cyber-attack. IEEE Access **6**, 2984–2995 (2017)
39. C.A. Sagaran, A. Dehghantanha, R. Ramli, A user-centered context-sensitive privacy model in pervasive systems, in *2010 Second International Conference on Communication Software and Networks* (2010), pp. 78–82
40. J. Wu, H. Li, S. Cheng, Z. Lin, The promising future of healthcare services: when big data analytics meets wearable technology. Inf. Manag. **53**(8), 1020–1033 (2016). Big Data Commerce
41. A.T. Gjerdrum, H.D. Johansen, D. Johansen, Implementing informed consent as information-flow policies for secure analytics on ehealth data: principles and practices, in *Proceedings - 2016 IEEE 1st International Conference on Connected Health: Applications, Systems and Engineering Technologies (CHASE 2016)* (2016), pp. 107–112
42. H.M. Ruzbahani, H. Karimipour, Optimal incentive-based demand response management of smart households, in *Conference Record - Industrial and Commercial Power Systems Technical Conference*, vol. 2018 (2018), pp. 1–7
43. H. Karimipour, V. Dinavahi, On false data injection attack against dynamic state estimation on smart power grids, in *2017 5th IEEE International Conference on Smart Energy Grid Engineering (SEGE 2017)* (2017), pp. 388–393
44. J. Yao, A ten-year review of granular computing, in *2007 IEEE International Conference on Granular Computing (GRC 2007)* (2007), pp. 734–734
45. T. Shah, A. Yavari, K. Mitra, S. Saguna, P.P. Jayaraman, F. Rabhi, R. Ranjan, Remote health care cyber-physical system: quality of service (QoS) challenges and opportunities, IET Cyber-Phys. Syst. Theory Appl. **1**(1), 40–48 (2016)
46. J. Zhang, G.Y. Tian, A.M. Marindra, A.I. Sunny, A.B. Zhao, A review of passive RFID tag antenna-based sensors and systems for structural health monitoring applications. Sensors **17**(2), 1–33 (2017)
47. M. Chen, Y. Ma, J. Song, C.F. Lai, B. Hu, Smart clothing: connecting human with clouds and big data for sustainable health monitoring. Mobile Netw. Appl. **21**(5), 825–845 (2016)
48. S. Walker-Roberts, M. Hammoudeh, A. Dehghantanha, A systematic review of the availability and efficacy of countermeasures to internal threats in healthcare critical infrastructure. IEEE Access **6**, 25167–25177 (2018)
49. M. Conti, T. Dargahi, A. Dehghantanha, *Cyber Threat Intelligence: Challenges and Opportunities* (Springer, Berlin, 2018), pp. 1–6

Chapter 13
Privacy Preserving Abnormality Detection: A Deep Learning Approach

Wenyu Han, Amin Azmoodeh, Hadis Karimipour, and Simon Yang

1 Introduction

Artificial Intelligence (AI) is the concept used to describe computer systems that can learn from their own experiences and solve complex problems in different situations [1]. Around 2010, the field of AI has been shaken by the broad and unforeseen successes of multi-layer Neural Networks (NNs). This success is due to the introduction of high performance computing, Graphic Processing Unit (GPUs), and the availability of large labeled data sets that could be used as training testbeds. This combination has allowed the rise of Deep Learning (DL) on Deep Neural Networks (DNNs), especially on the architecture called Convolutional Neural Networks (CNNs) [2, 3].

The development of AI has made major advances in recent years and its potential appears to be promising. In the healthcare sector, scientific competitions like ImageNet large-scale visual recognition challenges are providing evidence that computers can achieve human-like competence in image recognition. Researches demonstrated that AI is able to make clinical diagnoses at levels equal to clinicians in some specific cases using medical images [4, 5].

This venture will have a considerable impact on healthcare operation, management and research. However, there are still barriers and challenges that need to be addressed. Several growing trends in the healthcare, such as clinician mobility and wireless networking, health information exchange, and cloud computing are

W. Han · H. Karimipour (✉) · S. Yang
School of Engineering, University of Guelph, Guelph, ON, Canada
e-mail: whan01@uoguelph.ca; hkarimi@uoguelph.ca; Canada-hkarimi@uoguelph.ca;
syang@uoguelph.ca

A. Azmoodeh
Cyber Science Lab, School of Computer Science, University of Guelph, Guelph, ON, Canada
e-mail: amin@cybersciencelab.org

© Springer Nature Switzerland AG 2020
K.-K. R. Choo, A. Dehghantanha (eds.), *Handbook of Big Data Privacy*,
https://doi.org/10.1007/978-3-030-38557-6_13

increasing the concerns related to privacy and data protection [6]. Other trends that are aggravating the problem are the emergence of advanced persistent threats, targeted attacks against information systems, whose main purpose is to smuggle recoverable data by the attacker [7–10]. We cannot ignore the challenges in ethics, and security raised using AI, which is why on this chapter we will focus on one of this concern: privacy and the use of personal data in AI.

2 Background

2.1 Privacy and Healthcare

Preserving the privacy of healthcare information is a considerable challenge of the field [11]. Protecting patient and Health Information Systems (HIS) and maintaining the system security is a major obstacle to provide digital services in this context [12]. Critical role and imperative stored information stored in HIS turn it to a gold mine for cybercriminals for data breach and causing intentional system failures [13]. Despite a considerable attentions and researches to propose approaches to provide HIS with security and privacy, the research area is still controversial [14]. On the one hand, the digital revolution has affected the health industry. The cost of health and medical services has experienced a dramatic fall by employing information technology [15]. Besides, quality of medical services has been significantly increased according to using electronic health record systems [16]. On the other hand, during the past decades, security and privacy have became a challenging issue. A rapid escalate has occurred in data breaches somehow in 2016, CynergisTek has released the Redspin's seventh annual breach report [17].

AI is playing a significant role in the quality and quantity of HIS services. A wide range of medical activities are leveraging AI ranging from diagnostic, imaging to screening and genetic testing [18]. Firstly, an automated, accurate and on-time medical service decrease the possibility of data breach and privacy issues lie in human-centric traditional healthcare systems [19]. Secondly, AI techniques transfer knowledge from document and health records into hyperparameters and models which can not be easily being understood, recovered, or extracted. It is notable that while designing an AI-based healthcare system, careful surveillance is necessary to consider AI-based privacy issues such as differential privacy [20]. In this work, a privacy preserving abnormality detection technique is proposed which employs CNN for image classification without human interaction.

2.2 Convolutional Neural Network

A CNN is a deep network structure which can take image as input and adjust various aspect in the image to differentiate one from another [1, 21]. Compared to the other classification algorithms, CNN requires less pre-processing. The architecture of a CNN is inspired by the organization of the Visual Cortexis and is analogous to that of the connectivity pattern of Neurons in the Human Brain [22]. In 1982, Fukushima's proposed neurocognitive machine based on the wilderness concept (Neocognitron) which was the first implementation version of the CNN [22–25]. Later at 1989 a five-layer CNN, LeNet was proposed that completely solved hand-written digit recognition [26]. This was the start of the CNN from theory to practical implementation. However, the absence of sample and computing power resulted in the unpopularity of the CNN. Instead, the design methods for characteristics such as support vector machines have accomplished excellent outcomes on tiny sample sets and have become mainstream. The CNN itself has been continually enhanced after many years of silence, with the emergence of the age of large information, and the prevalence of parallel computing based on GPU [27, 28]. In 2012, AlexKrizhevsky and others used an eight-layer CNN, AlexNet, to win that year's championship in the ImageNet image classification competition, far exceeding the second place by 10% points, allowing the CNN to come back to the sight of people [29]. Thereafter, different enhanced NN structures have emerged, most notably VGG, GoogleNet and Residual Neural Network (ResNet) [30–33].

The first significant notion of CNNs is local perceptual field where each neuron only requires perceiving the image's local characteristics to achieve the image's worldwide characteristics [34]. This is also inspired by the human visual nervous system. When humans recognize images, the nerves of the cerebral cortex only respond to local stimuli, indicating that human cognition of images is also a process from partial to whole [35].

The second important concept of CNNs is weight sharing. CNN use convolution operations to extract features from images, and the same convolution kernel extracts the same feature on the image. For multiple features extraction, multiple convolution kernels is required [36]. It is called "weight sharing" because the same convolution kernel slides between multiple parts of the image, and a locally extracted feature can be used in other areas, or the features of the image are independent of position. The sharing of weights can greatly reduce the amount of computation of the neural network [37]. Figure 13.1 shows an example of weight sharing.

The third important property of the CNN is the image extraction function that uses kernels of convolution. The method of convolution is a method that reduces the amount of parameters. The most important part of the process of convolution is the

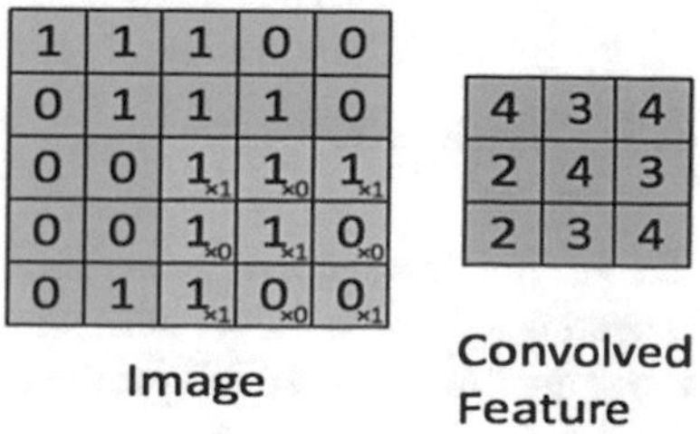

Fig. 13.1 Weight sharing

Image

Convolved Feature

Fig. 13.2 Convolution
operation

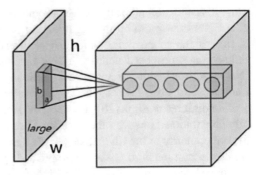

Fig. 13.3 Pooling operation

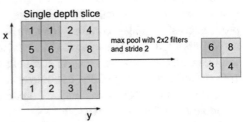

design of the step size and the number of kernels of convolution. The more number
of features are obtained, the more features are being extracted, but the network's
complexity is also increasing, which is susceptible to over-fitting issues. The
convolution kernel size influences the network structure's identification capacity,
and the size of the step determines the size and amount of image characteristics
taken [38, 39]. A sample convolution operation is shown in Fig. 13.2.

Pooling is another useful property of CNN. The pooling layer generally reduces
the eigenvector dimension of the convolutional layer output. The pooling method
minimizes image resolution and decreases the image's processing dimension, but
maintains the image's efficient data, decreases the processing complexity of the
subsequent convolution layer, and significantly decreases the image's network
rotation and translation. There are two particular techniques of pooling: mean
pooling and maximum pooling. The average pooling relates to calculating the
average value of the image target's local region as the unit value after pooling. The
maximum pooling is to pick as the pooled value the highest value of the target image
region [40, 41]. Pooling operation is described in Fig. 13.3.

2.3   TensorFlow

TensorFlow is a second-generation machine learning system created by Google that
overcomes the constraints of the first generation system, DistBelief, which can only
develop neural network algorithms, is difficult to configure, depends on Google's
internal hardware, is more widely used, and improves flexibility and portability [42,

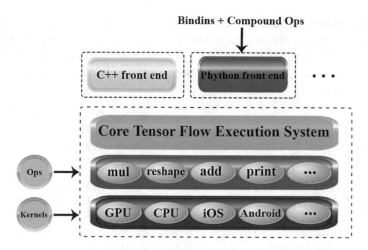

Fig. 13.4 TensorFlow architecture framework

43]. Architecture of TensorFlow is shown in Fig. 13.4. As shown in Fig. 13.4 the system architecture is divided into two parts:

- Front-end: provides a computer graphics programming model and offers assistance for various languages such as Python, C, Java, and Go.
- Backend: provides a runtime environment responsible for executing computational graphs, implemented in C.

Literally, it is a framework for the implementation of tensor flow on a graph and the implementation of machine learning algorithms, and has the following characteristics [44–46]:

- Flexibility—TensorFlow is not a rigorous library of NN. It can be used as partial differential solution in scientific computing, as long as the calculation can be represented as a data flow graph.
- Portability—the same code can be deployed to a PC, server or mobile device with any number of CPUs, GPUs or TPUs.
- Automatic differentiation—TensorFlow supports automatic differentiation, and the user does not need to solve the gradient by backpropagation.
- Multi-language support—TensorFlow officially supports Python, C, Go, and Java interfaces. Users can experiment with Python in a well-configured machine and deploy it in C in environments with tight resources or low latency.
- Performance—Although TensorFlow only supported stand-alone machines when it was first released, it is not good in performance evaluation, but with the strong development strength of Google, TensorFlow performance has caught up with other frameworks.

When constructing an algorithm, the user can construct a calculation graph according to personal preference and actual needs using a suitable front-end language. After the graph is built, the session is connected to the back end of the TensorFlow with the session as the bridge, and the calculation process of the graph is started and executed. The back end of the TensorFlow performs the specific calculation according to the current hardware environment calling the Kernel of Operation [47].

3 Medical Image Analysis Based on Deep Learning

Medical imaging technology plays a key role in early diagnosis, staging, and disease assessment. Medical image assessment has become an essential component of medical studies, clinical illness diagnosis and therapy with the ongoing growth and advancement of medical imaging technology and computer technology [48]. Medical imaging technologies include medical imaging, image processing, imaging analysis, and AI decision-making. Analysis of medical image is an interdisciplinary subject based on medical imaging, digital image processing and analysis, numerical algorithms, mathematical modeling and artificial intelligence [49, 50]. In the field of medical image analysis, it mainly includes image segmentation, image registration, image denoising, image fusion, image texture analysis, time series image analysis and image retrieval based on image content, as well as image understanding, image recognition and intelligent decision-making. In recent years, the increase of big data and computing power has made AI one of the key technology, which play a significant role in practical applications [51, 52]. AI and specifically DL can use complex neural network architecture to model patterns in data with unprecedented accuracy. In the field of medical health, the application of DL in medical imaging often appears as an application for assisted diagnosis or imaging detection [48].

Since 2006, DL has made important breakthroughs in many areas. The great success of deep learning in the field of computer vision has inspired many scholars at home and abroad to apply it to medical image analysis. Since 2016, in the medical image analysis, many specialists have summarized, evaluated and discussed the study position and issues of deep learning. A study released recently in Medical Image Analysis offers an extensive overview of deep learning in classification, identification and segmentation of medical images, registration and retrieval [53, 54].

3.1 CNN in Medical Image Classification

Medical image classification can be divided into image screening and target or lesion classification. Image screening is one of the earliest applications of deep learning in the field of medical image analysis [52]. It refers to taking one or more inspection images as input, predicting it through a trained model, and outputting a signal indicating whether it has a certain disease or severity. Nowadays, CNN is gradually becoming a standard technology in image screening classification, and its application is very extensive. For example, Arevalo et al. proposed a feature learning framework for breast cancer diagnosis, and used CNN to automatically learn the distinguishing features to classify mammogram lesions [55]. Kooi et al. compared the manual design and automatic CNN feature extraction methods in traditional Computer Aided Diagnosis (CAD), both of which were trained on large data sets of about 45,000 mammograms [52]. The results show that CNN is superior to traditional CAD system methods at low sensitivity, and both are comparable under high sensitivity. In addition, there are some work to combine CNN with Recurrent Neural Network (RNN). For example, [56] uses CNN to extract low-level local feature information in the slit lamp image, and further extracts high-level features in combination with RNN to classify nuclear cataract.

CNN is also widely used in the classification of targets or lesions [57]. used CNN to extract depth features at different levels, which improved the classification accuracy of breast cancer [58]. compared the tasks of detecting lung nodules in CT images and distinguishing between benign and malignant pulmonary nodules. The two types of end-to-end training artificial nerves were compared with Massive Training Artificial Neural Networks (MTANNs) and CNN. The experimental results show that the performance of MTANN is significantly higher than CNN only when minimum training data is used [58].

4   Proposed Case Study

This paper is focused on identifying abnormality detection in musculoskeletal radiographs using CNN as a binary classification task. Inspired by [59], Resnet and DenseNet models [30, 60] are used for classification task. Besides that, a network that separate local and global features and then combines them together is also proposed to improve the overall accuracy.

4.1   Dataset

MURA dataset [61], a large data set of bone X-rays provided by Stanford University School of Medicine is used in this work [61]. The main goal of this work is to train a CNN to perform the assignment of binary classification for normal and abnormal images. MURA is currently one of the largest X-ray dataset of 14,982 cases with 40,895 musculoskeletal X-rays. There were 9067 ordinary upper musculoskeletal and 5915 upper extremity unusual musculoskeletal X-rays in more than 10,000 instances, including the chest, arches, knees, forearms, wrists, palms, and toes.

The data is split by default into a training set (36,808 images) and a validation set (3197 images). The data is also partitioned based on studies. A study can consist of multiple X-ray images of a single patient and a single body part, but the images can be of different angles. Having multiple views helps radiologists to come to a more informed conclusion. This means that in the dataset, all the images belonging to a study would have the same class.

4.2 Data Augmentation

Data augmentation refers to the effect of appropriately transforming the original data to achieve an expanded data set based on some prior knowledge [62]. Specifically, in the image classification task, under the premise of keeping the image category unchanged, the following transformation can be performed on each image in the training set:

1. Random rotation, translation, scaling, cropping, filling, left and right flipping, etc. within a certain degree, these transformations correspond to observations of the same target at different angles.
2. Adding noise perturbations to pixels in the image, such as salt and pepper noise, Gaussian white noise, and so on.
3. Color conversion.
4. Changing the brightness, sharpness, contrast, sharpness, etc. of the image.

In the image classification task, image data expansion is generally one of the methods that most people will adopt. This is because deep learning has certain requirements on the size of the data set. If the original data set is small, the network cannot be well satisfied. The training of the model affects the performance of the model, and the image enhancement is to process the original image to expand the data set, which can improve the performance of the model to some extent.

In this work random sized crop in pre-processing stage is used. In other word, each input image is resized to 256×256 and then random-cropped to 224×224 before feeding into the network. Before applying the training process, each image is loaded in as a grayscale image with only one channel, and has the following augmentations applied to it:

- Zero padded and resized to be 256×256
- Random cropped to 224×224.
- Random rotation within $\pm 30°$.
- Randomly flipped horizontally.

For the preprocess improvement, the sharpen filter and contrast enhancing filter have also been applied to make dataset better for later training process. Figure 13.5 shows an example of an image of the shoulder part that was run through the data augmentation pipeline five times.

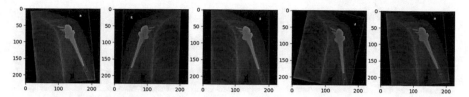

Fig. 13.5 Data augmentation

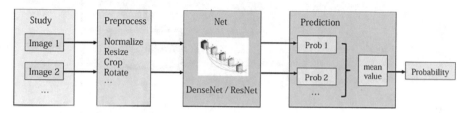

Fig. 13.6 Prediction pipeline of the model

4.3 Abnormality Detection Based on CNN

Figure 13.6 shows the prediction pipeline of the model used in this work which is adopted from [61]. The model feeds each image in the study into the network and evaluate the probability of abnormality for each image. Then it calculates the arithmetic mean value of the probabilities and outputs it as the final probability of the study.

If the probability is higher than 0.5, then can regard it as an abnormal study. The network uses DenseNet-169. The final fully connected layer is replaced with one that has a single output, and a sigmoid nonlinearity is added. To solve the problem of class imbalance, the loss function of each image X is defined by the weighted binary cross entropy:

$$L(X, y) = -w_{T,1} \, y \log P(Y = 1 | X) - w_{T,0} \, y \log P(Y = 0 | X) \tag{13.1}$$

where y is the label of the study, $P(Y = 1|X)$ is the probability that the network classifies the image as abnormal, $P(Y = 0|X)$ is the probability that the network classifies the image as normal, $w_{T,1}$ is the proportion of normal images and $w_{T,0}$ is the proportion of abnormal images in the dataset.

Since using only horizontal flip and rotation will cause overfitting, data-augmentation is also performed at training stage because. After trying different batch sizes 8, 16, 32, 64, 128 and the corresponding learning rate, batch size 16 and an initial learning rate 0:0001 is used which decays by a factor of ten each time the validation loss plateaus after an epoch as the hyper parameters.

Fig. 13.7 Resnet residual
learning module

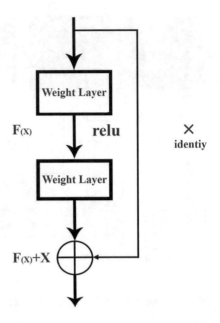

4.3.1 ResNet and DenseNet

ResNet's primary concept is to add a direct link channel to the network, which is the highway network concept [30]. ResNet's concept is very comparable to that of the highway network, enabling direct passage of the initial entry to the subsequent sections as shown in Fig. 13.7.

DenseNet was inspired by both ResNet and Inception Network [30, 60]. As with ResNet, in order to help reduce information and gradients being washed out due to the numerous layers, a convolution layer in DenseNet takes the feature maps produced by all the previous convolution layers within the dense block to which it belongs as input. However, the input from the different levels is not associated with the summation, but coupled with function maps similar to Inception Network. The BC in DenseNet-BC relates to the use and compression of bottleneck. The bottleneck layers assist to decrease the input size in terms of the number of channels for the tightly linked convolution layers while minimizing the quantity of missed data. Similarly, to decrease the amount of function maps generated between dense frames, compression is used. Structure of DenseNet is shown in Figs. 13.8 and 13.9.

4.3.2 Global and Local Features Combination

Considering that the abnormalities of bones usually happens in small areas, this work suggest a hierarchical feature selection to increase the accuracy of the abnormality detection. Inspired by the Attention Guided Convolutional Neural

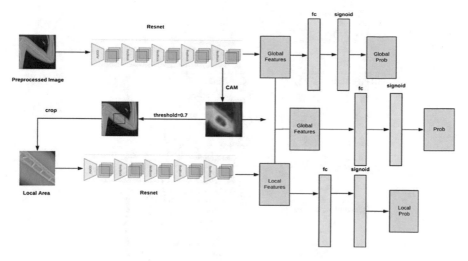

Fig. 13.8 Architecture of combined features network

Network [63], a combination of global and the local features on radiographs is proposed. The framework of the proposed network is shown in Fig. 13.8.

The network consists of three parts: global branch, local branch, and classifier. An input image (preprocessed image) first goes through the global branch and output the global feature (the 1-D feature after global average pooling). Then a heatmap is generated based on the feature maps (the 7×7 features before global average pooling).

After that, the heatmap is turned into a binary map under a threshold. By locating the maximum connected component on the binary map, the local area is cropped from the input image (preprocessed image). Afterwards, the cropped local image, after the same procedure of preprocessing, goes through the local branch and output the local feature. Finally, the global feature and the local feature are concatenated and fed into the fully-connected layer for classification.

For heatmap generation, the class activation map of the image is used as follows:

$$M_c = \sum_k w_k^c A^k \qquad (13.2)$$

where c is the given class, w_k^c is the weight corresponding to class c and A^1, A^2, $\ldots A^N$ are the feature maps.

The global branch and local branch are all based on ResNet-50 model. The ResNet-50 model which was trained previously is used in this model as the initialization for both global branch and local branch. Notice that the global branch needs no training.

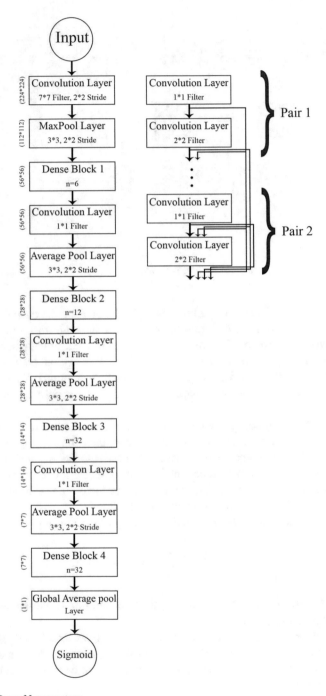

Fig. 13.9 DenseNet structure

5   Results

The learning abilities and memorization properties of the algorithms are measured by the False Positive Rate (FPR), True Positive Rate (TPR), and Accuracy (Acc) values, which are defined as [64]:

$$FPR = \frac{FP}{TN + FP}$$

$$TPR = \frac{TP}{TP + FN} \tag{13.3}$$

$$ACC = \frac{TP + TN}{TP + TN + FP + FN}$$

Figure 13.10 shows the results of training and validation loss during training. As can be seen the training loss is consistently being reduced, and the validation loss is decreasing on average.

Table 13.1 shows the summary of the results, including the accuracy of each type of the global branch, the local branch as well as the Area Under the Curve (AUC).

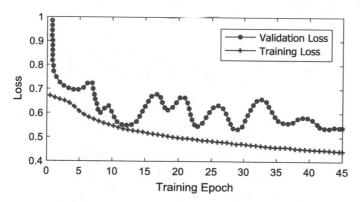

Fig. 13.10 Training and validation loss

Table 13.1 Summary of the results

Type	ResNet50 (b16, global)	ResNet50 (b16, local)	Combined features net
Elbow	0.8688	0.8438	0.8688
Finger	0.8400	0.8229	0.8171
Forearm	0.8394	0.8321	0.8467
Hand	0.7784	0.7605	0.8383
Humerus	0.8897	0.8603	0.9118
Shoulder	0.8000	0.7949	0.7897
Wrist	0.8950	0.8529	0.8908
All	0.8452	0.8237	0.8510
AUC	0.9049	0.8848	0.9076

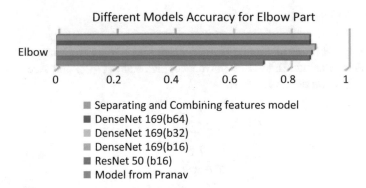

Fig. 13.11 Comparison of different models accuracy for Elbow part

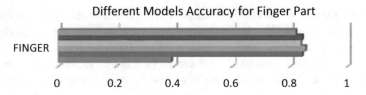

Fig. 13.12 Comparison of different models accuracy for Finger part

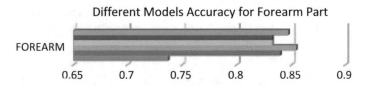

Fig. 13.13 Comparison of different models accuracy for Forearm part

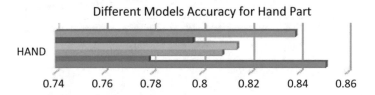

Fig. 13.14 Comparison of different models accuracy for Hand part

As seen from the results, local model of ResNet-50 performs slightly worse, due to the cropping process, which results in partial loss of information. However, the overall results for different body parts turns out to be higher on accuracy and AUC than the global branch, indicating that the idea of combine global and local features works better. Detailed results for different body parts are shown in Figs. 13.11, 13.12, 13.13, 13.14, 13.15, and 13.16.

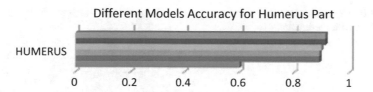

Fig. 13.15 Comparison of different models accuracy for Humerus part

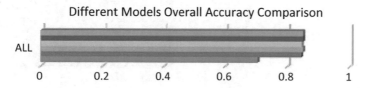

Fig. 13.16 Comparison of different models overall accuracy

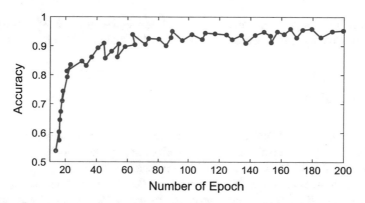

Fig. 13.17 Final model accuracy through epochs

Accuracy of the final model eventually converges into about 90% after training for 50 epochs as can be seen in Fig. 13.17. The final model's confusion matrix of performance on validation set is also shown below in Fig. 13.18. The confusion matrix is a situation analysis table that summarizes the prediction results of the classification model in data science, data analysis and machine learning. The records in the data set are summarized in a matrix form according to the two categories of classification and judgment made by the real category and the classification model. Since this task is a binary classification problem, the data set has two types of records: positive category and negative category, and the classification model may make a positive judgment on the record classification (the judgment record belongs to the positive category) or the negative judgment (the judgment record belongs to the negative category). This confusion matrix is a 2 × 2 situation analysis table showing the number of the following four groups of records: a positive record that makes a correct judgment (true positive), a positive record that makes a wrong

Fig. 13.18 Confusion Matrix of final model for validation dataset

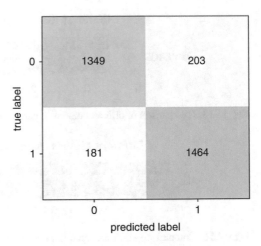

judgment (false negative), a negative record that makes a correct judgment (true Negative) and a negative record (false positive) that makes a false judgment.

6 Conclusion

DL and in particular CNN are among the most popular choices for medical or biomedical images analysis. In this work abnormality detection and abnormality localization using CNN is implemented on musculoskeletal radiographs in MURA dataset. At first, model are trained based on ResNet and DenseNet to classify the images as either normal or abnormal. In the second step, global and local feature are combined to improve the performance. Google GPU platform is used for DL implementation to reduce the computational burden. It should be noted that ResNet and DenseNet models are mainly used for nature image classification in the literature, which is quite different from a radiograph. It might be possible to get better results with a different models.

References

1. N. Milosevic, A. Dehghantanha, K.K.R. Choo, Machine learning aided Android malware classification. Comput. Electr. Eng. **61**, 266–274 (2017)
2. O.M.K. Alhawi, J. Baldwin, A. Dehghantanha, Leveraging machine learning techniques for windows ransomware network traffic detection, in *Advances in Information Security*, (Springer, Cham, 2018)
3. A. Shalaginov, S. Banin, A. Dehghantanha, K. Franke, Machine learning aided static malware analysis: a survey and tutorial, in *Advances in Information Security*, (Springer, Cham, 2018)
4. A. Eliasy, R. Ambrosio, B.T. Lopes, Artificial intelligence in corneal diagnosis: where are we? in *Current Ophthalmology Reports*, (Springer, Cham, 2019), pp. 1–8

5. A. Esteva, B. Kuprel, R.A. Novoa, J. Ko, S.M. Swetter, H.M. Blau, S. Thrun, Dermatologist-level classification of skin cancer with deep neural networks. Nature **542**, 115 (2017)
6. O. Osanaiye, H. Cai, K.K.R. Choo, A. Dehghantanha, Z. Xu, M. Dlodlo, Ensemble-based multi-filter feature selection method for DDoS detection in cloud computing. EURASIP J. Wirel. Commun. Netw. **2016**, 130 (2016)
7. H. Karimipour, V. Dinavahi, On false data injection attack against dynamic state estimation on smart power grids, in *2017 5th IEEE International Conference on Smart Energy Grid Engineering, SEGE 2017* (2017)
8. J. Sakhnini, H. Karimipour, A. Dehghantanha, Smart grid cyber attacks detection using supervised learning and heuristic feature selection, in *IEEE Int. Conf. on Smart Energy Grid Engineering, Oshawa* (2019)
9. H.K.S. Geris, Feature selection-based approach for joint cyber-attack detection and state estimation, in *IEEE Int. Conf. on Smart Energy Grid Engineering, Oshawa* (2019)
10. S. Grooby, T. Dargahi, A. Dehghantanha, A bibliometric analysis of authentication and access control in IoT devices, in *Handbook of Big Data and IoT Security*, (Springer, Cham, 2019)
11. M. Keil, E.H. Park, B. Ramesh, Violations of health information privacy: the role of attributions and anticipated regret in shaping whistle-blowing intentions. Inf. Syst. J. **28**, 818–848 (2018)
12. C.S. Kruse, B. Smith, H. Vanderlinden, A. Nealand, Security techniques for the electronic health records. J. Med. Syst. **41**, 127 (2017)
13. S. Walker-Roberts, M. Hammoudeh, A. Dehghantanha, A systematic review of the availability and efficacy of countermeasures to internal threats in healthcare critical infrastructure. IEEE Access **6**, 25167–25177 (2018)
14. W. Meng, K.R. Choo, S. Furnell, A.V. Vasilakos, C.W. Probst, Towards Bayesian-based Trust Management for Insider Attacks in healthcare software-defined networks, in IEEE Transactions on Network and Service Management **15**(2), 761–773 (June 2018)
15. P.C. Evans, M. Annunziata, *Industrial Internet: Pushing the Boundaries of Minds and Machines* (General Electric, Tech. Rep, 2012)
16. M. Begli, F. Derakhshan, H. Karimipour, A layered intrusion detection system for critical infrastructure using machine learning, in *IEEE Int. Conf. on Smart Energy Grid Engineering, Oshawa* (2019)
17. Y. Wang, L.A. Kung, T.A. Byrd, Big data analytics: understanding its capabilities and potential benefits for healthcare organizations. Technol. Forecast. Soc. Chang. **126**, 3–13 (2018)
18. F. Jiang, Y. Jiang, H. Zhi, Y. Dong, H. Li, S. Ma, Y. Wang, Q. Dong, H. Shen, Y. Wang, Artificial intelligence in healthcare: Past, present and future. Stroke Vasc Neurol **2**, 230–243 (2017)
19. M. Coeckelbergh, Health care, capabilities, and AI assistive technologies. Ethical Theory Moral Pract. **13**, 181–190 (2010)
20. W.N. Price, I.G. Cohen, Privacy in the age of medical big data. Nat. Med. **25**, 37–43 (2019)
21. H. HaddadPajouh, A. Dehghantanha, R. Khayami, K.K.R. Choo, A deep Recurrent Neural Network based approach for internet of Things malware threat hunting. Futur. Gener. Comput. Syst. **85**, 88–96 (2018)
22. Z. Jiao, X. Gao, Y. Wang, J. Li, A deep feature based framework for breast masses classification. Neurocomputing **197**, 221–231 (2016)
23. Q. Dou, H. Chen, Y. Jin, L. Yu, J. Qin, P.A. Heng, 3D deeply supervised network for automatic liver segmentation from CT volumes, in *Lecture Notes in Computer Science (Including Subseries Lecture Notes in Artificial Intelligence and Lecture Notes in Bioinformatics)* (2016)
24. H. Karimipour, A. Dehghantanha, R.M. Parizi, K.R. Choo, H. Leung, A deep and scalable unsupervised machine learning system for cyber-attack detection in large-scale smart grids. IEEE Access **7**, 80778–80788 (2019)
25. K. Fukushima, Neocognitron: A self-organizing neural network model for a mechanism of pattern recognition unaffected by shift in position. Biol. Cybern. **36**, 193–202 (1980)
26. Y. Le Cun, B. Boser, J.S. Denker, D. Henderson, R.E. Howard, W. Hubbard, L.D. Jackel, Backpropagation Applied to Handwritten Zip Code Recognition, Neural Computation, vol. 1 **551**, 541 (1989)

27. H. Karimipour, V. Dinavahi, Robust massively parallel dynamic state estimation of power systems against cyber-attack. IEEE Access **6**, 2984–2995 (2017)
28. H. Karimipour, V. Dinavahi, Extended Kalman filter-based parallel dynamic state estimation. IEEE Trans. Smart Grid **6**, 1539–1549 (2015)
29. A. Krizhevsky, I. Sutskever, G.E. Hinton, ImageNet classification with deep convolutional neural networks, in *Advances in Neural Information Processing Systems*, (2012)
30. K. He, X. Zhang, S. Ren, J. Sun, Deep residual learning for image recognition, in *Proceedings of the IEEE Computer Society Conference on Computer Vision and Pattern Recognition* (2016)
31. C. Szegedy, W. Liu, Y. Jia, P. Sermanet, S. Reed, D. Anguelov, D. Erhan, V. Vanhoucke, A. Rabinovich, Going deeper with convolutions, *in Proceedings of the IEEE Computer Society Conference on Computer Vision and Pattern Recognition* (2015)
32. X. Han, Y. Zhong, L. Cao, L. Zhang, Pre-trained alexnet architecture with pyramid pooling and supervision for high spatial resolution remote sensing image scene classification. Remote Sens. **9**, 848 (2017)
33. G. Zeng, Y. He, Z. Yu, X. Yang, R. Yang and L. Zhang, "Going Deeper with Convolutions," arXiv **1409**, 4842 (2014)
34. B.Q. Huynh, H. Li, M.L. Giger, Digital mammographic tumor classification using transfer learning from deep convolutional neural networks. J. Med. Imag. **3**, 034501 (2016)
35. J. Blumberg, G. Kreiman, How cortical neurons help us see: visual recognition in the human brain. J. Clin. Invest. **120**, 3054–3063 (2010)
36. S. Mohammadi, H. Mirvaziri, M. Ghazizadeh-Ahsaee, H. Karimipour, Cyber intrusion detection by combined feature selection algorithm. J. Inform. Secur. Appl. **44**, 80–88 (2019)
37. S. Mohammadi, V. Desai, H. Karimipour, Multivariate mutual information-based feature selection for cyber intrusion detection, in *2018 IEEE Electrical Power and Energy Conference, EPEC 2018* (2018)
38. T.D. Kulkarni, W.F. Whitney, P. Kohli, J.B. Tenenbaum, Deep convolutional inverse graphics network, in *Advances in Neural Information Processing Systems*, (2015)
39. D.-X. Zhou, Universality of deep convolutional neural networks, in *Applied and Computational Harmonic Analysis*, (2019)
40. S. Li, W. Song, H. Qin, A. Hao, Deep variance network: an iterative, improved CNN framework for unbalanced training datasets. Pattern Recogn. **81**, 294–308 (2018)
41. S. Li, W. Song, H. Qin, A. Hao, Deep variance network: An iterative, improved CNN framework for unbalanced training datasets. Pattern Recogn. **81**, 294–308 (2018)
42. S. Saha, E. Lange and S. Hehl-Lange, "A Comprehensive Guide to Convolutional Neural Networks- the ELI5 way", 2005, available online at: https://towardsdatascience.com/a-comprehensive-guide-to-convolutional-neural-networks-the-eli5-way-3bd2b1164a53
43. T. Hope, Y.S. Resheff, I. Lieder, *Learning TensorFlow: A Guide to Building Deep Learning Systems* (O'Reilly Media Inc., 2016)
44. N. Shukla, Machine Learning with Tensorflow, 2018
45. E.M. Dovom, A. Azmoodeh, A. Dehghantanha, D.E. Newton, R.M. Parizi, H. Karimipour, Fuzzy pattern tree for edge malware detection and categorization in IoT. J. Syst. Archit. **97**, 1–7 (2019)
46. A. Azmoodeh, A. Dehghantanha, K.-K.R. Choo, Robust malware detection for internet of (battlefield) things devices using deep eigenspace learning. IEEE Trans. Sustain. Comput. **4**, 88–95 (2018)
47. F. Nelli, F. Nelli, Deep learning with TensorFlow, in *Python Data Analytics*, (2018)
48. L. Carin, M.J. Pencina, On Deep Learning for Medical Image Analysis (2018)
49. J. Archenaa, E.A.M. Anita, A survey of big data analytics in healthcare and government. Proc. Comput. Sci. **50**, 408–413 (2015)
50. K. Suzuki et al., Radiol. Phys. Technol. **10**, 257–273 (2017)
51. A. Azmoodeh, A. Dehghantanha, M. Conti, K.K.R. Choo, Detecting crypto-ransomware in IoT networks based on energy consumption footprint. J. Ambient. Intell. Humaniz. Comput. **9**, 1141–1152 (2018)

52. G. Litjens, T. Kooi, B.E. Bejnordi, A.A.A. Setio, F. Ciompi, M. Ghafoorian, J.A.W.M. Laak, B. Ginneken, C.I. Sánchez, A survey on deep learning in medical image analysis. Med. Image Anal. **42**, 60–88 (2017)
53. G. Litjens, T. Kooi, B.E. Bejnordi, A.A.A. Setio, F. Ciompi, M. Ghafoorian, J.A.W.M. Laak, B. Ginneken, C.I. Sánchez, A survey on deep learning in medical image analysis. Med. Image Anal. **42**, 60–88 (2017)
54. G.E. Hinton, "A practical guide to training restricted Boltzmann machines machine learning group", Univ. of Toronto, Toronto, ON, Canada, tech. Rep., 2010–2003 (2010)
55. J. Arevalo, F.A. González, R. Ramos-Pollán, J.L. Oliveira, M.A. Guevara Lopez, Representation learning for mammography mass lesion classification with convolutional neural networks. Comput. Methods Prog. Biomed. **127**, 248–257 (2016)
56. P. Moeskops, M.A. Viergever, A.M. Mendrik, L.S. De Vries, M.J.N.L. Benders, I. Isgum, Automatic segmentation of MR brain images with a convolutional neural network. IEEE Trans. Med. Imaging **35**(5), 1252–1261 (2016)
57. J. Kawahara, G. Hamarneh, Multi-resolution-tract CNN with hybrid pretrained and skin-lesion trained layers, in *Lecture Notes in Computer Science (Including Subseries Lecture Notes in Artificial Intelligence and Lecture Notes in Bioinformatics)* (2016)
58. N. Tajbakhsh, K. Suzuki, Comparing two classes of end-to-end machine-learning models in lung nodule detection and classification: MTANNs vs. CNNs. Pattern Recogn. **63**, 476–486 (2017)
59. P. Rajpurkar, J. Irvin, K. Zhu, B. Yang, H. Mehta, T. Duan, D. Ding, A. Bagul, C. Langlotz, K. Shpanskaya, M.P. Lungren, CheXNet: radiologist-level pneumonia detection on chest X-rays with deep learning. arXiv.org (2017)
60. G. Huang, Z. Liu, L. van der Maaten, K. Q. Weinberger, Densely connected convolutional networks, in *Proceedings - 30th IEEE Conference on Computer Vision and Pattern Recognition, CVPR 2017* (2017)
61. P. Rajpurkar, J. Irvin, A. Bagul, D. Ding, T. Duan, H. Mehta, B. Yang, K. Zhu, D. Laird, R.L. Ball, C. Langlotz, MURA: large dataset for abnormality detection in musculoskeletal radiographs. arXiv (2018)
62. Y. Bar, I. Diamant, L. Wolf, S. Lieberman, E. Konen, H. Greenspan, Chest pathology detection using deep learning with non-medical training, in *Proceedings - International Symposium on Biomedical Imaging* (2015)
63. P. Beyer, S. Mihowicz, M. Boistelle, 2018-diagnose like a radiologist: attention guided convolutional neural network for thorax disease classification. Sem. des Hopitaux (1975)
64. D.P. MacKinnon, *Introduction to Statistical Mediation Analysis* (Taylor and Francis Group, London, 2014)

Chapter 14
Privacy and Security in Smart and Precision Farming: A Bibliometric Analysis

Sanaz Nakhodchi, Ali Dehghantanha ⓘ, and Hadis Karimipour

1 Introduction

Big data analytics are one of the prominent parts of data science and are becoming more significant year after year, because most companies both small and large, are collecting huge amounts of useful information [1, 2]. The information may contain data such as "national intelligence, cyber security, fraud detection, marketing, medical information" [3], agriculture information and financial information. Popular companies such as Microsoft and Google are using data analysis in the means of gaining perspective for their decision making, as well as further understanding the links between existing and next generation technologies [3–7]. Moreover, agriculture is another noteworthy domain that these new technologies have impacted that should not be overlooked. For instance, traditional agricultural systems used animal force instead of mechanic force as well as the simpler methods used for planting and collection of crops.

Merging the advanced technologies and agriculture, led to the appearance of smart farming resulting in an increase in the quality and quantity of products as well as helping to reduce the "heavy labor and tedious tasks" [8]. Internet of Things (IoT) and Artificial Intelligence (AI) technologies are two prominent tools with a crucial role in smart farming such as driverless tractors, automatic watering and irrigation, real-time monitoring and analysis, and the connected farms which is sensors and IoT [2, 9–13]. In addition, in the terms of big IoT data, security and privacy are becoming important especially in processing and storing data from sensors.

S. Nakhodchi (✉) · A. Dehghantanha
School of Computer Science, University of Guelph, Guelph, ON, Canada
e-mail: nakhodcs@uoguelph.ca; ali@cybersciencelab.org

H. Karimipour
School of Engineering, University of Guelph, Guelph, ON, Canada
e-mail: hkarimi@uoguelph.ca; Canada-hkarimi@uoguelph.ca

© Springer Nature Switzerland AG 2020
K.-K. R. Choo, A. Dehghantanha (eds.), *Handbook of Big Data Privacy*,
https://doi.org/10.1007/978-3-030-38557-6_14

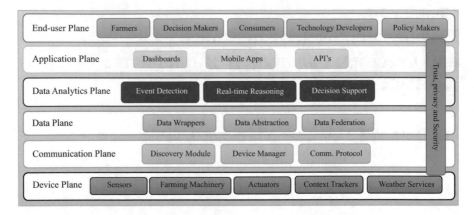

Fig. 14.1 Architecture of agri-IoT [14]

Figure 14.1 shows the architecture of agriculture IoT with different layers. As can be seen, all layers require to provide privacy and security approaches. Changes in agricultural systems and the processes of food production, create an opening for cyber-attack vectors and security implications. Meaning that structures and architecture of modern networks of food production can be vulnerable as a result of the high number of operations and systems. In addition, the system vulnerabilities may lead to "hybrid warfare tactics of both state and non-state actors". For instance, if there is a vulnerability in a major system, the risk will threat all dependent systems which can be financial, manufacturing and other sectors [15].

In 2016, FBI warned the farmers from the United States about industry devices hacks and data breaches. FBI reported that cyber-attackers can target any entities in the farms for stealing information such as soil content, past crop yields and planting. Moreover, attackers might encrypt data which is collected and ask for ransom along with damaging food process and production [16]. Although the large-scale companies can be more absorbable for attacks, the small and medium sized cannot be overlooked, due to the fact that over 60% of all compromised companies were small to medium in 2014. For instance, agribusiness enterprises and agricultural suppliers are directly targeted by attackers although small businesses compromised with 75% of spear-phishing attacks in 2015 [17].

Upon new technology, hackers can hide their intrusion in the systems. Although there are some existing approaches to boost smart farming systems, the significant spikes of the aforementioned agriculture statistic still need new approaches to have a better and secure system in agricultural sectors. In this regard, there are activities that researchers have been working on. For example, due to a variety of vulnerabilities in critical systems, researchers have been discussing and suggesting recommendation to tackle such vulnerability [18]. Moreover, [19] an algorithm have been presented for cyber-attack on wind farms. The method can detect attacks based on updating each node dynamically. Therefore, a reliable and secure framework for farming is introduced in [20] which can encrypt collected data and store them in a secure environment. The aforementioned examples indicate that researchers did significant effort in this domain, although there is no bibliometric article in this area.

"Bibliometrics encompasses the measurement of 'properties of documents, and of document related processes" [21]. It can help researchers to better understand the research patterns and activities. It is a comprehensive report which evaluate distribution of research. Energy analysis for hybrid electric vehicles [22] and technology mining [23] are the example used for bibliometrics. In addition, one of the benefits of using bibliometrics analysis is relying on authors who help them to represent the significance of their activities and papers. The second advantage is that institutions can assess the performance of publication and evaluate impact factor. Prediction of future research and effectivity in other areas along with increasing knowledge are the other advantages of studying bibliography.

In order to demonstrate the importance and increased number of cyberattack in agriculture sectors, this paper aims to provide an investigation of the domain by doing comprehensive assessment of cybersecurity in agriculture in the Web of Science from 2008 to 2018. The method includes the publication patterns, assessment on cybersecurity in agriculture and research topics. This study is based on two questions: (a) what is the trend of publications in cybersecurity approach of agriculture, and (b) how does this trend help to identify the future direction of this study?

Using "cybersecurity" and "agriculture" as the main keyword, 147 articles were found which were filtered and classified narrowing it down to 141 as the main result. All of these were collected from the Web of Science Core Collection. The exclusion parts were Arts and Humanities Citation Index (A&HCI) and Conference Proceedings Citation Index-Social Science and Humanities (CPCI-SSH) due to being unrelated. The English language was also another filter. The analysis was based on generating relationship between the abstract, title, publication, citation, research area, geographical location and the keywords used.

The following sections are organized as Sect. 2 which discusses the methodology used to retrieve information, Section 3 discusses the findings of the information and results and Sect. 4, includes the conclusion of the study.

2   Methodology

"Bibliometrics offers a powerful set of methods and measures for studying the structure and process of scholarly communication" [21]. It shows the information of publications and demonstrate that how publications can have an impact on institutes. According to [24] bibliometric is one of the oldest research techniques in library and information. The bibliometric method is divided into two sections based on [24]: general instruction, which is about using a search engine with researcher to avoid likely error in the search process, and publication analysis, which describes the evaluation methods of publications. This approach used different articles. For instance, [25] focused on researching about human resource training with 900 publications from 1975 to 2016. Furthermore, [26] considered 149,652 articles of obstetrics science between 2002 and 2013.

In this paper, general instruction with the manual and automatic methods are used for retrieving information. The main keywords are cybersecurity and agriculture which in the first search brought forth 147 articles which included articles, processing papers, reviews, books and so on. Although, after removing unrelated papers, 141 results remained between 2008 and 2018. The query used in this study is: ((cybersecurity OR cyber-security OR cyber-attack OR data theft OR malware detection OR privacy) AND ((agriculture OR farming OR agri-food OR smart farming OR dairy OR poultry OR livestock OR chattels) NOT (nuclear power plant))).

All the publication indexed in the Web of Science Core Collection. The exclusion included ignoring non-English articles, and Arts and Humanities Citation Index (A&HCI) and Conference Proceedings Citation Index-Social Science and Humanities (CPCI-SSH). The analysis was considered based on (a) productivity (b) research areas (c) institutions (d) authors (e) impact journals (f) highly cited article and (g) keyword frequency. In addition, for visualizing the results, VOSviewer tool was used.

2.1 Web of Science

There are a variety of databases which are indexing articles such as IEEE explore, Google Scholar, Science Direct, Web of Science, Elsevier and Springer. Web of Science (WoS) was a major database for bibliometric until 2004 before launching Scopus [27]. Moreover, Google Scholar is another popular database for searching [28]. In this study, WoS is selected for searching due to three reasons. First, WoS is a unique tool for bibliometric analysis before Google Scholar and Scopus [27]. Second, more than 90% of the highest impact factor journals indexes in WoS. Last but not least, because of avoiding overlap, WoS is the only search engine for this research [29].

3 Finding

This section considers the finding of the topic related to cybersecurity, privacy and agriculture which is divided into seven sections: productivity, research areas, institutions, authors, impact journals, highly-cited articles and keywords frequency. This finding is significant due to showing publication rate and bibliometric data. Figure 14.2 shows the number of publications from 2008 to 2018.

Figure 14.2 shows the different types of publication released during the period which are article, proceeding paper, review and editorial material. As can be seen,

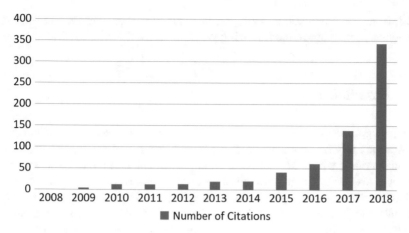

Fig. 14.2 Citation distribution

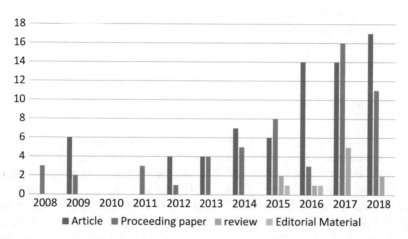

Fig. 14.3 Number of publications

in overall, the article has the highest ranking of publication and proceeding paper is in the follow as the second. 2015 and 2017 are the 2 years that the number of proceeding papers were just more than two publications rather than articles. Although there is a fluctuation in the number of review papers between 2015 and 2018, the number of materials is still the same in the 2015 and 2016 and do not appear during the other years. In general, the trend of articles increased from 2008 to 2018.

The frequency of journal is evaluated based on the citations indexed used during citation analysis. It also used for assessing researcher's performance in academic. Figure 14.3 shows the citation distribution over the last 10 years. It presents that the number of publications have an impact on the number of citations. The number of citations is 946 along with average citation per year which is 86 between 2008 and

2018. Based on publications during recent years, it is predicted that the number of citations will increase in the following years.

3.1 Productivity

This part considers productivity among continents. The frequency of number of publications rely on productivity. It can be used as a tool to evaluate the number of publications which are released among different continents. The significant impact of discussing about productivity is that the researcher can improve efficiency and productivity of the publications. Moreover, it is useful for contributing in new technology and identifying the best one. Table 14.1 shows the number of publications in different countries and continents between 2008 and 2018. It can be seen that continent of Europe had the most contributions (66) while North America with <10 difference is second one. In contrast, Australia and Africa continents have the lowest articles, 6 and 15 respectively. United Stated had significant effort in publication, 50 between 2008 and 2018.

3.2 Research Areas

This part considers the number of publications in a variety of research areas. Research area usually include one and two disciplinaries for developing specific areas and how it can impact on different research areas. WoS covers more than 150 different scientific research areas. Table 14.2 provides the information about top five research areas between 2008 and 2018 in this search. As can be seen, Engineering has 37.58% of publications which is the highest, followed by Computer Science with 28.36%. Moreover, after 21 publications in Telecommunications areas, agriculture and environmental sciences ecology are the least ones with 16 and 14 publications, respectively.

3.3 Institute

This part considers the number of publications based on institutes. The goal of this part is to recognize the active institutes and evaluate the quality of them based on publications. Table 14.3 shows top six institutions which have the publications in the cybersecurity and agriculture approaches. It can be seen that United States has 17 publications which is the highest number of papers. University of Oxford from England, University of Tennessee Knoxville and University of Tennessee System from United States are the prominent university with the majority publications.

Table 14.1 Productivity

List of continents	Number of articles	Number of articles (%)
Asia	51	36.06
India	14	9.92
Malaysia	1	0.70
Iran	2	1.41
China	15	10.63
Singapore	1	0.70
South Korea	6	4.25
Taiwan	3	2.12
Saudi Arabia	3	2.12
Pakistan	1	0.70
Jordan	1	0.70
Turkey	2	1.41
Kazakhstan	1	0.70
United Arab Emirates	1	0.70
North America	57	40.42
United States	50	35.46
Canada	7	4.96
South America	1	0.70
Bolivia	1	0.70
Europe	66	46.65
Spain	2	1.41
England	16	11.34
Greece	7	4.96
Hungary	1	0.70
Italy	3	2.12
Netherlands	5	3.54
Portugal	2	1.41
Belgium	4	2.83
Finland	2	1.41
Germany	5	3.54
France	4	2.83
Bulgaria	1	0.70
Denmark	4	2.83
Latvia	1	0.70
Romania	2	1.41
Scotland	2	1.41
Switzerland	2	1.41
Austria	1	0.70
Ireland	1	0.70
Sweden	1	0.70
Australia	6	4.24
Australia	5	3.54

(continued)

Table 14.1 (continued)

List of continents	Number of articles	Number of articles (%)
New Zealand	1	0.70
Africa	15	10.57
South Africa	6	4.25
Botswana	1	0.70
Ethiopia	1	0.70
Kenya	1	0.70
Morocco	2	1.41
Nigeria	2	1.41
Tanzania	1	0.70
Zimbabwe	1	0.70

Table 14.2 Research areas

Research areas	Number of publications	Number of publications (%)
Engineering	53	37.58
Computer science	40	28.36
Telecommunications	21	14.89
Agriculture	16	11.34
Environmental sciences ecology	14	9.92

Table 14.3 Institutions

Institutions	Publications	Country
University of Oxford	4	England
University of Tennessee Knoxville	4	United States
University of Tennessee System	4	United States
State University Of New York SUNY System	3	United States
United States Department of Agriculture USDA	3	United States
University of Wisconsin System	3	United States

3.4 Authors

This part considers the number of publications based on the authors under country. The goal of this part is to identify who is more active in this area. Table 14.4 shows top ten authors that who were more productive according to country as well. It can be seen that United States has the most authors with six publications. There also are four publications with British authors after china with five publications. Nigeria, Finland and Morocco are the countries that each author has one publication. Thus, North America has more contribution in terms of privacy, security and agri-food.

Table 14.4 Authors

Authors	Publications	Publications (%)	Country
Lan Li	3	2.12	China
P. K. Freeman	2	1.41	United States
R. S. Freeland	2	1.41	United States
Jay Graham	2	1.41	United States
Li Ming	2	1.41	China
Michael J. Tildesley	2	1.41	England
Hans Bauer	2	1.41	England
B. Adegbuyi	1	0.70	Nigeria
Elisa Aaltola	1	0.70	Finland
Youssef Abarghaz	1	0.70	Morocco

Table 14.5 Greatest journals based on the number of publications

Journals title	IF	Q	P	P (%)
Computers and Electronics in Agriculture	3.17	Q1	2	1.41
IEEE Communications Magazine	10.35	Q1	2	1.41
IEEE Internet Of Things Journal	9.51	Q1	2	1.41
IEEE Transactions on Smart Grid	7.364	Q1	2	1.41
PLOS One	2.77	Q1	2	1.41

3.5   Impact Journals

This part considers top four impact journals. The goal of this part is helping the researchers to publish their works in the good quality journals. Table 14.5 shows that although the number of publications in the list are the same, IEEE Communications Magazine has the better impact factor.

3.6   Highly-Cited Articles

This part considers the number of citations which received by journals from 2008 and 2018. The goal of this part can have impact on the quality of research. Table 14.6 shows top three cited articles. It provides information such as the number of times cited, title of published journal, year of publication and research area. As can be seen, "Big Data in Smart Farming—A review" had most citations. The article considers big data applications with smart farming approach [30].

Table 14.6 Top three cited articles

Titles	Times cited	Published journal	Year	Research area
Big Data in Smart Farming—A review [30]	123	Agricultural System	2017	Agriculture
Low-Altitude Unmanned Aerial Vehicles-Based Internet of Things Services: Comprehensive Survey and Future Perspective [31]	97	IEEE Internet of Thing Journal	2016	Computer science; engineering; telecommunications
A Database For Integrated Assessment of European Agricultural Systems [32]	51	Environmental Science and Policy	2009	Environmental sciences and ecology

Table 14.7 Frequency of titles and keywords

Title	Frequency	Keywords	Frequency
Framework	9	Wind farm	20
Farm	8	Identification	17
Application	7	theft	17
Analysis	6	Cyber attack	11
Wireless sensor network	6	Control system	11
Big data	5	Computer	8
Cyber security	4	Farm location	7
RFID	4	Livestock loss	7

3.7 Keywords Frequency

This part considers the variety of keywords which are used by researchers frequently. This section can help researchers to recognize current and past topic of research. Table 14.7 shows the list of keywords and titles frequencies. This list is created of 4298 keywords and 498 titles which were merged from 141 articles between 2008 and 2018. It is shown that most of titles are related to wireless systems, security and farm. It means that the majority of researches has used these keywords. Figure 14.4 provides more information for deep analysis. It shows that the word map has five clusters which has drawn from content analysis of publications. Moreover, Table 14.8 is another view of Fig. 14.4.

Figure 14.4 presents that the majority of research related to "IoT" technology and farming. These are the two main clusters (red and green). The highlighted of IoT key terms are "smart grid", "smart city", "smart farming" and "critical infrastructure" while "farmer", "bird", "livestock", "disease" are related terms for agriculture. Moreover, "rfid", "server" and. "science", "database" are the terms that create links between research topics.

Table 14.8 Keywords clustering

Red	Green	Purple	Yellow	Blue
IoT	Farmer	Protocol	Database	Threat
Thing	Factor	Server	Access	Disruption
Drone	Disease	Rfid	Life	Critical infrastructure
Architecture	Livestock	Cattle rustling	Business	Cyber security
Cloud	Household		Property right	Large number
Smart grid	Respondent		Science	
Information infrastructure	Bird		Water	
Smart grid	Link		Traceability	
Precision farming			Public access	
			Communal farmer	
			Nanotechnology	

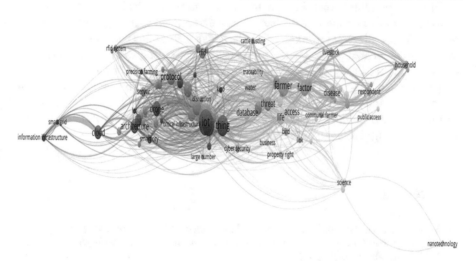

Fig. 14.4 Keywords clusters

4   Conclusion

Huge amounts of data have been produced which brings the concept of big
data which can be structural or nonstructural data. Thus, data management in
the environment which is expanding continuously, creates concerns about data
processing, analysis, privacy and security [33]. Critical infrastructures such as
power grid systems, precision agriculture and healthcare systems are some of the
prominent circumstances that face big data and challenges [34]. In addition, as with
any Internet-based technology, there tangible number of IoT with differences in
the scale of the networks [2]. IoT applications and technologies are vulnerable to
cyber threats from adversary attackers. Smart farming and their systems are not

exceptions. There was a lot of research in order to provide applications or solutions for having secure systems in farming.

In this paper, the trends of agriculture and cybersecurity, privacy research is considered from 2008 to 2018 by bibliometric method. In this study, there were seven (7) criteria including keywords frequency, impact journals, highly cited articles, productivity, research areas, authors and institutions. In the past 10 years, it was shown that the number of publications which are related to agriculture and security had grown. Moreover, the analysis demonstrated that the trends of the publications faced a significant increase in the last 2 years along with increasing the number of citations. Hence, it was mentioned that for having better quality of research and increasing citations, it is required to have a publication in highly ranked journals.

In this paper, the publication analysis is done between 2008 and 2018.

First, it presented that Europe based on continents had most publications followed by North America. Second, it was determined that Engineering domain had 37.58% of all research areas. Third, the active institutions were identified which were mostly located in the United States. Forth, according to active authors, data shown that Lan Li with three publications had the first rank. At last but not least, the map analysis of keywords demonstrated the trends of research activities which can be used for future study. In the period, the keywords such as "iot", "thing", "smart farming", "factor", "database", "protocol", "farmer" used as important terms related to security in agriculture approach.

References

1. S. Grooby, T. Dargahi, A. Dehghantanha, A bibliometric analysis of authentication and access control in IoT devices, in *Handbook of Big Data and IoT security* (Springer International Publishing, Cham, 2019), pp. 25–51
2. A. Azmoodeh, A. Dehghantanha, K.-K.R. Choo, Big data and internet of things security and forensics: challenges and opportunities, in *Handbook of Big Data and IoT Security* (Springer International Publishing, Cham, 2019), pp. 1–4
3. M.M. Najafabadi, F. Villanustre, T.M. Khoshgoftaar, N. Seliya, R. Wald, E. Muharemagic, Deep learning applications and challenges in big data analytics. J. Big Data **2**, 1 (2015)
4. S. Mohammadi, H. Mirvaziri, M. Ghazizadeh-Ahsaee, H. Karimipour, Cyber intrusion detection by combined feature selection algorithm. J. Inf. Secur. Appl. **44**, 80–88 (2019)
5. E.M. Dovom, A. Azmoodeh, A. Dehghantanha, D.E. Newton, R.M. Parizi, H. Karimipour, Fuzzy pattern tree for edge malware detection and categorization in IoT. J. Syst. Archit. **97**, 1–7 (2019)
6. H.H. Pajouh, R. Javidan, R. Khayami, A. Dehghantanha, K.K.R. Choo, A two-layer dimension reduction and two-tier classification model for anomaly-based intrusion detection in IoT backbone networks. IEEE Trans. Emerg. Top. Comput. **7**(2), 314–323 (2019)
7. A. Azmoodeh, A. Dehghantanha, K.-K.R. Choo, Robust malware detection for internet of (Battlefield) things devices using deep eigenspace learning. IEEE Trans. Sustain. Comput. **4**(1), 88–95 (Feb. 2018)
8. M. Brown, Smart farming—automated and connected agriculture (2018)

9. J. Sakhnini, H. Karimipour, A. Dehghantanha, Smart grid cyber attacks detection using supervised learning and heuristic feature selection, in *2019 IEEE 7th International Conference on Smart Energy Grid Engineering (SEGE)* (IEEE, 2019), pp. 108–112
10. A. Azmoodeh, A. Dehghantanha, M. Conti, K.K.R. Choo, Detecting crypto-ransomware in IoT networks based on energy consumption footprint. J. Ambient. Intell. Humaniz. Comput. **9**(4), 1141–1152 (2018)
11. M.R. Begli, F. Derakhshan, H. Karimipour, A layered intrusion detection system for critical infrastructure using machine learning, in *2019 IEEE 7th International Conference on Smart Energy Grid Engineering (SEGE)* (IEEE, 2019), pp. 120–124
12. S. Geris, H. Karimipour, A feature selection-based approach for joint cyber-attack detection and state estimation, in *IEEE Int. Conf. on Smart Energy Grid Engineering (SEGE)* (IEEE, 2019)
13. H. Karimipour, S. Geris, A. Dehghantanha, H. Leung, Intelligent anomaly detection for large-scale smart grids, in *2019 IEEE Canadian Conference of Electrical and Computer Engineering (CCECE)* (IEEE, 2019), pp. 1–4
14. A. Kamilaris, F. Gao, F.X. Prenafeta-Boldu, M.I. Ali, Agri-IoT: a semantic framework for Internet of Things-enabled smart farming applications, in *2016 IEEE 3rd World Forum on Internet of Things, WF-IoT 2016* (IEEE, 2017), pp. 442–447
15. M.M. Jahn et al., Cyber risk and security implications in smart agriculture and food systems (2019)
16. Z. Zorz, FBI warns farming industry about equipment hacks, data breaches (2016)
17. G. Information, APT28 under the scope – a journey into exfiltrating intelligence (2015)
18. B. Reaves, T. Morris, Analysis and mitigation of vulnerabilities in short-range wireless communications for industrial control systems. Int. J. Crit. Infrastruct. Prot. **5**, 154–174 (2012)
19. N. Trantham, A. Garcia, Reputation dynamics in networks: Application to cyber security of wind farms. Syst. Eng. **18**, 339–348 (2015)
20. H. Chi, S. Welch, E. Vasserman, E. Kalaimannan, A framework of cybersecurity approaches in precision agriculture (2017)
21. C.L. Borgman, Communication and Collaboration Scholarly Communication and Bibliometrics. Annu. Rev. Inf. Sci. Technol. **36**(1), 2–72 (2002)
22. P. Zhang, P. Yan, C. Du, A comprehensive analysis of energy management strategies for hybrid electric vehicles based on bibliometrics. Renew. Sust. Energ. Rev. **48**, 88–104 (2015)
23. F. Madani, 'Technology Mining' bibliometrics analysis: applying network analysis and cluster analysis. Scientometrics **105**, 323–335 (2015)
24. J. Koskinen et al., How to use bibliometric methods in evaluation of scientific research? An example from Finnish schizophrenia research. Nord. J. Psychiatry **62**(2), 136–143 (2008)
25. I. Danvila-del-Valle, C. Estévez-Mendoza, F.J. Lara, Human resources training: a bibliometric analysis. J. Bus. Res **101**, 627–636 (2019)
26. A.M. Palacios-Marqués et al., Worldwide scientific production in obstetrics: a bibliometric analysis. Ir. J. Med. Sci. **188**, 913–919 (2019)
27. É. Archambault, D. Campbell, Y. Gingras, V. Larivière, Comparing bibliometric statistics obtained from the web of science and Scopus. J. Am. Soc. Inf. Sci. Technol. **60**, 1320–1326 (2009)
28. J. Mingers, L. Leydesdorff, A review of theory and practice in scientometrics. Eur. J. Oper. Res. **246**(1), 1–19 (2015)
29. C. López-Illescas, F. de Moya-Anegón, H.F. Moed, Coverage and citation impact of oncological journals in the Web of Science and Scopus. J. Informetr. **2**, 304–316 (2008)
30. S. Wolfert, L. Ge, C. Verdouw, M.J. Bogaardt, Big data in smart farming – a review. Agric. Syst. **153**, 69–80 (2017)
31. N. Hossein Motlagh, T. Taleb, O. Arouk, Low-altitude unmanned aerial vehicles-based internet of things services: comprehensive survey and future perspectives. IEEE Internet Things J. **3**(6), 899–922 (2016)
32. S. Janssen, E. Andersen, I.N. Athanasiadis, M.K. van Ittersum, A database for integrated assessment of European agricultural systems. Environ. Sci. Pol. **12**(5), 573–587 (2009)

33. E. Ahmed et al., The role of big data analytics in Internet of Things. Comput. Netw. **129**, 459–471 (2017)
34. H. Karimipour, A. Dehghantanha, R.M. Parizi, K.K.R. Choo, H. Leung, A deep and scalable unsupervised machine learning system for cyber-attack detection in large-scale smart grids. IEEE Access **7**, 80778–80788 (2019)

Chapter 15
A Survey on Application of Big Data in Fin Tech Banking Security and Privacy

Mahdi Amrollahi, Ali Dehghantanha ⓘ, and Reza M. Parizi

1 Introduction

In 1988, an undergraduate student at Cornell University developed the first computer worm, causing computers to be infected and temporarily shut down. Although this was done merely as a breakthrough, it was the beginning of a new era in cyberspace. Since 2000, more than a million attacks have been reported against government agencies, private and financial centers [1, 2]. The number of reports is the only ones officially reported, while many might have never been registered. Every year, many organizations around the world are targeted by virus attacks to cybercrimes and commercial fraud. Cybercrimes differ from ordinary crimes. The most typical kinds of cybercrimes, regarding what has been published by CALUPTIX [3] are web attacks, malwares and application specific attacks (Fig. 15.1a).

Every day at least one news headlines in the world of malware, viruses, cyber warfare and espionage information is published. Between them, malware is the most common cyber attacks in 2016 as shown in Fig. 15.1a [3]. Malware is a malicious code which is developed to disorder or deny functions, collect confidential information, enter secret systems and more exploiting behaviors [4]. This sort of cyber threat is the spotlight in this paper because the most widespread financial threat since 2015 is FinTech (Financial technology) banking malware (Fig. 15.1b).

M. Amrollahi
School of Engineering, University of Guelph, Guelph, ON, Canada
e-mail: mamrollahi@uoguelph.ca

A. Dehghantanha
Cyber Science Lab, School of Computer Science, University of Guelph, Guelph, ON, Canada
e-mail: ali@cybersciencelab.org

R. M. Parizi (✉)
College of Computer and Software Engineering, Kennesaw State University, Marietta, GA, USA
e-mail: rparizi1@kennesaw.edu

© Springer Nature Switzerland AG 2020
K.-K. R. Choo, A. Dehghantanha (eds.), *Handbook of Big Data Privacy*,
https://doi.org/10.1007/978-3-030-38557-6_15

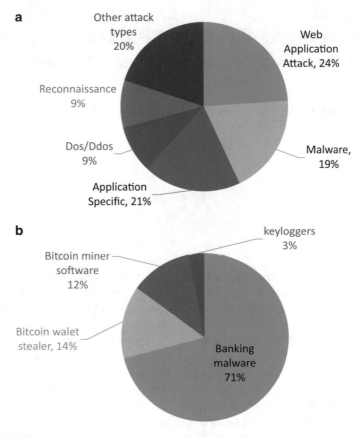

Fig. 15.1 (**a**) The most common cyber attacks in 2016. (**b**) The most widespread financial threat in 2015

There are various kinds of malwares but the most persistents are worms, viruses, trojans, rootkits, key-loggers and botnets [5, 6]. With the advent of the internet, the interactions and information exchanges have undergone tremendous changes. The internet environment is a dynamic and innovative environment, but this environment can make cyber threats more advanced than cyber defenses. The original design of the internet has been based on stable communication, not security. This issue has remained the same and no change has been made. Generally, most internet-based systems are vulnerable and available defensive methods have lost their functionality and current cyber security strategies are often inadequate and the gap between aggressive power and defensive power is on the rise. According to 2019 official annual cybercrime report by Herjavec Group [7], the cost of cyber attacks for the global economy is estimated at around $6 trillion annually by 2021 and this explains why cybercrime is a matter of day because the cost of direct and indirect injuries in the short and long term is as high as the cost of air and missile attacks. Malware detection with normal antivirus techniques is very difficult and a smart human

Fig. 15.2 Difference between big data and traditional approach to provide new security technologies for network monitoring

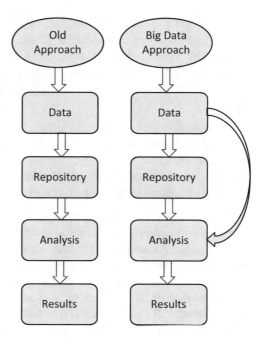

agent should also be used because in many cases the malware is the result of the combination of various malware and the complexity [8, 9].

Intelligent big data analytics is a promising technique which is already proved to be useful for malware detection [10]. In May 2012, Intel's IT Centre examined 200 IT managers in large companies to find out if/how they are performing big data analysis. The results show that big data analytic can be used in data security, private data maintenance technology, data transparency, performance benchmarking, data and system interoperability [11, 12].

In general, analysis of big data and machine learning approaches are providing new security techniques for network supervising, security information and event management (SIEM) and forensics which is highly important for financial industries to detect fraudulent activities, secure and analyze data. This research discusses about applying big data analytics methods in an effort to address the mentioned concerns. The difference between big data and traditional approach to provide new security technologies for network monitoring is shown in Fig. 15.2.

Big data includes lots of advantages:

1. It provides robust analytics and detailed insights into the problem.
2. It is good at analyzing big datasets. As malware corpus keeps increasing constantly, big data can adapt well in addressing this issue.
3. Big data can help explore data in real-time and take adequate decisions.
4. Big data improves machine learning models' prediction.

One of the dangers and threats of cyber security is spying and informational listening, in which an unauthorized person can listen to a copy of the data being streamed between the source and destination. In this regard, economic and banking issues have always been a priority. Therefore, in this study, malwares which target financial institute are studied. The basic questions are supposed to be answered are:

(1) How does malware affect on FinTech system?
(2) How malware steal banking information theft, such as the username and password?
(3) What are the malware detection techniques?
(4) How to implement the malware on FinTech system?

These issues are almost never explicitly disclosed in public. They are mainly criminals and hacker's concerns and in some cases for the governments to destroy, spy and steal information and money. Obviously, none of these groups are willing to expose their methods of malice and mistreatment.

The rest of this paper is structured as follows. In Sect. 2 research background and some related works are reviewed. Threats in Cyber Space (Challenges/Detection/Organization) is described in Sect. 3. Fin Tech Banking malware (Attitudes and approaches) and proposed cyber-attack detection with big data methods are presented in Sect. 4. Section 5 discusses the case studies and some results followed by the conclusion in Sect. 6.

2 Literature Review and Background

Accessing bank information can be achieved by criminals in a variety of hardware and software environments. According to statistics released by authoritative sources, information observation, especially confidential information in the field of finance and banking, has been paid attention more by cybercriminals in recent years. So far, several methods have been developed to counteract botnets, which of course, are less likely to be propagated. The first step in preventing these threats is to discover them. One of the techniques used in these structures is machine learning and data mining. Researchers from the security team, RSA, have discovered a new and dangerous Trojan called Pandemiya, which states that cybercriminals in the underworld are currently using it as a replacement for earlier versions of Zeus. The Trojan can easily steal banking information from users and companies. The Trojan has the ability to secretly steal information from forms and user credentials, which can then create fake web pages and display victim computer pictures. The source of the Trojan Bank Zeus has led to development over the last few years in undercover associations.

Malicious malware is more complex than Zeus, such as Ice IX, Citadel and Game Over. However, Pandemiya is far more complex and dangerous than the malware, which includes 25,000 lines of code written in C. According to McAfee's announcement, Gauss's major goal is to collect system specifications, network

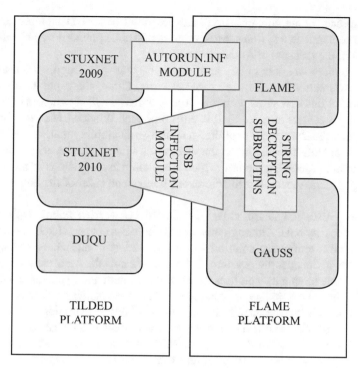

Fig. 15.3 The relationship of Duqu, Stuxnet, Flame and Gauss malware

card and BIOS specifications, e-mail licenses, social site licenses, and access permissions to electronic banking systems. The collection of each of these data is also responsible for various parts of the Gauss malware. According to McAfee's security alert, the malware such as Stuxnet and Flam viruses consists of separate partitions that work together in an integrated manner, and each liability department has a special function. Some parts of the Gauss malware that McAfee reviewers have analyzed include features like adding apps to browsers, infecting USB memory, and executing Java and ActiveX commands. Based on McAfee's announcement, Gauss malware is the ultimate goal of collecting system profiles, network card and BIOS specifications, e-mail licenses, social site licenses, and access permissions to electronic banking systems. Each of this information is also collected by Gauss malware (Fig. 15.3) [13, 14].

Experts from Kaspersky Lab also believe that the main purpose of Gauss malware is to control bank operations in Middle Eastern banks to collect information from financial transfers related to some regional political and military groups. According to Kaspersky, Gauss malware has the ability to identify and control bank accounts at Bank of Beirut, FBLF, Bloom Bank, Byblos Bank, Fransa Bank and Credit Lebanais. It has also been observed that operations by users in the Middle East at the Citibank and PayPal financial sites were also monitored by the malware. The level of infection with Gauss malware is not clear, but it is not thought to be widespread. Some contaminated statistics point to several hundred to several thousand contaminated systems. Most of these infected systems have been identified in Lebanon, the Palestinian Authority and Israel.

In 2011 there was lots of research about the malware, Duqu, which allegedly had a close relationship with the Stuxnet virus. Often, these points refer to the association of this new virus with the virus, Stuxnet, the likely authors of this virus and the major centers targeted by this virus. For each Windows user, it is important to know how the Duqu virus exploited a security vulnerability that was not detected so that it could infiltrate and infect the victim's computer. This security hole is in the TrueType font processing section, which is available in all versions of the Windows operating system. According to Microsoft, threats and risks of the Duqu virus are limited.

So more than the Duqu virus, we should be worried about exploiting the Windows security hole. Although this security hole has not been fixed yet, Microsoft has provided a temporary solution to prevent access to and abuse of vulnerable components in the operating system. So maybe it's not bad, users are advised to use and install this temporary solution. Most of the content and explanations that have been published about this security hole also refer to the malicious Word file. But the important point is that the security crash is in the Windows operating system, and not in Word. Word software is just one tool to exploit this cache. In the upgraded version, Microsoft's announcement states explicitly that using a malicious web page can also easily be exploited to crash. To get infected with the Duqu, it is just enough to visit a malicious site that includes TrueType fonts. No email, no Word, nor opening an attached file is necessary [15].

The Equation group uses malicious software for multiple operating systems, some of which are known as Regin. The Equation Group is undoubtedly one of the most experienced and skilled cyber team in the world, and acts in a complex and completely mysterious way. The tool developed by this group is unique in some cases and also works well in extraction and theft of information. The malware has the ability to program hard disk firmware and can make a hidden part of the hard disk accessible only by the API. Even after the malware has been installed, it's impossible to erase it, even formatting the hard disk normally. The malware attacks hard disks such as Seagate and can change the drivers of Toshiba, Samsung, Hitac hand Western Digital are known by two different platforms known as Equation Drug and Gray Fish. The vaguest and important point is whether the hard disk manufacturer is working with the NSA?

Seagate and Micron acknowledged that they unknowingly provided the source code for firmware to the NSA and this would require the NSA to change it in case of a violation. In fact, obtaining the source code for hard disk firmware for the NSA is very convenient for hiring a software developer or by stealing it from another method. The malware has the ability to program the firmware of the hard disk, and is able to build a hidden partition on a hard disk that is accessible only by the API.

Even after the malware has been installed, it's impossible to erase it, even formatting the hard disk does not have any effect at all. The malware hides hard disks such as Seagate Western Digital, Hitachi, Samsung, Toshiba and can change drivers and are known by two different platforms called Equationdrug and GrayFish. The vague and very important point is whether the hard disk manufacturer cooperates with the NSA. Seagate and Micron acknowledged that they unknowingly provided NSA with source code for firmware, and this would require the NSA to change it in case of an offense. In fact, obtaining the hard disk firmware source code for the NSA is very convenient with hiring a software developer or stealing it from another method. The Equation group infects its victims by relying on multiple techniques. These techniques include:

(1) Self replicating Code-Worm
(2) Physical media, CD-ROMs
(3) Uses the USB port − USB sticks + exploits
(4) Web based exploit Internet attacks

Kaspersky is one of the most prestigious companies active in network security and cyber space since 1997. According to data collected from November 2013 to October 2014, 12,100 mobile banking Trojans were detected, which is 9 times more than the Trojans discovered in 2013, and 45,032 users were minted at least once in the year (Fig. 15.4a) [16].

Internet fraudsters use different software to implement their goals. As seen in Fig. 15.4b, Java platform has the most prominence among internet fraudsters. Although many attempts have been made to formulate maladaptive math, there is not a common category that everyone agrees with. Instead of trying to precisely define the details of these words, the general characteristics of each of the varieties are as follows. Three features are about types of malware [17–19]:

(1) Malicious malware actively tries to reproduce by creating new or similar copies. Malware may also be reproduced passively, for example by a user who copies it incorrectly, but they do not say the same thing.
(2) The growth of the malware population is indicative of a change in the total number of malware-generated malformations as a result of reproduction. A malware that does not reproduce is always a population growth of zero, but malware that has zero population growth may also be as causal.
(3) Parasitic malware needs other executable codes to survive. The word "executable" here should be very general, which includes all types of valid code, such as the block boot code on the hard disk, the binary code of the software and the interpretative code. It also includes code-like scripting languages as well as codes that may need to be compiled before running.

3   Threats in Cyber Space (Challenges/Detection/Organization)

To be protected from all threats in cyber space, we should develop a comprehensive security program, and to achieve this goal, we should recognize the type of crimes

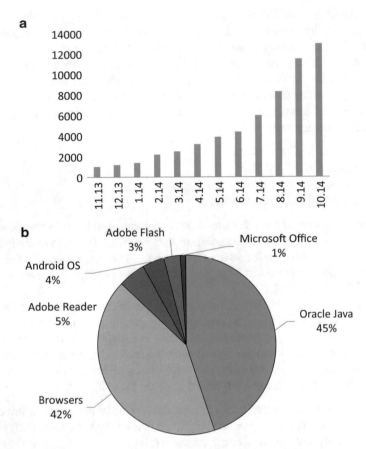

Fig. 15.4 (**a**) The amount of bank Trojans discovered on mobile 2013–2014 report are generated by Kaspersky lab. (**b**) The extent of the malware spread according to the target program

and cyber wars and strategies to overcome them. The detection of a spyware malware with normal antivirus techniques is very difficult, and in this case, a smart human agent should also be used, because in many cases the malware is the result of the combination of various malware and the complexity. In this regard, the spyware malware, anti-virus techniques and its performance in the field of banking information are being investigated. The financial industry overcomes difficulties in both to handle cyber-attacks and to provide secure customer protection against various cybercrimes such as malware attacks, phishing and fraudulent activities [20]. In these times, organizations are able to use security techniques in order to protect themselves from cyber-attacks. As an example, Minded Security has developed a cutting-edge technology called AMT (Agentless anti-Malware Technology) to detect and manage banking malware. Their program can detect all the different kinds of banking malware. The software can be developed for a particular bank to detect malwares precisely [21].

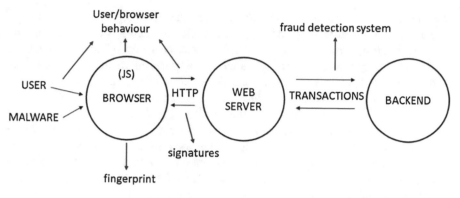

Fig. 15.5 Detection techniques [22]

3.1 Kałużny & Olejarka's Malware Detection Approach/Proposed Cyber-Attack Detection Method

Jakub Kałużny and Mateusz Olejarka [22] claim that the best method to prohibit malwares from obtaining financial information is to detect the web injections. In addition, special JavaScript codes in the bank's website can analyze the DOM (Document Object Model) tree and find patterns from web injection or fingerprints from gathering clients' data [22]. Figure 15.5 shows different detection techniques such as signatures, fingerprints and user behavior based on JavaScript.

To collect the information about malware infection, there is way of mixing three input data:

- browser fingerprint,
- HTTP response data,
- Browser behavior.

The JavaScript code includes the web injected signature check, which verifies the function name, JS object's name and type and the constant strings. Users are allowed to work only after the code verifies the website for any possible malware. The second useful way to detect malwares is to utilize browser fingerprints. The aim is to check the website for setting which is seemed to be suspicious. Moreover, the user behavior can also be used to detect malicious codes. It can be measured using measurements such as speed of the mouse movement and speed on tapping buttons. The result can represent the distinguish between humans and bots. Another way defined by Jakub Kałużny and Mateusz Olejarka [22] is designing a fraud detecting system which can use the output of the previous techniques and mix the results with the data gathered from other banking systems. A disadvantage of this detection method is that it uses the signature-based detection technique to identify malwares. In order to act properly, the signature of existing malware should be available in the system repository. In other words, this technique acts only with well-known malware and it fails to identify zero-day attacks [23]. However, lots of researches have been done in the telecommunication domain and a bit in the banking area. In addition, the majority of today's researchers aim at different kinds of tools or/and programs for detecting malicious software, but there is no information about their application in financial industries. Most of the researches they were done in this domain are not in official form of studies, but other than it, they have been published on websites or blogs (a.k.a. grey literature). Companies and organizations are under cyber-attacks persistently. Small delinquency can damage thousands of dollars where majors can cost millions for organizations [24]. Emails are very important for the businesses as a communication tool [25]. Even though the application of emails has made the communication faster and more efficient, some significant threats associated with emails have emerged [26].

3.2   SANS Institute Malware Detection

SANS Institute suggested number of solutions to stop cyber-attacks such as network supervising and analysis, files analysis, email analysis, URL analysis and data analysis. Regarding SANS Institute, malicious emails can be detected before reaching to end user by using email monitoring system. In cases that malicious emails have reached to the user undetected, the email security system should check all the links and attachments in a sandbox environment before the final user has been allowed to open it. The network monitoring is the key due to receive an instant detection and respond [27, 28]. Different tools can be used for network traffic monitoring such as IDS/IPS [27]. The functionality is the key differences between intrusion detection systems (IDS) and intrusion prevention systems (IPS). IDS creates alerts when an intrusion is found on the network. The main goal of these kinds of systems is to supervise the traffic, but it cannot ban network attacks [29]. On the other hand, IPS covers both functions of monitoring and preventing an attack. These systems can also block the traffic within a network. In most situations, IPS is used to stop the ongoing attacks. IDS and IPS are good for analyzing data came from internet and finding issues in the network traffic, but they are not developed to analyze the emails content when an email is involved in a network as one of the most important data. Both systems are good to be implemented in financial institutions as a defense layer, but they are not suitable to identify malwares which have been received by emails. In order to analyze and protect the content of an email, email scanning system is needed to run on the email server. The system needs to resolve the message body, attachments and URLs and considers the address from which the message has been sent [27]. Barracuda Networks Email Security Technology is one of the systems existing to check the network security with which companies can manage all email traffic and protect the company systems from threats. Anti-spam protection, email analysis, sender profile scanning and real time protection are the main functions of this system [30]. Infected files are another way for a malware to enter a network. Thus, developing a file analyzer is essential for the system to identify and remove malicious files. As an example, if an unknown file is figured out, it must be verified in a secure environment. URL and IP address monitoring is another method to improve security systems. The system should contain a list of suspicious URLs and IPs. This blacklist needs to be updated consistently. The blacklist is created by manual reports, web crawlers and website analysis [31].

4   Fin Tech Banking Malware (Attitudes and Approaches)

4.1   Fin Tech Banking Malware

The most dangerous malware in the financial industry are Zbot/Zeus, Zeus Gameover, SpyEye, Ice IX, Citadel and Botnets [32]. Zeus known as Zbot is a type of Trojan trying to achieve confidential information with infecting Windows users. The main goal of this malware is to penetrate the systems and collect passwords, bank credentials and other financial data. Zeus can be manipulated in order to work in different systems. To send and receive data over the network, this malware needs Command and Control servers. However, it was mentioned that this malware tends to change in order to penetrate different systems. Thus, the latest Zeus includes domain generation algorithm (DGA) to control the malware weakness which was mentioned above. This malware is still very active in the banking industry by affecting thousands of systems and achieving data being worth hundreds of millions dollars [33]. Banking malwares has the highest rate of threats in financial industries in 2015.

Zeus Gameover is a kind of Zeus relying on a peer-to-peer botnet infrastructure. It looks constantly for data on somebody's computer and when Gameover finds it, sends it to another peer. The data is transferred to another computer which is also on the same network that Zeus P2P uses [34]. The goal of Gameover is the same as the Zeus Malware. SpyEye is also a member of the Zeus family aim to steal money from bank accounts [35]. This malware includes different components working together. So, some parts of this bot can be improved to work in proper situations [36].

Ice IX is a Trojan which emerges from Zeus with some improved components and it has the same goal with Zeus. Another type of the Zeus banking malware is the Citadel Trojan. Regarding an article written by Jason Milletary, Citadel is used mainly for stealing information from online banking activities [37].

These are the top widely used malwares in the financial industry used by cybercriminals to achieve credentials and private information. However, there are lots of them aiming to penetrate the networks [38].

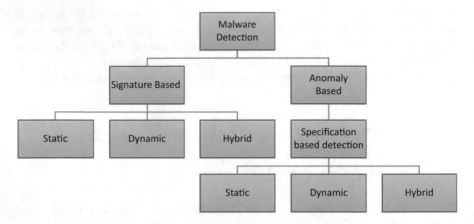

Fig. 15.6 Malware detection techniques

4.2 Malware Detection Techniques with Big Data Aspect

A program that aims to detect malicious efforts is called a malware detector that aims to help protect the system by detecting malware [39]. Of the various diagnostic methods, one can refer to the following: anomaly-based detection and signature-based detection. In addition, there is also a specific type of anomaly-based detection method called profile-based detection [40]. This section de-scribes the various malware detection techniques mentioned in the literature. As shown in Fig. 15.6, anomaly-based detection and signature-based detection, and specification-based detection are a subset of anomaly-based detection.

4.2.1 Anomaly-Based Detection

The behavior of a given network is characterized by detecting anomalies by separating normal behavior from suspicious [41–44]. The two main parts of this technique are: training phase and supervision phase. Firstly, the system tries to get familiar with the normal behavior of the monitored system. Network performance is determined dependent on predefined conduct, which is a lot of host and/or PARC UIs (PUIs).

The most important advantage of using indirect methods based on anomalies is the possibility to use this technique to detect unknown (zero-day) attacks, which are unfamiliar attacks to detect malware [45]. This is done by evaluating the deviations between normal and irregular behavior.

Another advantage of this procedure is that regular activity profiles dependent on a system make it hard for cybercriminals to recognize which safety efforts are low and can be assaulted without distinguishing them [46]. However, according to Jyothsna and Prasad research [47], one of the major limitations of anomaly-based detection is the process of defining the set of rules and establishing the system's acceptable behavior by the administrator. System performance relies upon the degree of system combination and protocol testing. Moreover, administrator knowledge assumes a significant role in characterizing appropriate net-work behavior [47]. There is a special type of anomaly-based diagnosis called profile-based diagnosis that plans to discover regular false alerts that happen in anomaly-based diagnosis [48].

4.2.2 Signature-Based Detection

Another way to detect malware is signature-based detection. This technique tries to find a sequence of bits that are inside the malware code [48]. Information on the code sequence (signature) is stored in a repository called signature-based recognition knowledge [49]. Signature-based diagnostics, unlike malware-based diagnostics, cannot detect anonymous attacks (i.e. zero-day attacks) because new malware code sequences are not available in the database, so signatures only work with well-defined behavior patterns. And failed to properly handle new malware with modified behavior characteristics [41, 45]. Another disadvantage of this technique is that the development of the new signature requircs human intervention, as suggested by Idika and Mathur [23]. Therefore, human errors may occur, which can reduce the security of a given network and may take developers a long time to sign. Another way to identify malware is by file size. Using this method, any antivirus program can easily detect whether a particular file is infected. Some viruses have their own code at the end of the file [49]. Furthermore, the most significant part of any antivirus program is the scan engine that that scans the file and measures it prior and afterward. In the event that the document is bigger than expected, it is probably going to be infected.

4.3 Spyware

Spyware is software that collects information from a computer and sends it to someone else. Before emerging as a serious threat in recent years, the word spyware was first used in 1995 in a post to joke and mock the Microsoft Business Competitive Model. The exact information that spyware collects may be different, but they can include anything potentially valuable:

- Usernames and passwords. This information can be obtained from files on the machine, or by using an event log, by recording the things the user types in. The incident is different from the Trojan, it only records the keys that are compressed by the user, without any response to it, and there is no trick.
- Email addresses that are valuable to mail spam senders.
- Bank account numbers and credit card numbers.
- Software activation keys to facilitate illegal duplication.

Viruses and worms may also collect similar information, but spyware is not considered because spyware can be transmitted in a different way in a different way, for example, with software that the user installs, or exploits the technical and security shortcomings of web browsers. The last method makes it easy for the spyware to be installed on the user's computer by opening and viewing an Internet page.

4.4   Key Logger Structure

The main idea behind the incident is the occurrence of the two connections in the chain of events. This is when the key is pressed on the keypad and when it is displayed on the screen. This is done by visual monitoring, a hardware bug on the keyboard or the computer system itself, replacing the keyboard driver, filtering the drivers in the keyboard stack, replacing the addresses in the system tables, and requesting information [50] from the keyboard [51]. Event reports are divided into hardware and software for development. In the hardware process, a small electronic piece is installed on the keyboards and is designed and implemented in software using a series of software applications. The most commonly used methods to build a software incident are as follows (Fig. 15.8):

- System hook method: When a key is pressed, a system message is sent. This is done with a Win API system function called Set Windows Hook Ex.
- Query information request from the keyboard: This is done by a WinAPI system function called Get (Async) Keystate or Get Keyboard State.
- Use Filter Driver

Key logger use rootkits to hide, and rootkits are often of two types: cover in user mode and kernel coverage [51]. The rate of use of key logger from various routocrats is shown in Fig. 15.7.

4.5   Core and User Level

Depending on the type of code that is running, the processor decides which mode to take. In brief, applications and some launches are executed in user mode. Also, the main operating system parts and most launchers are running in kernel mode. When an application runs in a user mode, Windows operates a process for it. A process involves two parts for each program: Private Handle Table, Private Virtual Address Space. Each program runs in an isolated environment, no program can access and modify the program's other program's space; also, when an application crashes and continues to work, only the program is affected and other programs are affected. All

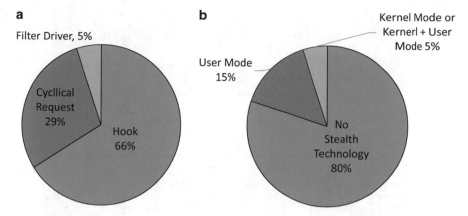

Fig. 15.7 (**a**) The extent to which malware is used in a variety of ways. (**b**) The incidence rate of incoming messages from different rootkits

core level programs use a single environment that shares all. Therefore, kernel level programs can change the amount of virtual memory that is at the disposal of others, and this change causes the operating system to encounter an error (Fig. 15.8) [52].

4.6   Protection Against Key Logger Attack

Banks must use a trusted device concept to ensure users' authentication when logging in. If the user is logged in from an untrusted device, the banking system must send an SMS alert to confirm that the user has been targeted. User training is one of the key components to ensuring a secure Internet banking experience. After successfully logging in, the bank can issue a security alert on its web pages to alert users to the threats it poses to Internet banking. Banks should use artificial intelligence or machine-based learning software that can judge user behavior and transfer large amounts of cash to the destination rather than the user's monthly pattern.

This software can be used to detect all electronic transactions including credit card transaction and will be able to detect if the user has made a purchase not within the customer's pattern and will alert and sometimes disable the credit card or Fin Tech banking account in extreme cases until the customer's identity is verified. The machine based learning or artificial intelligence should predict this anomaly and take appropriate action.

Information security is an important part of the Internet banking process. Therefore, banks can improve their security features by securing their own servers and linking between the user and the internet banking server. Figure 15.9 describes a list of security features that each bank must include to describe the security of user data and communications [53].

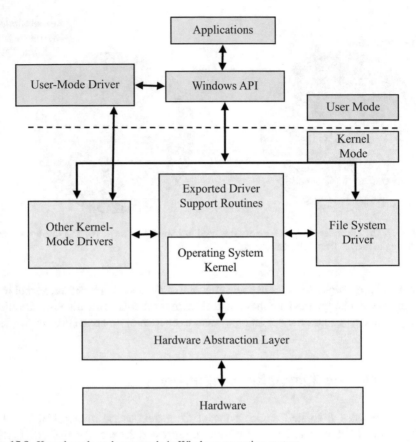

Fig. 15.8 Kernel mode and user mode in Windows operating system

Most antivirus software detects incident events as potentially malicious or potential undesirable software and stores them in their database. As the main goal of incident events is to obtain confidential data as described in Fig. 15.10. They can be summarized as follows:

- Use one-time password or two-step identification
- Use of active protection systems to detect incident events
- Use virtual keyboard
- Antivirus software updates
- Firmware update
- Failure to grant software user permission to normal users
- Limit the number of system administrators and apply strict policies to protect passwords
- Lack of trust in files and emails from invalid sources
- Inspection of computer keyboard and suspicious hardware

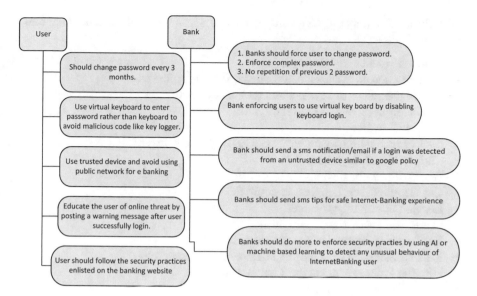

Fig. 15.9 Proposed security model required to decrease the security risks in Internet banking

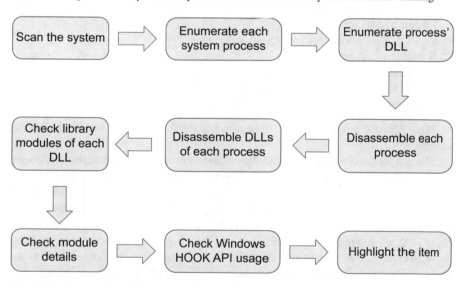

Fig. 15.10 Methods to confronting Fin Tech banking malware (key loggers)

4.7 Strategies of FinTech Banking Malware Attack (Spyware and Hacking Malware)

According to a study conducted on malware released in the past few years, it has been attempted to provide a comprehensive template for implementing this type of malware. A number of commonly used strategies/model for implementing these malware includes:

- Compress and encrypt information.
- Capture a screen at a specified time and from specified pages.
- Record the values of keys pressed on the keyboard.
- Use multiple servers to keep anonymity.
- Update malware.
- Lack of recognition by antivirus and antispyware software.
- Capture Visual Keyboard.
- Work with low bandwidth.
- Use Google Drive, Dropbox to dump the server.
- Logging of running processes.
- Create Shell access at certain times.
- Use backup programs to prevent Process Kill.
- Send all files such as photos and databases and compressed.
- Hide the Process name in the Task manager.
- Delete files in the registry.
- Create an infected file using non-infected files such as .jpg
- Disabling anti-viruses.
- Residing in inaccessible memory.
- Intelligent publishing and propagation process.
- Formation of Agent networks.
- Failure to identify the central server.
- Ability to fake as genuine services like Windows Services.
- Run on non-Windows operating systems.

Table 15.1 summarizes the response of some FinTech banking malwares to these attacks.

The results show comparative study of the proposed FinTech banking malwares attack and the effect of these attackers on server and settings of banking systems.

The results demonstrated that the all malwares mentioned in Table1 can be affected on FinTech banking systems through: command to run the server and settings, logging of running processes, ability to encrypt logs, ability to compress logs, lack of recognition by antivirus, ability to use multiple servers to keep anonymity and hide the process name in the Task manager. But some of them are resistant to these attackers technique such as "Use registry to destroy" for Flame malware.

Table 15.1 Compare the response of some FinTech banking malwares to some attacks model

	Zbot	Stuxnet	Duqu	Flame	Guass	Equation	Regin
Command to run the server and settings	Y[a]	Y	Y	Y	Y	Y	Y
Logging of running processes	Y	Y	Y	Y	Y	Y	Y
Ability to encrypt logs	Y	Y	Y	Y	Y	Y	Y
Ability to compress logs	Y	Y	Y	Y	Y	Y	Y
Infect shortcuts for user to run	Y	Y	N[a]	Y	N	N	N
Take a screenshot and record the key pressed	Y	N	Y	Y	Y	N	Y
Hide the process name in the task manager	Y	Y	Y	Y	Y	Y	Y
Use registry to destroy	Y	Y	Y	N	Y	Y	Y
Ability to use multiple servers to keep anonymity	Y	Y	Y	Y	Y	Y	Y
Lack of recognition by antivirus	Y	Y	Y	Y	Y	Y	Y
Clever releases	Y	Y	Y	Y	Y	Y	Y
Digital certificate abducting	Y	Y	Y	Y	N	N	N

[a]Y = Yes (it means responding (yes or no) of some Fin Tech banking malwares to some common attacks technique), and N = No

5   Case Study: Implement a Fin Tech Malware Model with Key Logger

Given the subject matter, it was necessary to implement malware similar to Zeus with the purpose of collecting confidential bank information. Therefore, a sample of spyware was designed and implemented. The purpose of producing this malware is to collect information from bank cards of the network of accelerated networks. This information is collected when the victim is entering his card information in an online payment system (such as buying a cell phone charge, paying a bill online, etc.), and after the payment, this information is sent to the attacker's host. Currently, the malware can only work when the victim is paying by using the Google Chrome browser.

The capabilities of this spyware include:

- Ability to compress and encrypt information.
- Ability to capture a screen at a specified time and from specified pages.
- Ability to record the values of keys pressed on the keyboard.
- Ability to use multiple servers to keep anonymity.
- Ability to update malware.
- Lack of recognition by antivirus and antispyware software.
- Ability to capture Visual Keyboard.
- Ability to work with low bandwidth.

After spyware runs on a victim machine, it starts its activity. The software will search for specific processes at chrome.exe at specified intervals. If this particular sheet is not found, the software continues to search for its period. But if you find the page you are interested in, it will collect the mouse and keyboard input knobs to get started. This will cause spyware to be transferred to spyware, as long as the desired sheet is active in the chrome.exe process, the values of the keys pressed on the keyboard, as well as the location of mouse clicks on the screen, are transmitted to the spyware in accordance with the messaging system on the Windows operating system. Since, information may be entered both from the physical keyboard and the virtual keyboard, the values entered by the keyboard are stored in a memory in a straightforward manner and the input values by mouse, in terms of the position of the cursor, as an image in size 60×60 pixels are stored on the memory. Usually, most users enter a 16-digit card number and expiration date of the card via the keyboard and the Internet code and CVV2 code via virtual keyboards. After paying out and leaving the Internet payment page, a string is generated from the values of the keys pressed from the keyboard in a file and in the direction where the screenshots have been saved. At this point, the collected data are sent to the attacker's host. Because of the low bandwidth usage and the lack of user access or network administrators (in the case of data observation) of the sent information, the data should first be stored in a packet, and then, using a compression method, the volume of the sent data are reduced. The method used to package data is an innovative method. In this way, binary saved data are stored in a new file. To avoid interference with different file information, a separator is used to separate the content of different files. In the next step, since the malware process is a client-server, a re-attack should be prevented on the server. For this reason, the prepared package overview is computed with the SHA-1 abstract method and re-integrates the result into the package. After receiving this packet, the server discards the abstract sent from the packet. Then separately calculates the package abstract with the SHA-1 method and compares with the received abstract. If both abstracts are the same, user can be sure that the data received along the path is unchanged. Also, by storing the abstract of each packet in the database, it is possible to accept packets received in the presence of abstracts in the database, and thus prevent a repeat attack. The compression method used to compress a packet is the Gzip method. The choice of this method is due to the proper function of the algorithm, as well as the low compression time and, therefore, the lack of user attention in the case of CPU usage observation. Also, to prevent disclosure of information, encryption should be performed on the compressed package. Using the AES encryption algorithm, we encrypt the file information. An important point at this point is the key exchange between the malware and the host, which should both use the same key for encryption and decryption. To use a single password key, we use a single-time password method. Malware, based on the current time on a global scale and the application of a fixed algorithm on it, obtains the key to the encrypted data. On the other hand, on the host side, the same algorithm is performed according to the current time, and as a result, the unit key is redefined. Given the number of servers provided to receive data from malware, data is sent to a server. On the server side, decryption, incompatibility and closing tasks are performed, and the files obtained are stored in a single path

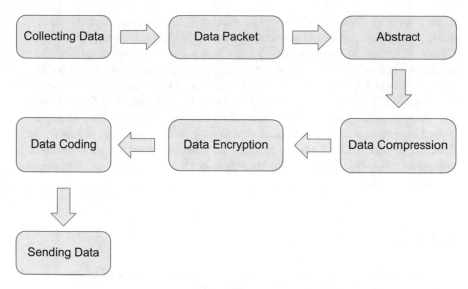

Fig. 15.11 Proposed malware model for operating on Fin Tech system with key logger

for each packet, and the attacker can reach their goal by analyzing and verifying. The malware producer method to operate on Fin Tech system is summarized in Fig. 15.11.

6   Conclusion

Currently, many countries have launched aggressive cyber-attacks under the name of spying. Such operations are not limited to governments. Individuals, groups and organizations can do this. All manufacturing and information services are now exclusively integrated into the Internet. This trend began in the 1990s with a shift in the focus of mass communication to the Internet and the growing demands in the area of production, distribution, communications and financial issues. Such a heavy reliance on the Internet has further exacerbated the potential damage caused by cybercrime attacks. Smart hackers disrupt vital websites to steal personal and confidential personal information from individuals and institutions. The most severe of these attacks occurs when hackers invade financially and military institutions that have been recently activated. Informational listening and observing is done in a variety of software and hardware.

In this study, Fin Tech banking malware is considered and the different methods of their detection were investigated. The malware is designed with the goal of collecting bank information in a native form, where bank card details of the network member will be accelerated and will be sent to the attackers after processing for specified purposes. The most important indicators of this malware include the ability to encrypt and compress information, as well as the lack of recognition by antivirus.

In case study section, by reviewing and evaluating the behavior of malware in this field, a malware model for implementation on Fin Tech system was purposed. Apart from the specific objectives targeted by attackers with the support of specific groups, the main target of the attackers is economic goals, and among them, the banks are the right target for them. In this regard, native malware have been designed and implemented to obtain victims' bank information. After installing the malware on the victim machine, the malware scans the browsers loaded pages and begins to collect information about bank cards after finding online electronic payment pages. This information will be sent to the attacker's servers after the victim's work is completed after various processing operations, such as encryption and compression of the information.

References

1. L.X. Yang, P. Li, X. Yang, Y.Y. Tang, Security evaluation of the cyber networks under advanced persistent threats. IEEE Access **5**, 20111–20123 (2017)
2. N. Boel, T. Olovsson, in *Security and Privacy for Big Data: A Systematic Literature Review*. IEEE International Conference on Big Data (2016), pp. 3693–3702
3. CALUPTIX, Top 5 Cyber Attack Types in 2016 So Far (2016), https://www.calyptix.com/top-threats/top-5-cyber-attack-types-in-2016-so-far. Caluptix Security
4. J. Lee, K. Jeong, H. Lee, in *Detecting Metamorphic Malwares Using Code Graphs*. ACM Symposium on Applied Computing (2010), pp. 1970–1977
5. M. Garnaeva, V. Chebyshev, D. Makrushinand, A. Ivanov, IT Threat Evolution in Q1 2015. Malware report, Kaspersky (2015)
6. V.S. Sathyanarayan, P. Kohli, B. Bruhadeshwar, in *Signature Generation and Detection of Malware Families*. Australasian Conference on Information Security and Privacy (2008), pp. 336–349
7. S. Morgan, Herjavec Group, 2019 Official Annual Cybercrime Report, Steve Morgan, Editor-in-Chief Cybersecurity Ventures (2019), https://www.HerjavecGroupherjavecgroup.com/wp-content/uploads/2018/12/CV-HG-2019-Official-Annual-Cybercrime-Report.pdf
8. T. Morris, S. Pan, J. Lewis, J. Moorhead, B. Reaves, N. Younan, R. King, M. Freund, V. Madani, in *Cyber Security Testing of Substation Phasor Measurement Units and Phasor Data Concentrators*. Proceedings of Cyber Security and Information Intelligence Research Workshop (CSIIRW) (2011), pp. 12–14
9. S. Mohammadi, H. Mirvaziri, M.G. Ahsaee, H. Karimipour, Cyber intrusion detection by combined feature selection algorithm. J. Inf. Secur. Appl. **44**, 80–88 (2019)
10. E. Modiri Dovom, A. Azmoodeh, A. Dehghantanha, D. Ellison, R. Modiri, H. Karimipour, Fuzzy pattern tree for edge malware detection and categorization in IoT. J. Syst. Archit. **97**, 1–7 (2019)
11. C. Tankard, Big data security. Netw. Secur. **7**, 5–8 (2012)
12. C. Everett, Big data–the future of cyber security or its latest threat? Comput. Fraud Secur. **9**, 14–17 (2015)
13. H. Karimipour, A. Dehghantanha, R.M. Parizi, K.R. Choo, H. Leung, A deep and scalable unsupervised machine learning system for cyber-attack detection in large-scale smart grids. IEEE Access **7**, 2169–3536 (2019)
14. B. Bencsáth, G. Pék, L. Buttyán, M. Felegyhazi, The cousins of Stuxnet: Duqu, Flame, and Gauss. Future Internet **4**, 971–1003 (2012)
15. B. Bencsáth, G. Pék, L. Buttyán, M. Felegyhazi, in *Duqu: Analysis, Detection, and Lessons Learned*. ACM European Workshop on System Security (EuroSec) (2012)

16. M. Garnaeva, V. Chebyshev, D. Makrushin, R. Unuchek, A. Ivanov, Kaspersky Security Bulletin, Overall statistics for 2014 (2014). https://securelist.com/kaspersky-security-bulletin-2014-overall-statistics-for-2014/68010/68010/

17. Kaspersky Cyber Threat Real-Time Map. https://cybermap.kaspersky.com

18. M. Nadir Bin Ali, M. Emran Hossain, M. Masud Parvez, Design and implementation of a secure campus network. Int. J. Emerg. Technol. Adv. Eng. **5**(7) (2015)

19. H. Darabian, S. Homayon, A. Dehghantanha, S. Hashemi, H. Karimipour, Deep learning and machine learning for detecting cryptomining malware: a study on static and dynamic analysis. IEEE Access, 1–13 (2019)

20. Lockheed Martin Corporation, Guide to Cyber security for Financial Services Firms. An eBook by: Lockheed Martin Corporation (2015), http://www.cutoday.info/content/download/26039/218761/version/1/file/Lockheed+Martin+Guide+to+Cybersecurity.pdf

21. AMT - Banking Malware Detector, Minded Security (2017), https://www.mindedsecurity.com/index.php/products/amt-banking-malwaredetector

22. J. Kałużny, M. Olejarka, *Script-Based Malware Detection in Online Banking Security Overview* (Black Hat Asia, 2015)

23. N. Idika, A. Mathur, *A Survey of Malware Detection Techniques* (Purdue University, 2007), p. 48

24. M. Behradfar, H. Haddadpajouh, A. Azmoodeh, A. Dehghantanha, H. Karimipour, in *RAT Hunter: Building Robust Model for Hunting RAT Based on Optimum Features*. 29th Annual International Conference on Computer Science and Software Engineering, Toronto, Canada (2019), pp. 1–10

25. A. Duane, P. Finnegan, in *Managing Email Usage: A Cross Case Analysis of Experiences with Electronic Monitoring and Control*. 6th International Conference on Electronic commerce (2004), pp. 229–238

26. J.H. Gottschalk, The risks associated with the business use of email. Intellect. Prop. Technol. Law J. **17**(7), 16 (2005)

27. T. Micro, Email Reputation Services (2007). Retrieved from: www: https://ers.trendmicro.com

28. B. Schneier, Monitoring: network security for the 21st century. Comput. Secur. **20**, 491–503 (2001). Retrieved from https://www.schneier.com/academic/paperfiles/paper-msm.pdf

29. A.S. Ashoor, A. Shaker, S. Gore, in *Difference Between Intrusion Detection System (IDS) and Intrusion Prevention System (IPS)*. International Conference on Network Security and Applications (2011), pp. 497–501

30. Barracuda Networks Inc., Barracuda Email Security Gateway (2017). Retrieved from https://assets.barracuda.com/assets/docs/dms/Barracuda_Email_Security_Gateway_DS_US.pdf

31. J. Ma, L.K. Saul, S. Savage, G.M. Voelker, Beyond Blacklists: Learning Malicious Web Sites from Suspicious URLs (2009). Retrieved from http://cseweb.ucsd.edu/~saul/papers/kdd09_url.pdf

32. A. Zaharia, The Top 10 Most Dangerous Malware That Can Empty Your Bank Account (2016). Retrieved from https://heimdalsecurity.com/blog/topfinancial-malware/

33. Secure Works Counter Threat Unit TM, Banking Botnets Persist Despite Take-downs (2015). Retrieved from https://www.secureworks.com/research/banking-botnets-persist-despite-takedowns

34. M. Kjaersgaard, Everything You Need to Know About the Notorious Zeus Game Over Malware (2014). Retrieved from https://heimdalsecurity.com/blog/zeus-gameover/

35. L. Constantin, Banking Malware Monitors Victims by Hacking Webcams and Micro-phones (2012). Retrieved from https://www.pcworld.com/article/255979/banking_malware_monitors_victims_by_hijacking_webcams_and_microphones_researchers_say.html

36. A.K. Sood, R.J. Enbody, R. Bansal, Dissecting spy eye–understanding the design of third generation botnets. Comput. Netw. **57**(2), 436–450 (2013)

37. J. Milletary, Citadel trojan malware analysis. Luettu **13** (2014)

38. Unisys Stealth Solution Team, Zeus Malware: Threat Banking Industry (2010). Retrieved from http://botnetlegalnotice.com/citadel/files/Guerrino_Decl_Ex1.pdf

39. M. Christodorescu, S. Jha, S.A. Seshia, D. Song, R.E. Bryant, in *Semantics-Aware Malware Detection*. 2005 IEEE Symposium on Security and Privacy (S&P'05) (2005), pp. 32–46
40. Z. Bazrafshan, H. Hashemi, S.M. Hazrati Fard, A. Hamzeh, in *A Survey on Heuristic Malware Detection Techniques*. The 5th Conference on Information and Knowledge Technology, IEEE (2013), pp. 113–120
41. A. Namavarjahromi, J. Sakhnini, H. Karimipour, A. Dehghantanha, in *A Deep Unsupervised Representation Learning Approach for Effective Control of Cyber-Physical Systems*. 29th Annual International Conference on Computer Science and Software Engineering, Toronto, Canada (2019), pp. 1–10
42. M.R. Begli, F. Derakhshan, H. Karimipour, in *A Layered Intrusion Detection System for Critical Infrastructure Using Machine Learning*. IEEE International Conference on Smart Energy Grid Engineering (SEGE) (2019), pp. 1–5
43. S. Geris, H. Karimipour, in *A Feature Selection-Based Approach for Joint Cyber-Attack Detection and State Estimation*. IEEE International Conference on Smart Energy Grid Engineering (SEGE), Oshawa, Canada (2019), pp. 1–5
44. J. Sakhnini, A. Dehghantanha, H. Karimipour, in *Smart Grid Cyber Attacks Detection Using Supervised Learning and Heuristic Feature Selection*. IEEE International Conference on Smart Energy Grid Engineering (SEGE), Oshawa, Canada (2019), pp. 1–5
45. S. Mohammadi, V. Desai, H. Karimipour, in *Multivariate Mutual Information-Based Feature Selection for Cyber Intrusion Detection*. IEEE Electrical Power and Energy Conference (EPEC), Toronto, ON (2018), pp. 1–6
46. A. Patcha, J.M. Park, An overview of anomaly detection techniques: existing solutions and latest technological trends. Comput. Netw. **51**(12), 3448–3470 (2007)
47. S. Dubey, N. Tripathi, A survey on intrusion detection systems. Int. J. Sci. Res. Sci. Eng. Technol. **1**, 29–40 (2015)
48. P.D. Kumar, A. Nema, R. Kumar, in *Hybrid Analysis of Executables to Detect Security Vulnerabilities: Security Vulnerabilities*. Proceedings of the 2nd India Software Engineering Conference ACM (2009), pp. 141–142
49. S. Choudhary, R. Saroha, M.S. Beniwal, How anti-virus software works? Int. J. Adv. Res. Comput. Sci. Softw. Eng. **3**(4), 5–7 (2013)
50. Hooking the System Service Dispatch Table (2014), INFOSEC, http://resources.infosecinstitute.com/hooking-system-service-dispatch-table-ssdt
51. N. Grebennikov, Keyloggers: How they work and how to detect them, securelist (2007), https://securelist.com/analysis/publications/36138/keyloggers-how-they-work-and-how-to-detect-them-part-1
52. Hooks Overview, Windows Dev Center (2007), https://msdn.microsoft.com/en-us/library/windows/desktop/ms644959(v=vs.85).aspx
53. I. Georgiev, D. Marc Eng, Schaaf, Cyber Security Fraud Prevention Using Data Analytics Developing a Layered Framework with Preconditions to Enable Fraud Identification in Bank Sector (2017). 10.13140/RG.2.2.21343.76965

Chapter 16
A Hybrid Deep Generative Local Metric Learning Method for Intrusion Detection

Mahdis Saharkhizan, Amin Azmoodeh, Hamed HaddadPajouh,
Ali Dehghantanha ⓘ, Reza M. Parizi, and Gautam Srivastava

1 Introduction

In recent times, the fast growing pace of industrialization and information technology has tightly connected the prevalence of using computerized system. Enormous amounts of data are being generated and communicated over computer networks that has turned these networks as an absorbing target for cyber-criminals [3, 8, 11]. In recent decades, the industrial revolution using information technology has penetrated into all aspects of our modern life ranging from agriculture, manufacturing to healthcare and urbanization [1, 7, 15, 23, 37]. The stream of data communication over networks is increasing and being targeting by attackers continuously [39]. On the other hand, Machine Learning based systems are increasingly being employed to enhance the accuracy and robustness of security mechanisms to cope with such cyber attacks [9, 20–22, 28, 40].

In order to secure and protect networks and infrastructure, Intrusion Detection Systems (IDSs) must be deployed as an critical module in the networks [13, 24, 29, 30, 45]. IDS system provide a safeguard for both inside and outside intrusion attacks

M. Saharkhizan
School of Electrical and Computer Engineering, Shiraz University, Shiraz, Iran
e-mail: mahdis@cybersciencelab.org

A. Azmoodeh (✉) · H. HaddadPajouh · A. Dehghantanha
Cyber Science Lab, University of Guelph, Guelph, ON, Canada
e-mail: amin@cybersciencelab.org; hamed@cybersciencelab.org; ali@cybersciencelab.org

R. M. Parizi
College of Computer and Software Engineering, Kennesaw State University, Marietta, GA, USA
e-mail: rparizi1@kennesaw.edu

G. Srivastava
Department of Mathematics and Computer Science, Brandon University, Brandon, MB, Canada
e-mail: srivastavag@brandonu.ca

© Springer Nature Switzerland AG 2020
K.-K. R. Choo, A. Dehghantanha (eds.), *Handbook of Big Data Privacy*,
https://doi.org/10.1007/978-3-030-38557-6_16

and are generally categorized into two taxonomies: signature-based and anomaly-based detection [14, 17].

Signature-based IDSs utilize patterns of previously identified malicious activities as signatures to recognize intrusions and Anomaly-based IDSs endeavor to detect deviations from normal patterns to hunt intrusions [6]. While signature-based IDSs are more accurate to detect previously known attacks, they operate ineffectively against unknown or polymorphic attacks [32].

In this chapter, we propose a hybrid machine learning approach to maximize detection rate for User to Root (U2R) and Root to Local (R2L) which are minor but more harmful attacks within NSL-KDD dataset which is a refined version of its predecessor the KDD'99 dataset [42]. The dataset includes 22 different categories of attacks that can be classified into four major classes as seen in Table 16.1.

In the first stage, the proposed method employs Deep Autoencoders [4] to cluster attacks and then it leverages Generative Local Metric Learning (GLML) to learn distance metrics within each cluster and mitigate the effect of overlapped and minor class on mis-classification.

Typically, the following criteria are used to evaluate the utility of machine learning aided techniques in intrusion detection:

- True Positive (TP): indicates that a intrusion is correctly identified.
- True Negative (TN): indicates that a benign is detected as a non-malicious activity correctly.
- False Positive (FP): indicates that a benign is falsely detected as a malicious activity.
- False Negative (FN): indicates that an intrusion is not detected and labeled as a non-malicious activity.

Table 16.1 NSL-KDD attacks

Attack class	Attack type
Probe	Satan, Ipsweep, Nmap, Portsweep, Mscan, Saint
DoS	Back, Land, Neptune, Pod, Smurf, Teardrop, Apache2, Udpstorm, Processtable, Worm
U2R	Buffer-overflow, Loadmodule, Rootkit, Perl, Sqlattack, Xterm, Ps
R2L	Guess-Password, Ftp-write, Imap, Phf, Multihop, Warezmaster, Warezclient, Spy, Xlock, Xsnoop, Snmpguess, Snmpgetattack, Httptunnel, Sendmail, Named

Based on the criteria described above, the following metrics will be introduced to quantify a given system:

Accuracy indicates the number of samples that a classifier correctly detects, divided by the number of all samples:

$$Accuracy = \frac{TP + TN}{TP + TN + FP + FN} \qquad (16.1)$$

Precision is another metric that indicates the ratio of predicted intrusion samples that are correctly predicted:

$$Precision = \frac{TP}{TP + FP} \qquad (16.2)$$

Recall indicates the ratio of intrusion samples that are correctly predicted:

$$Recall = \frac{TP + TN}{TP + FN} \qquad (16.3)$$

F-Measure is the harmonic mean of prediction and recall, and defined as follows:

$$F - Measure = \frac{2 * TP}{2 * TP + FP + FN} \qquad (16.4)$$

The rest of the chapter is organized as follows. In Sect. 2 we briefly review the related literature. Next, Sect. 3 presents our proposed method and Sect. 4 describes our dataset and the approach we prepare it for the learning task. We follow this with its evaluation in Sect. 5. Section 6 concludes this chapter and suggests a future research agenda.

2   Related Work

The importance of industrial networks and protecting them against harmful cyber-attacks has motivated researches to propose new approaches in this area. In order to protect ICS against advanced persistent group attacks, Grooby et al. [19] deeply analyzed some campaign attacks targeting industrial networks and proposed a triage defensive process based on Diamond model to protect ICSs. Zhang et al. [49] proposed a multi-layer, defense-in-depth based IDS system for robustly detecting intrusions in industrial control system (ICS). They employed an auto-associative kernel regression to strengthen early attack detection and used k-Nearest Neighbor, Decision Tree, Random Forest and Bagging Tree as base models and an optimizer to alongside an optimizer to build a multi-layer detection system. In a similar approach, Daryabar et al. [11] analyzed risks and vulnerabilities of Supervisory Control And Data Acquisition (SCADA) systems and presented strategies to improve the

SCADA security systems. Modiri et al. [12] applied fuzzy pattern tree on several datasets of malware and benign and obtained the average accuracy of 95.74%.

During the past decade, proposing novel and modified approaches to empower intrusion detection mechanisms has been an active area of research. Haddadpajouh et al. [34] proposed a two-tier classification models based on machine learning approaches namely Naïve Bayes, certainty factor voting version of KNN classifiers and also Linear Discriminant Analysis for dimension reduction and intrusion classification. Their method obtained detection rate of 67.16 and 34.18% for U2R and R2l attacks respectively. Using Fuzzy Rough Sets, Selvakumar [39] proposed a feature selection algorithm for intrusion detection system in Wireless Sensor Networks (WSN). The model is based on the fuzzy rough set-based nearest neighborhood classification (FRNN) model for training the classifier and robustly works with biased intrusion dataset and achived detection rate of 99.87% on their dataset.

Panda et al. [35] proposed a hybrid approach for detecting network intrusions using a combination of decision trees as classifiers and Principal Component Analysis for dimensionally reduction. They applied two-class classification approaches and achieved a low false alarm rate of 0.1%. In another recent project, Salo et al. [38] proposed a hybrid dimensional reduction algorithm that overcomes high-dimension data for anomaly-based intrusion detection. Their model includes information gain and principal component analysis with an ensemble classifier based on a support vector machine, Instance-based learning algorithms and multi layer perceptron. They obtained acceptable results for normal/attack detection scenarios on the majority of datasets. In another work, Haddadpajouh et al. [33] proposed a two-tier classification algorithm for anomaly-based intrusion detection for Internet of Things(IoT) backbone networks. The algorithm includes a dimension reduction component and two-tier classification module to recognize malicious activities belonging to User to Root (U2R) and Remote to Local (R2L) attacks and obtained accuracy of 70.15% for U2R and 42% for R2L class respectively.

Nowadays, machine learning has demonstrated its capabilities to combat challenging cybersecurity problems and to provide robust and accurate solutions for IT and OT networks [16, 25, 36, 40]. Azmoodeh et al. [2] proposed a novel approach to identify crypto-ransomeware in IoT nodes using energy consumption information of the node and achieved accuracy of 94.27% by applying a grinding mechanism on power signals and using KNN as classification. Darabian et al. [10] has presented a method using maximal frequent patterns to differentiate malware and benign IoT applications and achieved accuracy rate of 99% in the detection of unseen IoT malware. Complexity of overlapped data of network intrusions necessitates robust and modern techniques to deal with the complexity.

Deep Learning [27] methods have rapidly become a methodology of choice for analyzing wide range of cybersecurity problems [44]. Autoencoders (AE) [18] is a category of deep learners that can efficiently operate in unsupervised learning. Autoencoders learn a representation of data and encode higher dimensions of data to a compressed lower dimension code in the output layer. AEs have been widely used to overcome the curse of dimensionality [27] as well as unsupervised learning

[4]. Yousefi-Azar et al. [47] proposed a novel feature learning algorithm using AE to learn latent representation of cybersecurity datasets to maximize discrimination of classes in the new space and obtained accuracy of 95.7% for Microsoft Malware Classification dataset.

Performance of machine learning methods relies on distance metrics that they are using. Metric Learning is the task of discovering an alternative distance metric for the input space of data somehow the learned metric preserves the distance relation among the training data [31, 46]. Kong and Yang [26] proposed a framework that extracts function call graphs of malware and learns discriminant malware distance metrics and maximizes the margin between classes to increase the performance of classification. They achieved an accuracy rate of 86.67% Hupigon and 93.3% for benign class. In other security related research, Tao et al. [41] proposed regularized smoothing KISS metric learning method by integrating smoothing and regularization techniques to increase the performance of person identification and obtained matching rate 96%.

3   Proposed Method

The proposed method is a hybrid approach that in the first stage pre-processes data and then leverages AE to encode data into a more separable latent space. Next, the approach utilizes k-means to cluster data into a subset of data and then finds local metrics of each cluster. Figures 16.1 and 16.2 illustrate training and test phase of the proposed method respectively.

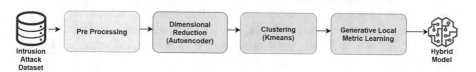

Fig. 16.1 Flowchart of training phase of the proposed method

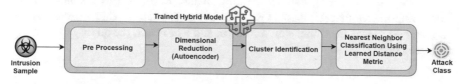

Fig. 16.2 Flowchart of test phase of the proposed method

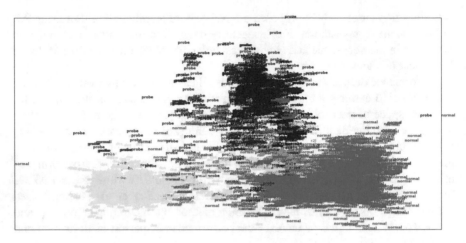

Fig. 16.3 NSL-KDD's class distribution

3.1 Autoencoders

Autoencoders (AEs) form a major category of unsupervised neural networks. An AE network accepts a tensor and tries to transmute it to another tensor of latent space [5]. In other words, AE are able to automatically learning a reasonable notion of semantic similarity among input features (Fig. 16.3).

The process of AE training consists of two parts namely encoders and decoders. An encoder is used for mapping the input data into hidden representation. A decoder is used for reconstructing input data from the hidden representation [31]. The hidden layer contains important information about original feature space in order to realize unsupervised feature extraction [43], Fig. 16.4 illustrates structure and data flow of a typical AE and Fig. 16.3 plots the dataset into a two-dimensional space to illustrate its complicated and overlapped data distribution.

In this case, we utilized AE with a ReLU activation function to learn the whole structure of dataset with no need of using explicit labels to reconstructing them. Indeed, reconstructing data can be helpful to avoid memorizing data and the consequent overfitting and underfitting in the result. In this chapter it is of crucial importance that AE learns the generality of dataset. In other words, it is not necessary to reduce the dimension of dataset and as a result, the quality of learning becomes better.

3.2 K-Means Clustering

A wide variety of machine learning based intrusion detection methods integrate both supervised and unsupervised learning to enhance detection performance.

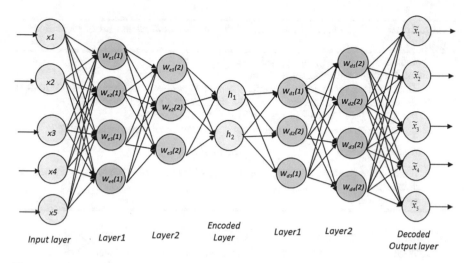

Fig. 16.4 Autoencoder structure

K-means is a popular unsupervised component in intrusion detection. While the majority of intrusion attack data includes complex and overlapped data distribution, a clustering component assists the proposed method to divide data into subsets that approximately include uncomplicated data distribution to learn. The general setting for the clustering algorithm is as follows:

- Accepts transmuted dataset from AE component.
- Partitions objects into k non-empty subsets.
- Identifies the cluster centroids (mean point) of the current partition.
- Assigns each point to a specific cluster.
- Computes the distances from each point and allot points to the cluster where the distance from the centroid is minimum.

3.3   Generative Local Metric Learning

In this study, the bias problem arising from overlapped attack distribution that causes misclassifying harmful attack scenario such as U2R and R2L has been the focus. From the empirical experience, Noh et al. [31] demonstrated that learning local metric by GLML enhances the discrimination ability of a nearest neighbour classifier on various datasets. Algorithm 1 describe GLML approach.

One of the main reasons that GLML is selected to apply on NSS-KDD is that it has demonstrated its performance to deal with high dimensional space. Indeed, complex distribution of attacks and imbalanced dataset as seen in Fig. 16.3 intensify hardship to learn from intrusion attack information.

Algorithm 1: Generative local metric learning for nearest neighbor classification

---

Input: data $D = x_i, y_i|_{i=1}^N$ and a point x in
Output: Predicted Attack Label $y_b(x)$ out
1: Estimate mean vector μ_c and covariance matrix $\sum_c$ of each class $c = \{1, \ldots, C\}$ from D.
2: Use the estimated parameters $\mu_c, \sum_c$ and obtain B matrix at the point x while
   $B = \sum_{i=1}^c H_{P_i}(\sum_{i \neq j} P_j^2 - \sum_{i \neq j} P_j)$. and H is Hessian Matrix
3: Use the eigenvectors and the eigenvalues of B and obtain the metric matrix A in
   $$A_{opt} = \beta[U_+ U_-] \begin{pmatrix} d_+ \Lambda_+ & 0 \\ 0 & -d_- \Lambda_- \end{pmatrix} [U_+ U_-]^T.$$
4: Use metric A, perform the nearest neighbor classification, and obtain $y_b(x)$ with the new distance.
5: **return** $y_b(x)$

Equation 16.5 is defined as the Mahalanobis distance between two samples x_1 and x_2 with a positive definite square matrix $A \in R^{D \times D}$ where D is the dimensionality of data space.

$$d(x_1, x_2) = \sqrt{(x_1 - x_2)^T A (x_1 - x_2)} \qquad (16.5)$$

Furthermore, The Hessian of the Gaussian density function is presented by Eq. 16.6.

$$H_{P_c(X)} = [\sum_c^{-1} (x - \mu_c)(x - \mu_c)^T \sum_c^{-1} - \sum_c^{-1}] \qquad (16.6)$$

This expression (Eq. 16.6) is used with estimated parameters to learn the local metric at each point x.

4 Dataset

NSL-KDD is a recognized dataset for intrusion detection which is the latter version of KDD99 dataset including 41 attributes (see Table 16.2) [33]. Table 16.3 gives information about distribution of samples over classes. In this research, GLML is trained with both training sets (KDDTrain+) and then evaluated using the test set (KDDTest+).

Table 16.2 NSL-KDD features

Type	Features
Nominal	Protocol-type(2), Service(3), Flag(4)
Binary	Land(7), logged-in(12), root-shell(14), su-attempted(15), is-host-login(21), is-guest-login(22)
Numeric	Duration(1), src-bytes(5), dst-bytes(6), wrong-fragment(8), urgent(9), hot(10), num-failed-logins(11), num-compromised(13), num-root(16), num-file-creations(17), num-shells(18), num-access-files(19), num-outbound-cmds(20), count(23), srv-count(24), serror-rate(25), srv-serror-rate(26), rerror-rate(27), srv-rerror-rate(28), same-srv-rate(29), diff-srv-rate(30), srv-diff-host-rate(31), dst-host-count(32), dst-host-srv-count(33), dst-host-same-srv-rate(34), dst-host-diff-srv-rate(35), dst-host-same-src-port-rate(36), dst-host-srv-diff-host-rate(37), dst-host-serror-rate(38), dst-host-srv-serror-rate(39), dst-host-rerror-rate(40), dst-host-srv-rerror-rate(41)

Table 16.3 NSL-KDD number of sample for each attack category

Training dataset		Testing dataset	
Class	Sample	Class	Sample
Normal	67,343	Normal	9711
DoS	45,927	DoS	7460
Probe	11,656	Probe	2421
U2R	995	U2R	2885
R2L	52	R2L	67
Total	125,973	Total	22,544

4.1 Nominal Attributes

According to Table 16.2, the dataset contains non-numerical attributes. Generally, the vale of these attributes are replaced with a number that represents the attribute value so as to distance calculation. For instance, dictionary $'tcp': 0, 'udp': 1, 'icmp': 2$ is used to replace protocol-type categorical value with numerical values in order to calculate distance. However, for a categorical attributes that includes m distinct items, $0 \leq distance(value_x, value_y) \leq m$ while it is not meaningful and all value should have equal distance to each other. Therefore, we have designed a transformation function that converts a feature with m distinct value to an m-dimensional feature somehow $\forall value_x$ and $value_y$ $distance(value_x, value_y) = 1$ as in Eq. 16.7.

$$feature_x \Rightarrow \widehat{feature}_x \tag{16.7}$$

$$while\ size(\widehat{feature}_x) = |distinct\ value\ of feature_x| \tag{16.8}$$

$$and\ \widehat{feature}_{x_i} = 1\ when\ feature_x = i \tag{16.9}$$

5 Experiments

The proposed method has been evaluated using the aforementioned dataset. While the dataset includes different sample sets for training and testing, we have trained dataset with $KDDTarin+$ set and assessed the proposed method performance by $KDDTest+$ on a Microsoft Windows 10 workstation with i7 Core CPU and 8GB of memory. All scripts were developed by Python (version 3.6).

Table 16.4 compares the performance of rival methods in terms of detection rate. As can be seen from the Table 16.4, the proposed method outperforms other approaches and obtained a detection rate of 77.61% and 46.92% for U2R and R2L attacks respectively (Table 16.5).

Table 16.4 Detection rate(Recall) performance comparison

Method	Normal	Probe	DoS	U2R	R2L
SVM with BIRCH [42]	99.3	**99.5**	**97.5**	28.8	19.7
Association rule IDS [45]	**99.5**	96.8	74.9	0.79	0.38
Two-tier [33]	94.56	79.76	84.68	67.16	34.81
TDTC[33]	94.43	87.32	88.2	70.15	42
GLML	86.09	67.96	50.19	64.18	44.12
Proposed method	88.94	65.05	73.03	**77.61**	**46.92**

Best (optimal) values are highlighted in bold

Table 16.5 Performance improvement comparison

Class	Accuracy	Precision	Recall	F-measure	False alarm rate
GLML					
Normal	86	86.4	86.09	89.25	14.7
DoS	84	88.2	67.96	76.76	26.3
Probe	84	41	50.19	45.13	10.58
U2R	92	3	64.18	5.73	7
R2L	88	67.14	44.12	53.24	4
Proposed method					
Normal	76.5	68	88.94	77	33
DoS	83.54	88	65.05	74	5
Probe	92.65	72	73.03	72	4
U2R	97.33	10	77.61	17	2.5
R2L	90.19	87	46.92	58	1.1

Table 16.6 Overall detection rate

Method	Detection rate
Nave Bayes	72
KNN	77.79
TDTC	84.86
Two-tier	81.97
Feature selection with SVM IDS [48]	82
GLML	71
Proposed method	81

Although the proposed approach has been designed so as to enhance the detection rate over harmful attacks which belong to minor classes, overall detection rate of the proposed method was evaluated. Table 16.6 describes detection rate of the compared method when they are trained by KDDTrain+ set and were tested by the KDDTest+ set. TDTC [33] obtained detection rate of 84.86%. However, the proposed method achieved 81% of recall which is approximately a close performance to the best value.

In order to evaluate the improvements of the proposed method compared with the GLML method, all performance metrics were examined for both method. Table 16.5 gives detailed information about performance of GLML and the proposed method. As can be seen from the Table 16.5, the proposed method outperforms GLML for all evaluation metric of R2L and U2R class that demonstrates its improvement. In addition, overall performance of the proposed method for all attack categories indicates overall improvement.

6 Conclusion

Rapid evolution of computerized networks has revealed several attack vectors for cyber-criminals. In addition, the importance of performing functionality and information stored and transfers over the networks encourage hackers to bypass security mechanisms to gain access to the network and its information. Intrusion detection systems are actively involved in attack scenarios and a robust IDS can significantly improve the defensive capability of network. While there have been several proposed approaches for boosting IDS functionality, there are dangerous attack scenarios that can be undetected while attribute and frequency of these attacks are difficult to learn from attack datasets. In this chapter, we have proposed a hybrid model that during different steps endeavour to maximize the discrimination of attack data and correctly classify them. Autoencoder transfer dataset into a more separable latent space and k-means clusters data to divide a complex data distribution into some simpler sets. Then, GLML has been utilized to learn distance metric within each cluster. Experiments demonstrate the usefulness and superiority of the proposed method for R2L ad U2R attack detection. The recommended future work includes integrating the proposed method and potential methods into a decision making system to leverage their outputs and develop a system that accurately detect all attacks.

References

1. A. Azmoodeh, A. Dehghantanha, K.K.R. Choo, *Big Data and Internet of Things Security and Forensics: Challenges and Opportunities* (Springer International Publishing, Cham, 2019), pp. 1–4
2. A. Azmoodeh, A. Dehghantanha, M. Conti, K.-K.R. Choo, Detecting crypto-ransomware in IoT networks based on energy consumption footprint. J. Ambient Intell. Humaniz. Comput. **9**(4), 1141–1152 (2018)
3. P.N. Bahrami, A. Dehghantanha, T. Dargahi, R.M. Parizi, K.R. Choo, H.H.S. Javadi, Cyber kill chain-based taxonomy of advanced persistent threat actors: analogy of tactics, techniques, and procedures. J. Inf. Process. Syst. **15**, 865–889 (2019). https://doi.org/10.3745/JIPS.03.0126
4. P. Baldi, Autoencoders, unsupervised learning, and deep architectures, in *Proceedings of ICML Workshop on Unsupervised and Transfer Learning* (2012), pp. 37–49
5. D.S. Berman, A.L. Buczak, J.S. Chavis, C.L. Corbett, A survey of deep learning methods for cyber security. Information **10**(4), 122 (2019)
6. M.H. Bhuyan, D.K. Bhattacharyya, J.K. Kalita, Network anomaly detection: methods, systems and tools. IEEE Commun. Surv. Tutorials **16**(1), 303–336 (2014). https://doi.org/10.1109/SURV.2013.052213.00046
7. M. Conti, A. Dehghantanha, K. Franke, S. Watson, Internet of things security and forensics: challenges and opportunities. Futur. Gener. Comput. Syst. **78**, 544–546 (2018). https://doi.org/10.1016/j.future.2017.07.060. http://www.sciencedirect.com/science/article/pii/S0167739X17316667
8. M. Damshenas, A. Dehghantanha, R. Mahmoud, S. bin Shamsuddin, Forensics investigation challenges in cloud computing environments, in *Proceedings Title: 2012 International Conference on Cyber Security, Cyber Warfare and Digital Forensic (CyberSec)* (2012), pp. 190–194. https://doi.org/10.1109/CyberSec.2012.6246092

9. M. Damshenas, A. Dehghantanha, R. Mahmoud, A survey on malware propagation, analysis, and detection. Int. J. Cyber-Secur. Digit. Forensics **2**(4), 10–30 (2013)

10. H. Darabian, A. Dehghantanha, S. Hashemi, S. Homayoun, K.K.R. Choo, An opcode-based technique for polymorphic internet of things malware detection, in *Concurrency and Computation: Practice and Experience* (Wiley, Hoboken, 2019), p. e5173

11. F. Daryabar, A. Dehghantanha, N.I. Udzir, N.F.b.M. Sani, S. bin Shamsuddin, Towards secure model for SCADA systems, in *2012 International Conference on Cyber Security, Cyber Warfare and Digital Forensic (CyberSec)* (June 2012), pp. 60–64

12. E.M. Dovom, A. Azmoodeh, A. Dehghantanha, D.E. Newton, R.M. Parizi, H. Karimipour, Fuzzy pattern tree for edge malware detection and categorization in IoT. J. Syst. Archit. **97**, 1–7 (2019)

13. S. Dua, X. Du, *Data Mining and Machine Learning in Cybersecurity* (Auerbach Publications, Boca Raton, 2016)

14. G. Epiphaniou, T. French, H. Al-Khateeb, A. Dehghantanha, H. Jahankhani, A novel anonymity quantification and preservation model for undernet relay networks, in ed. by H. Jahankhani, A. Carlile, D. Emm, A. Hosseinian-Far, G. Brown, G. Sexton, A. Jamal. *Global Security, Safety and Sustainability - The Security Challenges of the Connected World* (Springer International Publishing, Cham, 2016), pp. 371–384

15. I. Ghafir, M. Hammoudeh, V. Prenosil, L. Han, R. Hegarty, K. Rabie, F.J. Aparicio-Navarro, Detection of advanced persistent threat using machine-learning correlation analysis. Futur. Gener. Comput. Syst. **89**, 349–359 (2018)

16. S. Gerris, H. Karimipour, A feature selection-based approach for joint cyber-attack detection and state estimation, in *IEEE International Conference on Smart Energy Grid Engineering (SEGE)* (2019), pp. 1–5

17. T.R. Glass-Vanderlan, M.D. Iannacone, M.S. Vincent, Q. Chen, R.A. Bridges, A survey of intrusion detection systems leveraging host data, in *CoRR* (2018). http://arxiv.org/abs/1805.06070

18. I. Goodfellow, Y. Bengio, A. Courville, *Deep Learning* (MIT press, Cambridge, 2016)

19. S. Grooby, T. Dargahi, A. Dehghantanha, *Protecting IoT and ICS Platforms Against Advanced Persistent Threat Actors: Analysis of APT1, Silent Chollima and Molerats* (Springer International Publishing, Cham, 2019), pp. 225–255

20. S. Homayoun, A. Dehghantanha, M. Ahmadzadeh, S. Hashemi, R. Khayami, Know abnormal, find evil: Frequent pattern mining for ransomware threat hunting and intelligence. IEEE Trans. Emerg. Top. Comput. 1–1 (2017). https://doi.org/10.1109/TETC.2017.2756908

21. S. Homayoun, M. Ahmadzadeh, S. Hashemi, A. Dehghantanha, R. Khayami, *BoTShark: A Deep Learning Approach for Botnet Traffic Detection* (Springer International Publishing, Cham, 2018), pp. 137–153

22. S. Homayoun, A. Dehghantanha, M. Ahmadzadeh, S. Hashemi, R. Khayami, K.-K.R. Choo, D.E. Newton, DRTHIS: deep ransomware threat hunting and intelligence system at the fog layer. Futur. Gener. Comput. Syst. **90**, 94–104 (2019)

23. H. Karimipour, V. Dinavahi, Robust massively parallel dynamic state estimation of power systems against cyber-attack. IEEE Access **6**, 2984–2995 (2018). https://doi.org/10.1109/ACCESS.2017.2786584

24. H. Karimipour, A. Dehghantanha, R.M. Parizi, K.R. Choo, H. Leung, A deep and scalable unsupervised machine learning system for cyber-attack detection in large-scale smart grids. IEEE Access **7**, 80778–80788 (2019)

25. H. Karimipour, S. Geris, A. Dehghantanha, H. Leung, *Intelligent Anomaly Detection for Large-Scale Smart Grids* (IEEE, Piscataway, 2019), pp. 1–4

26. D. Kong, G. Yan:, Discriminant malware distance learning on structural information for automated malware classification, in *Proceedings of the 19th ACM SIGKDD International Conference on Knowledge Discovery and Data Mining, KDD '13* (ACM (2013), pp. 1357–1365. https://doi.org/10.1145/2487575.2488219

27. Y. LeCun, Y. Bengio, G. Hinton, Deep learning. Nature **521**(7553), 436 (2015)

28. N. Milosevic, A. Dehghantanha, K.K.R. Choo, Machine learning aided android malware classification. Comput. Electr. Eng. **61**, 266–274 (2017)
29. S. Mohammadi, V. Desai, H. Karimipour, *Multivariate Mutual Information-Based Feature Selection for Cyber Intrusion Detection* (2018), pp. 1–6. https://doi.org/10.1109/EPEC.2018.8598326
30. S. Mohammadi, H. Mirvaziri, M. Ghazizadeh-Ahsaee, H. Karimipour, Cyber intrusion detection by combined feature selection algorithm. J. Inf. Secur. Appl. **44**, 80–88 (2019). https://doi.org/10.1016/j.jisa.2018.11.007. http://www.sciencedirect.com/science/article/pii/S2214212618304617
31. Y. Noh, B. Zhang, D.D. Lee, Generative local metric learning for nearest neighbor classification. IEEE Trans. Pattern Anal. Mach. Intell. **40**(1), 106–118 (2018). https://doi.org/10.1109/TPAMI.2017.2666151
32. O. Osanaiye, K.K.R. Choo, M. Dlodlo, Distributed denial of service (DDoS) resilience in cloud: review and conceptual cloud ddos mitigation framework. J. Netw. Comput. Appl. **67**, 147–165 (2016)
33. H.H. Pajouh, R. Javidan, R. Khayami, D. Ali, K.K.R. Choo, A two-layer dimension reduction and two-tier classification model for anomaly-based intrusion detection in iot backbone networks. IEEE Trans. Emerg. Top. Comput. **7**, 314–323 (2016)
34. H.H. Pajouh, G. Dastghaibyfard, S. Hashemi, Two-tier network anomaly detection model: a machine learning approach. J. Intell. Inf. Syst. **48**(1), 61–74 (2017)
35. M. Panda, A. Abraham, M.R. Patra, A hybrid intelligent approach for network intrusion detection. Proc. Eng. **30**, 1–9 (2012)
36. J. Sakhnini, H. Karimipour, A. Dehghantanha, Smart grid cyber attacks detection using supervised learning and heuristic feature selection, in *IEEE International Conference on Smart Energy Grid Engineering (SEGE)* (2019), pp. 1–5
37. J. Sakhnini, H. Karimipour, A. Dehghantanha, R. Parizi, G. Srivastava, Security aspects of internet of things aided smart grids: a bibliometric survey. Elsevier J. Internet Things 1–13 (2019). https://doi.org/10.1016/j.iot.2019.100111
38. F. Salo, A.B. Nassif, A. Essex, Dimensionality reduction with IG-PCA and ensemble classifier for network intrusion detection. Comput. Netw. **148**, 164–175 (2019). https://doi.org/10.1016/j.comnet.2018.11.010. http://www.sciencedirect.com/science/article/pii/S1389128618303037
39. K. Selvakumar, M. Karuppiah, L. SaiRamesh, S.H. Islam, M.M. Hassan, G. Fortino, K.K.R. Choo, Intelligent temporal classification and fuzzy rough set-based feature selection algorithm for intrusion detection system in WSNs. Inf. Sci. **497**, 77–90 (2019). https://doi.org/10.1016/j.ins.2019.05.040. http://www.sciencedirect.com/science/article/pii/S0020025519304438
40. A. Shalaginov, S. Banin, A. Dehghantanha, K. Franke, *Machine Learning Aided Static Malware Analysis: A Survey and Tutorial* (Springer International Publishing, Cham, 2018), pp. 7–45
41. D. Tao, L. Jin, Y. Wang, Y. Yuan, X. Li, Person re-identification by regularized smoothing kiss metric learning. IEEE Trans. Circuits Syst. Video Tech. **23**(10), 1675–1685 (2013)
42. M. Tavallaee, E. Bagheri, W. Lu, A.A. Ghorbani, A detailed analysis of the kdd cup 99 data set, in *2009 IEEE Symposium on Computational Intelligence for Security and Defense Applications* (IEEE, Piscataway, 2009), pp. 1–6
43. T.Wen, Z. Zhang, Deep convolution neural network and autoencoders-based unsupervised feature learning of eeg signals. IEEE Access **6**, 25399–25410 (2018)
44. Y. Xin, L. Kong, Z. Liu, Y. Chen, Y. Li, H. Zhu, M. Gao, H. Hou, C. Wang, Machine learning and deep learning methods for cybersecurity. IEEE Access **6**, 35365–35381 (2018)
45. W. Xuren, H. Famei, X. Rongsheng, Modeling intrusion detection system by discovering association rule in rough set theory framework, in *2006 International Conference on Computational Inteligence for Modelling Control and Automation and International Conference on Intelligent Agents Web Technologies and International Commerce (CIMCA'06)* (2006), pp. 24–24
46. L. Yang, R. Jin, Distance metric learning: a comprehensive survey. Mich. State Univ. **2**(2), (2006)

47. M. Yousefi-Azar, V. Varadharajan, L. Hamey, U. Tupakula, Autoencoder-based feature learning for cyber security applications, *2017 International Joint Conference on Neural Networks (IJCNN)* (2017), pp. 3854–3861. https://doi.org/10.1109/IJCNN.2017.7966342
48. J. Zhang, M. Zulkernine, A. Haque, Random-forests-based network intrusion detection systems. IEEE Trans. Syst. Man, Cybern., Part C (Applications and Reviews) **38**, 649–659 (2008)
49. F. Zhang, H.A.D.E. Kodituwakku, W. Hines, J.B. Coble, Multi-layer data-driven cyber-attack detection system for industrial control systems based on network, system and process data. IEEE Trans. Indust. Inf., 1–1 (2019). https://doi.org/10.1109/TII.2019.2891261

Chapter 17
Malware Elimination Impact on Dynamic Analysis: An Experimental Machine Learning Approach

Mohammad Nassiri, Hamed HaddadPajouh, Ali Dehghantanha (iD),
Hadis Karimipour, Reza M. Parizi, and Gautam Srivastava

1 Introduction

Malware includes any malicious software that enters a computer system with intentions of sabotage. According to the annual report by Ponemon Institute, 11.7 million dollars spent on cybersecurity in 2018 [19]. Daily increasing expansion of malware is indicative of the idea that the developers are highly interested in gaining profits through them. The emergence of digital currency has caused issues in legally ramifications for cyber-criminals [3]. Computer system misuses have reached their highest peak [8]. Against such threats, the techniques of malware analysis has also been advanced [17], and we are now bearing witness to the development of new methods of malware identification. Malware analysis is divided into two groups, named as static and dynamic [10, 12]. Static analysis recognizes the malicious behaviour of software with no need to actually run it. There are many constraints in this method of analysis, including the obfuscation technique and encoding methods

M. Nassiri
Computer Engineering Department, Urmia University, Urmia, Iran

H. HaddadPajouh (✉) · A. Dehghantanha
Cyber Science Lab, University of Guelph, Guelph, ON, Canada
e-mail: hamed@cybersciencelab.org; ali@cybersciencelab.org

H. Karimipour
School of Engineering, University of Guelph, Guelph, ON, Canada
e-mail: hkarimi@uoguelph.ca; Canada-hkarimi@uoguelph.ca

R. M. Parizi
College of Computer and Software Engineering, Kennesaw State University, Marietta, GA, USA
e-mail: rparizi1@kennesaw.edu

G. Srivastava
Department of Mathematics and Computer Science, Brandon University, Brandon, MB, Canada
e-mail: srivastavag@brandonu.ca

© Springer Nature Switzerland AG 2020
K.-K. R. Choo, A. Dehghantanha (eds.), *Handbook of Big Data Privacy*,
https://doi.org/10.1007/978-3-030-38557-6_17

359

[15]. As a result, dynamic analysis entered the field to reduce the limitations of static analysis. An executable sample of malware runs in this method, and its behaviour is observed as it runs [22].

The main problem in dynamic analysis is the omission of many of the samples from the dataset. This is due to improper running and crashing of logs files. By running improperly, the cause of corruption by malware in the virtual machine and the subsequent improper forwarding of the log files to the server is the result. Additionally, a log file may be useless if not satisfying the executable sample in the Sandbox environments (Virtual Machine). Such malware usually serves specific purposes, and written for a system featuring specific characteristics or making use of protectors preventing their execution in the virtual machine or under the supervision of an observer. Due to the same reason, researchers clear any logs sized below 70 Kb [20] or files where the logs below are 10 APIs record [1]. The other cases cause the results to be optimum only under experimental conditions, and improper results would be obtained in case of entering the samples that are either part of or similar to the eliminated samples.

In this chapter, the static and dynamic analysis methods are combined to present an appropriate hybrid solution. Outstanding results were obtained with no deletion of samples from the dataset, even ones having used the packing method. For reaching the desirable result, conducting of dynamic analysis on software, and also not eliminating samples even if problems occur. In contrast, static analysis is carried out on the experimented sample as a substitution and a preliminary detection only serves as a preliminary prevention.

1.1 Static Analysis

In the static analysis method, the experimented sample is not executed, which causes the offering of numerous methods for bypassing it. One such solution widely applied in static analysis is the use of Optional Headers in the Portable Executable (PE) structure and then supervising the Import Table section [13, 16]. PE is a structure that every file that runs on the Microsoft Windows operating system has to follow. In the Import Table section in PE structure, the entire API is required by the program to be used so that the PE can adequately execute. As a result, it is clear that techniques such as dynamic API calling or unnecessary APIs, used only for misleading, can be applied to bypass the method. After extracting the name of APIs from the Import Table portion, a list names is created and used in the data mining process. Figure 17.1 illustrates an example of the Import Table and its functions that pertain to malware.

OFTs	FTs (IAT)	Hint	Name
Dword	Dword	Word	szAnsi
00011208	00011208	04EF	VirtualProtect
0001121A	0001121A	0218	GetModuleHandleW
0001122E	0001122E	01EC	GetFileInformationByHandle
0001124C	0001124C	0464	SetFileInformationByHandle
0001126A	0001126A	000C	AddSecureMemoryCacheCallback
0001128A	0001128A	009A	CreateMemoryResourceNotification
000112AE	000112AE	016B	GetApplicationRecoveryCallback
000112D0	000112D0	01F5	GetFinalPathNameByHandleW
000112EC	000112EC	0212	GetMaximumProcessorGroupCount
0001130C	0001130C	021D	GetNamedPipeClientComputerNa...
00011814	00011814	008F	CreateFileW

Fig. 17.1 Functions of Import Table of a malware's PE

1.2   Dynamic Analysis

A method that is complementary to static analysis is called dynamic analysis. In this approach, the examined sample executes, and its behaviour is investigated and recorded during execution. The entire APIs recalling cases, input arguments, and functions' outputs as well as all the registry values are recorded and stored in log files. These log files, which usually have XML format, are transferred to the next stage and processed. Next, they are ready to be applied in a data mining phase.

2   Related Work

To perform a study of the works done in this regard, Sami et al. [21] offered a static analysis to discover malware. In their study, the required properties were preliminary extracted from PE following which the Fisher algorithm was applied to score the properties so that those repeatedly utilized in data mining could be determined and used. The selection matrix obtained from this part transferred as an input to the data mining algorithm. In the data mining phase, they made use of WEKA software [25], which is an open-source software frequently employed by many researchers. The majority of the data mining and classification algorithms are implemented in this tool which makes is very useful. Their proposed method showed an accuracy rate of 98.3%.

Based on static analysis, Belaoued et al. [4] dealt with the statistical study of the APIs used in the majority of malware. They, as well, extracted their required properties from PE in a static manner and then selected the frequently repeated one among them. To determine whether an API was used in the malware or not, they utilized the Chi-Square test. This also assisted in learning if it has a positive effect on data mining. The results obtained in their study indicated that the malware mostly applies the functions used for the creation of new processes, replications, reading, and writing in memory. They extracted from the system functions obtained for the malicious and benign files over 60 cases with the highest frequency in each group. In the end, the experiments and Chi-Square test provided for the extraction of 22 of the most important APIs recalled by the malware. The selected functions are from three libraries, named *Advapi32.dll, Kerel32.dll* and *User32.dll*.

In [5], we see the use of static analysis to perform Multiple Comparison Analysis (MCA) for the detection of APIs used in each specific group of malware. 12 special groups of malware were applied in the study, and each contained 10 PE files. In total, 120 PE files were analyzed for malware and 90 other PE files were taken into account for the benign files. The APIs used in PE files were extracted using static analysis, and 30% of the APIs with the highest iteration applied in the end. After the creation of the MCA matrix, it is fed into statistical software. Moreover, the output of the software determines the classification of the malware groups in the end. Also, Manhattan distance was used to perform APIs assignment to each of the groups. Once the distance between an API and the defined threshold, the API is assigned to the group. This research was a supplement to their prior studies in [4] and the APIs extracted from it classified in the malware groups.

There are numerous studies undertaken in dynamic analysis. Ding et al. [9] employed Object-Oriented Association Mining and focused on the cost and time reduction for experimenting and classifying the malware groups. The main problem of these methods arises when the number of association rules becomes too many with the reduction of minimum support following which a considerable time has to be spent on malware analysis. The objective of their work is increasing OOA speed with an emphasis on the following two principles:

- Increasing the quality of the association rules
- Increasing the accuracy of classification in OOA

First, useless APIs are eliminated. This causes an increase in quality and speed. Consequently, API datasets incorporate APIs used in the sample dataset sample formed otherwise the intended API is eliminated. As for the benign cases, as well, the APIs list is extracted only employing the static method. The dataset used in their study gave 6181 APIs out of which 1000 frequently applied functions were selected, and the information gain algorithm was subsequently utilized to select the functions with the highest rate of turbulence. In their method, a min_obj_support value makes it clear whether the function used both in the malicious and benign software should be retained or deleted from the dataset. In summary, their method is twice as fast and provides an accuracy rate of 91.2% as compared to basic OOA.

Yang et al. [18] first extracted APIs list using dynamic analysis. The sample analysis reports have been excerpted from Cuckoo sandbox, usually used for dynamic analysis. This data is transformed into a data sequence to be input into Malheur Software for clustering and undergo classification. Also, BBIS was employed to analyze the reports and make preparations for clustering. They achieved an accuracy equal to 90.9% through accelerating the clustering and reducing the volume consumed by the reports.

Cho et al. [7] applied multiple sequence alignment to detect malware. The Cuckoo sandbox was utilized to extract the APIs. To be able to make use of the MSA method, the entire API tails should have a fixed length. Similarly, they have to be uniquely encoded. In their paper, 13 types of classification are applied in consideration for APIs. Each API is shown in a three-letter designation. The first letter is indicative of API classification and the rest are the indices used to set where the API belongs. For example, CAA is reflective of API's belonging to Process set. MSA is applied to find the standard segments in API tails in each family of malware. In the end, 15 malware groups were applied for evaluation, and the obtained results are generally suggestive of 83% accuracy.

Fan et al. [11] extracted APIs through dynamic analysis. Their proposed method highly concentrated on APIs extraction in a dynamic manner and implementation of data mining on the logs extracted from software. In their study, two sets of the used essential functions have also been pointed out, with the functions required for the creation of a new process and the functions needed for performing code injection. For evaluation, two experiments were conducted. The first experiment encompassed 263 malware, and the second one used 773 malware. Both experiments included 251 benign software. Naive Bayes, SVM, and J48 were employed to perform classification. Also, k-fold cross-validation, with $k = 10$, was utilized. In the end, 180 features were obtained and the *InfoGainAttributeEval* algorithm was used to reduce it. This was followed with experiments being conducted for 20 to about 1800 features. The statistics are expressive of the idea that about 100 features provide an optimum result, and there is no need for performing experiments with a large number of features. In the last experiment, an accuracy of 95.3% was attained with a large number of malware and only 80 total features.

3   Proposed Method

In this study, the static and dynamic analysis methods are applied concomitantly. The method offered for hybrid analysis in this chapter, is presented in Fig. 17.2.

As shown in Fig. 17.2, the samples are examined in a virtual machine, and their behaviours recorded. Then, the obtained logs passed to the classification phase. There is a possibility of observing the unauthentic logs twice during execution and once during processing, in which case they are subjected to static analysis. Next, the

Fig. 17.2 Model of the
proposed method

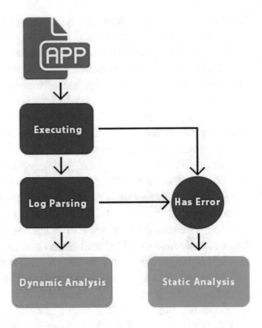

logs, as mentioned earlier, along with the logs obtained from the dynamic analysis,
are transferred to the classification phase.

3.1 Data Processing

Every sample has to undergo processing by a machine learning model. Regarding
the dynamic analysis, the sample should execute, and afterwards, its behaviour is
recorded. The bytes of the sample and its structure should be processed in static
analysis so that the useful information could be extracted from the APIs list used.

In previous work, there is a possibility of error emergence for samples in all
stages of executing, processing, and analysis before data mining. These types of
samples are omitted from the datasets, and they do not enter the classification phase.
However, the present study firstly explains why each of the errors has occurred, and
the analysis follows it so that the obtained results could be perfect and pervasive.

3.2 Virtual Environment Execution

In this phase, the samples are executed in a virtual machine so that their behaviours
can be recorded. One of the methods of monitoring the sample behaviour is the use
of hooking technique. In this method, a DLL is injected into examined software
address space. Then, there is a written jump code at the beginning of each function

that is required to investigate. Thus, the injected function could execute in place of the primary function. One of the highly applied software types in this regard is *WinAPIOverride32*, which is an open-source software type and perfectly fits such research tasks. Most of the previous works examined based manual execution of each sample and to store its corresponding log files. But the proposed method is replaced by the command line of *WinAPIOVerride32* software. Furthermore, the entire execution, recording, and management stages of the virtual machine is conducted automatically [6, 14, 26, 27]. Typically, each sample executed for about 2 min, and its behaviour was recorded. It is essential for a monitoring file capable of determining the functions required by a hook, of recording the sample behaviour using *WinAPIOVerride32*. The selection of the functions is crucial and can influence the classification task because such a selection determines the data mining features. A large number of the functions mentioned for monitoring purposes in this study are amongst the functions applied in Cuckoo sandbox [2].

In this stage of analysis, errors can come about in two forms. First, when the virtual machine is troubled, and the log file not appropriately transferred, or the malware affects the virtual machine and causes the misbehavior, saying, its network that causes the failure in log file sending. Second, when the studied sample fails working correctly due to the absence of its requirements, and an error emerges accordingly. Furthermore, this case can come about in some examples through the techniques used by malware developers in such a way that malware undergoes malfunctioning or does not execute its malicious part upon observing the virtual machine or under the supervision of a given software type. The technique is a method of bypassing the dynamic analysis. The researchers can seminally remove the first case from the dataset and the second case is eliminated when the sample file size investigated in such a manner that the researchers usually delete the files less than 70 KB size, or samples using log files below 10 APIs. In this chapter, static analysis is employed for the first and second case so that a preliminary result can be obtained by eliminating them and through a quick method. For the second scenario, there is a possibility of experimenting with dynamic analysis. In the beginning, data mining results obtained with no deletion of the sample. Therefore, the samples as mentioned earlier are analyzed statically in the next stage so that they can subject to data mining along with the other authentic examples brought in from the dynamic analysis part, and the result of these two stages compared with one another.

3.3   Log Processing

In discussions on the processing of logs, the samples' logs, usually in XML format, are parsed. Moreover, the features used in the classification task extracted in this section. There is a possibility of error emergence in this stage in such a way that XML file is imperfect or it has been corrupted during the transferring stage the result of which is its lack of proper obedience of XML structure following which it will not be parsed. In all of these cases, the file is deleted from the dataset by the researchers. In this method, static analysis conducted for these types of files after the detection of improper cases. After performing static analysis, the results obtained along with the other results from the dynamic analysis of the authentic samples will be allowed to enter data mining phase.

4 Dataset

The dataset used in this method is one of the most novel extant datasets. This dataset pertains to June 2018, and it has been procured from VirusShare Website [24]. Many of the studies performed on malware utilize the VXHeaven dataset [23]. This dataset is old and excellent results can be obtained in many of the cases through simple static analysis while many of the packing techniques are not applied thereto, though the majority of the researchers delete these files in case they come across them. In the present study, we use not only a new dataset but also none of the examined samples, and even the packed ones were not omitted so that the results could be completely pervasive. There are used 1056 software samples in the experiments out of which 550 were malware. The benign software used in the present study reaches a number equal to 506, and they have extracted from a newly installed Windows 7 system folder and several other verified resources.

5 Evaluation and Experimental Result

Three experimental scenarios for evaluating the proposed method were conducted. The first experiment deals with the investigation of omitting the logs with small sizes or the lack of using a minimum number, 10, of APIs. In this scenario, the possibility of making comparisons without using static analysis was verified since the samples able to execute and passe the first stage of monitoring. In the second experiment, the samples were eliminated due to the lack of correct execution, and the result of performing static analysis on them has been explained earlier. The final experiment, as well, deals with the pooling of the two above mentioned experiments so that the overall result of the implementation of the proposed method could be obtained. In the last experiment, all samples, even the packed cases, are involved, and the obtained results are a lot more pervasive than has been seen in similar research. Moreover, Python with the Scikit-learn library was applied to perform data mining. The algorithms selected for data mining from the aforesaid library were Random Forest, Decision Tree, Naive Bayes, and SVM. It is worth mentioning here that the k-fold cross-validation method, with $k = 10$, has been used in all experiments for authenticating the results. In this method, the dataset is divided into 10 sections, and each section is used once for the test and the other times for training so that the mean value of all the results could be announced as the final result in the end.

5.1 Experiment I

In this experiment, as it is observed in Table 17.1, the results of the dynamic analysis have been obtained for the dataset containing authentic log files and also the log files omitted for their smaller size. This shows the potential results of not eliminating these files. The best performance of the tested algorithms belongs to Random Forest with an accuracy of 92%.

Table 17.2, in contrast, indicates potential results in case of replacing the files featuring smaller sizes and having been obtained from dynamic analysis with files obtained from just static analysis. The experiment results are completely satisfactory and declares the proper functioning of the proposed method. In this stage, as well, Random Forest algorithm, with an accuracy equal to 97%, obtains the best result and the proposed method has succeeded in enhancing the accuracy by 5.43%.

Also, Fig. 17.3 shows the comparison of these two methods.

5.2 Experiment II

In experiment II, we show our results in Table 17.3. There are a few scenarios we focus on in this run. First, we look at all samples that could not be executed. Second, we look at samples that when executing the virtual machine found their execution to be problematic. Lastly, we focus on samples that have not generally undergone any dynamic analysis. Based on the obtained results, the best results were from Random Forest. The proposed method has been able to achieve very good accuracy at 97%.

Table 17.1 Results of classification on dynamic analyzed samples with the small size

Classifier	Accuracy	Precision	F1	Recall
Random Forest	0.92	0.98	0.91	0.88
Decision Tree	0.89	0.91	0.88	0.87
Naive Bayes	0.87	0.89	0.83	0.75
SVM	0.89	0.95	0.86	0.77

Table 17.2 Results of classification on static analyzed samples with the small size

Classifier	Accuracy	Precision	F1	Recall
Random Forest	0.97	0.99	0.97	0.96
Decision Tree	0.94	0.91	0.94	0.96
Naive Bayes	0.70	0.64	0.77	0.96
SVM	0.95	0.99	0.94	0.91

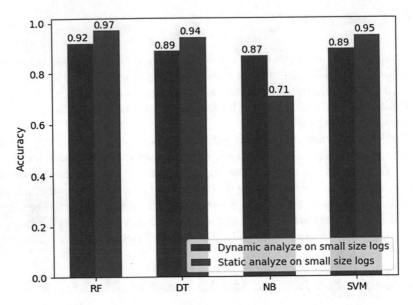

Fig. 17.3 Comparison of static and dynamic analysis of samples with the small size

Table 17.3 Results of classification of samples that could not be executed

Classifier	Accuracy	Precision	F1	Recall
Random Forest	0.97	0.99	0.98	0.98
Decision Tree	0.93	0.92	0.95	0.97
Naive Bayes	0.80	0.96	0.83	0.73
SVM	0.93	0.99	0.95	0.94

Table 17.4 Results of classification of all samples without any omitted

Classifier	Accuracy	Precision	F1	Recall
Random Forest	0.97	0.99	0.97	0.97
Decision Tree	0.95	0.93	0.95	0.96
Naive Bayes	0.65	0.61	0.74	0.98
SVM	0.95	0.99	0.95	0.94

5.3 Experiment III

In the final experiment, all of the samples were included to obtain a pervasive result without the elimination of any samples from the dataset. Table 17.4 is indicative of the results obtained from this experiment. The results indicated that the selected features and the implementation of the proposed method have been in a very good condition and the malware and software classes have been classified in an accuracy equal to 97%.

6 Conclusion

The expansion of the malware has caused offerings of new methods of malware analysis. Static analysis limitations have discouraged the use of this method alone. Additionally, sample elimination from datasets to increase detection accuracy dragged the present study towards the offering of a method for overcoming such problems. This chapter tries combining the two analyses and making use of a hybrid analysis so that the entire samples, both the ones with problems in execution and the ones using dynamic analysis bypassing techniques, could be examined. The proposed method showed that through carrying out three experiments on the unpack and packed samples which using bypassing techniques that it is capable of increasing the detection accuracy by 5.43% and getting it to a level as high as 97%. Furthermore, the results have been optimal for all of the samples without any omission in general and only a limited number of features provided for malware detection in an accuracy equal to 97%. The results here were obtained under up-to-date and new dataset examination, unlike prior studies. Efforts will be made in the future research to meet the software sample needs it is possible so that the samples could be subjected more increasingly to the dynamic analysis for its high detection accuracy.

References

1. M. Ahmadi, A. Sami, H. Rahimi, B. Yadegari, Malware detection by behavioural sequential patterns. Comput. Fraud Secur. **2013**(8), 11–19 (2013)
2. Automated Malware Analysis, Cuckoo sandbox—automated malware analysis. https://cuckoosandbox.org/. Accessed 17 Aug 2018
3. P.N. Bahrami, A. Dehghantanha, T. Dargahi, R.M. Parizi, K.R. Choo, H.H.S. Javadi, Cyber kill chain-based taxonomy of advanced persistent threat actors: analogy of tactics, techniques, and procedures. J. Inf. Process. Syst. **15**(4), 865 889 (2019). https://doi.org/10.3745/JIPS.03.0126
4. M. Belaoued, S. Mazouzi, Statistical study of imported APIs by PE type malware, in *2014 International Conference on Advanced Networking Distributed Systems and Applications* (2014)
5. M. Belaoued, S. Mazouzi, Towards an automatic method for API association extraction for PE-malware categorization, in *Proceedings of the International Conference on Intelligent Information Processing, Security and Advanced Communication (IPAC15)* (2015)
6. L. Cheng, J. Liu, G. Xu, Z. Zhang, H. Wang, H.N. Dai, Y. Wu, W. Wang, SCTSC: a semi-centralized traffic signal control mode with attribute-based blockchain in IoVs. IEEE Trans. Comput. Soc. Syst. (in press). https://doi.org/10.1109/TCSS.2019.2904633
7. K. Cho, E.G. Im, Extracting representative API patterns of malware families using multiple sequence alignments, in *Proceedings of the 2015 Conference on Research in Adaptive and Convergent Systems (RACS)* (2015)
8. M. Damshenas, A. Dehghantanha, R. Mahmoud, A survey on malware propagation, analysis, and detection. Int. J. Cyber Secur. Digit. Forensics **2**(4), 10–30 (2013)
9. Y. Ding, X. Yuan, K. Tang, X. Xiao, Y. Zhang, A fast malware detection algorithm based on objective-oriented association mining. Comput. Secur. **39**, 315–324 (2013)

10. E.M. Dovom, A. Azmoodeh, A. Dehghantanha, D.E. Newton, R.M. Parizi, H. Karimipour, Fuzzy pattern tree for edge malware detection and categorization in IoT. J. Syst. Archit. **97**, 1–7 (2019). https://doi.org/10.1016/j.sysarc.2019.01.017

11. C.-I. Fan, H.-W. Hsiao, C.-H. Chou, Y.-F. Tseng, Malware detection systems based on API log data mining, in *2015 IEEE 39th Annual Computer Software and Applications Conference* (2015)

12. E. Gandotra, D. Bansal, S. Sofat, Malware analysis and classification: a survey. J. Inf. Secur. **5**(2), 56–64 (2014)

13. H. HaddadPajouh, A. Dehghantanha, R. Khayami, K.K. Choo, A deep recurrent neural network based approach for Internet of Things malware threat hunting. Futur. Gener. Comput. Syst. **85**, 88–96 (2018)

14. Y. Ma, Y. Wu, J. Li, J. Ge, APCN: a scalable architecture for balancing accountability and privacy in large-scale content-based networks. Inf. Sci. (in press). https://doi.org/10.1016/j.ins. 2019.01.054

15. A. Moser, C. Kruegel, E. Kirda, Limits of static analysis for malware detection, in *Twenty-Third Annual Computer Security Applications Conference (ACSAC 2007)* (2007)

16. H.H. Pajouh, A. Dehghantanha, R. Khayami, K.K. Choo, Intelligent OS X malware threat detection with code inspection. J. Comput. Virol. Hack. Tech. **14**(3), 213–23 (2018)

17. R.M. Parizi, A. Dehghantanha, K.R. Choo, Towards better ocular recognition for secure real-world applications, in *2018 17th IEEE International Conference On Trust, Security And Privacy In Computing And Communications/12th IEEE International Conference On Big Data Science And Engineering (TrustCom/BigDataSE), New York* (2018), pp. 277–282

18. Y. Qiao, Y. Yang, J. He, C. Tang, Z. Liu, CBM: free, automatic malware analysis framework using API call sequences, in *Advances in Intelligent Systems and Computing Knowledge Engineering and Management* (2013), pp. 225–236

19. K. Richards, R. LaSalle, F.V.D. Dool, 2017 cost of cyber crime study. https://www.ponemon. org/library/2017-cost-of-cyber-crime-study. Accessed 14 Aug 2018

20. Z. Salehi, M. Ghiasi, A. Sami, A miner for malware detection based on API function calls, and their arguments, in *The 16th CSI International Symposium on Artificial Intelligence and Signal Processing (AISP 2012)* (2012)

21. A. Sami, B. Yadegari, N. Peiravian, S. Hashemi, A. Hamze, Malware detection based on mining API calls, in *Proceedings of the 2010 ACM Symposium on Applied Computing - SAC'10* (2010)

22. A. Shalaginov, S. Banin, A. Dehghantanha, K. Franke, Machine learning aided static malware analysis: a survey and tutorial, in *Cyber Threat Intelligence* (Springer, Cham, 2018), pp. 7–45

23. VirusShare, VirusShare.com. https://virusshare.com/. Accessed 17 Aug 2018

24. VX Heaven, http://83.133.184.251/virensimulation.org/. Accessed 17 Aug 2018

25. I.H. Witten, E. Frank, *Data Mining: Practical Machine Learning Tools and Techniques* (Morgan Kaufmann, Burlington, 2016)

26. Z. Yao, J. Ge, Y. Wu, L. Jian, A privacy preserved and credible network protocol. J. Parallel Distrib. Comput. **132**, 150–159 (2019)

27. R. Zhou, X. Zhang, X. Wang, G. Yang, H. Wang, Y. Wu, Privacy-preserving data search with fine-grained dynamic search right management in fog-assisted Internet of Things. Inf. Sci. **491**, 251–264 (2019)

Chapter 18
RAT Hunter: Building Robust Models for Detecting Remote Access Trojans Based on Optimum Hybrid Features

Mohammad Mehdi BehradFar, Hamed HaddadPajouh, Ali Dehghantanha ⓘ**, Amin Azmoodeh, Hadis Karimipour, Reza M. Parizi, and Gautam Srivastava**

1 Introduction

Malware is malfunction working software that can be used to steal information, compromise computer activities, bypassing access controls, or causing harm to its victim's system (even IoT devices [1, 2]). Malware is a broad term that refers to a variety of malicious programs. These include viruses, worms, trojans, rootkits, adware, spyware, and others [3]. Trojans refer to malicious software that runs in a normal way and seems useful but working in a malicious way [4, 5]. A Trojan malware usually opens access to the infected systems for malicious groups remotely. When an attacker accesses a victim's system, he/she will able to steal needed information, prepare the platform for installing more malware, edit files, monitor user activity and anonymous Internet activity [6].

M. M. BehradFar
Computer Engineering Department, Pishtazan Institute of Higher Education, Shiraz, Iran

H. HaddadPajouh (✉) · A. Dehghantanha · A. Azmoodeh
Cyber Science Lab, University of Guelph, Guelph, ON, Canada
e-mail: hamed@cybersciencelab.org; ali@cybersciencelab.org; amin@cybersciencelab.org

H. Karimipour
School of Engineering, University of Guelph, Guelph, ON, Canada
e-mail: hkarimi@uoguelph.ca; Canada-hkarimi@uoguelph.ca

R. M. Parizi
College of Computer and Software Engineering, Kennesaw State University, Marietta, GA, USA
e-mail: rparizi1@kennesaw.edu

G. Srivastava
Department of Mathematics and Computer Science, Brandon University, Brandon, MB, Canada
e-mail: srivastavag@brandonu.ca

© Springer Nature Switzerland AG 2020
K.-K. R. Choo, A. Dehghantanha (eds.), *Handbook of Big Data Privacy*,
https://doi.org/10.1007/978-3-030-38557-6_18

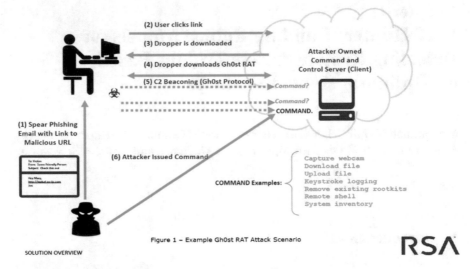

Figure 1 – Example Gh0st RAT Attack Scenario

SOLUTION OVERVIEW

Fig. 18.1 The process of malicious operation by gh0st RAT [9]

Remote Access Trojan (RAT) is a member of the trojan family. RAT works through an attacker who gains access to a system and is able to control the victim's system by sending commands, images, videos or any file type from wherever he/she wants. Predominantly even defensive mechanisms like Anti-Viruses cannot detect these types of malware. RAT attacks are generally carried out in the form of spear-phishing or social engineering [7, 8]. Figure 18.1 shows the process of infiltration and malware use of RAT [9] in gh0st RAT from APT18 [10].

When the RAT is installed on the victim's computer system, the attacker can control the system through network connectivity and perform malicious activities such as:

- Infecting system files
- Download, send, delete and rename files
- Destroy hardware with overclocking
- System Registry modification
- Formatting Disk Drives
- Stealing passwords and credit card numbers
- Installing programs in stealth mode
- Voice recording with the microphone connected
- Display fake errors
- Recording and remote control of the victim's screen [11].

1.1   RAT Structure and Architecture

Remote Access Trojans are a class of Backdoors that are used to control the victim's machine remotely. It is a program or set of related programs that the hacker installs on the target system in order to access the system later. Backdoors can embed inside an email. The secret is that the hacker knows how to get access to the information without having to identify it, and use it to gain more access to the targeted system hack [12]. Before installing a backdoor, attackers asses the system in order to find the running services. Usually, the attacker installs a backdoor that adds a new service, giving the service an unrecognizable name, or using a service that has never been used or disabled in the process list [13].

The service generation technique is beneficial because when a hacking attempt occurs, the system administrator usually seeks out strange things on the system and leaves all inactive services untouched. Thus, the intruder can then access the system at any time without any identification. Backdoor services allow the intruder to have the highest level of access and permission to the system in most cases.

When the RAT starts up, it acts as an executable (exe) file, and it interacts with some registry keys that are responsible for starting the processing and creation of system services. Unlike conventional backdoor machines, RATs connect to the victim's system and always wrap with two files: one server file and another client file.

(a) the server file is installed on the victim's system
(b) the client file is used to control the victim's system.

One of the symptoms of an infected system is that it displays abnormal behavior [14], but in the system infected by RATs it is difficult to diagnose and track abnormal indications due to the following reasons:

- They will open legal ports on infected machines. For this reason, security products not detect as a bug.
- They imitate commercial and legal remote management tools.
- They use methods that do not make malware common.

The life cycle of each RAT from when it is initialized to their installation phase can be seen in Fig. 18.2 and counted as follows:

1. Select the target system by the attacker.
2. Stimulate the system to get specific software or open link or attachment.
3. Malware installation operations automatically and secretly on the victim system.
4. Start malware activity with the first system connected to the network.
5. Connect RAT to the Command and Control (C&C) server to receive control commands.
6. After connecting the system, it waits for receiving commands.
7. Receive information and conduct attacks.
8. Connect to the C&C server for updating information and getting instructions for future attacks or terminates itself.

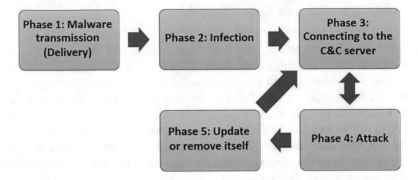

Fig. 18.2 RAT life cycle from initial to attack phase

In this chapter we propose an intelligence methodology for extracting a prominent feature set from RATs behaviors. The main contributions of this chapter for hunting RAT malware are listed as follows:

- Collecting an appropriate dataset from real-world RAT malware,
- Applying feature analyzing from dynamic analysis of RATs,
- And selecting the optimum hybrid (from dynamic and static) and prominent features for RAT hunting.

1.2 Measurement Metrics

To show the performance of the model we use statistical metrics in machine learning for malware detection as given in [15, 16].

1.2.1 Confusion Matrix

A confusion matrix is a summary of prediction results on a classification problem. Table 18.1 shows this matrix and its values. Each element of this matrix has a meaning as follows:

- **True Positive (TP):** the ratio of RATs sample which classified correctly.
- **True Negative (TN):** the ratio of RATs sample which classified as normal sample.
- **False Positive (FP):** the ratio of normal samples which classified as RAT.
- **False Negative (FN):** the ratio of normal samples which classified correctly.

There are some other statistical metrics that we used for evaluating of the proposed methodology as follows:

Table 18.1 Confusion matrix for RAT classification task

	Normal	RAT
Normal	TN	FP
RAT	TP	FN

$$\text{False Alarm Rate } (FAR) : \frac{FP}{FP + TN} \tag{18.1}$$

$$\text{Recall} : \frac{TP}{TP + FN} \tag{18.2}$$

$$\text{Accuracy } (ACC) : \frac{TP + TN}{TP + FP + TN + FN} \tag{18.3}$$

$$\text{Precision} : \frac{TP}{FP + TP} \tag{18.4}$$

$$F - measure : 2 * \frac{Precision * Recall}{Precision + Recall} \tag{18.5}$$

2   Related Work

The efforts for hunting RAT malware by machine learning approaches has increased in recent years. Jiang et al. [17] presented the idea of detecting RATs in the early stage of communication and implemented the process of detection. Their proposed method on the network behavior features which extract from the TCP header. Hence, their approach could execute quickly, even possible to detect an unknown RAT while it communicates through TCP protocol. DT and RF detection models of show better results than other machine learning algorithms in detecting RAT sessions, due to their accuracy of greater than 96% together with their FNR of less than 20%.

Wu et al. [14] proposed a framework to detect RATs at area network borders using time slicing algorithm to cut the IP flow into flow slices. They used frequent sequence mining to filter heartbeat and Naïve Bayes to classify the slices. Then, they performed tests on a week of their lab continuous traffic data and two types of internet traffic storage. The experiments on the datasets show their proposed methods are excellent in tracking external control and data exfiltration through analyzing only a few packets of the flows. Since the external control stands for a beginning or ongoing attack, their work meets actual demands for security. Their methods have worked well on real-world traces with a false positive rate of less than 0.6%.

Yamada et al. [18] analyzed the RAT-based reconnaissance behaviors on internal networks, and also proposed a detection technique for their communication sequences that based on the behavioral features. It extracts RAT connection candidates from the inbound and outbound communications, and the administrative operations analyzed from the protocol headers of SMB and DCE/RPC packets. It also integrates and detects the RAT connection candidates and related administrative communications. Their obtained results showed that the proposed technique can detect the reconnaissance of 99.26% of the 34 real RATs (29 families) on the experimental environment, and also accurately distinguish between the behaviors of the reconnaissance of Advanced Persistent Threat (APT) from that of the normal users on an actual organization's internal network.

Awad et al. [19] looked at a host-based framework introduced for RAT bot detection. The proposed framework depends on the behavior analysis of the running system of the host machine by capturing the running activities using the monitoring module. After that, a feature vector for each running process is constructed and sends to the classifier stage. In the classifier, the decision of whether this process is benign or malicious is taken raising the alarm to the administrator in malicious cases. Several classifiers at the classifier stage are evaluated choosing the best performance one. The proposed framework tested against unknown samples providing accuracy of about 95% with a low false-positive rate.

Kolosnjaji et al. [20] construct deep neural networks to improve modeling and classification of system calls sequences as also seen in [21]. By combining convolutional and recurrent layers in one neural network architecture, they obtain optimal classification results. Using a hybrid neural network containing two convolutional layers and one recurrent layer, they get a novel approach to malware classification. Their neural network outperforms not only other simpler neural architectures, but also previously widely-used Hidden Markov Models and Support Vector Machines.

Wang et al. [22] developed an automatic malware detection system by training an SVM classifier based on behavioral signatures. A cross-validation scheme used for solving classification accuracy problems by using SVMs associated with 60 families of real malware. The experimental results reveal that the classification error decreases as the sizing of testing data increased. For different sizing (N) of malware samples, the prediction accuracy of malware detection goes up to 98.7% with $N = 100$. The overall detection accuracy of the SVC is more than 85% for unspecific mobile malware.

Xu et al. [23], introduced a framework for malware detection based on online analysis of virtual memory access patterns using machine learning. This framework applied to the application-specific malware detection scenario which targets detecting malware-infected runs of known applications. They addressed the challenge of online memory data collection using a system/function-call epoch based memory access summary. They experimentally covered both kernel and user level threats and demonstrated very high detection accuracy against kernel-level rootkits (100% detection rate with less than 1% false positives) and user-level memory corruption attacks (99.0% detection rate with less than 5% false positives). A key value of the proposed methodology is using machine learning to determine malware signatures for classification in contrast to the traditional reliance on human insight, a major step in automating this critical analysis problem.

Fig. 18.3 The conducted research methodology for hunting RAT malware

3   Proposed Methodology

With regards to achieving an optimum model for RAT hunting, we investigated the characteristics of RAT malware, as shown in Fig. 18.3. After collecting the real-world samples from public repositories, we run them under Cuckoo Sandbox environment. The behavioral characteristics of this type of malware are vectorized in this environment. Next, we applied different machine learning models to obtain the best match model.

3.1   Dataset

In this chapter, we collected a batch of 450 real-world RAT samples and studied the behavior of this malware by optimized Cuckoo Sandbox environment. In order to detect malware with a behavioral analysis method, it is necessary to implement them to observe specific behavioral characteristics. Because of the inability to observe the exploitation of RAT malware during real-world execution of system resources and functions, it is essential to parse the given results that generated from running of the malicious sample. In this work, we developed a script to parse Cuckoo results for RAT hunting goal. We also collected benign wares samples from Microsoft Store platform.

For creating our dataset, we conducted both dynamic and static analysis. In the Static Analysis section, the DLL files were examined, and all relevant library functions recorded. Table 18.2 lists commonly used DLLs [24].

In the behavioral (dynamic) analysis section, all suspicious and distinct behavioral APIs between RAT and normal samples exploited in the file and network section.

RATs mainly rely on network-based invocations to do their malicious work on this platform by sending targeted communications between the hacker, the C&C server, and the victim machine. In this context, several Windows API functions are commonly used for these communications. Of the Windows network options, malware most commonly uses Berkeley compatible sockets, functionality that is almost identical on Windows and UNIX systems.

We implement Berkeley compatible sockets' network functionality in Windows in the Winsock libraries, primarily in ws2_32.dll. Of these, the

Table 18.2 Common DLLs in Windows executable files

DLL	Description
Kernel32.dll	This is a very common DLL that contains core functionality, such as access and manipulation of memory, files, and hardware
Advapi32.dll	This DLL provides access to advanced core Windows components such as the Service Manager and Registry
User32.dll	This DLL contains all the user-interface components, such as buttons, scroll bars, and components for controlling and responding to user actions
Gdi32.dll	This DLL contains functions for displaying and manipulating graphics
Ntdll.dll	This DLL is the interface to the Windows kernel. Executable generally do not import this file directly, although it is always imported indirectly by Kernel32.dll. If an executable imports this file, it means that the author intended to use functionality not normally available to Windows programs. Some tasks, such as hiding functionality or manipulating processes, will use this interface
WSock32.dll and Ws2_32.dll	These are networking DLLs. A program that accesses either of these most likely connects to a network or performs network-related tasks
Wininet.dll	This DLL contains higher-level networking functions that implement protocols such as FTP, HTTP, and NTP

Table 18.3 Berkeley compatible socket networking functions [24]

Function name	Description
Socket	Creates a socket
Connect	Attaches a socket to a particular port, prior to the accept call
Bind	Indicates that a socket will be listening for incoming connections
Listen	Opens a connection to a remote socket and accepts the connection
Accept	Opens a connection to a remote socket; the remote socket must be waiting for the connection
Send	Sends data to the remote socket
recv	Receives data from the remote socket

`socket`, `connect`, `bind`, `listen`, `accept`, `send`, and `recv` functions are the most common [24], and these are described in Table 18.3.

4   Experimental Results

In order to hunt the RAT samples, we applied feature selection process on the collected samples and observed empirical results from malware implementation in the sandbox environment, tracking suspicious behavioral activities. Clearly, we saw a tangible difference in the use of malware with benign files from Behavioral APIs. These differences were in file sections, networks, and dropped files. In this regard, the following features selected, and the relevant data recorded as follows:

- **DLL files:** Includes include and export DLL files name.

Table 18.4 Distributions of each class of the label which extracted from modified sandbox

Class of feature	Number of feature
DLL	69
Behavioral	129
Dropped file	37

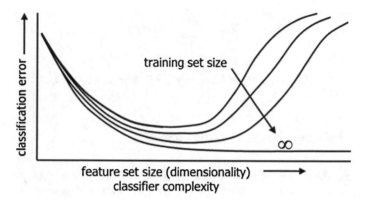

Fig. 18.4 Peaking phenomenon; with an increasing number of features from one point to the next, classification error increases [25]

- **Behavioral APIs**: include all API which called during the execution of malware under sandbox environment. This feature set also include networks features.
- **Dropped files:** This set consists the feature of dropped file that RAT downloaded and dropping in victim's system.

Table 18.4 also shows the distribution of each class of feature which extracted from the modified sandbox.

By summarizing the analysis of RATs, we eventually managed to create a data set with 235 attributes related to RAT files and normal files. Feature Selection, known as Variable Selection and Attribute Selection, as well as Variable Subset Selection, the sub-selection process is among the features [13]. A classifier error designed by real data displays a different behaviour in the mode of increasing the number of attributes. The increase in the number of attributes, in some cases, can lead to an increase in classification error. This is because in practical cases, the best number of features is not the highest number of features. Figure 18.4 shows the peaking phenomenon [25].

4.1   Information Gain

One way to achieve the goal is to eliminate unrelated or excess variables, and entropy mainly use in the information theory scale, which describes the net amount of an arbitrary set of specimens as seen in Eqs. (18.6) and (18.7). Entropy is the basis of various grading and selection methods in Information Gain [26]. This measure is considered an unpredictable scale of the system [19]. In this paper, with the implementation of this algorithm, the number of features from 235 attributes decreased to 149 ones.

$$E(S) = \sum_{2}^{C} -p \log_2 p_i \qquad (18.6)$$

$$Gain(T, X) = Entropy(T) - Entropy(T, X) \qquad (18.7)$$

4.2 Correlation-Based Feature Selection

We evaluate the value of a subset of attributes by using the ability to predict individual characteristics of each feature as well as the degree of redundancy between them. The subset of the features that match the class is preferred, compared to less consistency [27]. In this chapter, with the implementation of this algorithm, the number of features decreased from 235 to 45 using this criteria.

4.3 Classification

With regards to evaluation of the selected feature sets, we applied the traditional machine learning algorithms such as Bayes Network, Naive Bayes, K-Nearest Neighbor (with $K = 1, 3, 5$) trees/J48 as well as Convolutional Neural Network (CNN).

At the first stage of the classification task, we applied the machine learning models on the entire obtained features ($n = 235$) from Sandbox. The results of overall evaluation of the dataset before the Feature Selection procedure are given in Table 18.5.

By examining the impact of existing features, based on the classification results, the main features that are most important in the process of detecting healthy files and

Table 18.5 The obtained classification results before applying feature selection phase

Model	FAR	Precision	Recall	F-measure	Accuracy
Bayes network	0.115	0.907	0.885	88.30%	88.50%
Naive bayes	0.085	0.927	0.915	91.40%	91.50%
KNN ($K = 1$)	0.205	0.855	0.795	78.60%	79.50%
J48	0.03	0.97	0.97	97.00%	97.00%
Deep learning (CNN)	0.025	0.9737	0.925	94.87%	95.00%

RAT are distinguished. As shown in Fig. 18.5, the most important of these features are the connection functions.

By Applying the information gain algorithm, we obtained 149 features with the Ranker method, which results from the executed models as described in Table 18.6.

In the second round of the feature selection process, we applied Correlation-based feature selection algorithm and obtained promising results as it can be seen in Table 18.7.

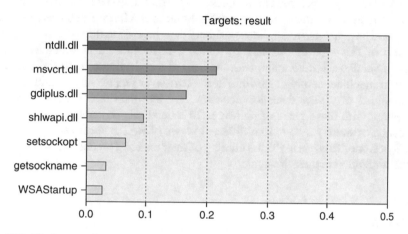

Fig. 18.5 The impact of prominent features on classification results

Table 18.6 The obtained classification results after applying feature selection phase (*No. of feature* = 149)

Model	FAR	Precision	Recall	*F*-measure	Accuracy
Bayes network	0.005	0.995	0.995	99.50%	**99.50%**
Naive bayes	0.003	0.998	0.998	99.70%	**99.75%**
KNN	0.05	0.955	0.95	95.00%	95.00%
J48	0.028	0.973	0.97	97.20%	97.25%
Deep learning (CNN)	**0**	**1**	**0.975**	**98.73%**	98.75%

The bold entries demonstrate the highest value which reached for each metric

Table 18.7 The obtained classification results after applying feature selection phase (*No. of Feature* = 45)

Model	FAR	Precision	Recall	*F*-measure	Accuracy
Bayes network	0.005	0.995	0.995	99.50%	99.50%
Naive bayes	0.003	0.998	**0.998**	**99.70%**	**99.75%**
KNN (*K* = 1)	0.05	0.955	0.95	95.00%	95.00%
J48	0.028	0.973	0.973	97.20%	97.25%
Deep learning (CNN)	**0**	**1**	0.975	98.73%	98.75%

The bold entries demonstrate the highest value which reached for each metric

5   Conclusion and Future Work

Malicious activities are entering a new phase in which malicious code, instead of infecting computers, seeks to access users' information for personal gain. Accordingly, the number of malware and its harmful effect are increasing. These attacks include various aspects such as blackmail, revenge, terror, information theft, and misuse. Amongst the total set of malware, Remote Access Trojans (RAT) have gained increasing popularity among hackers and information thieves. In this chapter, we presented an optimum feature set for hunting RATs. We collected over 400 real-world samples from a valid repository, then investigated over 235 behavioral features of this type of malware by running them under a modified version of Cuckoo Sandbox. Furthermore, with the help of a collection of data and execution different machine learning algorithm and a two-layer feature selection algorithms, we obtained over 99% detection accuracy and less than 0.03% false alarm rate in dealing with these types of malware. To extend this research, we propose the collection of more features from different views of RAT malware such as Opcode and ByteCode. This can assist the hunting of their exact intent and identify the stage of their infection in their life-cycle.

References

1. E.M. Dovom, A. Azmoodeh, A. Dehghantanha, D.E. Newton, R.M. Parizi, H. Karimipour, Fuzzy pattern tree for edge malware detection and categorization in IoT. J. Syst. Archit. **97**, 1–7 (2019). https://doi.org/10.1016/j.sysarc.2019.01.017
2. J. Sakhnini, H. Karimipour, A. Dehghantanha, R.M. Parizi, G. Srivastava, Security aspects of internet of things aided smart grids: a bibliometric survey. Internet of Things **2019**, 100111 (2019). https://doi.org/10.1016/j.iot.2019.100111
3. R.T. Shoniwa, G. George, Scanning tool for the detection of images embedded with malicious programs, in *2015 International Conference on Electrical, Electronics, Signals, Communication and Optimization (EESCO)* (2015)
4. D. Kiwia, A. Dehghantanha, K.-K.R. Choo, J. Slaughter, A cyber kill chain based taxonomy of banking Trojans for evolutionary computational intelligence. J. Comput. Sci. **27**, 394–409 (2018)
5. P.N. Bahrami, A. Dehghantanha, T. Dargahi, R.M. Parizi, K.R. Choo, H.H.S. Javadi, Cyber kill chain-based taxonomy of advanced persistent threat actors: analogy of tactics, techniques, and procedures. J. Inf. Process. Syst. **15**, 865–889 (2019). https://doi.org/10.3745/JIPS.03.0126
6. S.C. Pallaprolu, J.M. Namayanja, V.P. Janeja, C.S. Adithya, Label propagation in big data to detect remote access Trojans, in *2016 IEEE International Conference on Big Data (Big Data)* (IEEE, Piscataway, 2016), pp. 3539–3547
7. R. HosseiniNejad, H. HaddadPajouh, A. Dehghantanha, R. M. Parizi, A cyber kill chain based analysis of remote access Trojans, in *Handbook of Big Data and IoT Security*, ed. by A. Dehghantanha, K.-K.R. Choo (Springer, Cham, 2019), pp. 273–299. https://doi.org/10.1007/978-3-030-10543-3_12
8. T. Dargahi, A. Dehghantanha, P.N. Bahrami, M. Conti, G. Bianchi, L. Benedetto, A Cyber-Kill-Chain based taxonomy of crypto-ransomware features. J. Comput. Virol. Hack Tech. **15**(4), 277–305 (2019). https://doi.org/10.1007/s11416-019-00338-7

9. S. Samuel, J. Graham, C. Hinds, Hunting Malware: An example using Gh0st, in *2017 International Conference on Computational Science and Computational Intelligence (CSCI)* (IEEE, 2017 Dec), pp. 97–102

10. H. Mwiki, T. Dargahi, A. Dehghantanha, K.-K.R. Choo, Analysis and triage of advanced hacking groups targeting western countries critical national infrastructure: APT28, RED October, and Regin, in *Critical Infrastructure Security and Resilience* (Springer, Berlin, 2019), pp. 221–244

11. M. Rezaeirad, B. Farinholt, H. Dharmdasani, P. Pearce, K. Levchenko, D. McCoy, Schrödinger's RAT: profiling the stakeholders in the remote access Trojan ecosystem, in *27th USENIX Security Symposium (USENIX Security 18)* (2018), pp. 1043–1060

12. M. Mimura, Y. Otsubo, H. Tanaka, Evaluation of a brute forcing tool that extracts the rat from a malicious document file, in *2016 11th Asia Joint Conference on Information Security (AsiaJCIS)* (IEEE, Piscataway, 2016), pp. 147–154

13. A. Pektaş, T. Acarman, Classification of malware families based on runtime behaviors. J. Inform. Secur. Appl. **37**, 91–100 (2017)

14. S. Wu, S. Liu, W. Lin, X. Zhao, S. Chen, Detecting remote access Trojans through external control at area network borders, in *Proceedings of the Symposium on Architectures for Networking and Communications Systems* (IEEE Press, New York, 2017), pp. 131–141

15. H.H. Pajouh, G. Dastghaibyfard, S. Hashemi, Two-tier network anomaly detection model: a machine learning approach. J. Intell. Inf. Syst. **48**(1), 61–74 (2017). https://doi.org/10.1007/s10844-015-0388-x

16. R.M. Parizi, A. Dehghantanha, K.-K.R. Choo, A. Singh, Empirical vulnerability analysis of automated smart contracts security testing on blockchains, in *Proceedings of the 28th Annual International Conference on Computer Science and Software Engineering, CASCON '18* (2018), pp. 103–113

17. D. Jiang, K. Omote, An approach to detect remote access Trojan in the early stage of communication, in *2015 IEEE 29th International Conference on Advanced Information Networking and Applications* (IEEE, Piscataway, 2015), pp. 706–713

18. M. Yamada, M. Morinaga, Y. Unno, S. Torii, M. Takenaka, RAT-based malicious activities detection on enterprise internal networks, in *2015 10th International Conference for Internet Technology and Secured Transactions (ICITST)* (IEEE, Piscataway, 2015), pp. 321–325

19. A.A. Awad, S.G. Sayed, S.A. Salem, A network-based framework for RAT-bots detection, in *2017 8th IEEE Annual Information Technology, Electronics and Mobile Communication Conference (IEMCON)* (IEEE, Piscataway, 2017), pp. 128–133

20. B. Kolosnjaji, A. Zarras, G. Webster, C. Eckert, Deep learning for classification of malware system call sequences, in *Australasian Joint Conference on Artificial Intelligence* (Springer, 2016), pp. 137–149

21. H. HaddadPajouh, A. Dehghantanha, R. Khayami, K.-K.R. Choo, A deep Recurrent Neural Network based approach for Internet of Things malware threat hunting. Futur. Gener. Comput. Syst. **85**, 88–96 (2018)

22. P. Wang, Y.-S. Wang, Malware behavioural detection and vaccine development by using a support vector model classifier. J. Comput. Syst. Sci. **81**(6), 1012–1026 (2015)

23. Z. Xu, S. Ray, P. Subramanyan, S. Malik, Malware detection using machine learning based analysis of virtual memory access patterns, in *Proceedings of the Conference on Design, Automation and Test in Europe, European Design and Automation Association* (2017), pp. 169–174

24. M. Sikorski, A. Honig, *Practical Malware Analysis: The Hands-on Guide to Dissecting Malicious Software* (No Starch Press, San Francisco, 2012)

25. J.M. Van Campenhout, On the peaking of the Hughes mean recognition accuracy: The resolution of an apparent paradox. IEEE Trans. Syst. Man Cybern. **8**(5), 390–395 (1978 May)

26. Y. Yang, J.O. Pedersen, A comparative study on feature selection in text categorization, in *Proceedings of the International Conference on Machine Learning*, vol. 97 (1997), p. 35

27. M.A. Hall, Correlation-based feature selection for machine learning. Ph.D Thesis, The University of Waikato, Hamilton, 1999

Chapter 19
Active Spectral Botnet Detection Based on Eigenvalue Weighting

Amin Azmoodeh, Ali Dehghantanha ⓘ **, Reza M. Parizi, Sattar Hashemi, Bahram Gharabaghi, and Gautam Srivastava**

1   Introduction

Advances in a computerized system and its penetration to all aspects of life has motivated cyber-criminals to target these systems so as to attain private and sensitive stored information or cause disorders in their services [17]. A typical botnet is a network of infected systems such as computer, an Internet of Things node or smartphone that are controlled by cyber attackers to scheme a massive harmful attack [4, 23, 38]. Botnets can be used to drop malicious programs [24], re-distribute malware [18, 29], and even run Denial of Service (DoS) attacks [37].

Recognizing botnets and their attacks is an active research sphere in computer security and several approaches have been proposed for botnet detection [5, 49]. Machine learning techniques have demonstrated their potential for robust and accurate botnet detection [8]. Zhang et al. [50] proposed a system that identified the

A. Azmoodeh (✉) · A. Dehghantanha
Cyber Science Lab, University of Guelph, Guelph, ON, Canada
e-mail: amin@cybersciencelab.org; ali@cybersciencelab.org

R. M. Parizi
College of Computer and Software Engineering, Kennesaw State University, Marietta, GA, USA
e-mail: rparizi1@kennesaw.edu

S. Hashemi
Department of Computer Science and Engineering, Shiraz University, Shiraz, Iran
e-mail: s_hashemi@shirazu.ac.ir

B. Gharabaghi
School of Engineering, University of Guelph, Guelph, ON, Canada
e-mail: bgharaba@uoguelph.ca

G. Srivastava
Department of Mathematics and Computer Science, Brandon University, Brandon, MB, Canada
e-mail: srivastavag@brandonu.ca

© Springer Nature Switzerland AG 2020
K.-K. R. Choo, A. Dehghantanha (eds.), *Handbook of Big Data Privacy*,
https://doi.org/10.1007/978-3-030-38557-6_19

probable host in a Peer-to-Peer botnet and then statistically generated a profile for network traffic and distinguished between them to identify malicious activities using a flow-based clustering algorithm. Stevanovic and Pedersen [44] presented a flow-based method that analyzed network traffic and employed traditional supervised machine learning algorithms such as a Bayesian network, Neural Network and Support Vector Machines and accurately detected botnets. Homayoun et al. [23] introduced a deep learning-based botnet traffic analyzer called *BotShark* that uses only network transactions and therefore, avoiding inherent restrictions such as the inability to analyze encrypted data and precisely identified botnets.

Clustering is a prevalent machine learning technique for botnet detection [33]. *BotMiner*, proposed by Gu et al. in [21], clustered malicious and benign network traffic and performed cross cluster correlation to detect bots that share both similar communication and malicious activity patterns. In related work, Al-Jarrah et al. [2] proposed a novel traffic based intrusion detection system by data reduction and feature selection, randomized data partitioning, and recognize malicious activities using comparison with the center of clusters.

Graph mining is an active and promising research area to apply to cybersecurity problems [3, 22]. Graph clustering is a broad category of machine learning which aims to group vertices of a given graph based on its edges structure and discover densely connected groups of nodes in a graph [12, 13, 31]. Graph clustering is an inherent issue in a wide-range of application such as community detection in social networks, VLSI design, image processing, bioinformatics and and many others [39]. There are two main categories in graph clustering, namely Local and Global methods. Local methods are mainly based on a local search criteria and crawl inside the graph to partially discover partitions and find locally optimal clusters [43]. On the other hand, global methods cluster the vertices by considering the entire structure of the graph and make an effort to minimizing a partitioning criterion.

Spectral Clustering [35] as a subset of global clustering algorithms utilizes eigenspace properties of the graph to perform clustering. Similar to the majority of graph clustering algorithms, spectral methods presume that the adjacency matrix of the graph is wholly available and use their intended eigen-decomposition [15] for clustering. However in wide-range of problems preparation of similarity matrix arises a potential cost, uncertainty or unavailability.

The rest of the chapter is organized as follows. In Sect. 2 we briefly review related subjects such as spectral clustering, active learning, perturbation theory. Section 3 is dedicated to describing related methods and Sect. 4 contains the proposed method and three suggestions regarding eigenvalue weighting. Section 5 presents the experiments on botnet dataset and in Sect. 6, we discuss the proposed method and some future agenda is suggested.

2   Background

2.1   Spectral Clustering

Spectral Clustering [3, 35] is a significant, analytical and prevalent category of global graph clustering algorithms which leverages eigen-decomposition of a graph's matrix to cluster vertices. These methods are an alternative solution for the graph partitioning problem and have demonstrated performance especially when the dataset contains complex data shape and structure. Spectral methods embed the graph into eigenspace and run a traditional clustering algorithm such as K-means [27] on it. Basic and major reference study for this field was proposed by Shi and Malik in [42]. The authors start with a normalized cut criteria, convert it to linear algebra and finally solve it somehow answer proves eigenspace of *Laplacian* matrix is an alternative space for graph clustering. Algorithm 1 shows the basic procedure of these methods.

After proposing spectral clustering in [42], various versions were presented. To obtain more knowledge about the concept of Spectral Clustering we refer readers to [32] and to know the most common variations we refer readers to [35]. In addition, to obtain deep knowledge about spectral graph theory, concepts and the mathematics of graph spectrums are given in [15]. In some of the studies, proposed algorithms perform two-way clustering and suggest the recursive approach to construct k-clusters. In others, authors focus on multi-way clustering. Most of the k-way methods endeavor to find an appropriate alternative embedding by using k eigenvectors of the matrix [11, 32].

2.2   Active Learning

Active Learning is an idea to perform on machine learning algorithms to achieve admissible performance by consuming less learning material. Active learning algorithms attempt to iteratively find more important data for learning and then query it. In other words, they adaptively generate a sequence of decisions under a hypothesis and past experience outcomes [40]. Although supervised learning is an included part of active learning, there are significant research for unsupervised learning. The majority of research related to active clustering focus on certain

---

Algorithm 1: Basic spectral clustering

Input: Graph Adjacency Matrix W
Output: Cluster C_1, C_2
1. *Set $D = DegreeMatrix(W)$ & $L = D - W$*
2. *Find the second eigenvector v_2 of L*
3. *Run Kmeans on v_2*

---

constraints to consider during actively data partitioning. Constraints mainly include pairwise *must-link* and *cannot-link* criteria between instances [1, 20, 46]. In some other approaches, authors have proposed an active learning algorithm to generate a representative point from the whole of the dataset for data clustering based on spectral graph partitioning [7, 28]. From a similarity consumption viewpoint, as mentioned in Sect. 1, Eriksson et al. [19] introduced and analyzed an efficient active hierarchical clustering algorithm that could robustly cluster noisy graphs. Similarly, Krishnamurthy et al. [30] presented another framework that can apply to a traditional clustering algorithm as an input argument and actively perform clustering in a hierarchical structure.

2.3 Matrix Perturbation

Perturbation Theory [6, 45] is a mathematical approach to analyze the effect of an argument's perturbation on the output of a function to approximate its value. Perturbation theory aids to approximate a function that exact solutions and equations cannot be derived from when perturbing. Perturbation theory has a wide range of usefulness in science and engineering and by joining it with sensitivity analysis [9] we would be able to notify the amount of sensitivity of an arbitrary function to its arguments' perturbation.

Matrix Perturbation theory works on matrix functions especially eigenfunctions, where eigenfunctions can be defined as Eigenvalues and Eigenvectors. Since eigenfunctions are functions of matrix indices, we are able to apply perturbation theory on them to evaluate the effects of slight changes to eigenvectors and eigenvalues. Analyzing the effect of perturbation on Spectral Clustering has been the main or part of contribution in many works [25, 26, 36, 48].

2.4 Notation and Settings

In this chapter, W refers to similarity matrix of Graph (or distance matrix of the dataset) with n vertices and therefore, size W is $n \times n$. L denotes *Laplacian* of W. λk and vk are used for kth eigenvalue and eigenvector respectively. D is a $n \times n$ non-diagonal degree matrix which entries are zero and diagonal indices generate by $D_{i,j} = \sum_{j=1}^{n} W_{i,j}$. All hatted sign variables are related to the non-complete matrix $\widehat{W}$ that active clustering algorithms aim to work on it by perturbation theory to achieve the same clustering performance despite the minimum similarity consumption.

3   Related Methods

Similarity challenge is an important issue in botnet detection and on many occasions, preparing a complete similarity matrix is impossible, costly or uncertain. On the other hand, spectral clustering requires the whole similarity matrix to perform acceptable partitioning. Hence, proposing an active learning strategy for minimizing the cost of similarity usage is significantly beneficial. Shamir and Tishby [41] restricted their proposed method to consume only b number of similarities and introduced two novel algorithms. A random algorithm for choosing the next similarity to query randomly and the other was an active query approach, given in Algorithm 2.

During each iteration, the $S\&T$ method tries to find the index that maximizes the norm-2 of changes in second laplacian eigenvector. Since the beginning of the algorithm gives all non-diagonal indices inputed to zero, their corresponding points in eigenspace is also zero. So matrix entries that they are perturbing, or in other words actual similarity values, will change the second eigenvector which will help the algorithm to minimize error between $\widehat{v_2}$ and v_2 and iteratively approximate $\widehat{v_2}$ close to v_2. The $S\&T$ method employs the perturbation theory to calculate the $\|\frac{\partial \widehat{v_2}}{\partial \widehat{W_{i,j}}}\|$. The idea behind partial derivative roots in sensitivity analysis [9] to discover the most important matrix entry that maximizes changes in the second eigenvector at each step and aims K-means to perform more accurate clustering. From a spectral graph theory viewpoint, an eigenvector could well represent two clusters and therefore, the $S\&T$ method would be practical in two-way clustering and for multi-way clustering, we should apply recursive approach on each discovered cluster.

Besides the $S\&T$ method, considering some intuitive contributions, Wauthier et al. [47] proposed an active spectral clustering which tracked the most sensitive entry to perturbation around the uncertain point of the second eigenvector. They hypothesized that points around K-means's discrimination point has maximum error and endeavored to minimize it. We see their algorithm given as Algorithm 3.

Algorithm 2: Shamir and Tishby ($S\&T$) [41] method

Input: inital zero matrix $\widehat{W}$ and b
Output: Cluster C_1, C_2
$S = \{(i, j) : i, j \epsilon \{1, \ldots, n\}, i < j\}$
$for \ t = 1 \ to \ b$
$\quad \widehat{L} = \widehat{D} - \widehat{W}$
$\quad (i^*, j^*) = \arg\max_{(i,j)\epsilon S} \|\frac{\partial \widehat{v_2}}{\partial \widehat{W_{i,j}}}\|$
$\quad \widehat{W_{i^*,j^*}} = W_{i^*,j^*} \quad (query \ W_{i^*,j^*})$
$run \ Kmeans \ on \ \widehat{v_2}$

Algorithm 3: Wauthier et al. (IU-RED) [47] method

Input: inital zero matrix $\widehat{W}$
Output: Cluster C_1, C_2
$S = \{(i, j) : i, j \epsilon \{1, \ldots, n\}, i < j\}$
$q = number\ of\ queries$
$for\ t = 1\ to\ q$
$\quad \widehat{L} = \widehat{D} - \widehat{W}$
$\quad k_{min} = argmin_k |\widehat{v_2}(k)|$
$\quad (i^*, j^*) = \arg\max_{(i,j)\epsilon S} |\frac{\partial \widehat{v_2}(k_{min})}{\partial \widehat{W}_{i,j}}|$
$\quad \widehat{W}_{i^*,j^*} = W_{i^*,j^*}\quad (query\ W_{i^*,j^*})$
$run\ Kmeans\ on\ \widehat{v_2}$

IU-RED algorithm structure is close to the $S\&T$ algorithm, but the main difference between described methods is that $S\&T$ maximizes global changes of $\widehat{v_2}$, but IU-RED maximizes change around uncertain point k_{min}. As mentioned for the $S\&T$ method, the IU-RED algorithm just performs active spectral clustering for two-cluster problems and for multi-way implementation authors used recursive approach.

From graph theory, each eigenvector can represent two clusters properly. Therefore, in multi-way clustering, algorithms use at least $k-1$ eigenvectors for detecting k clusters. As seen in the schematic of Fig. 19.1, yellow and orange clusters are not separable using the 2nd eigenvector. Both of the $S\&T$ and IU-RED methods should run twice, the first time for detecting red and blue sections, and the second time on a red segment for detecting yellow and orange clusters. It is evident that every learner with similarity cost reduction goals should attempt to find similarities in the intra-cluster regions (e.g. yellow, orange and blue) as seen in Fig. 19.1 and avoid finding inter-cluster similarities inside the black and gray regions. An ideal algorithm endeavors to query intra-cluster similarities and thus eigenvectors tend to be sharper and more separable due to their corresponding clusters.

There are two major inefficiencies in a combination of described methods with a recursive approach for multi-way clustering. First, there is ambiguity in recursion since in actual implementation for real problem datasets, we are not aware of the correct path to continue recursion and choose proper cluster to divide. Another problem refers to the inconsistency between the algorithm's goal and modus operandi. As seen in Fig. 19.1, algorithms try to separate blue and red part sin 2nd eigenvector at the first step. Therefore, some chosen similarities in the red part are inside the black region, or in graph clustering literature this is known as inter-cluster similarities. Neglecting the fact that a sizable number of inter-cluster edges results in reducing the performance of any graph clustering algorithm, it is obvious that queried inter-cluster edges (entries in the black part of Fig. 19.1) to discover red cluster in the first step, are useless in the second step and will increase similarity cost.

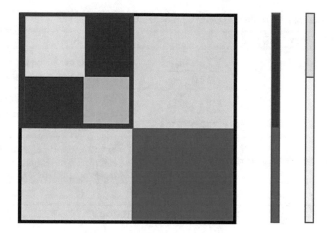

Fig. 19.1 Schematic view of an ideal block diagonal similarity matrix and its 2nd and 3rd eigenvectors

4   Proposed Method

In order to perform multi-way active clustering on botnet dataset, we propose a general function which considers a linear combination of eigenvalues and eigenvectors in Eq. (19.1). Then, we suggest three different optimization function based on Eq. (19.1).

$$(i^*, j^*) = argmax_{i,j} \| \frac{\sum_{l=2}^{k} \partial(f_v(\widehat{W}, l) \times g_\lambda(\widehat{W}, l))}{\partial \widehat{W}_{i,j}} \| \tag{19.1}$$

$f_v(\widehat{W}, l)$ calculates the kth eigenvector of matrix $\widehat{W}$ or a variation of it such as Laplacian or Normalized Laplacian [10] and similarly $g_\lambda(\widehat{W}, l)$ calculates the kth eigenvalue of matrix $\widehat{W}$ or a variation of it. Function g_λ plays a key role in this study and enables us to tune algorithms by changing the g_λ for different detection goals.

Table 19.1 provides information about the proposed method's suggested combinational function.

The main difference between Normalized Laplacian and standard Laplacian is that L_{norm}'s eigenvalues are normalized. Algorithm 4 demonstrates implementation for Suggested Method III of Table 19.1.

An important preference of Suggested Method III compared with Suggested Method I and II is its normalized eigenvalues which prevents neglecting small clusters and focusing on large clusters when graph's partitions are unbalanced [34].

Table 19.1 Summary of three suggestive variations of general function

Method	Objective Function	Description
Suggested method I	$(i^*, j^*) = argmax_{i,j} \| \dfrac{\sum_{l=2}^{k} \partial(\widehat{\lambda}_l \widehat{v}_l)}{\partial \widehat{W}_{i,j}} \|$	$\widehat{v}_i$ and $\widehat{\lambda}_i$ are ith eigenvector and eigenvalue of matrix $\widehat{W}$ respectively
Suggested method II	$(i^*, j^*) = argmax_{i,j} \| \dfrac{\sum_{l=2}^{k} \partial(\frac{\widehat{v}_l}{\widehat{\lambda}_l})}{\partial \widehat{W}_{i,j}} \|$	$\widehat{v}_i$ and $\widehat{\lambda}_i$ are ith eigenvector and eigenvalue of Laplacian matrix $\widehat{L}$ respectively
Suggested method III	$(i^*, j^*) = argmax_{i,j} \| \dfrac{\sum_{l=2}^{k} \partial((1 - \widehat{\lambda}l)\widehat{v}_l)}{\partial \widehat{W}_{i,j}} \|$	$\widehat{v}_i$ and $\widehat{\lambda}_i$ are ith eigenvector and eigenvalue of Normalized Laplacian matrix $\widehat{L}_{norm}$[10] respectively

---

Algorithm 4: Suggested method III implementation

Input: inital zero matrix $\widehat{W}$
Output: Cluster $C_1, C_2, \ldots, C_k$
$S = \{(i, j) : i, j \epsilon\{1, \ldots, n\}, i < j\}$
$q = number\ of\ queries$
$for\ t = 1\ to\ q$
$\quad \widehat{L}_{norm} = I - \widehat{D}^{\frac{-1}{2}} \widehat{W} \widehat{D}^{\frac{-1}{2}}$
$\quad (i^*, j^*) = argmax_{i,j} \| \dfrac{\sum_{l=2}^{k} \partial((1 - \widehat{\lambda}_l)\widehat{v}_l)}{\partial \widehat{W}_{i,j}} \|$
$\quad \widehat{W}_{i^*, j^*} = W_{i^*, j^*}\ \ (query\ W_{i^*, j^*})$
$run\ Spectral\ Clustering\ on\ \widehat{W}$

---

5 Experiments

5.1 Dataset

In this study, the performance of the proposed method evaluated using ISOT,[1] which is a widely cited dataset for botnet detection. Furthermore, to extract information from log files, *Tranalyzer*[2] is utilized, and a subset of data which included Storm, Zeus, and Waledac attacks was selected. In order to generate a similarity matrix of the dataset, Cosine similarity [14] ($W_{i,j} = \dfrac{X_i X_j}{\|X_i\| \|X_j\|}$) method was applied.

---

[1] https://www.uvic.ca/engineering/ece/isot/datasets/.
[2] https://tranalyzer.com/.

5.2   Evaluation Metric

5.2.1   Purity

Purity is an evaluation benchmark to measure performance of clustering algorithms that identifies which cluster was assigned to the class and then the accuracy of this assignment is measured using Eq. (19.2).

$$Purity(\Omega, C) = \frac{1}{N} \sum_{k} argmax_j |\omega_k \cap c_j| \qquad (19.2)$$

where $\Omega = \omega_1, \omega_2, \ldots, \omega_k$ is the set of clusters and $C = c_1, c_2, \ldots, c_j$ is the set of classes.

5.2.2   PEDK (Proportionate Eigenvectors Direction Keeping)

PEDK is a measurement metric which is designed with considering the concept of both Active Learning and Spectral Clustering. PEKD allows users to apply it on unlabeled datasets and measure the ability of the active clustering method for preserving the k most important eigenvectors' direction of $\widehat{W}$ aligned with those of W (see Eq. (19.3)).

$$PEDK(W, \widehat{W}) = \frac{\sum_{i=2}^{k} \sum_{j=2}^{k} |\theta(v_i, v_j) - \theta(\widehat{v}_i, \widehat{v}_j)|}{2k\pi} \qquad (19.3)$$

where $\theta(x, y) = cos^{-1}(\frac{x.y}{\|x\|.\|y\|})$ and $\theta(v_i, v_j) - \theta(\widehat{v}_i, \widehat{v}_j)$ are terms that calculate the difference of pairwise angles between the ith and jth eigenvectors of W and $\widehat{W}$. Summations would calculate it for all pairs of eigenvectors. The denominator term $2k\pi$ is to normalize measurement.

5.3   Results

To evaluate our proposed method's performance, we measured Purity on ISOT dataset to compare the detection rate of active clustering algorithms. Figure 19.2 illustrates and compares Purity of methods. To compare the active clustering algorithms' purity, we measured the Purity of complete matrix W using standard Normalized Cut algorithm [42]. As can be seen from Fig. 19.2, Suggested Method III outperforms others while consuming less similarity material. Furthermore, its Purity for 60% of similarity consumption overtakes the Normalized Cut. Another striking feature of the graph is better performance of suggested methods compared with $S\&T$ and IU-RED for multi-way botnet dataset.

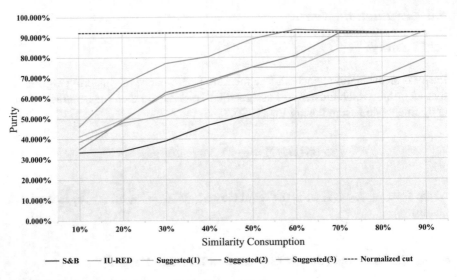

Fig. 19.2 Purity measurement over similarity consumption

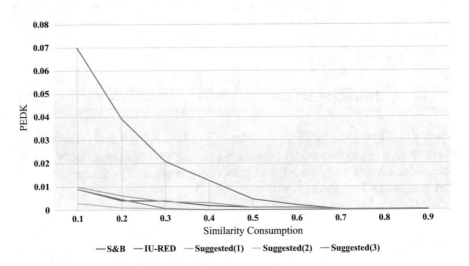

Fig. 19.3 PEDK measurement over similarity consumption

In order to realize the level of algorithm succession for constructing $\widehat{W}$ structure similar to W, PEDK is designed. Figure 19.3 depicts that PEDK is a proper metric to assess this category of methods. Moreover, PEDK value for suggested method III experienced a substantial decline to reach its minimum value using less similarity material.

6 Discussion and Future Work

The increasing pervasiveness of internet-connected devices and the importance of stored information and provided services necessitate imposing security mechanism to protect them against cyber-threats [16]. Botnets are networks of infected nodes controlled by cyber-criminals to organize a group of attackers. Graph clustering is a prevalent technique to detect botnets that leverages similarity matrix of graph to perform graph partitioning. However, in many situations preparing complete matrix of graph is impossible. In this chapter we reviewed two recognized algorithm in this domain, *S&T* [41] and IU-RED [47] which proposed for a dataset of two clusters. Recursive implementation for $k, (k > 2)$ partitions lead to two basic problems: ambiguity in recursion path for actual executions and low performance due to query inter-cluster similarities. The proposed method extends its operational eigenspace to k eigenvectors and leverages a linear combination of eigenvalues-eigenvectors. Combining eigenvalues assists the algorithm to adaptively control itself regarding the effect of each eigenvector importance. Then, we evaluated our approach over a benchmark botnet dataset and demonstrates practical usefulness of the proposed method. Furthermore, we introduced and measured specific metrics to compare active graph clustering algorithms. Since calculating the partial derivative of eigenvectors and eigenvalues is a time-consuming task, future work could include proposing an approximate model for the proposed method. In addition, scheming a distributed active clustering algorithm for the Internet of Things [3] and edge computing could potentially be considered.

References

1. A.A. Abin, H. Beigy, Active selection of clustering constraints: a sequential approach. Pattern Recogn. **47**(3), 1443–1458 (2014)
2. O.Y. Al-Jarrah, O. Alhussein, P.D. Yoo, S. Muhaidat, K. Taha, K. Kim, Data randomization and cluster-based partitioning for botnet intrusion detection. IEEE Trans. Cybern. **46**(8), 1796–1806 (2016). https://doi.org/10.1109/TCYB.2015.2490802
3. A. Azmoodeh, A. Dehghantanha, K.K.R. Choo, Robust malware detection for internet of (battlefield) things devices using deep eigenspace learning. IEEE Trans. Sustain. Comput. **4**(1), 88–95 (2019)
4. P.N. Bahrami, A. Dehghantanha, T. Dargahi, R.M. Parizi, K.R. Choo, H.H.S. Javadi, Cyber kill chain-based taxonomy of advanced persistent threat actors: analogy of tactics, techniques, and procedures. J. Inf. Process. Syst. **15**, 865–889 (2019). https://doi.org/10.3745/JIPS.03.0126
5. M. Bailey, E. Cooke, F. Jahanian, Y. Xu, M. Karir, A survey of botnet technology and defenses, in *2009 Cybersecurity Applications and Technology Conference for Homeland Security* (IEEE, Piscataway, 2009), pp. 299–304
6. R. Bhatia, Review of matrix perturbation theory: by G.W. Stewart and Ji-Guang Sun. Linear Algebra Appl. **160**, 255–259 (1992). https://doi.org/10.1016/0024-3795(92)90451-F
7. Z. Bodó, Z. Minier, L. Csató, Active learning with clustering, in *Active Learning and Experimental Design Workshop in Conjunction with AISTATS 2010* (2011), pp. 127–139
8. A.L. Buczak, E. Guven, A survey of data mining and machine learning methods for cyber security intrusion detection. IEEE Commun. Surv. Tutorials **18**(2), 1153–1176 (2016). https://doi.org/10.1109/COMST.2015.2494502

9. D.G. Cacuci, *Sensitivity and Uncertainty Analysis*, vols. 1, 2 (Chapman & Hall/CRC Press, Boca Raton)

10. M.S. Cavers, The normalized laplacian matrix and general randic index of graphs. Ph.D. Thesis, University of Regina, 2010

11. P.K. Chan, M.D. Schlag, J.Y. Zien, Spectral K-way ratio-cut partitioning and clustering. IEEE Trans. Comput. Aided Des. Integr. Circuits Syst. **13**(9), 1088–1096 (1994)

12. S. Chester, B.M. Kapron, G. Srivastava, S. Venkatesh, Complexity of social network anonymization. Soc. Netw. Anal. Min. **3**(2), 151–166 (2013)

13. S. Chester, G. Srivastava, Social network privacy for attribute disclosure attacks, in *2011 International Conference on Advances in Social Networks Analysis and Mining* (IEEE, Piscataway, 2011), pp. 445–449

14. S.S. Choi, S.H. Cha, C.C. Tappert, A survey of binary similarity and distance measures. J. Syst. Cybern. Inform. **8**(1), 43–48 (2010)

15. F.R. Chung, F.C. Graham, *Spectral Graph Theory*, vol. 92 (American Mathematical Society, Providence, 1997)

16. M. Conti, T. Dargahi, A. Dehghantanha, *Cyber Threat Intelligence: Challenges and Opportunities* (Springer, Cham, 2018), pp. 1–6

17. M. Conti, A. Dehghantanha, K. Franke, S. Watson, Internet of things security and forensics: challenges and opportunities. Futur. Gener. Comput. Syst. **78**, 544–546 (2018)

18. E.M. Dovom, A. Azmoodeh, A. Dehghantanha, D.E. Newton, R.M. Parizi, H. Karimipour, Fuzzy pattern tree for edge malware detection and categorization in IoT. J. Syst. Archit. **97**, 1–7 (2019). https://doi.org/10.1016/j.sysarc.2019.01.017

19. B. Eriksson, G. Dasarathy, A. Singh, R. Nowak, Active clustering: robust and efficient hierarchical clustering using adaptively selected similarities, in *Proceedings of the 14th International Conference on Artificial Intelligence and Statistics* (2011), pp. 260–268

20. N. Grira, M. Crucianu, N. Boujemaa, Active semi-supervised fuzzy clustering. Pattern Recogn. **41**(5), 1834–1844 (2008)

21. G. Gu, R. Perdisci, J. Zhang, W. Lee, Botminer: clustering analysis of network traffic for protocol- and structure-independent botnet detection, in *Proceedings of the 17th Conference on Security Symposium, SS'08* (USENIX Association, Berkeley, 2008), pp. 139–154. http://dl.acm.org/citation.cfm?id=1496711.1496721

22. H. Hashemi, A. Azmoodeh, A. Hamzeh, S. Hashemi, Graph embedding as a new approach for unknown malware detection. J. Comput. Virol. Hack. Tech. **13**(3), 153–166 (2017)

23. S. Homayoun, M. Ahmadzadeh, S. Hashemi, A. Dehghantanha, R. Khayami, *BoTShark: A Deep Learning Approach for Botnet Traffic Detection* (Springer, Cham, 2018), pp. 137–153

24. S. Homayoun, A. Dehghantanha, M. Ahmadzadeh, S. Hashemi, R. Khayami, Know abnormal, find evil: frequent pattern mining for ransomware threat hunting and intelligence. IEEE Trans. Emerg. Top. Comput. (1), 1–1 (2017)

25. L. Huang, D. Yan, N. Taft, M.I. Jordan, Spectral clustering with perturbed data, in *Advances in Neural Information Processing Systems*, ed. by D. Koller, D. Schuurmans, Y. Bengio, L. Bottou, vol. 21 (Curran Associates, Red Hook, 2009), pp. 705–712

26. B. Hunter, T. Strohmer, Performance analysis of spectral clustering on compressed, incomplete and inaccurate measurements (2010). arXiv:1011.0997

27. A.K. Jain, M.N. Murty, P.J. Flynn, Data clustering: a review. ACM Comput. Surv. **31**(3), 264–323 (1999)

28. T. Joachims, Transductive learning via spectral graph partitioning, in *Proceedings of the 20th International Conference on Machine Learning (ICML-03)* (2003), pp. 290–297

29. D. Kiwia, A. Dehghantanha, Choo, K.K.R., J. Slaughter, A cyber kill chain based taxonomy of banking trojans for evolutionary computational intelligence. J. Comput. Sci. **27**, 394-409 (2018)

30. A. Krishnamurthy, S. Balakrishnan, M. Xu, A. Singh, Efficient active algorithms for hierarchical clustering (2012). arXiv:1206.4672

31. C. Li, T. Amagasa, H. Kitagawa, G. Srivastava, Label-bag based graph anonymization via edge addition, in *Proceedings of the 2014 International C* Conference on Computer Science & Software Engineering* (ACM, 2014), p. 1

32. U. von Luxburg, A tutorial on spectral clustering. Stat. Comput. **17**(4), 395–416 (2007). https://doi.org/10.1007/s11222-007-9033-z

33. L. Mai, M. Park, A comparison of clustering algorithms for botnet detection based on network flow, in *2016 8th International Conference on Ubiquitous and Future Networks (ICUFN)* (IEEE, Piscataway, 2016), pp. 667–669

34. L. Malina, G. Srivastava, P. Dzurenda, J. Hajny, R. Fujdiak, A secure publish/subscribe protocol for internet of things, in *Proceedings of the 2019 14th International Conference on Availability, Reliability and Security (ARES 2019)* (Canterbury, 2019), pp. 26–29

35. M.C. Nascimento, A.C. de Carvalho, Spectral methods for graph clustering—a survey. Eur. J. Oper. Res. **211**(2), 221–231 (2011). https://doi.org/10.1016/j.ejor.2010.08.012

36. A.Y. Ng, M.I. Jordan, Y. Weiss, On spectral clustering: analysis and an algorithm, in *Advances in Neural Information Processing Systems* (2002), pp. 849–856

37. O. Osanaiye, H. Cai, K.K.R. Choo, A. Dehghantanha, Z. Xu, M. Dlodlo, Ensemble-based multi-filter feature selection method for ddos detection in cloud computing. EURASIP J. Wirel. Commun. Netw. **2016**(1), 130 (2016)

38. J. Sakhnini, H. Karimipour, A. Dehghantanha, R.M. Parizi, G. Srivastava, Security aspects of internet of things aided smart grids: a bibliometric survey. Internet of Things **2019**, 100111 (2019). https://doi.org/10.1016/j.iot.2019.100111

39. S.E. Schaeffer, Graph clustering. Comput. Sci. Rev. **1**(1), 27–64 (2007). https://doi.org/10.1016/j.cosrev.2007.05.001

40. B. Settles, Active learning. Synth. Lect. Artif. Intell. Mach. Learn. **6**(1), 1–114 (2012)

41. O. Shamir, N. Tishby, Spectral clustering on a budget, in *Proceedings of the 14th International Conference on Artificial Intelligence and Statistics* (2011), pp. 661–669

42. J. Shi, J. Malik, Normalized cuts and image segmentation. IEEE Trans. Pattern Anal. Mach. Intell. **22**(8), 888–905 (2000). https://doi.org/10.1109/34.868688

43. D.A. Spielman, S.H. Teng, A local clustering algorithm for massive graphs and its application to nearly linear time graph partitioning. SIAM J. Comput. **42**(1), 1–26 (2013)

44. M. Stevanovic, J.M. Pedersen, An efficient flow-based botnet detection using supervised machine learning, in *2014 International Conference on Computing, Networking and Communications (ICNC)* (2014), pp. 797–801. https://doi.org/10.1109/ICCNC.2014.6785439

45. L.N. Trefethen, D. Bau III, *Numerical Linear Algebra*, vol. 50 (SIAM, 1997)

46. X. Wang, I. Davidson, Active spectral clustering, in *2010 IEEE International Conference on Data Mining* (IEEE, Piscataway, 2010), pp. 561–568

47. F.L. Wauthier, N. Jojic, M.I. Jordan, Active spectral clustering via iterative uncertainty reduction, in *Proceedings of the 18th ACM SIGKDD International Conference on Knowledge Discovery and Data Mining* (ACM, New York, 2012), pp. 1339–1347

48. D. Yan, L. Huang, M.I. Jordan, Fast approximate spectral clustering, in *Proceedings of the 15th ACM SIGKDD International Conference on Knowledge Discovery and Data Mining* (ACM, New York, 2009), pp. 907–916

49. H.R. Zeidanloo, M.J.Z. Shooshtari, P.V. Amoli, M. Safari, M. Zamani, A taxonomy of botnet detection techniques, in *2010 3rd IEEE International Conference on Computer Science and Information Technology (ICCSIT)*, vol. 2 (IEEE, Piscataway, 2010), pp. 158–162

50. J. Zhang, R. Perdisci, W. Lee, X. Luo, U. Sarfraz, Building a scalable system for stealthy p2p-botnet detection. IEEE Trans. Inf. Forensics Secur. **9**(1), 27–38 (2014). https://doi.org/10.1109/TIFS.2013.2290197

Printed in the United States
by Baker & Taylor Publisher Services